Setting Conservation Targets for Managed Forest Landscapes

Forests host a disproportionate share of the world's biodiversity. They are increasingly being seen as a refuge for genetic diversity, native species, natural structures, and ecological processes yet intensive forestry threatens their value for biodiversity. The authors present concepts, approaches, and case studies illustrating how biodiversity conservation can be integrated into forest management planning. They address ecological patterns and processes taking place at the scale of landscape, or forest mosaics. This book is intended for students and researchers in conservation biology and natural resource management, as well as forest land managers and policy-makers. It presents case studies and examples from many forest regions of the world and addresses multiple components of biodiversity. With contributions from researchers who are familiar with forest management and forest managers working in partnership with researchers, this book provides insight and concrete tools to help shape the future of forest landscapes worldwide.

MARC-ANDRÉ VILLARD is a Professor of Biology at Université de Moncton, where he holds a Canada Research Chair in Landscape Conservation. He is a Fellow of the American Ornithologists' Union and co-editor of the journal *Avian Conservation and Ecology*.

BENGT GUNNAR JONSSON is a Professor of Plant Ecology at Mid Sweden University. He has been an active part of several national conservation projects initiated by the Swedish Forest Agency and the Swedish EPA, and has acted as scientific advisor within the Convention of Biological Diversity.

Conservation Biology
This series aims to present internationally significant contributions from leading researchers in particularly active areas of conservation biology. It focuses on topics where basic theory is strong and where there are pressing problems for practical conservation. The series includes both authored and edited volumes and adopts a direct and accessible style targeted at interested undergraduates, postgraduates, researchers and university teachers.

1. *Conservation in a Changing World*, edited by Georgina Mace, Andrew Balmford and Joshua Ginsberg 0 521 63270 6 (hardcover), 0 521 63445 8 (paperback)
2. *Behaviour and Conservation*, edited by Morris Gosling and William Sutherland 0 521 66230 3 (hardcover), 0 521 66539 6 (paperback)
3. *Priorities for the Conservation of Mammalian Diversity*, edited by Abigail Entwistle and Nigel Dunstone 0 521 77279 6 (hardcover), 0 521 77536 1 (paperback)
4. *Genetics, Demography and Viability of Fragmented Populations*, edited by Andrew G. Young and Geoffrey M. Clarke 0 521 782074 (hardcover), 0 521 794218 (paperback)
5. *Carnivore Conservation*, edited by John L. Gittleman, Stephan M. Funk, David Macdonald and Robert K. Wayne 0 521 66232 X (hardcover), 0 521 66537 X (paperback)
6. *Conservation of Exploited Species*, edited by John D. Reynolds, Georgina M. Mace, Kent H. Redford, and John G. Robinson 0 521 78216 3 (hardcover), 0 521 78733 5 (paperback)
7. *Conserving Bird Biodiversity*, and edited by Ken Norris and Deborah J. Pain 0 521 78340 2 (hardcover), 0 521 78949 4 (paperback)
8. *Reproductive Science and Integrated Conservation*, edited by William V. Holt, Amanda R. Pickard, John C. Rodger and David E. Wildt 0 521 81215 1 (hardcover), 0 521 01110 8 (paperback)
9. *People and Wildlife*, edited by Rosie Woodroffe, Simon Thergood and Alan Rabinowitz 0 521 82505 9 (hardcover), 0 521 53203 5 (paperback)
10. *Phylogeny and Conservation*, edited by Andrew Purvis, John L. Gittleman and Thomas Brooks 0 521 82502 4 (hardcover), 0 521 53200 0 (paperback)
11. *Large Herbivore Ecology*, edited by Kjell Danell, Roger Bergstrom, Patrick Duncanand John Pastor 0 521 83005 2 (hardcover), 0 521 53687 1 (paperback)
12. *Top Predators in Marine Ecosyems*, edited by Ian Boyd, Sarah Wanless and C. J. Camphuysen 0 521 84773 7 (hardcover), 0 521 61256 X (paperback)
13. *Coral Reef Conservation*, edited by Isbelle Côté and Jogn Reynolds 0521 85536 5 (hardcover), 0 521 67145 0 (paperback)
14. *Connectivity Conservation*, edited by Kevin R. Crooks and M. Sanjayan 0 521 85706 6 (hardcover), 0 521 67381 X (paperback)
15. *Zoos in the 21st Century*, edited by Alexandra Zimmermann, Matthew Hatchwell, Lesley Dicheie and Chris West 9780521853330 (hardcover) 9780521618588 (paperback)

Setting Conservation Targets for Managed Forest Landscapes

Edited by

MARC-ANDRÉ VILLARD

Université de Moncton, Canada

BENGT GUNNAR JONSSON

Mid Sweden University, Sweden

CAMBRIDGE
UNIVERSITY PRESS

CAMBRIDGE UNIVERSITY PRESS
Cambridge, New York, Melbourne, Madrid, Cape Town, Singapore, São Paulo, Delhi

Cambridge University Press
The Edinburgh Building, Cambridge CB2 8RU, UK

Published in the United States of America by Cambridge University Press, New York

www.cambridge.org
Information on this title: www.cambridge.org/9780521877091

© Cambridge University Press 2009

First published 2009

Printed in the United Kingdom at the University Press, Cambridge

A catalog record for this publication is available from the British Library

Library of Congress Cataloging in Publication data
Setting conservation targets for managed forest landscapes / edited by Marc-André Villard, Bengt
Gunnar Jonsson. – 1st ed.
   p.   cm.
Includes index.
ISBN 978-0-521-87709-1
1. Forest biodiversity conservation.   2. Forest conservation.   I. Villard, Marc-André, 1963–
II. Jonsson, Bengt Gunnar.
QH75.S472   2009
639.9 – dc22   2008037123

ISBN 978-0-521-87709-1 hardback
ISBN 978-0-521-70072-6 paperback

Contents

Contributors

Per Angelstam
School for Forest Engineers, Swedish
University of Agricultural Sciences (SLU),
Box 43, SE-73931, Skinnskatteberg,
Sweden

Doug P. Armstrong
Wildlife Ecology Group, Institute of
Natural Resources, Massey University, PB
11222, Palmerston North, New Zealand

Emin Zeki Baskent
Karadeniz Technical University, Faculty of
Forestry, Department of Forest
Management, 61080 Trabzon, Turkey

Andrew F. Bennett
Landscape Ecology Research Group,
School of Life and Environmental
Sciences, Deakin University, 221 Burwood
Highway, Burwood, Victoria 3125,
Australia

Yves Bergeron
Centre d'étude de la forêt, Chaire
industrielle CRSNG-UQAT-UQAM,
Université du Québec en
Abitibi-Témiscamingue, Rouyn-Noranda,
QC J9X 5E4, Canada

Matthew G. Betts
Department of Forest Science, Oregon
State University, Corvallis, OR 97331, USA

Béatrijs Bossuyt
Ghent University, Terrestrial Ecology
Unit, K. L. Ledeganckstraat 35, B-9000
Ghent, Belgium

Dave Cheyne
Alberta-Pacific Forest Industries Inc., Box
8000, Boyle, AB ToA oMo, Canada

Don R.Church
Conservation International, 2011 Crystal
City Drive, Arlington, VA 22202, USA

Pierre Drapeau
Centre d'étude de la forêt, Université du
Québec à Montréal, C.P. 8888, Succursale
Centre-Ville, Montréal, QC H3C 3P8,
Canada

Simon Dyer
The Pembina Institute, 200 606 – 7th
Street SW, Calgary, AB T2P 1Z2,
Canada

Elston Dzus
Alberta-Pacific Forest Industries Inc., Box
8000, Boyle, AB ToA oMo, Canada

Claude Gascon
Conservation International, 2011 Crystal
City Drive, Arlington, VA 22202, USA

Brigitte Grover
Alberta-Pacific Forest Industries Inc., Box
8000, Boyle, AB ToA oMo, Canada

Bruno Hérault
Centre d'Ecologie Végétale et
d'Hydrologie, Institut de Botanique, rue
Goethe 28, F-67083 Strasbourg,
France

Olivier Honnay
University of Leuven, Division of Plant
Systematics and Ecology, Arenbergpark 31,
B-3001 Heverlee, Belgium

Eija Hurme
Department of Biology, POB 3000,
FIN-90014, University of Oulu,
Finland

Bengt Gunnar Jonsson
Department of Natural Sciences,
Engineering and Mathematics Mid
Sweden University, SE-851 70 Sundsvall,
Sweden

Artti Juutinen
Faculty of Economics, POB 4000,
FIN-90014, University of Oulu,
Finland

Alain Leduc
Centre d'étude de la forêt, Université du
Québec à Montréal, C.P. 8888, Succursale
Centre-Ville, Montréal, QC H3C 3P8,
Canada

David A. MacLean
Faculty of Forestry and Environmental
Management, University of New
Brunswick, PO Box 44555, Fredericton,
NB E3B 6C2, Canada

Christian Messier
Centre d'étude de la forêt, Université du
Québec à Montréal, C.P. 8888, Succursale
Centre-Ville, Montréal, QC H3C 3P8,
Canada

Mikko Mönkkönen
Department of Biological and
Environmental Science, POB 35,
FIN-40014, University of Jyväskylä,
Finland

Michael K. Montigny
New Brunswick Department of Natural
Resources, Hugh John Flemming Forestry
Centre, C.P. 6000 Fredericton, NB E3B
5H1, Canada

Sven G. Nilsson
Department of Ecology, Animal Ecology,
University of Lund, Ecology Building,
S-223 62 Lund, Sweden

Don Pope
Alberta-Pacific Forest Industries Inc.,
Box 8000, Boyle, AB T0A 0M0,
Canada

James Q. Radford
Landscape Ecology Research Group,
School of Life and Environmental
Sciences, Deakin University, 221 Burwood
Highway, Burwood, Victoria 3125,
Australia

Thomas Ranius
Department of Ecology, Swedish
University of Agricultural Sciences, Box
7044, SE-750 07 Uppsala, Sweden

John S. Richardson
Department of Forest Sciences, University
of British Columbia, Vancouver, BC V6T
1Z4, Canada

Jean-Michel Roberge
Department of Biological and
Environmental Science, University of
Jyväskylä, POB 35, FIN-40014, Jyväskylä,
Finland

Jim Schieck
Alberta Research Council, Bag 4000
Vegreville, AB T9C 1T4, Canada

Robert S. Seymour
School of Forest Resources, University of
Maine, Orono, ME 04469, USA

Luis A. Solorzano
Gordon and Betty Moore Foundation, PO
Box 29910, San Francisco, CA 94129,
USA

Ross M. Thompson
School of Biological Sciences and
Australian Centre for Biodiversity,
Monash University, Melbourne, VIC
3800, Australia

Megan Van Fossen
Andean Center for Biodiversity
Conservation, Conservation International
Venezuela, Ave. San Juan Bosco, Piso 8,
Officina 8-A, Altamira, Caracas, Venezuela

Grisel Velasquez
Andean Center for Biodiversity
Conservation, Conservation International
Venezuela, Ave. San Juan Bosco, Piso 8,
Officina 8-A, Altamira, Caracas, Venezuela

Marc-André Villard
Canada Research Chair in Landscape
Conservation, Département de Biologie,
Université de Moncton, Moncton, NB E1A
3E9, Canada

Heiko U. Wittmer
Wildlife, Fish and Conservation Biology,
University of California, One Shields Ave.,
Davis, CA 95616, USA

Foreword

As landscape ecology has developed over the past quarter-century, applications of its basic results have become widespread in applied conservation biology. Some applications have been distortions of the basic research results by oversimplification. For example, the original meaning of connectivity became streamlined into "corridors" and applied as a simple solution to all fragmentation problems. Many such applications have been essentially random and without demonstrable measures of success or failure. At the opposite extreme, results of simulation models have been applied globally without measures of effect that would constitute real tests of the reality of the model results. In both these extreme cases, the missing link was some quantitative measure capable of demonstrating statistically what had been achieved by the conservation application derived from the results of fundamental research.

The contributors to this volume each advance ways to increase the connectivity between the advancing front of fundamental ecological knowledge and the application of that knowledge in conservation. Managers and applied ecologists attempt to correct, improve, or guide ecological processes or the structural surrogates of those processes. Without a target, quantitatively defined in terms of the system's processes or structures, the effect of applications cannot be assessed.

Conservation applications can be better connected to the knowledge base, current theory, and valid statistical analysis if basic research provides targets that can be used in applications. Those targets and how to provide them is what this volume is about. Here, conservation targets are any quantitative objective based on empirical data or realistic models used to adjust intensity of conservation management.

Several chapters explicitly recognize the commonness of non-linear ecological responses to changes in landscape structure, often requiring applications to detect critical thresholds. Simulation models are combined with realistic data sets to project likely responses. Whatever the current knowledge and projections, they must be treated as an evidence-based model to be tested and updated from additional evidence. The challenge for basic research is to set targets before every facet of complexity is detailed by empirical data sets. Basic researchers seek evidence-based generalities that will apply as broadly as possible but in setting targets, they also need to recognize that applications normally focus on specific conservation goals and localized management units.

Contributions in this volume aim not at setting aside reserves as the main thrust of conservation management but, instead, recognize the need to manage all the landscape between reserves as well as the reserves. The strategy is to manage conservation issues at the scale of the entire landscape including all the reserves.

The audiences that can benefit from these contributions include: research ecologists who wish to see their concepts and new knowledge used in management applications, the appliers who have the same desire from the other side of the gap, those who wish to make their policies effective on the ground, administrators who need a sound basis for funding decisions in applied ecology, and politicians who find it necessary to make political adjustments in translating basic ecological knowledge into practicable programs in the current sweep of environmental discussions.

The editors acknowledge the need for some allowance to vary targets in consideration of socio-economic parameters, but that should not be taken to mean that basic researchers in ecology should be responsible for putting the "political spin" on targets. In Canada, and probably globally, there have been blatant examples of scientists being blamed for applications that have gone wrong because politicians bent the scientific findings and recommendations. Scientists, basic and applied, are not responsible for producing politically acceptable ecological applications and must stay well clear of politically adjusted targets; the professional hazard is already too great.

Application of ecology to conservation needs to move to a state where defensible targets are based on peer-reviewed scientific findings and the efficacy of applications is judged by the degree of attainment of those targets. This volume is intended to move conservation applications toward that state.

Gray Merriam
Professor Emeritus, Landscape Ecology and Environmental Science
Arden, Ontario, Canada

Acknowledgements

This book represents the collective accomplishment of 38 contributors, 31 reviewers, and numerous colleagues who have encouraged us in this endeavour through stimulating discussions. Each chapter was reviewed by two experts. We are thus indebted to a lot of excellent people, namely: A. Arponen, A. Bennett, M. Betts, S. Boutin, J. Brunet, R. Cormier, E. Fleishman, S. Fraver, J. Humphrey, K. Hylander, T. Kuuluvainen, T. Lämås, T. Lehesvirta, D. Ludwig, M. McCarthy, B. McComb, G. Merriam, G. Mikusinski, P. Nantel, R. Noss, O. Ovaskainen, B. Pettersson, H. Possingham, J. Radford, J.-M. Roberge, A. Rodrigues, J. Rolstad, A. Saint-Hilaire, R. Scheller, J. Stokland, and D. Whitaker.

We thank Cambridge University Press, especially D. Lewis and A. C. Evans, for the support they provided throughout the development of the project and the production of the book, respectively.

M.-A. Villard dedicates this book to Arianne and Maude, who provided constant motivation to work for a better future. B. G. Jonsson thanks the participants of the Baltic Forest project for providing insights on the different aspects and inherent conflicts in sustainable forest management.

A plea for quantitative targets in biodiversity conservation

MARC-ANDRÉ VILLARD AND BENGT GUNNAR JONSSON

Ecological degradation is both ubiquitous and relentless. Human activities have left a footprint even in the most remote locations. Some species benefit from certain forms of degradation whereas many others are expected to decline to extinction under current or increasing land-use intensity (Vitousek *et al.* 1997; Norris and Pain 2002). While the optimal allocation of conservation efforts and funding at the global scale is being debated (Myers *et al.* 2000; Balmford *et al.* 2002; O'Connor *et al.* 2003; Lamoreux *et al.* 2006), target setting at the landscape scale should be viewed as equally important because, for many taxa, this is the scale over which most human activities take place and management regulations are applied. A landscape can be defined as a mosaic of habitat types whose extent reflects the perspective of target species or taxa (Wiens *et al.* 2002). However, it should be noted that this organism-centered perspective of the landscape must interact with human perception and action. Forest managers perceive the landscape as that of the "forest" or "forest management unit", which may cover hundreds of square kilometers.

The landscapes we tend to envision when considering human activities such as timber harvesting or agriculture may match those perceived by many birds and mammals, but not those over which the dynamics of most species (e.g. plants and insects) take place. With the exception of some mega-projects, most human activities tend to alter relatively small patches (e.g. a forest stand or a field). Each of these activities may not pose a serious threat to biological diversity, but their cumulative effects across the landscape

Setting Conservation Targets for Managed Forest Landscapes, ed. M.-A. Villard and B. G. Jonsson. Published by Cambridge University Press.

can be severe. Hence, it is not surprising that human societies have also established more or less intricate regulations to coordinate these activities so that they do not threaten basic human needs (water supply, protection against landslides or avalanches, food production). In fact, landscapes have been "planned" for centuries either by design (e.g. royal gardens, certain settlements) or as a result of interacting social, political, and economic forces.

After millennia of overexploitation of ecological systems through agriculture, hunting, fishing, mining, and forestry, a few pioneers proposed landscape planning principles derived from an understanding of "how the land works" (e.g. Leopold 1933; McHarg 1969). Meanwhile, ecosystems around the world continue to be pushed to the limits of their resilience and often beyond. The resilience of ecosystems depends heavily on the continued presence of certain species and structures which develop or recruit very slowly, such as large-diameter trees or snags or certain lichen or invertebrate species (Bengtsson et al. 2003).

So far, the main strategy of conservation biologists to reduce the rate of ecological degradation has been to set aside reserves. Quantitative targets have been established through international treaties such as those of Rio (1992) and Johannesburg (2002). To guide the selection of protected area networks, sophisticated procedures are being developed to optimize certain parameters of biodiversity (Margules and Pressey 2000). Unfortunately, the range of possibilities is often limited and some reserve networks have to be intensively managed to meet conservation goals owing to resource use and development pressures in the intervening space, also known as the "matrix".

In this book, we submit that biodiversity conservation would greatly benefit from the development of quantitative targets. These targets should not only pertain to reserves, but also to the matrix (Lindenmayer and Franklin 2002), "production landscapes", or simply "managed landscapes". Site-specific, "snapshot" conservation through discrete reserves should be replaced by landscape-scale strategies embracing ecological variability in space and time (e.g. Lindenmayer and Franklin 2002; Bengtsson et al. 2003). Conservation objectives, and corresponding numerical targets, can be established for critical local structures such as dead and dying trees, ecological processes (e.g. fire, insect outbreaks, or flooding by beavers), or landscape elements such as grasslands or old forest. Ultimately, this approach aims to ensure that managed landscapes contribute positively to the conservation of biological diversity, whether in conjunction with or independently from nature reserves. Even arbitrary targets can be useful by focusing conservation efforts (Margules and Pressey 2000). However, this book emphasizes empirical approaches to set targets more objectively by using the responses of certain species, structures, or ecological processes to habitat alteration.

DON'T WE SET TARGETS ALREADY?

Surprisingly few attempts have been made to set quantitative targets because this is both a difficult and risky endeavour. The scientific challenge comes from the multiplicity of relevant factors that must be addressed whereas the risk for those setting targets and the ecosystems involved comes from this very complexity. Researchers naturally tend to shy away from such risks, being trained to collect large data sets and to analyse these data very thoroughly before stating any conclusion about a system under study. In addition, few authors have focused their attention on conservation target setting at the landscape scale. The realization that "the matrix matters" and that reserves must be "functionally connected" to form networks is relatively recent (Merriam 1984; Ricketts 2001; Lindenmayer and Franklin 2002). Furthermore, the empirical knowledge required to implement this holistic vision of conservation lags far behind theoretical forays. None the less, empirically-based, quantitative targets should help focus attention toward particularly important issues and they will empower the forest manager, because one can only manage measurable parameters. In this book, we will define conservation targets as *any quantitative objective determined by using empirical data or realistic models to adjust management intensity with the purpose of maintaining forest biodiversity.*

We submit that research-based conservation targets represent the most efficient way to incorporate conservation values or priorities into the socio-economic agenda of a region or country. Establishing targets helps (1) to focus the attention of all stakeholders (e.g. environmentalists, land owners, land managers, regional or national politicians, conservation biologists) and, when an agreement has been reached, (2) to coordinate the efforts of these various parties. Setting targets also represents a good approach to link basic research to public needs without stifling the curiosity driving it. To be stimulated and efficient, researchers must explore new issues or phenomena; there is no shortage of unexplored areas in the world of conservation target setting! Finally, conservation targets provide useful checkpoints for feedback into adaptive management programs (see Chapter 17, this volume). Conservation planners and ecosystem managers increasingly realize that they cannot "get it right the first time". Targets must evolve along with the global environment. Hence, human activities must be planned by using scientifically rigorous yet flexible approaches. Quantitative targets can thus be implemented in an attempt to keep land use within certain bounds, and they can be adjusted when necessary in ecosystems where we still have the luxury of making mistakes.

When it is based on shaky scientific procedures or "expert advice", target setting can also lead to a massive waste of time and energy or, more dramatically, to the disengagement of stakeholders. Thus, it is critical that scientific standards be established and gradually refined to ensure that the targets set are robust to scrutiny and, thus, easily defensible. This book aims to provide guidance to those who want to contribute to the establishment of a scientific foundation for conservation target setting.

TYPES OF CONSERVATION TARGET

Biodiversity conservation targets can take a variety of forms, depending on the species or functional group, or the space and time scales considered. None the less, we can divide ecological parameters for which we could set targets into four broad categories: (1) local habitat features associated with the presence or abundance of individual species or guilds; (2) landscape structure; (3) demographic parameters; and (4) ecosystem processes.

Critical habitat features

This category pertains to structures that are critical to certain life-history requirements of a species or set of species. Because some of these structures may be relatively rare in the environment, targets may have to be established specifically for them. Suitable sites for reproduction or shelter are an obvious example. Several species nest or roost in tree cavities or "hollows" (e.g. Whitford and Williams 2002; Martin *et al.* 2004). Suitable trees or snags may be relatively rare, especially when the primary excavator or secondary users have a large body size. Trees or logs of a certain type and size may also play a critical role as substrates for certain species of lichen and moss (Berg *et al.* 2002). Large mammals such as canids or bears have fairly specific requirements for denning sites (Fernandez and Palomares 2000). Resources may also be very patchily distributed in the case of insects whose larvae feed on a single species of plant (Hanski and Singer 2001; Hanski and Heino 2003; Paivinen *et al.* 2003). Finally, some species have very specific requirements when selecting mating sites. Well-known cases are species congregating in lekking or rutting sites, such as certain grouse species and ungulates, respectively (Helle *et al.* 1994; Apollonio *et al.* 1998; Hanowski *et al.* 2000).

Landscape structure

Even when a given site provides suitable habitat for a species, its presence or abundance may still be significantly influenced by the proportion of habitat in the surroundings (Mazerolle and Villard 1999; Cushman and McGarigal 2004). This may simply reflect the probability of immigration into the site (Venier and Fahrig 1996) or the fact that the species requires several slightly different habitat types depending on its life-stage, climatic conditions, etc. For example, the probability that larvae of the Bay checkerspot butterfly (*Euphydryas editha bayensis*) will reach the adult stage may vary considerably between different slopes of the same mountain range according to the climatic conditions that year. In wet years, larvae will be more likely to reach the adult stage on warmer, south-facing slopes whereas in dry years, north-facing slopes will provide better conditions (Ehrlich and Murphy 1987). In landscapes where forest, pastures, and cropfields are interspersed, the reproductive success of forest birds may vary greatly as a function of the particular crops or the spatial extent of pastures and their use by potential nest predators (Andrén 1992) or brood parasites (Robinson *et al.* 1995).

Landscape structure designates the particular extent and arrangement of resource patches beyond the scale of a species' home range. Maintaining connectivity among resource patches is an important challenge in managed forest landscapes. For a plant, the concept is equally relevant, because landscape context may influence the seed rain, the availability of pollinators, the intensity of grazing, parasitism, competition, etc. (Jacquemyn *et al.* 2001; Verheyen *et al.* 2003).

Population parameters

Managers of protected areas have often used quantitative targets to guide their interventions when developing conservation strategies for species at risk. Such targets may pertain to the minimum number of individuals required in a population to reduce the loss of genetic variability (Frankel and Soulé 1981) or extinction (Marshall and Edwards-Jones 1998). Procedures to set recovery targets for threatened species are discussed at length by Armstrong and Wittmer (Chapter 13, this volume). Population-viability analysis (PVA) is often used to estimate the extinction risk associated with various scenarios or conservation strategies (Beissinger and McCullough 2002). PVA can in turn be used to define targets for population size or various demographic parameters, e.g. maintaining fecundity above a certain limit.

Ecological processes

Ecologists and land managers now realize the critical importance of certain processes in maintaining the integrity of ecosystems. Natural processes such as fire (Perera *et al.* 2004) and flooding (Naiman and Décamps 1997) may play critical roles in the persistence of certain species or species assemblages. Effects of fire on stand and landscape dynamics have been widely documented. Fire creates optimal conditions for many species associated with dead wood (Hoyt and Hannon 2002; Nappi *et al.* 2003) and its effects on soil and understory vegetation may be critical to the maintenance of long-term forest productivity (Nilsson and Wardle 2005). Managing these processes undoubtedly represents one of the key challenges facing both land stewards and conservation planners.

OBJECTIVES OF THIS BOOK

This book aims to (1) review past attempts and approaches used to set quantitative conservation targets; (2) present empirical approaches that are being used in various forest regions of the world to develop targets; and (3) summarize key statistical and practical issues associated with target setting. Ultimately, we aim to provide a conceptual framework for all the individuals involved in the management of forest lands and interested in developing conservation targets for their own forest region. Although we recognize that tradeoffs are required between ecological principles and socio-economic considerations when implementing conservation targets, the book will focus on the ecological dimension of conservation planning and forest management. The reasons for this are outlined in detail in Chapter 3, this volume.

References

Andrén, H. 1992. Corvid populations and nest predation in relation to forest fragmentation – a landscape perspective. *Ecology* **73**:794–804.

Apollonio, M., M. Festa-Bianchet, F. Mari, E. Bruno and M. Locati. 1998. Habitat manipulation modifies lek use in fallow deer. *Ethology* **104**:603–12.

Balmford, A., A. Bruner, P. Cooper *et al.* 2002. Ecology-economic reasons for conserving wild nature. *Science* **297**:950–3.

Beissinger, S. R. and D. R. McCullough (eds.) 2002. *Population Viability Analysis.* Chicago, IL: University of Chicago Press.

Bengtsson, J., P. Angelstam, T. Elmqvist *et al.* 2003. Reserves, resilience and dynamic landscapes. *Ambio* **32**:389–96.

Berg, Å., U. Gardenfors, T. Hallingback and M. Noren. 2002. Habitat preferences of red-listed fungi and bryophytes in woodland key habitats in southern Sweden – analyses of data from a national survey. *Biodiversity and Conservation* 11:1479–503.

Cushman, S. A. and K. McGarigal. 2004. Hierarchical analysis of forest bird species-environment relationships in the Oregon Coast Range. *Ecological Applications* 14:1090–105.

Ehrlich, P. R. and D. D. Murphy. 1987. Conservation lessons from long-term studies of checkerspot butterflies. *Conservation Biology* 1:122–31.

Fernandez, N. and F. Palomares. 2000. The selection of breeding dens by the endangered Iberian lynx (*Lynx pardinus*): implications for its conservation. *Biological Conservation* 94:51–61.

Frankel, O. H. and M. E. Soulé. 1981. *Conservation and Evolution*. Cambridge, UK: Cambridge University Press.

Hanowski, J. M., D. P. Christian and G. J. Niemi. 2000. Landscape requirements of prairie sharp-tailed grouse *Tympanuchus phasianellus campestris* in Minnesota, USA. *Wildlife Biology* 6:257–63.

Hanski, I. and M. Heino. 2003. Metapopulation-level adaptation of insect host plant preference and extinction-colonization dynamics in heterogeneous landscapes. *Theoretical Population Biology* 64:281–90.

Hanski, I. and M. C. Singer. 2001. Extinction-colonization dynamics and host-plant choice in butterfly metapopulations. *American Naturalist* 158: 341–53.

Helle P., T. Helle and H. Linden. 1994. Capercaillie (*Tetrao urogallus*) lekking sites in fragmented Finnish forest landscape. *Scandinavian Journal of Forest Research* 9:386–96.

Hoyt, J. S. and S. J. Hannon. 2002. Habitat associations of black-backed and three-toed woodpeckers in the boreal forest of Alberta. *Canadian Journal of Forest Research* 32:1881–8.

Jacquemyn, H., B. Butaye and M. Hermy. 2001. Forest plant species richness in small, fragmented mixed deciduous forest patches: the role of area, time and dispersal limitation. *Journal of Biogeography* 28:801–12.

Lamoreux, J. F., J. C. Morrison, T. H. Ricketts *et al.* 2006. Global tests of biodiversity concordance and the importance of endemism. *Nature* 440:212–14.

Leopold, A. 1933. *Game Management*. New York, NY: Scribners.

Lindenmayer, D. B. and J. F. Franklin. 2002. *Conserving Forest Biodiversity: A Comprehensive Multiscaled Approach*. Washington, DC: Island Press.

Margules, C. R. and R. L. Pressey. 2000. Systematic conservation planning. *Nature* 405:243–53.

Marshall, K. and G. Edwards-Jones. 1998. Reintroducing Capercaillie (*Tetrao urogallus*) into southern Scotland: identification of minimum viable populations at potential release sites. *Biodiversity and Conservation* 7:275–96.

Martin, K., K. E. N. Aitken and K. L. Wiebe. 2004. Nest sites and nest webs for cavity-nesting communities in interior British Columbia, Canada: nest characteristics and niche partitioning. *Condor* 106:5–19.

Mazerolle, M. J. and M.-A. Villard. 1999. Patch characteristics and landscape context as predictors of species presence and abundance: a review. *Ecoscience* 6:117–24.

McHarg, I. L. 1969. *Design with Nature*. Garden City, NY: The American Museum of Natural History: Doubleday.

Merriam, G. 1984. Connectivity: a fundamental ecological characteristic of landscape pattern. Pp. 5–15 in J. Brandt and P. Agger (eds.) *Proceedings of the First International Seminar on Methodology in Landscape Ecological Research and Planning*. Roskilde, Denmark: International Association for Landscape Ecology.

Myers, N., R. A. Mittermeier, C. G. Mittermeier, G. A. B. da Fonseca and J. Kent. 2000. Biodiversity hotspots for conservation priorities. *Nature* **403**:853–8.

Naiman, R. J. and H. Décamps. 1997. The ecology of interfaces: riparian zones. *Annual Reviews of Ecology and Systematics* **28**:621–58.

Nappi, A., P. Drapeau, J.-F. Giroux and J.-P. L. Savard. 2003. Snag use by foraging black-backed woodpeckers (*Picoides arcticus*) in a recently burned eastern boreal forest. *Auk* **120**:505–11.

Nilsson, M.-C. and D. A. Wardle. 2005. Understory vegetation as a forest ecosystem driver: evidence from the northern Swedish boreal forest. *Frontiers in Ecology and the Environment* **3**:421–8.

Norris, K. and D. Pain (eds.) 2002. *Conserving Bird Biodiversity: General Principles and their Application*. Cambridge, UK: Cambridge University Press.

O'Connor, C., M. Marvier and P. Kareiva. 2003. Biological vs. social, economic and political priority-setting in conservation. *Ecology Letters* **6**:706–11.

Paivinen, J., P. Ahlroth, V. Kaitala *et al.* 2003. Species richness and regional distribution of myrmecophilous beetles. *Oecologia* **134**:587–95.

Perera, A. H., L. J. Buse and M. G. Weber. 2004. *Emulating Natural Forest Landscape Disturbances: Concepts and Applications*. New York, NY: Columbia University Press.

Ricketts, T. 2001. The matrix matters: effective isolation in fragmented landscapes. *American Naturalist* **158**:87–99.

Robinson, S. K., F. R. Thompson, T. M. Donovan, D. R. Whitehead and J. Faaborg. 1995. Regional forest fragmentation and the nesting success of migratory birds. *Science* **267**:1987–990.

Venier, L. A. and L. Fahrig. 1996. Habitat availability causes the species-abundance relationship. *Oikos* **76**:564–70.

Verheyen, K., O. Honnay, G. Motzkin, M. Hermy and D. R. Foster. 2003. Response of forest plant species to land-use change: a life-history trait-based approach. *Journal of Ecology* **91**:563–77.

Vitousek, P. M., H. A. Mooney, J. Lubchenco and J. M. Melillo. 1997. Human domination of Earth's ecosystems. *Science* **277**:494–9.

Whitford, K. R. and M. R. Williams. 2002. Hollows in jarrah (*Eucalyptus marginata*) and marri (*Corymbia calophylla*) trees. II. Selecting trees to retain for hollow dependent fauna. *Forest Ecology and Management* **160**:215–32.

Wiens, J. A., B. Van Horne and B. R. Noon. 2002. Integrating landscape structure and scale into natural resource management. Pp. 23–67 in J. Liu and W. W. Taylor (eds.) *Integrating Landscape Ecology into Natural Resource Management*. Cambridge, UK: Cambridge University Press.

Setting conservation targets: past and present approaches

BENGT GUNNAR JONSSON AND MARC-ANDRÉ VILLARD

INTRODUCTION

Biodiversity is a term now commonly used in the political arena. However, it has a fairly strict definition that is widely recognized in ecology. In essence, biodiversity refers to genes, species, and ecosystems as levels of organization, and it includes ecosystem structure and function (Noss 1990). These different aspects of biodiversity must also be the starting point for setting conservation goals for forest landscapes. However, when applied to forest management, biodiversity objectives must be broken down into measurable targets based on clear and, preferably, functional links to the overall goals.

Around the world, relatively pristine forest ecosystems have been preserved through the foresight of a few individuals, have been restored at great cost, or they simply persisted by default owing to slow economic development. In regions that are still undeveloped (e.g. portions of the boreal forest or the Amazon basin), targets may be set as proactive measures to limit impacts of foreseeable economic development (see also Chapter 4, this volume). In regions where conservation planning has maintained an intermediate level of ecological integrity, targets must still be set to protect sensitive species or critical ecological processes (see Chapters 8, 9, and 10, this volume). Finally, conservation targets may also represent useful tools to monitor the success of ecological restoration (see Chapter 11, this volume) in regions where major habitat loss and conversion have taken place.

Setting Conservation Targets for Managed Forest Landscapes, ed. M.-A. Villard and B. G. Jonsson. Published by Cambridge University Press.
© Cambridge University Press 2009.

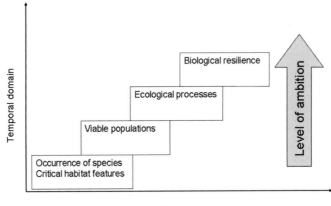

Figure 2.1. Target setting is needed for conservation goals representing different levels of conservation ambition, relating to increasing temporal and spatial domains (based on Angelstam *et al.* 2004).

Any specific target is relevant to a temporal and spatial domain. In addition, it may relate to different levels of conservation ambition. In this respect, at least four levels can be distinguished (Fig. 2.1): (i) occurrence of individual species, community types, or critical habitat features; (ii) viability of populations; (iii) maintenance of ecosystem processes; and (iv) biological resilience. Here, resilience refers to the ability of an ecosystem to withstand external disturbances (e.g. climate change). For each of the four levels, quantitative targets can be set. In this chapter, we will limit the discussion to the first three levels.

To set conservation targets, researchers and land managers have mainly relied on expert opinion, empirically derived rules of thumb, complex ecological models, or a combination thereof. Each approach has strengths and weaknesses, as illustrated by the chapters in this book. In spite of its relative cost-efficiency, expert opinion appears to have limited value compared to purely objective, empirically based modeling (Seoane *et al.* 2005, but see Martin *et al.* 2005). Empirically based rules of thumb may also be misleading and their application should be accompanied by active adaptive management (see Chapter 17, this volume). Finally, more complex ecological models (e.g. population viability analysis, Akçakaya 2004) may represent powerful tools but (a) they are relatively costly, (b) they are highly sensitive to the quality of the data upon which they are based, and (c) their outcome may vary according to the modeling frame selected. Burgman *et al.* (2005)

present a thorough review of the strengths and weaknesses of different landscape modeling approaches.

Rules of thumb have a negative connotation among many conservation biologists. They are often considered to be simplistic, unsubstantiated solutions to conservation problems (e.g. Agardy *et al.* 2003; Westphal *et al.* 2003). Alternatively, case-specific rules of thumb might represent useful quantitative targets when they are based on sound empirical data (Bergman *et al.* 2004; Guénette and Villard 2005) or realistic theoretical models (Etienne and Heesterbeek 2001; Frank 2004; Chapter 7, this volume). For research ecologists trained to explore, understand, and report on the complexity of nature, recommending targets that may be construed as rules of thumb is not a natural tendency. None the less, because overly complex rules cannot be applied to real-world ecosystems, case-specific rules of thumb may represent an efficient starting point to move toward more complex conservation strategies (Frank 2004, 2005). They may also represent a first step when launching an adaptive management scheme because they favor early action rather than the all too common "paralysis by analysis" leading to the development of ever more sophisticated models.

In this chapter, we review a variety of quantitative biodiversity targets that have been proposed, addressing levels of organization ranging from genes to communities and ecosystems. Throughout this exercise, however, we assume that planning and evaluation should be conducted at the landscape level. We will examine approaches used to derive targets, and their apparent influence on real-world forest management.

APPROACHES USED TO SET CONSERVATION TARGETS

In this section, we review the main approaches used to determine quantitative conservation targets, which may in turn be integrated into landscape-level conservation strategies (Table 2.1). Examples of approaches and applications are given in the other chapters in this volume.

Genetic targets

The loss of genetic variation in forest species is a cause for concern in many regions of the world; several studies have analysed the genetic structure and variation in forest plants and animals, especially in relation to ongoing habitat loss, fragmentation, and population reduction. The emerging consensus is that loss of genetic variation increases extinction risk (Frankham 2003; Ouborg *et al.* 2006). However, it appears that specific targets,

Table 2.1. *Types of quantitative target that can be applied to the conservation of forest biodiversity, along with the main approach(es) used by their proponents*

Type of biodiversity target	Approach used	Examples	Reference(s)
	Genetic targets		
Effective population size		Analysis of inbreeding and genetic drift as a function of population size	Nunney and Campbell (1993)
Natural level of genetic variation		Variation in allelic diversity as a function of sample size	Blakesley *et al.* (2004)
	Species-level targets		
Probability of occurrence		Habitat models – linear regressions with stand attributes; Habitat Suitability Index	Edenius *et al.* (2004)
Minimum viable population		Fitness estimates – plant populations; Population viability analysis (PVA) – vertebrates	Reed (2005), Reed *et al.* (2003), Akçakaya (2004)
Minimum viable metapopulation		Population viability analysis; Incidence function; Simulation modeling	Guttierez (2005), Baguette and Schtickzelle (2003), Snäll *et al.* (2005)
Metapopulation persistence		Metapopulation capacity of the landscape	Hanski and Ovaskainen (2000)
	Community-level targets		
Species richness		Species–area relationship	Desmet and Cowling (2004)
Community composition		Indicator species analysis	Macdonald (2007)

Habitat and ecosystem targets

Minimum habitat area	Threshold in species occurrences; Species–area relationship	Hayden et al. (1985), Watson et al. (2001)
Structural characteristics of the habitat, local (stand) level	Thresholds in species occurrence – logistic regression and ROC analysis	Guénette and Villard (2005)
Habitat amount (territory level or landscape context)	Thresholds in patch occupancy – piecewise regression and logistic regression	Homan et al. (2004), Suorsa et al. (2005)
	Segmented logistic regression; Logistic regression and ROC analysis	Betts et al. (2007), Chapter 9 (this volume)
Connectivity	Simulation modeling	Flather and Bevers (2002), Ovaskainen and Hanski (2003)
	Incidence function model and spatially explicit simulation	Schultz and Crone (2005)
Natural disturbance (frequency, extent, intensity)	Landscape division according to disturbance regime	Angelstam (1998)
	Forest edge structure	McIntire and Fortin (2006)
	Stand age distribution in the landscape	Pennanen and Kuuluvainen (2002)

e.g. minimum population size or fraction of natural variation maintained, are rarely included in forest management plans.

Based on empirical data and statistical analyses, effective population size estimates to reduce the risk of inbreeding and genetic drift are in the range 500–5,000 reproducing individuals (i.e. effective population size). This often translates into actual population sizes of more than 10,000 individuals (Thomas 1990). Genetic variation is often difficult to manage except in breeding and restoration programs, where the genetic material can be controlled. Blakesley et al. (2004) provide a good example of forest restoration in the tropics. They used microsatellite markers to define the need to sample seeds from many sites and the number of seed trees required to obtain the level of genetic variation observed in natural settings.

Species-level targets

Conservation target setting is perhaps most common at the level of single species or a limited set of species. This stems in part from the observed decline in the populations of many species, but probably also from the tendency of ecologists to study the detailed biology of individual species. This has resulted in policies and conservation measures directed to these species. Perhaps a more pragmatic argument for focusing on species is the fact that there is a risk that management of stand structure or landscape composition, even when fulfilling stated goals, may be accompanied by some degree of species loss (Lambeck 1997; Simberloff 1998; Chapter 7, this volume).

One of the main objectives of policies addressing biodiversity conservation is to halt species loss. Therefore, species must be part of conservation strategies and monitoring programs at one level or another. By using the requirements of focal species as conservation targets, the hope is to achieve efficiency in conservation actions (Simberloff 1998; Caro and Doherty 1999). However, strict species-specific approaches are generally ineffective to conserve entire ecosystems and most researchers argue for some kind of multi-species approach (e.g. Lambeck 1997; Chapter 6, this volume).

The focal species approach assumes that the demands of a limited group of species may encapsulate the demands of many other species. That is, they do not only show statistical correlation with other species, but are functionally linked in terms of ecological requirements (see Edenius and Mikusiński 2006). This assumption is not fully supported by empirical studies (Lindenmayer et al. 2002). For example, Andelman and Fagan (2000) showed that a random selection of species as "indicators" was just as efficient as those species targeted as umbrella species. Other authors, however, found that certain species may indicate the richness within larger species groups (e.g. Bonn and Schröder 2001; Mikusiński *et al.* 2001; Roberge and Angelstam 2006).

Population-level targets

Population-level targets fall into two broad categories. They may either focus on habitat conditions predicting the occurrence of species (e.g. habitat suitability models; Guisan and Zimmermann 2000; Pearce and Boyce 2006) or on the long-term persistence of local populations (population viability models; Morris and Doak 2002). Both approaches have the potential to provide quantitative targets applicable in forest management. Habitat suitability models can be used to map the probability of occurrence of particular species in the landscape with fairly limited data, which can then be included in forest management plans integrating multiple goals (Edenius and Mikusiński 2006; Chapter 15, this volume). Population viability models, on the other hand, incorporate much-needed temporal aspects of the dynamics of the populations at hand. Although they require higher-quality data than habitat suitability models, they allow comparing the putative outcomes of different management scenarios on the focal species and, thus, they can meet higher levels of conservation ambition. Population viability analysis has seen rapid development over the past decades (e.g. Beissinger and McCullough 2002; Akçakaya 2004).

In addition to temporal trends in population size, the rapid fragmentation of most forest landscapes calls for the consideration of spatial aspects. Metapopulation theory has opened the door to the quantitative analysis of complex population dynamics in a spatially explicit context (Levins 1968; Hanski 1999). The metapopulation concept implies that local extinction and recolonization of habitat patches drive the occurrence and persistence of species in fragmented landscapes. It highlights critical demographic characteristics such as dispersal ability and local persistence time. As modeling tools, the incidence function model (Hanski 1999) and other spatially explicit approaches are increasingly used in forest management planning (e.g. Wintle *et al.* 2005; Guttierez 2005; Venier *et al.* 2007). However, for certain species, managed forest landscapes may be too permeable to the movements of individuals (e.g. Gobeil and Villard 2002) to allow us to apply the metapopulation approach because local extinctions and recolonizations are relatively rare. In such cases, where dispersal is not limiting, conservation targets should focus on critical habitat features at the local scale (Edman *et al.* 2004; Guénette and Villard 2005).

Community-level targets

The relationship between area and species richness (see Box 2.1) is perhaps the best established pattern in nature. Owing to the strength of this relationship, it has frequently been invoked as a basis for target setting (Tjorve 2002; Desmet and Cowling 2004; Chapter 16, this volume). This approach allows us either to predict the number of species lost as a certain fraction of habitat is removed, or to estimate the area needed to retain a certain fraction of species. Although it is based on a snapshot of the system at hand, this approach has the advantage of requiring only species richness data from a range of spatial scales.

Site selection algorithms (Pressey *et al.* 1997) are closely related to species area curves as they provide information on how species richness increases with the inclusion of potential sites. These algorithms aim to maximize the representation of species over a limited number of sites considered for conservation. They are powerful and can include weights for different species and other "marginal restrictions" (Arponen *et al.* 2005; Moilanen 2007) to put more emphasis on, for instance, threatened species or certain habitat features.

The application of species–area curves and site-selection algorithms to conservation is not without problems. By only representing species in a network of protected sites, there is no guarantee that their populations will be viable over the long term. In a worst case scenario, sites selected to obtain the minimal set required to represent a given group of species may actually maximize the risk of extinction because small sites, which host small populations, will be favored. In an attempt to analyse site selection and population persistence, Cabeza and Moilanen (2003) exemplify how metapopulation models can be integrated into site-selection algorithms to avoid this type of problem.

Species richness estimates disregard actual species identity, which limit the value of this parameter as a primary target. Changes in species assemblages associated with forest management have been well documented (e.g. Hobson and Schieck 1999; Økland *et al.* 2003). Forestry operations may include ditching, fertilization, and changes in tree species composition and stand structure, which all potentially influence the overall structure and composition of species assemblages. Protection against forest fires will prolong succession at the expense of early successional stages. This suggests that the composition of species assemblages could be used as a target. The standard approach is ordination, which provides a numerical description of the species composition (Legendre and Legendre 1998). Ordination may be used for quantitative description and delineation of successional stages

(Klenner *et al.* 2000) and types of species assemblage (Ito *et al.* 2006). Instead of referring only to time since disturbance or management intervention, ordination techniques could provide a stronger link to, for instance, assemblage structures typical of unmanaged systems undergoing natural disturbance regimes.

Habitat and ecosystem targets

In some respects, setting targets in terms of habitat components, landscape structure, or ecosystem processes is just the flip side of the coin compared with target setting for species occurrence and population viability. In many cases, the same modeling approaches can be applied. There is, however, a fundamental difference in their application. Species-based targets are appropriate for scientific evaluation of conservation actions (Larson *et al.* 2004). They can thus serve as components in both strategic planning and monitoring of conservation actions (Rempel *et al.* 2004). Habitat and ecosystem targets, on the other hand, may actually correspond to the tactical and operational tools that forest managers can utilize to achieve conservation goals. The latter type of target has a clear "currency" (e.g. number of retained trees, area of protected forest), which allows comparison of the economic tradeoffs among competing conservation approaches (Kliskey *et al.* 1999; Marzluff *et al.* 2002). This is not to deny the importance of protecting habitats and ecosystems *per se*, but it is a fact that, on an operational level, species-based targets may be less likely to be implemented.

The majority of forest species are dependent on specific forest components. Different tree species as well as old or dead trees are important habitat components for many species (Berg *et al.* 1994). Thus, it is clear that the description and quantification of these structures should be included in the target-setting process (Bütler *et al.* 2004a; Penttilä *et al.* 2004). However, their application to conservation can be problematic. Targets determined for individual species or species guilds may not be applicable to the full range of biodiversity under consideration. Also, the assumption of a clear shift in ecological conditions around a threshold level in the focal habitat component needs to be validated (Muradian 2001; Guénette and Villard 2004; Ranius and Fahrig 2006; Chapter 10, this volume).

One major advantage of quantitative targets for specific substrates and habitats at the level of forest stands is that they are amenable to modeling (e.g. Ranius and Kindvall 2004; Chapter 10, this volume). The possibility of predicting stand attributes related to biodiversity by using models also allows us to predict volumes and timber quality, which makes it an efficient decision support system (Li *et al.* 2000). Thus, the ecological and economic tradeoffs associated with different management options may be analysed (Jonsson *et al.* 2006). They might also be used as objectives in more sophisticated statistical optimization analyses (e.g. simulated annealing, taboo search, heuristic models), which have proven to be valuable when analysing landscape scale issues (e.g. Öhman and Lämås 2005; Öhman and Eriksson 1998; Chapter 15, this volume).

Patch area and composition

Predicting the presence or absence of a particular species in individual stands or forest patches is a frequent objective of conservation biology studies. Numerous researchers have addressed the links between species occurrence and different sets of environmental variables. A major tool for this purpose is logistic regression. For a given a set of independent variables, this method provides a prediction of the probability of occurrence of a species. Given that some functional relationship exists, such models may have a strong impact on management as they identify levels of specific habitat features that are required for the occurrence of focal species. When a threshold is identified in the occurrence of the focal species, this critical value may guide the development of quantitative targets for conservation and management (Bütler *et al.* 2004a; Guénette and Villard 2005). Statistical methods in this field have evolved rapidly; several methods for comparing alternative models and detecting thresholds are readily available (Cumming 2000; Manel *et al.* 2001; Chapter 9, this volume). A limitation of classical logistic regression is that it assumes a linear relation between the independent variables and the occurrence of the species. This may be mitigated by applying appropriate transformations to the independent variables but, in some cases, the relations are complex and interactions among variables may reduce the strength and also the biological relevance of the derived models. Promising approaches to address this limitation are being developed, including Generalized Additive Models (Guisan *et al.* 2002) and Non-parametric Multiplicative Regression (McCune 2006).

Landscape structure and connectivity

Local, stand-level variables are known to influence the occurrence of species. However, a growing body of evidence suggests that landscape composition plays a role in regulating local biodiversity patterns. With the development of metapopulation theory and associated modeling approaches, the role of dispersal is increasingly being considered. With the recognition that location matters and that isolation of forest patches may cause severe declines in the local populations and metapopulations of certain species, landscape connectivity is now the focus of a lot of attention (Crooks and Sanjayan 2006). In its simplest form, the isolation of a forest patch can be measured as the distance to the nearest similar patch. However, from the metapopulation perspective, all patches within the dispersal range of a focal species may influence the probability of colonization of any particular patch. To measure this, the concept of the landscape metapopulation capacity was developed (Hanski and Ovaskainen 2000). Metapopulation capacity is indexed by using the area, the spatial location, and, in some cases, the quality of the habitat patches. Although we are unaware of any real-world application of this concept to landscape planning, it clearly is a valuable tool to guide conservation strategies in order to increase the probability of persistence of the (meta)populations in question. Without explicitly modeling species dynamics, Aune et al. (2005) used a common connectivity function (see Moilanen and Nieminen 2002) to analyse the degree of structural connectivity among small protected areas (woodland key habitats) and the established protected area network in northern Sweden. Their results indicated that, although widely distributed, the protected areas were likely too small and scattered to improve functional connectivity for most forest species except those with very high dispersal ability.

Natural disturbances

Natural disturbance is an integral component of any forest ecosystem. It influences age structure and species composition of the tree layer and is thus the basis for most forest classification schemes. Restoring forest ecosystems by focusing on natural disturbances has become a popular approach for conservation planning (e.g. Attiwill 1994; Angelstam 1998). To set targets for the restoration of natural disturbance regimes, detailed historical data are required. Based mainly on forest fires, a number of modeling approaches reconstructing past disturbance are available (e.g. Chapter 7, this volume). These may be traced back to early gap models like JABOWA (Botkin et al. 1972), individual tree models like SORTIE (Pacala et al. 1993), and recently developed models such as LANDIS (Mladenoff 2004) and derivatives thereof such as FIN-LANDIS (Pennanen and Kuuluvainen 2002) that simulate disturbance, succession, and seed dispersal over large landscapes. Although challenging to parameterize, these models do generate predictions of forest structure under natural disturbance that might be used to formulate conservation targets. If predictions on natural forest type and stand age distributions are available, they may provide baseline information against which the present landscape can be compared.

EXAMPLES OF TARGET-SETTING APPROACHES

This section presents selected case studies where quantitative approaches to target setting have been developed for the conservation of particular values. Additional examples can be found throughout the book.

Habitat requirements of species may be quantified by using snapshot data on occurrence of individual species and translated into habitat suitability maps or minimum levels of critical resources. For example, Guénette and Villard (2005) examined the relationship between the probability of occurrence of forest bird species, tree species composition (mainly the proportion of deciduous trees), and stand structure variables using logistic regression. Then, they used ROC analysis to identify threshold values in species responses to those habitat gradients (see Chapters 3 and 9, this volume, for details). ROC (receiver-operating characteristic) analysis allows identifying points optimizing model performance, here the prediction of species presence/absence. ROC threshold values obtained for individual species were then combined to suggest target levels for key variables, such as the density of large-diameter trees (Fig. 2.2). Following this study, the target value for this parameter was substantially increased in management guidelines for "old hardwood habitat" in New Brunswick, Canada (NB-DNR 2005).

The American three-toed woodpecker (*Picoides dorsalis*) is one of the most demanding bird species in boreal forests with respect to dead wood; it is also considered as a keystone species (Imbeau and Desrochers 2002). It feeds on insects in large dying and recently dead trees (snags). In a study addressing the habitat requirements of a closely related species, the Eurasian three-toed woodpecker (*P. tridactylus*), Bütler *et al.* (2004b) applied two different approaches: one theoretical, that was based on the energy demands of a woodpecker breeding pair, and an empirical one whereby the relationship between snag density and woodpecker occurrence was examined in a number of small landscapes in Switzerland. Independently, both approaches yielded a roughly similar prediction of the required density of snags. For a 90% probability of occurrence, the species required on average 14 snags ($\geq$21 cm in diameter at breast height) per hectare (corresponding to 18 m^3 ha^{-1}) over a habitat area of 100 ha. Predictions from the energetic model strengthened the conclusion that observed occurrence patterns reflect actual habitat requirements of the species.

In a long-term research program on arboreal marsupials in Australian mountain ash forests (*Eucalyptus* spp.), Lindenmayer and McCarthy (2006) presented an evaluation of the application of population viability analysis

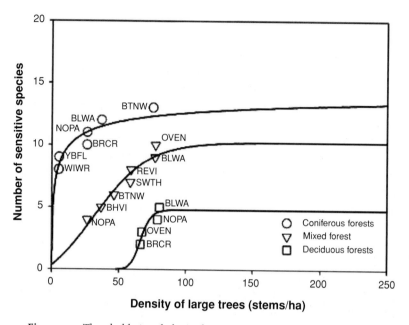

Figure 2.2. Thresholds (symbols) in the occurrence of forest birds as a function of the density of trees ≥30 cm in diameter at breast height in three different stand types. Four-letter codes refer to bird species (modified from Guénette and Villard 2005).

(PVA) models to guide forest management. One of their main aims was to assess the value of integrating monitoring data and PVA models. Early modeling attempts had identified certain targets for nesting sites (old trees with hollows) and food resources (amount of Acacia forage), as these were key drivers in the population dynamics. These factors were further translated into extinction risks expressed as a function of forest patch area. The original models for two species, Leadbeater's Possum (*Gymnobelideus leadbeateri*) and the Greater Glider (*Petauroides volans*), were evaluated by using long-term monitoring data. Although shown not to fully capture the biological demands of the two species, the models largely confirmed the area requirements for viable populations. Based on modified versions of the original models that better captured the biology of the species, new potential management guidelines have emerged, including retention patches for both nesting sites and foraging habitat. This is a good example of quantitative targets based on statistical models that influenced both the management of particular species but also how PVA models may be used to redirect management as well as monitoring schemes. A key lesson here is that although the early models were not perfect, they still guided management in a direction that turned out to be favorable to the species. However, the close monitoring of the system was also very important to assess the validity of early management interventions (see Chapter 17, this volume).

The three previous examples show how targets can be based on individual species or groups of ecologically similar species. However, forest management at the landscape scale can (or should) rarely be based on only a limited set of species. A complementary approach in strategic target setting is to consider the natural disturbance regimes and to draw from them conclusions on the distribution of different forest types and successional stages. The study conducted by Scheller *et al.* (2005) in the Boundary Waters Canoe (BWC) area of northern Minnesota provides a good example. The authors applied the LANDIS simulation (He and Mladenoff 1999) to model effects of continued fire suppression compared to a reintroduction of fires with fire intervals of 50, 100, or 200 years. The model suggested that a reintroduction of fires at intervals of 50–100 years would most likely restore and maintain the natural structure of forest and successional stages. Hence, the LANDIS model provided clear targets for the management of forest fires and other disturbances at the landscape scale (e.g. Akçakaya *et al.* 2004).

Many other relevant examples showing the value of quantitative targets in forest management could be mentioned. They illustrate significant progress compared to qualitative assumptions or expert opinion. As they are model-driven, the targets can be objectively adjusted (as the Australian example is clearly showing) when additional biological data are obtained, making them increasingly relevant to the system at hand. The examples also represent increasing levels of conservation ambition, from finding individual sites that are likely to host a species, to models that explicitly include the dynamics of the species and its habitat to, finally, a model that incorporates the main driving process at landscape scale and thus should be able to maintain a dynamic ecosystem.

We strongly believe that applying a more stringent quantitative approach to conservation target setting will increase the efficiency of management actions. However, we also stress the importance of making sure that the tools and models applied are relevant to the spatial and temporal domain of the system at hand. Further, a distinction should be made between strategic, tactical, and operational planning. At the strategic level, quantitative goals and targets are set. Then, tactical choices must be made to specify, for example, the timing and location of different activities. Finally, operational procedures must be chosen and implemented in the field (see also Chapter 17, this volume).

Box 2.1 Species–area relationship

It is considered an ecological law that the number of species (species richness) increases with habitat area. For saproxylic species, this may be either the area of a suitable forest stand or the actual volume of dead wood. The reasons for this general relationship are several. (1) More individuals fit into a larger area; assuming random distribution of species, more individuals translate into more species. (2) A larger area would be expected to be characterized by a more heterogeneous environment and, therefore, more distinct habitats for specialized species. (3) A larger area will host larger populations of component species, decreasing the risk of extinction of individual populations.

The relationship is well defined mathematically by;

$$S = c\,A^z$$

where S represents the number of species and A the area of habitat. Two parameters, c and z, define the actual relation between richness and area. The associated graphical representation is given in Figure A, below. The relationship is easier to represent if we take the logarithm of species richness and the area, i.e.

$$\log S = \log c + z \log A.$$

This transforms the relationship into a straight line. An interesting and important aspect is that the z-value provides the rate at which species richness decreases with decreasing area regardless of which initial area we consider. A certain percent decrease in area is always associated with a certain percent decrease in species richness, set by the z-value. Numerous studies have explored this relationship and the range of z-values is surprisingly narrow, most studied reporting z-values between 0.15 and 0.35 (Rosenzweig 1995). Setting even a modest z-value of 0.20 translates to a loss of 37% of species given a habitat loss of 90%.

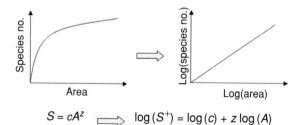

Figure A. Theoretical relationship between species richness and habitat area in arithmetic space (left) and logarithmic space (right). Area can be substituted for dead wood volumes, as many studies show a strong relation between habitat availability in the form of dead wood volume and the richness of saproxylic species.

References

Agardy, T., P. Bridgewater, M. P. Crosby *et al.* 2003. Dangerous targets? Unresolved issues and ideological clashes around marine protected areas. *Aquatic Conservation – Marine and Freshwater Ecosystems* 13:353–67.

Akçakaya, H. R. 2004. Using models for species conservation and management. Pp. 3–14 in H. R. Akçakaya *et al.* (eds.) *Species Conservation and Management.* New York, NY: Oxford University Press.

Akçakaya, H. R., V. C. Radeloff, D. J. Mladenoff and H. S. He. 2004. Integrating landscape and metapopulation modeling approaches: viability of the Sharp-tailed Grouse in a dynamic landscape. *Conservation Biology* 18:526–37.

Andelman, S. J. and W. F. Fagan. 2000. Umbrellas and flagships: efficient conservation surrogates or expensive mistakes? *Proceedings of the National Academy of Sciences of the United States of America* 97:5954–9.

Angelstam, P. K. 1998. Maintaining and restoring biodiversity in European boreal forests by developing natural disturbance regimes. *Journal of Vegetation Science* 9:593–602.

Angelstam, P., S. Boutin, F. Schmiegelow *et al.* 2004. Targets for biodiversity conservation – a rationale for macroecological research and adaptive management. *Ecological Bulletins* 51:487–509.

Arponen, A., R. K. Heikkinen, C. D. Thomas and A. Moilanen. 2005. The value of biodiversity in reserve selection: representation, species weighting, and benefit functions. *Conservation Biology* 19:2009–14.

Attiwill, P. M. 1994. The disturbance of forest ecosystems: the ecological basis for conservative management. *Forest Ecology and Management* 63:247–300.

Aune, K., B. G. Jonsson and J. Moen. 2005. Isolation and edge effects among woodland key habitats in Sweden: making fragmentation into forest policy? *Biological Conservation* 124:89–95.

Baguette, M. and N. Schtickzelle. 2003. Local population dynamics are important to the conservation of metapopulations in highly fragmented landscapes. *Journal of Applied Ecology* 40:404–12.

Beissinger, S. R. and D. R. McCullough (eds.) 2002. *Population Viability Analysis.* Chicago, IL: University of Chicago Press.

Berg, Å., B. Ehnström, L. Gustafsson *et al.* 1994. Threatened plant, animal, and fungus species in Swedish forests – distribution and habitat associations. *Conservation Biology* 8:718–31.

Bergman, K. O., J. Askling, O. Ekberg *et al.* 2004. Landscape effects on butterfly assemblages in an agricultural region. *Ecography* 27:619–28.

Betts, M. G., G. J. Forbes and A. W. Diamond. 2007. Thresholds in songbird occurrence in relation to landscape structure. *Conservation Biology* 21:1046–58.

Blakesley D., G. Pakkad, C. James, F. Torre and S. Elliott. 2004. Genetic diversity of *Castanopsis acuminatissima* (Bl.) A. DC. in northern Thailand and the selection of seed trees for forest restoration. *New Forests* 27:89–100.

Bonn, A. and B. Schröder. 2001. Habitat models and their transfer for single and multi species groups: a case study in an alluvial forest. *Ecography* 24:483–96.

Botkin, D. B., J. F. Janak and J. R. Wallis. 1972. Some ecological consequences of a computer model of forest growth. *Journal of Ecology* 60:849–73.

Burgman, M. A., D. B. Lindenmayer and J. Elith. 2005. Managing landscapes for conservation under uncertainty. *Ecology* 86:2007–17.

Bütler, R., P. Angelstam, P. Ekelund and R. Schlaepfer. 2004a. Dead wood threshold values for the three-toed woodpecker presence in boreal and sub-Alpine forest. *Biological Conservation* 75:227–43.

Bütler, R., P. Angelstam and R. Schlaepfer. 2004b. Quantitative snag targets for the three-toed woodpecker *Picoides tridactylus*. *Ecological Bulletins* 51:219–32.

Cabeza, M. and A. Moilanen. 2003. Site-selection algorithms and habitat loss. *Conservation Biology* 17:1402–13.

Caro, T. M. and G. Doherty. 1999. On the use of surrogate species in conservation biology. *Conservation Biology* 13:805–14.

Crooks, K. R. and M. Sanjayan (eds.) 2006. *Connectivity Conservation.* Cambridge, UK: Cambridge University Press.

Cumming, G. S. 2000. Using between model comparison to fine-tune linear models of species ranges. *Journal of Biogeography* 27:441–55.

Desmet, P. and R. Cowling. 2004. Using the species-area relationship to set baseline targets for conservation. *Ecology and Society* 9(2):11. Available online at www.ecologyandsociety.org/vol9/iss2/art11/.

Edenius, L., T. Brodin and N. White. 2004. Occurrence of Siberian jay *Perisoreus infaustus* in relation to amount of old forest at landscape and home range scale. *Ecological Bulletins* 51:241–7.

Edenius, L. and G. Mikusiński. 2006. Utility of habitat suitability models as biodiversity assessment tools in forest management. *Scandinavian Journal of Forest Research* 21 (suppl. 7):62–72.

Edman, M., M. Gustafsson, J. Stenlid, B. G. Jonsson and L. Ericson. 2004. Spore deposition of wood-decaying fungi – importance of landscape composition. *Ecography* 27:103–11.

Etienne, R. S. and J. A. P. Heesterbeek. 2001. Rules of thumb for conservation of metapopulations based on a stochastic winking-patch model. *American Naturalist* 158:389–407.

Flather, C. H. and M. Bevers. 2002. Patchy reaction-diffusion and population abundance: the relative importance of habitat amount and arrangement. *American Naturalist* 159:40–56.

Frank, K. 2004. Ecologically differentiated rules of thumb for habitat network design – lessons from a formula. *Biodiversity and Conservation* 13:189–206.

Frank, K. 2005. Metapopulation persistence in heterogeneous landscapes: lessons about the effect of stochasticity. *American Naturalist* 165:374–88.

Frankham, R. 2003. Genetics and conservation biology. *Comptes Rendus Biologie* 326:S22-S29.

Gobeil, J.-F. and M.-A. Villard. 2002. Permeability of three boreal forest landscape types to bird movements as determined from experimental translocations. *Oikos* 98:447–58.

Guénette, J.-S. and M.-A. Villard. 2004. Do empirical thresholds truly reflect species tolerances to habitat alteration? *Ecological Bulletins* 51:163–71.

Guénette, J.-S. and M.-A. Villard. 2005. Thresholds in forest bird response to habitat alteration as quantitative targets for conservation. *Conservation Biology* 19:1168–80.

Guisan, A. and N. E. Zimmermann. 2000. Predictive habitat distribution models in Ecology. *Ecological Modelling* 135:147–86.

Guisan A., T. C. Edwards and T. Hastie. 2002. Generalized linear and generalized additive models in studies of species distributions: setting the scene. *Ecological Modelling* 157:89–100.

Guttierez, D. 2005. Effectiveness of existing reserves in the long-term protection of a regionally rare butterfly. *Conservation Biology* 19:1586–97.

Hanski, I. 1999. *Metapopulation Ecology*. Oxford, UK: Oxford University Press.

Hanski, I. and O. Ovaskainen. 2000. The metapopulation capacity of a fragmented landscape. *Nature* 404:755–8.

Hayden, T. J., J. Faaborg and R. L. Clawson. 1985. Estimates of minimum area requirements for Missouri (USA) forest birds. *Transactions of the Missouri Academy of Sciences* 19:11–22.

He, H. S. and D. J. Mladenoff. 1999. Spatially explicit and stochastic simulation of forest landscape fire disturbance and succession. *Ecology* 80:81–99.

Hobson, K. A. and J. Schieck. 1999. Changes in bird communities in boreal mixedwood forest: harvest and wildfire effects over 30 years. *Ecological Applications* 9:849–63.

Homan, R. N., B. S. Windmiller and J. M. Reed. 2004. Critical thresholds associated with habitat loss for two vernal pool-breeding amphibians. *Ecological Applications* 14:1547–53.

Imbeau, L. and A. Desrochers. 2002. Foraging ecology and use of drumming trees by three-toed woodpeckers. *Journal of Wildlife Management* 66:222–31.

Ito, S., S. Ishigami, N. Mizoue and G. P. Buckley. 2006. Maintaining plant species composition and diversity of understory vegetation under strip-clearcutting forestry in conifer plantations in Kyushu, southern Japan. *Forest Ecology and Management* 231:234–41.

Jonsson, M., T. Ranius, H. Ekvall *et al.* 2006. Cost-effectiveness of silvicultural measures to increase substrate availability for red-listed wood-living organisms in Norway spruce forests. *Biological Conservation* 127:443–62.

Klenner, W., W. Kurz and S. Beukema. 2000. Habitat patterns in forested landscapes: management practices and uncertainty associated with natural disturbances. *Computers and Electronics in Agriculture* 27:243–62.

Kliskey, A. D., E. C. Lofroth, W. A. Thompson, S. Brown and H. Schreier. 1999. Simulating and evaluating alternative resource-use strategies using GIS-based habitat suitability indices. *Landscape and Urban Planning* 45:163–75.

Lambeck, R. J. 1997. Focal-species: a multi-species umbrella for nature conservation. *Conservation Biology* 11:849–56.

Larson, M. A., F. R. Thompson, J. J. Millspaugh, W. D. Dijak and S. R. Shifley. 2004. Linking population viability, habitat suitability, and landscape simulation models for conservation planning. *Ecological Modelling* 180:103–18.

Legendre, P. and L. Legendre. 1998. *Numerical Ecology*. Amsterdam: Elsevier.

Levins, R. 1968. *Evolution in Changing Environments*. Princeton, NJ: Princeton University Press.

Li, H., D. I. Gartner, P. Mou and C. C. Trettin. 2000. A landscape model (LEEMATH) to evaluate effects of management impacts on timber and wildlife habitat. *Computers and Electronics in Agriculture* 27:263–92.

Lindenmayer, D. B. and M. A. McCarthy. 2006. Evaluation of PVA models of arboreal marsupials: coupling models with long-term monitoring data. *Biodiversity and Conservation* 15:4079–96.

Lindenmayer, D. B., A. D. Manning, P. L. Smith *et al.* 2002. The focal-species approach and landscape restoration: a critique. *Conservation Biology* 16:338–45.

Macdonald, S. E. 2007. Effects of partial post-fire salvage harvesting on vegetation communities in the boreal mixedwood forest region of northeastern Alberta, Canada. *Forest Ecology and Management* 239:21–31.

Manel, S., H. C. Williams and S. J. Ormerod. 2001. Evaluating presence–absence models in ecology: the need to account for prevalence. *Journal of Applied Ecology* 38:921–31.

Martin, T. G., P. M. Kuhnert, K. Mengersen and H. P. Possingham. 2005. The power of expert opinion in ecological models using Bayesian methods: impact of grazing on birds. *Ecological Applications* 15:266–80.

Marzluff, J. M., J. J. Millspaugh, K. R. Ceder *et al.* 2002. Modeling changes in wildlife habitat and timber revenues in response to forest management. *Forest Science* 48:191–202.

McCune, B. 2006. Non-parametric habitat models with automatic interactions. *Journal of Vegetation Science* 17:819–30.

McIntire, E. J. B. and M. J. Fortin. 2006. Structure and function of wildfire and mountain pine beetle forest boundaries. *Ecography* 29:309–18.

Mikusiński, G., M. Gromadzki and P. Chylarecki. 2001. Woodpeckers as indicators of forest bird diversity. *Conservation Biology* 15:208–17.

Mladenoff, D. J. 2004. LANDIS and forest landscape models. *Ecological Modelling* 180:7–19.

Moilanen, A. 2007. Landscape zonation, benefit functions and target-based planning: unifying reserve selection strategies. *Biological Conservation* 134:571–9.

Moilanen, A. and M. Nieminen. 2002. Simple connectivity measures in spatial ecology. *Ecology* 83:1131–45.

Morris, W. F. and D. F. Doak. 2002. *Quantitative Conservation Biology.* Sunderland, MA: Sinauer Associates.

Muradian, R. 2001. Ecological thresholds: a survey. *Ecological Economics* 38:7–24.

NB-DNR. 2005. *Habitat Definitions for Old Forest Habitat in New Brunswick.* Fredericton, NB: Department of Natural Resources, Government of New Brunswick.

Noss, R. F. 1990. Indicators for monitoring biodiversity: a hierarchical approach. *Conservation Biology* 4:355–64.

Nunney, L. and K. A. Campbell. 1993. Assessing minimum viable population size: demography meets population genetics. *Trends in Ecology and Evolution* 8:234–9.

Öhman, K. and T. Lämås. 2005. Reducing forest fragmentation in long-term forest planning by using the shape index. *Forest Ecology and Management* 212:346–57.

Öhman, L. and L. O. Eriksson. 1998. The core area concept in forming contiguous areas for long-term forest planning. *Canadian Journal of Forest Research* 28:1032–9.

Økland, T., K. Rydgren, R. H. Økland, K. O. Storaunet and J. Rolstad. 2003. Variation in environmental conditions, understorey species number, abundance and composition among natural and managed Piceabies forest stands. *Forest Ecology and Management* 177:17–37.

Ouborg, N. J., P. Vergeer and C. Mix. 2006. The rough edges of the conservation genetics paradigm for plants. *Journal of Ecology* **94**:1233–48.

Ovaskainen, O. and I. Hanski. 2003. How much does an individual habitat fragment contribute to metapopulation dynamics and persistence? *Theoretical Population Biology* **64**:481–95.

Pacala, S. W., C. D. Canham and J. A. Silander. 1993. Forest models defined by field measurements. I. The design of a northeastern forest simulator. *Canadian Journal of Forest Research* **23**:1980–8.

Pearce, J. L. and M. S. Boyce. 2006. Modelling distribution and abundance with presence-only data. *Journal of Applied Ecology* **43**:405–12.

Pennanen, J. and T. Kuuluvainen. 2002. A spatial simulation approach to natural forest landscape dynamics in boreal Fennoscandia. *Forest Ecology and Management* **164**:157–75.

Penttilä, R., J. Siitonen and M. Kuusinen. 2004. Polypore diversity and old-growth boreal *Picea abies* forests in southern Finland. *Biological Conservation* **117**:271–83.

Pressey, R. L., H. P. Possingham and J. R. Day. 1997. Effectiveness of alternative heuristic algorithms for identifying indicative minimum requirements for conservation reserves. *Biological Conservation* **80**:207–19.

Ranius, T. and L. Fahrig. 2006. Targets for maintenance of dead wood for biodiversity conservation based on extinction thresholds. *Scandinavian Journal of Forest Research* **21**:210–18.

Ranius, T. and O. Kindvall. 2004. Modelling the amount of coarse woody debris produced by the new biodiversity-oriented silvicultural practices in Sweden. *Biological Conservation* **119**:51–9.

Reed, D. H. 2005. Relationship between population size and fitness. *Conservation Biology* **19**:563–8.

Reed, D. H., J. J. O'Grady, B. W. Brook *et al.* 2003. Estimates of minimum viable population sizes for vertebrates and factors influencing those estimates. *Biological Conservation* **113**:23–34.

Rempel, R. S., D. W. Andison and S. J. Hannon. 2004. Guiding principles for developing an indicator monitoring framework. *Forestry Chronicle* **80**:82–90.

Roberge, J.-M. and P. Angelstam. 2006. Indicator species among resident forest birds – a cross-regional evaluation in northern Europe. *Biological Conservation* **130**:134–47.

Rosenzweig, M. L. 1995. *Species Diversity in Space and Time*. Cambridge, UK: Cambridge University Press.

Scheller, R. M., D. J. Mladenoff, T. R. Crow and T. A. Sickley. 2005. Simulating the effects of fire reintroduction versus continued fire absence on forest composition and landscape structure in the Boundary Waters Canoe Area Wilderness, northern Minnesota, USA. *Ecosystems* **8**:396–411.

Schultz, C. B. and E. E. Crone. 2005. Patch size and connectivity thresholds for butterfly habitat restoration. *Conservation Biology* **19**:887–96.

Seoane, J., J. Bustamante and R. Diaz-Delgado. 2005. Effect of expert opinion on the predictive ability of environmental models of bird distribution. *Conservation Biology* **19**:512–22.

Simberloff, D. 1998. Flagships, umbrellas, and keystones: is single-species management passé in the landscape era? *Biological Conservation* **84**:247–57.

Snäll, T., Pennanen, J., Kivisto, L. and Hanski, I. 2005. Modelling epiphyte metapopulation dynamics in a dynamic forest landscape. *Oikos* **109**:209–22.

Suorsa, P., E. Huhta, A. Jantti *et al.* 2005. Thresholds in selection of breeding habitat by the Eurasian treecreeper (*Certhia familiaris*). *Biological Conservation* **121**:443–52.

Thomas, C. D. 1990. What do real populations tell us about minimum viable population sizes? *Conservation Biology* **4**:324–7.

Tjorve, E. 2002. Habitat size and number in multi-habitat landscapes: a model approach based on species-area curves. *Ecography* **25**:17–24.

Venier, L. A., J. L. Pearce, B. A. Wintle and S. A. Bekessy. 2007. Future forests and indicator-species population models. *Forestry Chronicle* **83**:36–40.

Watson, J., D. Freudenberger and D. Paull. 2001. An assessment of the focal-species approach for conserving birds in variegated landscapes in southeastern Australia. *Conservation Biology* **15**:1364–73.

Westphal, M. I., M. Pickett, W. M. Getz and H. P. Possingham. 2003. The use of stochastic dynamic programming in optimal landscape reconstruction for metapopulations. *Ecological Applications* **13**:543–55.

Wintle B. A., S. A. Bekessy, L. A. Venier *et al.* 2005. Utility of dynamic-landscape metapopulation models for sustainable forest management. *Conservation Biology* **19**:1930–43.

Designing studies to develop conservation targets: a review of the challenges

MARC-ANDRÉ VILLARD

INTRODUCTION

The emphasis of this volume is on quantitative approaches to conservation. This calls for the consideration of key issues related to study design, statistical analyses, and interpretation of quantitative results. In Chapter 1, we argued that conservation targets should be developed from sound empirical data. Chapter 2 reviewed some of the approaches that have been used to establish numerical targets. In this chapter, I examine challenges posed by conservation target setting from a quantitative perspective. Although setting targets is crucial to achieve conservation goals, this does not mean that it is an easy proposition!

Among the challenges associated with conservation target setting, I will focus on the following:

1. Determining appropriate benchmarks for conservation target development. Setting targets implies that ecological conditions of reference have been agreed upon by the members of a research team.
2. Selecting the level(s) of organization for which we will develop targets. Should targets be set for species/populations? Species assemblages? Ecosystems/habitat patches/landscape units? Ecological processes? Ecological stressors?
3. Choosing appropriate units to express targets. For example, a land manager might prefer to express targets in terms of timber volume that can be harvested annually, whereas ecologists might focus on the area

Setting Conservation Targets for Managed Forest Landscapes, ed. M.-A. Villard and B. G. Jonsson. Published by Cambridge University Press.

and configuration of habitat that should be present at all times over the landscape to maintain viable populations of focal species. Each unit has advantages and disadvantages. Ideally, a statistical relation can be established between them to meet multiple needs simultaneously.

4. Selecting the most appropriate study design to guide the development of conservation targets. What are the options and tradeoffs in study design associated with the investigation of species/species assemblage/ecosystem response to ecological gradients in space and time?

This chapter is structured around these four challenges. Undoubtedly there are many others, such as how to fit conservation targets derived from a scientific approach within the particular management regime or policy framework in place. Although this is a critical final step in target setting, I focus on the development of evidence-based targets. To be scientifically credible, conservation targets must be determined in the absence of value-driven pressures. Then, society will revisit and implement conservation targets in the light of scientific recommendations (Tear *et al.* 2005; Svancara *et al.* 2005). Policy may not strictly follow scientific guidance for a variety of reasons. However, researchers should strive to maintain scientific objectivity in the face of economic or political pressures when making recommendations on conservation targets because sound science will form the basis for later adjustments if policy fails.

I finish by illustrating the main challenges listed above with a conservation issue that has received considerable attention from forest managers, policy makers, and conservation scientists throughout the world: the design of riparian buffer strips. Given the diversity of stated conservation benefits of buffer strips and their widespread application, this seems like an ideal example to illustrate how a specific conservation issue has been addressed by scientists, managers, and policy-makers in different forest regions of the world.

DETERMINING BENCHMARK CONDITIONS

In ecology and conservation, there is no one-size-fits-all approach. Conservation targets should be developed based on the best ecological understanding available for the focal system. For example, it is important to have at least partial knowledge of the range of natural variation in key ecological processes in the study region so that benchmarks can be established to develop a conservation strategy (see Chapter 7, this volume). The ecological features to be maintained or restored should correspond to those typical for the region when it evolved in the absence of major human activities. Although this step seems obvious, it is not an easy one to address by any means. In cultural landscapes, ecologists and land managers may choose to establish a benchmark reflecting a given period in the management history of the study region (see Chapter 5, this volume). Elsewhere, benchmark conditions are generally defined based on the best approximation of the range of natural variation in ecological features associated with natural disturbance regimes prior to major human influence on the landscape.

Paleoecology provides a context into which one can define conservation goals with some degree of objectivity (Willis and Birks 2006). However, it does not offer an answer to the question "how far back is enough?", or "how far back is too far?" Answering these questions is clearly beyond the scope of this chapter. For now, it would seem reasonable to examine variations in ecosystem properties (fire return intervals, frequency of extreme climatic events, abundance of various species, etc.) over periods that correspond to the contemporary climatic period. Unfortunately, in some forest regions of the world, human activity has had non-trivial effects on biodiversity for such a long time that it is impossible to obtain data on the natural range of variation for the contemporary climatic period. Among the challenges facing researchers and forest managers, establishing an agreed-upon benchmark will likely remain one of the greatest. When a benchmark condition has been defined, stakeholders may also disagree about management intensities compatible with the maintenance or restoration of key features/processes. Hence, there is undoubtedly some subjectivity involved at this stage, especially if we elect to restore or maintain a "cultural landscape". None the less, plenty of science exists to develop the targets needed to achieve the stated goal/benchmark, or at least to move the ecosystem toward it.

SELECTING APPROPRIATE LEVEL(S) OF ORGANIZATION

Conservation targets and indicators can be selected at different levels of ecological organization, from genes to ecosystems. Several chapters of this book address the various tradeoffs associated with the selection of ecological indicators at different levels of organization. Roberge and Angelstam (Chapter 6) assess the value of species as tools for conservation target setting. Drapeau *et al.* (Chapter 7) focus on ecosystem-level indicators and try to bridge the gap between them and multi-species approaches. Nilsson (Chapter 5) contrasts the value of indicators at species, species assemblage, and ecosystem levels. Therefore, this chapter will only briefly review the issues at hand.

Genes

In Chapter 2, we referred to effective population size and allelic diversity as parameters which could be used to derive conservation targets. However, there are few examples on the use of quantitative targets at the genetic level in forest management. Concern for genetic diversity is mainly associated with extreme fragmentation of the original forest, selective harvesting of commercially valuable trees, or plantation forestry. A recent review on conservation genetics in tropical agroforestry systems concludes that "fragmentation thresholds for gene flow must be determined and the possible selection pressures exerted by farmers elucidated" (Boshier 2004:308). Nevertheless, the same review indicates that research investigating isolation effects on pollen flow for commercial tree species with different pollination mechanisms suggests that gene flow may be high across landscapes with low forest cover. Selective harvesting of large-diameter trees (diameter-limit harvesting) has been shown to have detrimental effects on residual tree performance (Sokol *et al.* 2004), suggesting a detrimental effect on genotype. In the case of plantation forestry, it consists in the genetic selection of high-yield or disease-resistant tree clones for plantation purposes. Genetic resource management has become especially relevant with the expansion of plantation forestry in many forest regions and the potential consequences of climate change on future timber yields. Strategies have been proposed to optimize genetic conservation (Yanchuk 2001) and seed-transfer guidelines are being developed (Ying and Yanchuk 2006).

Species and species assemblages

Policy on species at risk has led to the development and implementation of conservation strategies for individual species or narrow sets of species (Chapter 13, this volume). More generally, target setting may be focused on groups of species particularly sensitive to specific threats, namely focal species (Lambeck 1997). In managed forest landscapes, species most at risk may be those with a strong association with old forests and their attributes, such as dead wood; species with large area requirements; species associated with threatened plant assemblages (e.g. mixedwood stands in some regions) or rare microhabitat features (e.g. large snags, hollow trees or logs, vernal pools). Rempel (2007) proposed to select subsets of species representing all major habitat/landscape types present. This approach has value, but when it is applied to forest landscapes that are actively managed, it may not be efficient to address the requirements of old forest associates. Patterns of species co-occurrence may be used to select focal species indicating the presence of many others in a given assemblage (Mikusinski *et al.* 2001;

Chapter 6, this volume). Conservation targets can then be set based on the ecological requirements of those species. For example, Bennett and Radford (Chapter 8) and Betts and Villard (Chapter 9) used the response of focal species to habitat amount at the landscape scale to derive conservation targets. The recommended targets may reflect the response of the region's most sensitive species, or the combined response of a narrow set of focal species (see Fig. 2.2). Although this approach seems promising, translating response curves into actual conservation targets must be done carefully, owing to the potential influence of various sources of statistical bias (see Guénette and Villard 2004). Similarly, variations in species richness as a function of habitat amount may reveal sharp thresholds, but these thresholds do not necessarily correspond to appropriate conservation targets. Indeed, species richness may drop dramatically below specific habitat amounts in the landscape, but populations of the corresponding species may actually start declining at higher habitat amounts (Chapter 8, this volume). Biases in ecological responses may also be associated with the particular status of populations at the time of the study, i.e. stable, increasing, or declining. In this chapter, I will strictly focus on quantitative aspects of target setting.

Ecosystems, landscapes, and ecological processes

The advantages and disadvantages of fine- versus coarse-filter approaches to biodiversity conservation have been debated elsewhere (e.g. Franklin 1994; Tracy and Brussard 1994; Wilcove 1994). As pointed out by Block et al. (1995), the selection of one approach or the other represents a series of tradeoffs. Coarse-filter approaches have the benefit of addressing the needs of many species at once. For example, Lindenmayer et al. (2006) have proposed five "guiding principles" for biodiversity conservation that they deemed "broadly applicable to any forested area": the maintenance of (1) connectivity; (2) landscape heterogeneity; (3) stand structural complexity; and (4) aquatic ecosystem integrity; as well as (5) the use of natural disturbance regimes to guide human disturbance regimes. However, at least some of these principles require the study or monitoring of focal species (fine filter), especially the maintenance of connectivity. From a conservation perspective, connectivity pertains not only to landscape structure (structural connectivity), but also mainly to its effects on the movement of genes, organisms, disease, or natural disturbances across the landscape (functional connectivity) (Taylor et al. 2006). It is through their consequences on gene flow, (meta)population dynamics, or overall landscape structure that these movements become important (Wiens 2006) and they can hardly be inferred solely from knowledge of structural connectivity. Landscape heterogeneity and stand structural complexity also can hardly be inferred without some knowledge of the habitat requirements of actual species.

CHOOSING UNITS TO EXPRESS TARGETS

The choice of appropriate units for expressing conservation targets and, thereafter, monitoring the performance of management plans/conservation strategies pertains specifically to the "currencies" commonly used by the various stakeholders. Professional foresters are trained to monitor parameters such as basal area of trees or timber volume per unit area, and they generally manage the landscape as a function of optimal harvest block placement given a number of criteria ranging from market value of the wood to social or ecological considerations (e.g. aboriginal trap lines; watershed protection). Forest inventories may also classify as "non-merchantable" a variety of habitat types that may be considered as distinct by researchers, from the perspective of plant or animal species. Researchers tend to use units that correspond to their response variables, e.g. abundance or fitness parameter(s) associated with focal species, an index reflecting landscape heterogeneity, or frequency of management intervention. Finally, researchers and managers sometimes use the same currency, but express targets for this currency over different spatial scales (e.g. /ha; /100 ha). With the strong push for ecosystem management in many countries, researchers, managers, and policy-makers have had to leave behind their disciplinary approaches and to develop a common language (Meffe *et al.* 2002). This common language may mean that relationships must be examined between the various currencies until all parties are satisfied that the selected parameter(s) or metric(s) is (are) appropriate for the task at hand. For example, various methods may be used (field transects; relascope) to measure something as simple as basal area or stem density. One method (and common currency) can be selected *a priori*, or else different methods can be calibrated so that a single currency can be used to establish targets.

STUDY DESIGN CONSIDERATIONS

The word *target* refers to a level or situation which one intends to achieve. As explained in Chapter 1, this book specifically refers to *levels* rather than to *situations*. Target levels are inherently quantitative in nature and therefore call for statistical approaches or techniques, which in turn come with specific study design considerations. Conservation target development implies that researchers understand the behavior of their focal ecosystem when conditions vary over spatial scales and temporal scales as a result of disturbance. A first quantitative approach to examine this behavior is threshold detection. Other approaches (reviewed in Chapter 2) include the definition of minimum viable (meta)populations or population viability analysis. These approaches have received book-length treatment elsewhere (e.g. Hanski 1999; Beissinger and McCullough 2002) and they will not be reviewed here.

Thresholds as guides for conservation target setting

Ecological thresholds may provide valuable insight for the development of conservation targets. They can be defined as sudden shifts in a given response variable along an ecological gradient in space or time. For example, the probability of detecting a species at a given site might increase suddenly with an increase in habitat amount at the landscape scale (Fig. 3.1, top left). In the real world, this increase is generally more gradual, as the species is detected in some study sites surrounded by low amounts of habitat and it is not detected in other sites that are embedded within suitable habitat (Fig. 3.1, 5–25% "noise").

The interest in threshold detection among ecologists was sparked by papers such as those of Andrén (1994, 1996), as well as simulation modeling by Fahrig (1997, 2001) and Flather and Bevers (2002). Empirical studies soon followed to assess the relative influence of habitat amount (or loss) and configuration (or fragmentation) on species presence, abundance, or reproductive performance. These studies featured a variety of methods to determine threshold values, when present. Because presence–absence data are easily collected over a large number of sites, initial efforts featured logistic regression as a method to detect sudden shifts in the probability of detecting a species along an ecological gradient (e.g. in habitat amount). It was assumed that such shifts would correspond to inflexion points in the response curve, i.e. sudden changes in slope. However, when examining the behavior of the logistic curve by using simulated data (Fig. 3.1), the slope of the curve appeared to be extremely sensitive to an increasing amount of noise around the simulated threshold value. In fact, the logistic curve became virtually linear when the proportion of points falling outside the predicted zones reached 15%. In contrast, the threshold values obtained by using ROC (receiver-operating characteristic) analysis remained unchanged. This suggests that ROC analysis may be useful when researchers need to identify changes in ecological response in the absence of sharp, non-linear shifts in the system (see also Chapter 9, this volume).

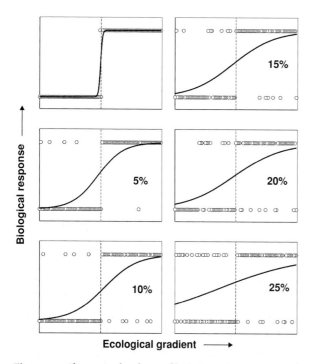

Figure 3.1. Change in the shape of logistic regression curve as an increasing proportion of noise is added to the simulated relationship between a biological response variable (e.g. presence or absence of a species) and an ecological gradient (e.g. habitat amount). The threshold values obtained from ROC (receiver-operating characteristic) analysis are shown by broken vertical lines. Corresponding AUC (area under the ROC curve) values ranged from 0.72 (model with 25% noise) to 1.00 (no noise). A model with an AUC>0.70 is deemed to provide a good discrimination between positive and negative responses.

ROC analysis is an iterative procedure whereby the user may decide to optimize the sensitivity of the model, or its specificity, or both (Manel *et al.* 2001). Sensitivity measures the model's ability to correctly identify true positives (e.g. sites where a species was actually present) whereas specificity reflects its ability to correctly identify true negatives (sites where it was actually absent). Here, I chose to maximize the sum of sensitivity and specificity or, in other words, to minimize the noise. Graphically (Fig. 3.1), this threshold value corresponds to the position on the *x* axis where the sum of false positives and false negatives is minimized. A threshold value may be obtained for any logistic model; such thresholds should only be considered valid when goodness of fit meets acceptable levels (area under the ROC curve ≥ 0.70; Swets 1988).

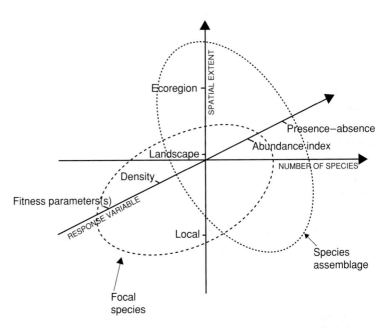

Figure 3.2. Schematic representation of the tradeoffs associated with the time-efficiency of a response variable, the spatial extent of the study area, and the generality of the conservation strategy in terms of number of species considered. Time-efficient response variables allow moving up from local to regional extent, and from one or a few focal species to species assemblages. On the other hand, focusing on one or a few species may allow measuring more informative (e.g. fitness) parameters.

Although presence–absence data can be obtained relatively easily over large areas, absences must be validated or the probability of detection of a species at a given sampling point must be explicitly considered (e.g. MacKenzie 2006). Species presence may also fail to indicate reproductive activity, let alone successful reproduction. The tradeoffs between sensitivity of the response variable, generality (e.g. in terms of number of species considered), and spatial extent of the study area are illustrated in Fig. 3.2.

When it is possible to obtain data on abundance, density, species richness, or other continuous variables, piecewise regression (Toms and Lesperance 2003) can be used to detect thresholds in relationships. It is a broken-stick model whereby two or more regression lines are joined at "breakpoint(s)" corresponding to thresholds (see Fig. 8.3 and Chapter 8, this volume). This modeling procedure can be used either with linear or polynomial regression segments, and it has been extended to model thresholds in binary response variables, i.e. segmented logistic regression (Muggeo 2003;

Box 9.1). Alternatively, one may use generalized additive models (GAMs), whereby one can test the fit of various "smoothed" curves to the data and detect significant changes in slope (Fewster *et al.* 2000). One might also want to fit a response surface to a large set of independent variables. In such cases, GAMs or non-parametric multiplicative regression (NPMR; McCune 2006) may be used.

The choice of a statistical method to detect thresholds is largely determined by the nature of the response variable (binary, such as presence–absence data, or continuous, such as abundance index values or species richness). Fitting response surfaces allows the examination of more complex systems where several independent variables interact to predict a species' probability of occurrence or abundance. However, objective methods to identify critical values corresponding to multidimensional thresholds have yet to be developed. Even when considering threshold detection methods applicable to simple, univariate models, their robustness to biases in sampling design, sample size, and other considerations should be examined to ensure that they can be used appropriately. Statistical simulations such as those illustrated in Fig. 3.1 can be very useful in this respect. Guénette and Villard (2004) performed such simulations to examine the robustness of ROC-derived thresholds to variations in sample size or in the thoroughness of sampling along a gradient. For example, a threshold might coincide with a gap in sampling along a gradient. In turn, such a threshold might have very little ecological relevance. Their results indicate that ROC thresholds are surprisingly robust, as long as sample size is fairly large. Results were less reliable when they randomly removed observations and sample size fell below *c.* 100.

Statistical thresholds as conservation targets

As pointed out by Bennett and Radford (Chapter 8, this volume), conservation targets often should not be set according to statistically significant threshold values themselves. Thresholds may actually correspond to the phenomena we are trying to prevent (local or regional extinction of species; loss of a critical ecological process, etc.). However, threshold values provide key insight about a given system's endpoints or critical parameters. Using thresholds obtained for several species or phenomena to develop conservation targets also appears to be a better approach than defining targets from the perspective of a single species or criterion (Chapter 2, this volume). Targets inspired from thresholds should always err on the side of caution (Chapters 8 and 9, this volume).

DEVELOPING TARGETS FOR RIPARIAN BUFFER STRIPS: A CASE STUDY

Forestry can have a wide range of effects on the integrity of freshwater ecosystems (Chapter 12, this volume). In many countries, legislation protecting water supply, fish habitat, or watersheds in general has been accompanied by a variety of guidelines and regulations applicable to managed forest landscapes (e.g. Anon. 2000; Lee *et al.* 2004). In turn, a vast literature has developed to provide guidance for riparian buffer strip design and management, or to test the efficiency of established guidelines. The overall conservation goal of forested buffer strips is clear: to maintain or restore riparian and freshwater ecosystems. Specific objectives may pertain to the protection of surface and ground water, the provision of suitable habitat for a range of living organisms, or the maintenance of functional connectivity for particular species. In a review of riparian buffer width guidelines in the United States and Canada, Lee *et al.* (2004) found no fewer than 60 jurisdictions with a published policy specific to this issue. Hence, riparian buffer management represents a widely used practice that can be informed by conservation biology. Richardson and Thompson (Chapter 12, this volume) review the various aspects of watershed management pertaining to freshwater ecosystems themselves. Here, I will focus on the efficiency of riparian buffer strips as a conservation tool for terrestrial organisms.

In spite of the concrete nature of the conservation goal being pursued, designing studies to assess the ecological relevance of guidelines for riparian buffer strips is far from simple. Replication may be especially hard to achieve owing to differences among (a) streams of different orders, (b) streams of the same order but located in different watersheds or catchments, or (c) lakes and streams. In addition to variation in stream characteristics *per se*, differences may pertain to riparian forest stand composition or structure, topography of the site, aspect, etc. Hence, quantitative guidelines pertaining to buffer strip width may have to be qualified to account for several site-specific variables. Specifically, the main quantitative aspect considered here (buffer width) must be accompanied by "modifying factors" (*sensu* Lee *et al.* 2004) to properly address site-specific variations. From an ecological perspective, a major decision pertains to the intended function(s) of the riparian buffer strips. Are they designed to provide habitat for all native species or only for species with relatively small area requirements or elongated home ranges, while connecting habitat patches for others?

I conducted a survey of the peer-reviewed literature addressing riparian buffer strip design to determine whether (1) the conservation objective(s) being tested was (were) explicitly stated; (2) sites were true replicates, considered as such, or treated as unique statistical objects along gradients; and (3) quantitative targets were defined based on empirical data. The review does not pretend to be exhaustive, but it covers a wide range of forest regions and response variables.

Observations

Interesting patterns emerged from this exercise (Table 3.1). First, very few studies referred to benchmarks to design riparian buffer strips. The reason for this is simple: all studies pertained to managed forest landscapes. Therefore, maintaining the extent of riparian forest that was present prior to large-scale human activities is rarely an option unless woodland around watercourses was naturally fragmented and woody vegetation was present as distinct strips, e.g. in arid or frequently burned landscapes. Second, although conservation objectives were generally stated, they were either vague (e.g. buffer width needed to conserve species) or unrealistic (e.g. ability to maintain pre-logging community). Third, most studies compared response variables among categories of buffer strip width. This experimental design has the advantage of allowing comparisons among clearly distinct sites, greatly simplifying statistical analyses. A drawback, however, is that conclusions are restricted to the particular width categories chosen *a priori*. It should be mentioned, however, that in many cases legislation setting buffer widths preceded the research, thus constraining study design options. Only two studies treated buffer width as a continuous variable in at least one analysis (Kilgo *et al.* 1998; Whitaker and Montevecchi 1999). Another (Spackman and Hughes 1995) examined the rate of increase in species richness of different taxa as distance from stream increased in untreated watersheds.

This case study nicely illustrates both the complexity of determining quantitative conservation targets and the philosophical shift required to properly address this type of issue. Again, the conservation goal is clear (protection of riparian and freshwater ecosystems), and the parameters requiring quantitative targets are relatively few. With respect to the conservation of terrestrial species, one can imagine that buffer width should be carefully determined as a function of modifying factors such as slope and aspect (e.g. Hylander *et al.* 2005), or forest stand type. Yet the vast majority of studies reviewed approached the question by using a classical experimental design (replicated treatments and controls). In most forest landscapes, one may question whether true replicates exist, not to mention appropriate controls. In studies where buffer widths were replicated, there were only

Table 3.1. *Review of studies addressing the design of riparian buffer strips (RBS) and their efficiency to reach conservation objectives* All but one study assessed the effects of riparian buffer strip width on various biotic or abiotic indicators.

Indicator(s)	Study design	Duration (pre/post)	Location	Explicit conservation objective?	Quantitative targets?	Reference
Bryophyte species richness and composition	25 stream sites pre- and post-harvest; (clearcut; clearcut with 10 m RBS; control)	2 (1/3)	Sweden	Yes – assessment of the ability of RBS to moderate the effects of clearcutting	No – "wider buffer strips"; account for prevailing wind direction	Hylander *et al.* (2005)
Species richness of vascular plants, birds and mammals	6 unmanaged stream sites	4? (?/?)	Vermont, USA	Yes – RBS width needed to "conserve species"	Yes – >75–150 m (90% species richness)	Spackman and Hughes (1995)
Salamander abundance and species richness	29 stream sites; RBS widths: 0–64 m and controls; adjacent clearcuts <5 yr old	1 yr	Oregon, USA	Yes – assessment of RBS width required to protect amphibian populations	No – recommend to "extend RBS requirements"	Vesely and McComb (2002)
Amphibian, songbird and small mammal abundance/ species composition	12 lakes; 3 replicates for each RBS width (20–100–200– 800 m)	4 yrs (2/2)	Alberta, Canada	Yes – assessment of RBS width required to protect species/ maintain abundances	Yes – RBS ≥200 m, but also mention that RBS design should be flexible and tailored to local conditions	Hannon *et al.* (2000)

Focus	Study design	Duration	Location	Assessment	RBS effective	Reference
Songbird abundance/species composition	25 river segments; RBS widths: 20, 40, 60 m; controls: >300 m	3 yrs (0/3)	Québec, Canada	Yes – assessment of effects of RBS width and thinning on community composition and species density	Yes – RBS ≥60 m	Darveau et al. (1995)
Songbird abundance/species composition	17–18 stream sites; RBS widths: 7–48 m and controls	3 yrs (1/2)	W Washington State, USA	Yes – assessment of RBS ability to maintain pre-logging community	Yes – RBS >45 m	Pearson and Manuwal (2001)
Songbird species richness and diversity	9 watersheds; RBS widths: 0–10; 20–25; 36–44; 100–144 m; controls	3 yrs	SW British Columbia, Canada	Yes – maintain species richness and abundance	Yes – RBS >100 m	Shirley and Smith (2005)
Bird abundance/species composition	20 stream segments; RBS widths: 20–100 m; controls: >400 m; adjacent sites clearcut 4–11 yrs before study	1 yr	Maine, USA	Yes – assessment of community similarity between RBS and controls	No	Meiklejohn and Hughes (1999)

(cont.)

Table 3.1. (cont.)

Indicator(s)	Study design	Duration (pre/post)	Location	Explicit conservation objective?	Quantitative targets?	Reference
Bird species richness and abundance	20 sites (4 replicates of 5 RBS width classes; <50 m–>1,000 m)	3 yr	South Carolina, USA	Yes – assessment of RBS width required to maintain regional community of bottomland hardwoods	Yes – RBS ≥500 m	Kilgo et al. (1998)
Bird species richness and abundance	29 stream sites; RBS widths: 20–50 m and controls	2 yr	Newfoundland, Canada	Yes – assessment of RBS value as habitat for riparian vs. "interior forest" species	No – distinct strategies needed for riparian and interior forest birds	Whitaker and Montevecchi (1999)
Small mammal density	25 river segments, RBS widths: 20, 40, 60, >300 m; thinned and unthinned	7 yr[a] (0/7)	Québec, Canada	Yes – assessment of RBS value as refuges for wildlife, and effects of RBS width	No – recommend to manage for heterogeneity in RBS width	Darveau et al. (2001)

[a] Sampling in 4 of the 7 years.

four or five width categories, the broader width often being considered as a control. Control widths varied from >300 m to 800 m (or unspecified width). Only Kilgo et al. (1998) would have had a design amenable to a quantitative, threshold detection approach, either in species abundance or in species richness as a function of buffer width. Instead, they grouped buffer widths into broad (50–700 m) categories to examine species-specific patterns in abundance.

Detection of thresholds in various biotic or abiotic parameters (e.g. microclimate, species richness, growth/reproductive success of focal species) as a function of buffer width would provide valuable insight for the design of riparian buffer strips. However, such thresholds would likely correspond to a range of different values, depending on the parameter considered. Target widths would also have to be adjusted as a function of abiotic parameters specific to particular sites (stand type, slope, aspect, prevailing wind direction, etc.). None the less, by restricting comparisons to a relatively narrow range of buffer strip widths, researchers restrict their ability to learn about stream–upland forest gradients, and therefore they miss an opportunity to develop better-informed target recommendations.

Going back to the stated conservation objectives, a conspicuous pattern across studies was how little attention was devoted to them. Most authors seemed to assume that the only objective of buffer strips could be the maintenance of "original" biodiversity, or an approximation of the structure of species assemblages found in controls. Yet an equally valid objective would be to provide movement corridors for certain taxa (e.g. Robichaud et al. 2002; Tewksbury et al. 2002). Whitaker and Montevecchi (1999) stressed the importance of clearly identifying the intended function(s) of the riparian buffers being designed. They were careful to distinguish species directly associated with the riparian ecosystem from those associated with upland forest habitats, because distinct conservation strategies should be developed to address their needs. A strategy designed strictly to protect riparian plants, animals, and the freshwater ecosystem itself would obviously require a buffer width very different from that required by an omnibus strategy aiming to include protection of upland forest species.

CONCLUSION

This chapter aimed to review the critical steps involved in the development of research-based, quantitative conservation targets. It does not pretend to provide a comprehensive overview of all quantitative approaches or issues. However, the case study nicely illustrates some of the practical challenges involved. These challenges pertain both to the difficulty of designing empirical studies to develop meaningful targets and to the philosophical shift required to succeed. It is no longer acceptable to blame inadequate study designs on the challenges of large-scale experiments. We have to collectively change our approach to conservation target setting, both in terms of clarity in our conservation objectives, innovative study designs, and appropriate analytical procedures. This book aims to bring us closer to this goal.

ACKNOWLEDGEMENTS

This work was supported by a Discovery Grant from the Natural Sciences and Engineering Research Council of Canada. I sincerely thank Jean-Sébastien Guénette for preparing Fig. 3.1 and for fruitful discussions around the notion of threshold detection. Darroch Whitaker, Kristoffer Hylander, and Bengt Gunnar Jonsson made insightful comments on the manuscript.

References

Andrén, H. 1994. Effects of habitat fragmentation on birds and mammals in landscapes with different proportions of suitable habitat – a review. *Oikos* 71:355–66.

Andrén, H. 1996. Population responses to habitat fragmentation: statistical power and the random sample hypothesis. *Oikos* 76:235–42.

Anonymous. 2000. Directive 2000/60/EC of the European parliament and of the Council of 23 October 2000 establishing a framework for community action in the field of water policy. *Official Journal of the European Communities* L327: 1–72.

Beissinger, S. R. and D. R. McCullough (eds.) 2002. *Population Viability Analysis.* Chicago, IL: University of Chicago Press.

Block, W. M., D. M. Finch and L. A. Brennan. 1995. Single species vs. multiple species approaches for management. Pp. 461–76 in T. E. Martin and D. M. Finch (eds.) *Ecology and Management of Neotropical Migratory Birds: A Synthesis and Review of Critical Issues.* New York, NY: Oxford University Press.

Boshier, D. H. 2004. Agroforestry systems: important components in conserving the genetic viability of native tropical tree species? Pp. 290–313 in G. Schroth, G. A. B. da Fonseca, C. A. Harvey *et al.* (eds.) *Agroforestry and Biodiversity Conservation in Tropical Landscapes.* Washington, D.C.: Island Press.

Darveau, M., P. Beauchesne, L. Bélanger, J. Huot and P. Larue. 1995. Riparian forest strips as habitat for breeding birds in boreal forest. *Journal of Wildlife Management* 59:67–78.

Darveau, M., P. Labbé, P. Beauchesne, L. Bélanger and J. Huot. 2001. The use of riparian forest strips by small mammals in a boreal balsam fir forest. *Forest Ecology and Management* 143:95–104.

Fahrig, L. 1997. Relative effects of habitat loss and fragmentation on population extinction. *Journal of Wildlife Management* **61**:603–10.

Fahrig, L. 2001. How much habitat is enough? *Biological Conservation* **100**:65–74.

Fewster, R. M., S. T. Buckland, G. M. Siriwardena, S. R. Baillie and J. D. Wilson. 2000. Analysis of population trends for farmland birds using generalized additive models. *Ecology* **81**:1970–84.

Flather, C. H. and M. Bevers. 2002. Patchy reaction-diffusion and population abundance: the relative importance of habitat amount and arrangement. *American Naturalist* **159**:40–56.

Franklin, J. F. 1994. Preserving biodiversity – species, ecosystems, or landscapes? *Ecological Applications* **4**:202–5.

Guénette, J.-S. and M.-A. Villard. 2004. Do empirical thresholds truly reflect species tolerance to habitat alteration? *Ecological Bulletins* **51**:163–71.

Hannon, S. J., C. A. Paszkowski, S. Boutin *et al.* 2000. Abundance and species composition of amphibians, small mammals, and songbirds in riparian buffer strips of varying widths in the boreal mixedwood of Alberta. *Canadian Journal of Forest Research* **32**:1784–800.

Hanski, I. 1999. *Metapopulation Ecology*. Oxford, UK: Oxford University Press.

Hylander, K., M. Dynesius, B. G. Jonsson and C. Nilsson. 2005. Substrate form determines the fate of bryophytes in riparian buffer strips. *Ecological Applications* **15**:674–88.

Kilgo, J. C., R. A. Sargent, B. P. Chapman and K. V. Miller. 1998. Effect of stand width and adjacent habitat on breeding bird communities in bottomland hardwoods. *Journal of Wildlife Management* **62**:72–83.

Lambeck, R. J. 1997. A multi-species umbrella for nature conservation. *Conservation Biology* **11**:849–56.

Lee, P., C. Smyth and S. Boutin. 2004. Quantitative review of riparian buffer width guidelines from Canada and the United States. *Journal of Environmental Management* **70**:165–80.

Lindenmayer, D. B., J. F. Franklin and J. Fischer. 2006. General management principles and a checklist of strategies to guide forest biodiversity conservation. *Biological Conservation* **131**:433–45.

MacKenzie, D. I. 2006. Modeling the probability of resource use: the effect of, and dealing with, detecting a species imperfectly. *Journal of Wildlife Management* **70**:367–74.

Manel, S., H. C. Williams and S. J. Ormerod. 2001. Evaluating presence-absence models in ecology: the need to account for prevalence. *Journal of Applied Ecology* **38**:921–31.

McCune, B. 2006. Nonparametric habitat models with automatic interactions. *Journal of Vegetation Science* **17**:819–30.

Meiklejohn, B. A. and J. W. Hughes. 1999. Bird communities in riparian buffer strips of industrial forests. *American Midland Naturalist* **141**:172–84.

Meffe, G. K., L. A. Nielsen, R. L. Knight and D. A. Schenborn. 2002. *Ecosystem Management*. Washington, D.C.: Island Press.

Mikusinski, G., M. Gromadzki and P. Chylarecki. 2001. Woodpeckers as indicators of forest bird diversity. *Conservation Biology* **15**:208–17.

Muggeo, V. M. R. 2003. Estimating regression models with unknown break points. *Statistics in Medicine* **22**:3055–71.

Pearson, S. F. and D. A. Manuwal. 2001. Breeding bird response to riparian buffer width in managed Pacific Northwest Douglas-fir forests. *Ecological Applications* 11:840–53.

Robichaud, I., M.-A. Villard and C. S. Machtans. 2002. Effects of forest regeneration on songbird movements in a managed forest landscape of Alberta, Canada. *Landscape Ecology* 17:247–62.

Rempel, R. S. 2007. Selecting focal songbird species for biodiversity conservation assessment: response to forest cover amount and configuration. *Avian Conservation and Ecology – Écologie et conservation des oiseaux* 2(1): 6. Available online at www.ace-eco.org/vol2/iss1/art6/.

Shirley, S. M. and J. N. M. Smith. 2005. Bird community structure across riparian buffer strips of varying width in a coastal temperate forest. *Biological Conservation* 125:475–89.

Sokol, K. A., M. S. Greenwood and W. H. Livingston. 2004. Impacts of long-term diameter-limit harvesting on residual stands of red spruce in Maine. *Northern Journal of Applied Forestry* 21:69–73.

Spackman, S. C. and J. W. Hughes. 1995. Assessment of minimum stream corridor width for biological conservation: species richness and distribution along mid-order streams in Vermont, USA. *Biological Conservation* 71:325–32.

Svancara, L., R. Brannon, J. M. Scott *et al.* 2005. Policy-driven versus evidence-based conservation: a review of political targets and biological needs. *BioScience* 55:989–95.

Swets, J. A. 1988. Measuring the accuracy of diagnostic systems. *Science* 240:1285–93.

Taylor, P. D., L. Fahrig and K. A. With. 2006. Landscape connectivity: a return to the basics. Pp. 29–43 in K. R. Crooks and M. Sanjayan (eds.) *Connectivity Conservation*. Cambridge, UK: Cambridge University Press.

Tear, T. H., P. Kareiva, P. L. Angermeier *et al.* 2005. How much is enough? The recurrent problem of setting measurable objectives in conservation. *BioScience* 55:835–49.

Tewksbury, J. J., D. J. Levey, N. M. Haddad *et al.* 2002. Corridors affect plants, animals, and their interactions in fragmented landscapes. *Proceedings of the National Academy of Sciences of the United States of America* 99:12923–6.

Toms, J. D. and M. L. Lesperance. 2003. Piecewise regression: a tool for identifying ecological thresholds. *Ecology* 84:2034–41.

Tracy, C. R. and P. F. Brussard. 1994. Preserving biodiversity – species in landscapes. *Ecological Applications* 4:205–7.

Vesely, D. G. and W. C. McComb. 2002. Salamander abundance and amphibian species richness in riparian buffer strips in the Oregon Coast Range. *Forest Science* 48:291–7.

Whitaker, D. M. and W. A. Montevecchi. 1999. Breeding bird assemblages inhabiting riparian buffer strips in Newfoundland, Canada. *Journal of Wildlife Management* 63:167–79.

Wiens, J. A. 2006. Introduction: connectivity research – what are the issues? Pp. 23–27 in K. R. Crooks and M. Sanjayan (eds.) *Connectivity Conservation*. Cambridge, UK: Cambridge University Press.

Wilcove, D. S. 1994. Preserving biodiversity – species in landscapes – response. *Ecological Applications* **4**:207–8.

Willis, K. J. and H. J. B. Birks. 2006. What is natural? The need for a long-term perspective in biodiversity conservation. *Science* **314**:1261–5.

Yanchuk, A. D. 2001. A quantitative framework for breeding and conservation of forest tree genetic resources in British Columbia. *Canadian Journal of Forest Research* **31**:566–76.

Ying, C. C. and A. D. Yanchuk. 2006. The development of British Columbia's tree seed transfer guidelines: purpose, concept, methodology, and implementation. *Forest Ecology and Management* **227**:1–13.

Testing the efficiency of global-scale conservation planning by using data on Andean amphibians

DON R. CHURCH, CLAUDE GASCON, MEGAN VAN FOSSEN, GRISEL VELASQUEZ, AND LUIS A. SOLORZANO

INTRODUCTION

Conservation planning at any scale (global, regional, or local) requires the best scientific input. For biodiversity conservation planning, detailed information on species distributions is needed. In addition, knowledge of the conservation status of species and of the present threats acting on those species is essential to enable some form of prioritization of conservation targets. To date, many valuable conservation planning approaches have been applied at these different scales, but often the quality and nature of the information varies among spatial scales, creating a disconnect between priorities at the local and global scales. Recent work on the global assessment of the conservation status of all amphibian species provides the conservation community with a unique opportunity to integrate conservation planning at the global, regional, and local scales using the same scientific information. Such information can help us establish global priorities for conservation action, design regional landscapes or conservation corridors based on the most highly threatened endemic species and their responses to different land uses, as well as define key gaps in existing networks of protected areas that need formal protection. Using the same detailed global information ensures that priorities at all scales are related and form an integrated strategy for addressing the most urgent conservation needs.

Although protected areas are critical to safeguarding global biodiversity, many species occur largely or entirely outside of protected areas.

Setting Conservation Targets for Managed Forest Landscapes, ed. M.-A. Villard and B. G. Jonsson. Published by Cambridge University Press.

Conservation goals must therefore address how populations and their habitats should be managed not only in protected areas but also in the matrix that surrounds these areas while also identifying targets for how protected area networks should be expanded. A primary objective for the conservation community is therefore to set conservation targets based on explicit knowledge of how species distributions overlap both existing protected areas and the intervening managed landscapes. A gap analysis can achieve this objective by overlaying species distribution maps onto protected area and land-use maps using Geographic Information Systems. To this end, a global gap analysis was recently conducted by the Center for Applied Biodiversity Science (CABS) at Conservation International (CI) to identify regions of the world that are missing protected areas for amphibians, birds, and mammals (Rodrigues *et al.* 2004). Globally, amphibians were found to be less well covered than birds or mammals. The Andes Region was identified as being among the regions with the most critical gaps in protected area coverage for birds, mammals, and, especially, amphibians. This high irreplaceability of the Andes Region means that a large proportion of the world's biodiversity can only be maintained if new critical areas within the Andes are protected and landscapes outside of protected areas are managed for threatened amphibian fauna; a result that stems directly from the high degree of endemism and species richness (Fig. 4.1) within the region. However, the scale of the recent analysis was global and did not incorporate several strategies currently being pursued by international and regional conservation groups. For example, Conservation International's conservation corridors target landscape conservation and sustainable use of over 60 million hectares in four primary areas of the Andes. There is a need, therefore, to identify areas where these conservation corridors fall short of protecting the region's biodiversity.

Sanderson *et al.* (2006) define a biological conservation corridor as a strategically and biologically defined sub-regional space within which conservation can be implemented, in part, without the restrictions usually associated with protected areas such as complete inaccessibility to economic development. Under their definition, socio-economic factors may help define the borders of conservation corridors but the main criteria are the distributions of species at risk of extinction, as measured by the IUCN Red List of Threatened Species compiled by the Species Survival Commission of the World Conservation Union. Conservation International has implemented this corridor concept in many parts of the world while recognizing that the more traditional practice of establishing protected areas within conservation corridors is often still critical for areas

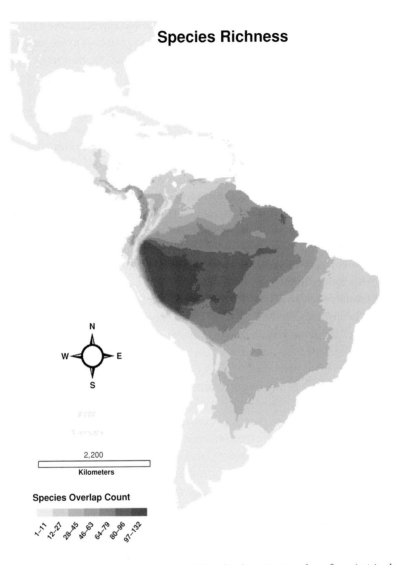

Species Richness

N
W—◇—E
S

2,200
Kilometers

Species Overlap Count

1–11 12–27 28–45 46–63 64–79 80–96 97–132

Figure 4.1. Spatial patterns of amphibian biodiversity (number of species) in the tropical Andes.

with globally threatened species, most notably in Key Biodiversity Areas (Eken *et al.* 2004) and Alliance for Zero Extinction Sites (Ricketts *et al.* 2006). It is important to note that management efforts are not necessarily fully implemented within CI's conservation corridors but, rather, that these are the areas where CI is actively planning or initiating actions such as improvement of agroforestry practices, restoration of degraded forests, and establishment of government and private protected areas for threatened species. Within the Andes Region, CI's delineation of conservation corridors took place before the threatened status of amphibians had been globally assessed and their distributions mapped.

Conservation research over the past 20 years has taught us a great deal about the impact of land use on species persistence. Specifically, much information has been assimilated on how tropical rainforests are affected by habitat loss and fragmentation, logging, hunting, road building, and increasingly encroaching agricultural frontiers. These findings support three basic statements. First, deforestation leads to forest fragments embedded in a non-forest matrix of habitats (Corlett 2000; Tabarelli *et al.* 2004). Second, ecological degradation, including disruption of species interactions, species loss, biomass collapse, exotic species invasion, and other processes, can be accounted for by relatively few factors: habitat loss, edge effects, land use in the surrounding matrix (i.e. matrix effects), and hunting/harvesting in the remaining forest fragments (Zuidema *et al.* 1996; Bierregaard *et al.* 2001; Laurance and Cochrane 2001). Finally, these four degradation factors may act simultaneously and synergistically, greatly exacerbating their individual effects (see Fahrig 2003; Tabarelli *et al.* 2004).

Scientists have now begun to translate information into specific guidelines and actions to counter additional biodiversity loss (Laurance and Gascon 1997; Bierregard *et al.* 2001; Laurance *et al.* 2002). Tabarelli *et al.* (2004) reviewed empirical studies to produce guidelines for the management of fragmented landscapes (i.e. fragments and matrix). These guidelines aim to mitigate or eliminate the negative impacts of human-induced landscape transformation, particularly on species persistence in fragmented forests. Such a level of generalization is possible because many organisms present similar responses to large-scale landscape transformations. In our discussion (below), we review four guidelines that are especially relevant to what landscape-level processes need to be addressed to ensure long-term persistence of threatened amphibian species within protected areas.

Conservation in the Andes

Within the Andes Region, forests are threatened by several specific factors including forest clearing for cattle pastures, commercial timber harvest, cultivation of illegal crops, flooding of valleys for reservoirs associated with hydroelectric dams, oil exploration, and subsistence agriculture

Box 4.1 Threats to amphibians

Amphibians are declining globally owing to a variety of threats. Habitat loss and degradation is the leading threat and is the primary trigger for threatened status of the over 1,800 IUCN red-listed species. Over 800 species globally have been identified as not having a distribution that overlaps with an existing protected area. Disease, pollution, invasive species, and overharvesting of amphibians are also severely threatening species around the globe and have directly led to the extinction of dozens of species in the past 20 years alone.

(Rodriguez-Mahecha *et al.* 2004). Forests in some areas remain largely intact whereas they are completely denuded or largely fragmented in others. Overall, it is estimated that no more than 25%, or 385,661 km², of forest remains throughout the region and only 7.9% is protected in reserves or parks (Rodriguez-Mahecha *et al.* 2004). In general, the forests within the inter-Andean valleys of Colombia and Ecuador are virtually gone whereas forests on the eastern slopes of the Andes in Peru and Bolivia are largely intact. The inter-Andean valleys are most hospitable to humans and are therefore most densely populated, but poor economies in these regions are leading to increasing migrations of people to the eastern slopes, thereby increasing the rates of forest degradation and loss in the largest remaining tracts of forests in the region (Rodriguez-Mahecha *et al.* 2004).

Amphibian species are still being discovered in the Andes at a high rate and it is expected that many more endemics will be formally recognized by science in the next few years. The discovery rate is especially high in Peru, where fewer surveys have been conducted relative to Ecuador and Colombia. This species-rich fauna captures some of the greatest evolutionary history among amphibians in one region anywhere on the planet. In addition to encompassing highly divergent lineages, including one monotypic family and 16 total families across the three amphibian orders, the Andes Region also has exceptional species radiations within several groups. The small, often highly specialized *Eleutherodactylus* frogs, in particular, constitute the most speciose vertebrate radiation in the world.

Andean amphibians have distribution and endemism patterns that reflect a finer resolution of biodiversity than do those of other vertebrates. In particular, amphibians have high beta-diversity – their species composition changes rapidly across the landscape – making them especially useful for a fine-grained approach to identifying areas in need of protection for biodiversity conservation. Using groups that are typically represented by large range species may result in missing many key sites for protection of broader biodiversity. However, the high beta-diversity of species within a region also poses a great challenge to conservation planners because a few large protected areas are unlikely to represent all species. Also, high beta-diversity reflects small distributions and narrowly defined ecological niches for individual species. Such an ecological pattern may demand fine-scale occupancy data of species within specific sites for accurate interpretation of what areas need protection to represent the biodiversity of a region. Without such data, there may be a risk of falsely concluding that a subset of species occur within the boundaries of a proposed protected area when they are actually largely or entirely extralimital.

Due to the dearth of high resolution data on species occupancy and the speed with which habitats are being degraded, conservation planning must usually settle for inputting relatively coarse data on species distributions into analyses as a first cut for defining priorities within a region. To date, there have been few opportunities to test the effectiveness of proposed conservation measures that emerge from such broad-scale analyses that, by necessity, have used relatively coarse data on species distributions. In this chapter, we explore the limits of current conservation planning in the Andes and identify priorities for expanding conservation initiatives in the region in the context of systematic conservation planning (Margules and Pressey 2000). Our primary goal is to identify the proportion of threatened species that collectively constitute a new conservation target within the Andes because their distributions fall outside both existing protected areas as well as CI's already delineated conservation corridors for the region. Second, using a focal species, we illustrate how broad-scale regional planning is ideally followed by relatively fine-scale analyses to identify specific site-level targets for conservation of threatened species on-the-ground. We address these questions in the context of landscape-level processes known to be important for amphibians and discuss the potential ramifications of our findings to the broader conservation of the region's biodiversity.

MATERIALS AND METHODS

Identifying new regional conservation targets

For our regional analyses, we used the Global Amphibian Assessment database (Stuart *et al.* 2004), first updating the IUCN criteria for each listed species according to the 2006 Red List, to identify the species whose range intersected the boundaries of the five Andean countries (Venezuela,

Colombia, Ecuador, Peru, and Bolivia) that CI incorporates within their Andes Center for Biodiversity Conservation (CBC). All species whose distribution intersects the boundaries of these five countries were used in our analyses. Global Amphibian Assessment data in geospatial format, compatible with modern Geographical Information Systems (GIS), depict estimated distribution ranges for individual species. In combination with fine-scale land cover monitoring studies and historical species presence records, these Global Amphibian Assessment data significantly contribute to identifying remnant habitat areas meriting further site-level evaluation for conservation intervention.

In 2006, Conservation International completed a deforestation study for the entirety of the Andes Region by using Landsat TM satellite imagery. This study generated coverages for remaining natural as well as degraded habitats within the region. These two habitat coverages were first overlaid with the distributions of all threatened amphibian species in the region in order to identify the extent to which the threatened Andean amphibian fauna species have conservation options in terms of habitat protection. Second, the habitat coverages and amphibian distributions were overlaid by a coverage of CI's Andean conservation corridor to identify the extent to which an existing conservation plan for the region could protect the remaining natural habitats that fall within the distributions of threatened species in the region. Summary statistics of potential conservation areas most relevant to the conservation of the threatened amphibians were calculated by clipping their distributions with respect to remaining habitats and borders of CI's conservation corridor.

Identifying priority target sites for species conservation

We define conservation site options, or sites, as species localities that, if appropriately managed, may contribute to improving the likelihood that extinction is avoided. Conservation resources are often limited and other challenges associated with habitat management for threatened species often exist. We therefore believe that it is important to prioritize sites in such a way that conservation measures can be focused where the greatest conservation benefits for species can be achieved. This is not to say that all sites for threatened species should not be managed appropriately but, rather, that the most important sites should be identified as targets for initial implementation of habitat management in case financial or political delays postpone actions across all sites.

For our fine-scale analysis, we focused on a species that occurs within Conservation International's NorAndean conservation corridor,

Atelopus carbonerensis in the Venezuelan Andes

The known distribution range for *Atelopus carbonerensis* is very restricted in size, not exceeding 10 km2. The entirety of its known population is associated with cloud forest areas in the state of Mérida in the highlands (2,000-2,800m above sea level) of Venezuela (La Marca, E., Rodríguez, A. & García-Pérez, J.E., 2004).

Although a portion of its known range coincides with national park, adjacent unprotected sites with recorded occurrences of this species face deforestation attributable to the expansion of small-holder agriculture and dairy cattle farming.

Legend

🏙 City of Mérida

Andes political divisions

☐ NorAndean conservation corridor

1,500
Kilometers

Figure 4.2. Conservation International's NorAndean conservation corridor.

which extends from Colombia to Venezuela (Fig. 4.2). This region is of significant importance for the conservation of endemic and range-restricted, amphibian species. Figure 4.3 depicts numerous areas along the flank of this region of the Andes mountain range where range-restricted species are concentrated. Concentrations of range-restricted species often indicate the presence of unique environmental conditions. Range-restricted species are

Amphibian Range Restrictedness in the NorAndean Corridor

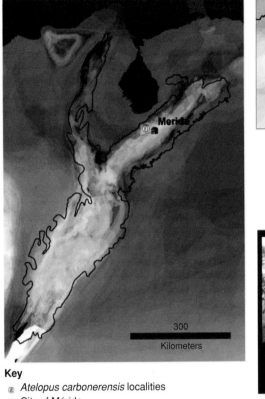

Key
- ☒ *Atelopus carbonerensis* localities
- ♠ City of Mérida
- ☐ NorAndean conservation corridor

Concentrations of range restricted species
High : 0.997193

Low : 0.000000

Figure 4.3. Density distribution in terms of number of range-restricted amphibian species within Conservation International's NorAndean conservation corridor.

frequently highly susceptible to the loss or degradation of such habitats. Once areas exhibiting high concentrations of endemic, range-restricted, and threatened species are identified at the landscape level, site-level options for the conservation of individual species or groups of species may be evaluated.

The harlequin toad, *Atelopus carbonerensis*, occurs in the San Eusebio Forest in La Carbonera in the state of Mérida (Fig. 4.2). The last recorded sighting of this species was in 1998 (La Marca *et al.* 2006). Prior research on this species identified cloud forest environments and their associated stream networks as primary habitat types for *A. carbonerensis*. This species is known to rely on freshwater streams for reproduction. Populations of this species are therefore susceptible to changes in water quality and quantity, as well as loss of forest habitat. Population decline for this species has led to its listing as Critically Endangered on the IUCN/SSC Red List of threatened species (La Marca *et al.* 2006).

The best site option for conservation of *A. carbonerensis* was identified in four steps. First, the four known localities for the species were georeferenced with respect to the existing protected area in the region, Sierra de la Culata National Park. Second, the localities and nearby protected area were overlaid with coverages for forest cover including both forest core and a 270 m forest edge habitat which comes close to the 300 m recommendation for a minimum forest buffer for amphibians (Semlitsch 1998). A 270 m buffer was selected because the data on forested areas come from satellite imagery where each pixel was slightly degraded to a resolution of approximately 90 m in order to compose a mosaic for a regional (Andes) deforestation assessment. GIS systems can rarely handle large data sets effectively at high resolution for analytical purposes. Buffer distances are effectively calculated in pixels (in this case 90 m distance per pixel). Third, the stream network and watershed sub-basin that encompasses three of the four localities were overlaid with the protected area and forest coverages. Fourth, distances between nearest known species localities and remaining patches of core forest habitat were measured in order to identify the best site option for conservation of the species. Identification of the patch of core forest habitat nearest to a known locality for the species was the target of our analysis as we assumed that this would be the highest priority site option for conservation of the species.

RESULTS

Species richness and endemism of amphibians in the tropical Andes

The ranges of 1,398 neotropical amphibian species intersect the political borders of the five Andes countries. Although the portion of their ranges intersecting with the country boundaries varies from 100% to less than 1%, the degree of endemism is striking. About 75.9% of the species (1,061) have more than 99% of their ranges within the borders of the five tropical

Table 4.1. *Extent of geographical correspondence between amphibian species distributions and the Andes Region*

% range area in Andes Region	species count	% total	(%) cumulative
90–100	1,100	78.68	78.68
80–90	16	1.14	79.82
70–80	13	0.93	80.75
60–70	15	1.07	81.82
50–60	26	1.86	83.68
40–50	31	2.22	85.90
30–40	38	2.72	88.62
20–30	53	3.79	92.41
10–20	33	2.36	94.77
5–10	25	1.79	96.56
0.1–5	48	3.44	100
Total	1,398	100	

Andean countries and 78.7% have more than 90% of their ranges in the region (Table 4.1). More than 90% of the species that intersect the Andean region have 30% or more of their total range within the region (Table 4.1). Only 3.4% of the species (48) have less than 5% of their range within the Andean region (Table 4.1).

Broad spatial patterns

The highest diversity of amphibians is found along the eastern foothills of the Andes and piedmont Amazonian lowlands of Ecuador and Peru (Fig. 4.1). The lowest diversity values are observed along the dry coastal zones of western Peru where there are areas without any reported amphibian species. There are clear concentrations of species with restricted ranges (Fig. 4.4).

Threat status and distribution patterns of tropical Andean amphibians

Within the greater Andes, 44% of amphibian species are threatened according to IUCN Red List criteria (Table 4.2). All Critically Endangered (CR) species that intersect the Andean region are endemics (99.9% of their range is within the five tropical Andean countries). Within the Endangered (EN) and Vulnerable (VU) categories, 97.9% and 96.3% of species, respectively, are endemic to the Andes. More than 60% of all threatened amphibians in the Andes have a range size of less than 2,000 km² (Fig. 4.5).

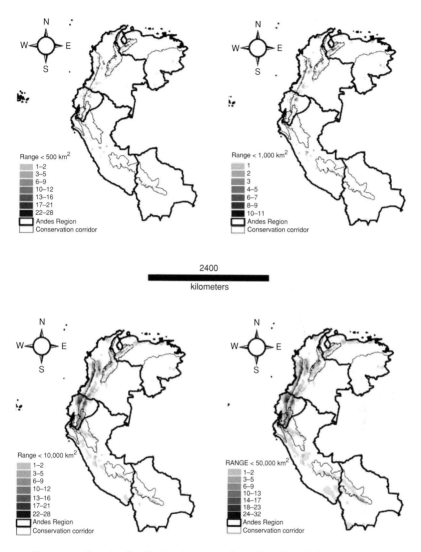

Figure 4.4. Density distribution in terms of number of amphibian species with extents of occurrence between less than 500 km² and 10,000–50,000 km² for species residing within the countries (Bolivia, Peru, Ecuador, Colombia, and Venezuela) representing Conservation International's Andean Centers for Biodiversity Conservation (CBC).

Table 4.2. *Number of amphibian species in the Andes Region in each IUCN Red List category*

IUCN 2006 Red List status	Species count
Critically Endangered (CR)	120
Endangered (EN)	187
Vulnerable (VU)	162
Near Threatened (NT)	71
Least Concern (LC)	530
Data Deficient (DD)	325
Extinct (EX)	3
Total	1,398

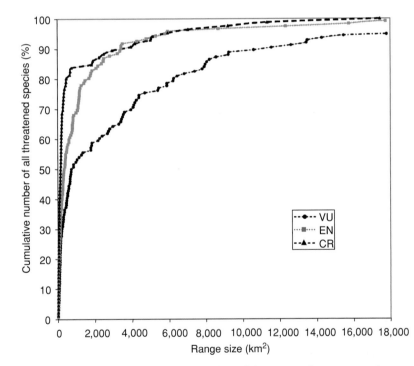

Figure 4.5. Percentage of all threatened amphibians according to range size. For example, 80% of all threatened amphibians have a range size less than 7,000 km². Critically Endangered (CR) species tend to reduce the percentage of threatened species within a given range size threshold. EN, endangered species; VU, vulnerable species.

Distributions of threatened amphibians and conservation corridors

There are a total of 1,061 amphibian species endemic to the Andes Region. In total, the conservation corridors overlap with the distributions of 68% of the region's amphibian fauna. The corridors overlap with 60% of the threatened amphibians in the region. Of these threatened species that occur within the conservation corridor boundaries, 97% are endemic to the Andes Region. Of those species whose distribution ranges overlap with the corridors, 50% have at least 90% of their total distribution range located outside of the corridor system. Of this 50%, only 6% have remaining forested habitat outside the corridors. The majority of remaining habitat for all threatened amphibians combined occurs within the conservation corridors (Fig. 4.6).

Results of fine-scale analysis of a focal species

According to the Global Amphibian Assessment, the estimated extent of occurrence for *Atelopus carbonerensis* is based on only a few historically occupied sites (Fig. 4.7). It is clear that, prior to 1986, extensive deforestation occurred around the south-western boundaries of Sierra de la Culata National Park (Fig. 4.8). The park occupies an area of approximately 2,004 km². It was officially declared a national park in 1989. We took a threefold approach to identify those sites that may now be too badly affected by anthropogenically induced forest degradation, that may represent ecotones (such as transitions from forest to shrub), or that may not have suitable habitats for reproduction. First, we examined sites in the context of present conservation regimes (i.e. the Sierra Culata National Park). Second, a 270 m edge buffer was calculated for remnant forested areas to differentiate those fragments whose form and size indicate the presence of potentially unfavorable habitat conditions (Fig. 4.8). Third, taking into consideration the dependence of *Atelopus carbonerensis* on streams for reproduction, sub-basins whose headwaters flow downstream to forest areas with species records were delineated as important contributors for the regulation of quality and quantity of hydrological resources (Fig. 4.9).

A close-up view of the locality records for *Atelopus carbonerensis* depicts three distinct and alarming conservation scenarios (Fig. 4.10). Site 1 depicts recent deforestation in close proximity of a historical species sighting record. Site 2 depicts a denuded landscape where past human settlement has likely led to the clearing of the original habitat associated with this observation record. Finally, site 3 depicts the nearly complete deforestation of a small and isolated forest patch on the landscape.

Remnant Habitat Distribution for Threatened Species

Key
Threatened Species Habitat

☐ Convervation corridor
☐ Andes Region
▨ Anthropogenically degraded amphibian habitat
■ Remnant amphibian habitat within corridor

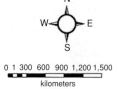

Figure 4.6. Total distribution of combined ranges for threatened amphibians (Critically Endangered, Endangered, and Vulnerable) in the Andes Region within remaining and human disturbed habitats. The maps depict the countries (Bolivia, Peru, Ecuador, Colombia, and Venezuela) representing Conservation International's Andean Centers for Biodiversity Conservation (CBC).

Site 1 offers the best scenario for locating existing populations and protecting critical habitat for the species. This site offers a potential 8.5 km² of intact forest core area, encompassing 1.5 km² of area outside the protected area network and 7.0 km² within the protected area network

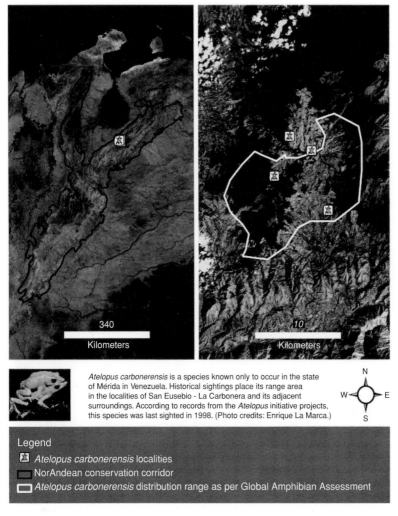

Figure 4.7. Localities for *Atelopus carbonerensis* with respect to the northern portion of CI's Andean conservation corridor (left image) and the Global Amphibian Assessment's (Stuart *et al.* 2004) published extent of occurrence for the species (right image).

(Fig. 4.11). Despite the fact that a portion of the forest area nearest the observation record lies outside of the immediate boundaries of the national park network, the edge-afflicted areas are contiguous and form a connective network between several patches of core forest area within the nearby national park and the proximity of species locality records to existing intact forest suggests that the species may extend into neighboring contiguous areas.

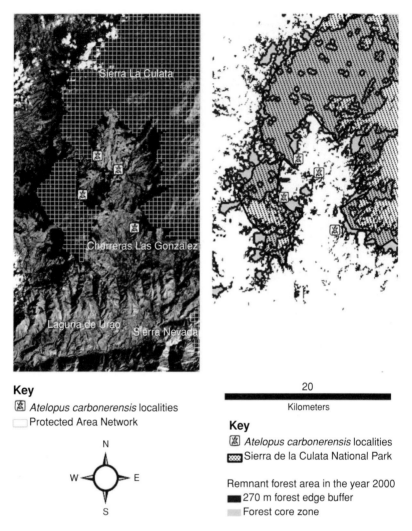

Key

🖼 *Atelopus carbonerensis* localities
▢ Protected Area Network

N
W ⬥ E
S

20
Kilometers

Key

🖼 *Atelopus carbonerensis* localities
▨ Sierra de la Culata National Park

Remnant forest area in the year 2000
■ 270 m forest edge buffer
▨ Forest core zone

Figure 4.8. Protected area coverage in relation to locality records for *Atelopus carbonerensis*. The left image in the figure depicts the landscape in the year 1986 as seen from the Landsat TM satellite platform and shows the current extent of the Sierra de la Culata National Park located in the vicinity of the observed species records. The right image shows the extent of forest cover in 2000, including core and edge forest habitats, with respect to the known localities for the species.

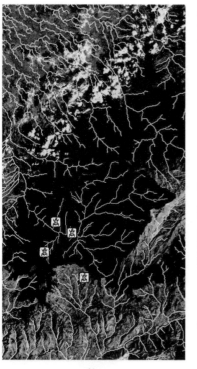
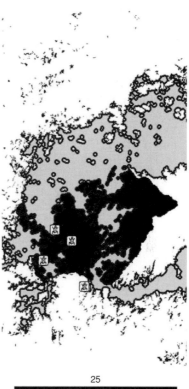

Key

🔲 *Atelopus carbonerensis* localities
NorAndean corridor stream network
▬ Watershed sub-basin

25
Kilometers

Key

🔲 *Atelopus carbonerensis* localities
▬ Watershed sub-basin

Remnant forest area in the year 2000
▬ 270 m forest edge buffer
░ Forest core zone

Figure 4.9. Watershed sub-basin in which *Atelopus carbonerensis* occurs. The left image depicts the stream network and extent of the watershed in which most of the localities for the species occur. The right image shows an overlay of the extent of forest cover for the region with the watershed.

DISCUSSION

Systematic conservation planning

From a regional conservation planning perspective, the small, highly allopatric distributions of many threatened species across a fragmented landscape require simultaneous analysis of species distributions and their

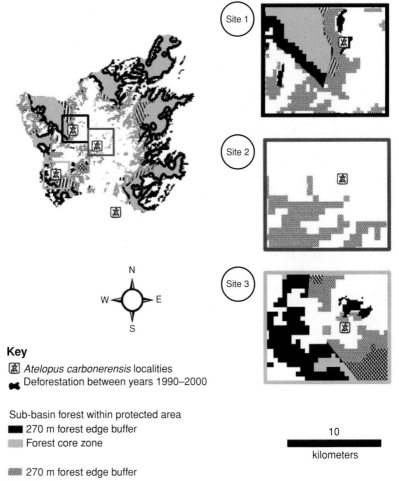

Key

🔏 *Atelopus carbonerensis* localities
🔸 Deforestation between years 1990–2000

Sub-basin forest within protected area
◼ 270 m forest edge buffer
▨ Forest core zone

▨ 270 m forest edge buffer
▨ Forest core zone

Figure 4.10. Conservation site options for *Atelopus carbonerensis*. In order to evaluate the conservation site options for the species, the three localities for the species that are within the same watershed sub-basin are each displayed together with the extent of forest core and edge habitats in immediate proximity. Only site 1 has core forest habitat within 1 km of a known locality for the species making it the best option for long-term protection of the species. Site 2 has core forest habitat within 3 km and site 3 has only edge habitat in near vicinity.

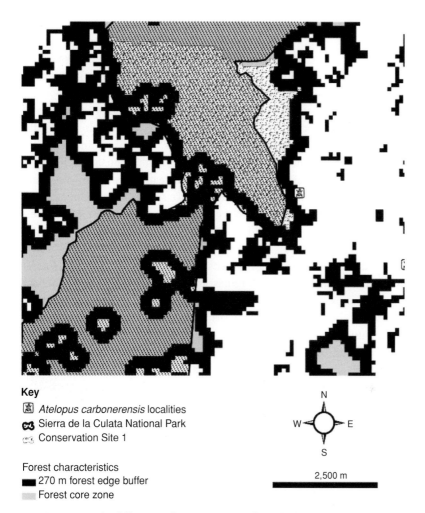

Key

 Atelopus carbonerensis localities
 Sierra de la Culata National Park
 Conservation Site 1

Forest characteristics
■ 270 m forest edge buffer
▨ Forest core zone

N
W—○—E
S

2,500 m

Figure 4.11. The full extent of contiguous core forest habitat at the best conservation site option for *Atelopus carbonerensis* (site 1) with respect to other nearby fragments of core and edge forest habitat and the boundary of the nearest existing protected area.

remaining habitats together with existing and proposed conservation areas. The effectiveness of such regional planning exercises may be limited by the coarse resolution of data that are often used in the absence of more detailed data on species distributions. Species extent of occurrence data are generally available and utilized, but high-resolution occupancy data are far less likely to introduce errors whereby species are assumed to be within a protected area when they actually are not. Consequently, a challenge to regional planning is to understand how such commission errors for multiple species cumulatively reduce the overall accuracy by which the regional planning analysis assesses how well conservation initiatives will protect a region's fauna.

Despite the spatial refinement limitations associated with the quality of coarse-scale information, regional analyses such as ours do provide the means to analyse pattern at landscape levels. These may influence the selection of priority sites for protection, while simultaneously providing key information regarding the potential importance of landscape, topographic, and climatologic characteristics that influence species distributions. Identifying significant patterns within a region, such as concentrations or clusters of species that are endemic to a region or that have very restricted distribution ranges, facilitates the identification and selection of sites where conservation investments can potentially optimize the number of species included by new reserves (Margules and Pressey 2000). Many political, socio-economic, and cultural factors tend to influence the size and location of reserves, but only spatial analyses of species distributions and threats can identify sites that, if protected, will complement the suite of species already within existing reserves. From the perspective of global biodiversity conservation, basing regional and national plans for reserve networks on such systematic conservation planning is more likely to meet goals of reducing the number of gap species even when data are spatially coarse or taxonomically incomplete (Margules and Pressey 2000).

Regional planning for Andean amphibian conservation

The amphibians of the Andes Region represent one of the most diverse and most threatened faunas on the planet. The combined high threat and alpha-diversity of this fauna together pose one of the global conservation community's greatest priorities (Stuart *et al.* 2004). At a broad scale, our analysis indicates that Conservation International's Andean conservation corridor design will protect 59% of threatened and 47% of non-threatened amphibian species within the region. This result indicates that the conservation planning efforts that determined the corridor boundaries were successful at capturing a majority of the region's threatened amphibian fauna and, presumably, a high degree of diversity within other groups that are distributed similarly to amphibians. However, limits of the conservation corridor system were also identified. First, 41% of the region's threatened amphibians occur entirely or mostly outside of the corridors. Conservation plans must quickly be developed for these species. Ideally, such plans would consider what new boundaries would most cost-effectively encompass the largest number of species that are currently extralimital to the existing corridors. Second, more than 50% of the threatened species that are within corridor boundaries only occur within degraded habitats, suggesting that many may have already been or are close to extirpation within the corridor. Different actions need to be taken for these species. First, at a minimum, rapid habitat restoration projects must be implemented for species that cannot maintain viable populations in degraded habitats and that cannot be saved by protecting suitable habitats outside of the existing corridor. Such efforts must include restoration not only of specific sites where some amphibians typically congregate (e.g. water bodies) but also forest habitats that may ensure the viability of regional metapopulations that are dependent on landscape-level processes such as dispersal and asynchrony among local population dynamics (Gascon *et al.* 1999; Lima and Gascon 1999). Second, for some species already in rapid decline and because of the real and potential spread of the fungal disease chytridiomycosis (Lips *et al.* 2006), such habitat restoration projects may not be sufficient in the short term and, in these cases, *ex situ* captive assurance colonies should be established until habitats have been sufficiently restored.

An important remaining question is how well amphibians serve as an effective surrogate for the region's total biodiversity. Amphibians are possibly more representative of biodiversity as a whole in tropical humid forests than other taxa because their high species turnover across the landscape better represents the highly speciose and often small-ranged invertebrates and plants. However, the extent to which amphibians may be a better surrogate for other high beta-diversity groups than birds and other low beta-diversity groups remains untested. Specifically, the extent of overlap among groups should be studied explicitly in at least a few areas to determine if amphibians may serve as good indicators of priority sites for overall biodiversity conservation in forests of the Andes and elsewhere. Within the Andes, it would be critical to do such a test prior to basing region-wide reserve networks largely on amphibian distribution data given that the region has some of the highest diversity of vascular plants anywhere in the world with approximately 10% of the world's species and an estimated 50%–60% of species endemic to the region (Rodriguez-Mahecha *et al.* 2004).

Importance of landscape-level processes

Another challenge to regional planning for a reserve network is that the viability of populations, and ultimately species, may often be dependent on landscape-level processes such as those that influence dispersal of individuals among populations. Landscape-level processes are sometimes not addressed in multi-species regional planning exercises although they should be considered for many taxa. Here we review four guidelines that are especially relevant to what landscape-level processes need to be addressed to provide threatened amphibian species with long-term protection within protected areas.

First, it is critical to protect large areas and prevent the fragmentation of currently contiguous large patches of forest. Research indicates that extinctions are expected to rapidly reduce biodiversity in fragments smaller than 100 ha (Laurance *et al.* 2002). In addition to supporting larger populations and hence protecting them against the demographic and genetic diversity problems that can occur in small populations (Gilpin and Soulé 1986; Menges 1992), large areas may be a source of immigrants for recolonization of small fragments (see Venticinque and Fowler 2001; Naughton-Treves *et al.* 2002).

Such recolonization opportunities may be especially critical given the likelihood of rampant local extirpations due to disease (Lips *et al.* 2006) and periods of drought associated with climate change (Pounds *et al.* 2006). To permit movements of individuals through corridors of suitable habitat, forest patches should remain connected through naturally vegetated corridors. An absence of vegetation cover around forest remnants represents a significant barrier for many species. Studies have shown that gallery forests left along stream gullies represent suitable habitat for litter frogs (Lima and Gascon 1999). These narrow areas (average of 160 m wide) were undistinguishable from adjacent primary forest with regards to the number of species and community composition of these two taxonomic groups. Moreover, many frogs and small mammals showed evidence of breeding in these habitats and a few individuals of small mammals were found to move between adjacent primary forest and the narrow gallery forest corridors. In addition, the width of the stream valley forest was directly related to the total number of species (Lima and Gascon 1999). Utilizing natural features, such as stream gullies, to maintain areas of forest cover between forest patches will greatly enhance functional connectivity and help prevent local extinctions through a rescue effect (Laurance and Gascon 1997; Bierregaard *et al.* 2001).

Second, it is important to promote reforestation and overall forest cover in critical areas of landscapes. Loss of primary forest results in the creation of a new matrix habitat that leads to additional changes in forest patches. First, the matrix habitat filters which species move through the landscape. Second, species that are associated with disturbed habitat, now more widely distributed and present in greater abundance, can invade forest patches and edge habitats (Tabarelli *et al.* 1999; Scariot 2001). Finally, depending on how the landscape is utilized, the matrix habitat (e.g. pasture, degraded pasture, second growth forest) can increase the severity of edge effects on fragments (Williamson *et al.* 1998; Mesquita *et al.* 1999; Gascon *et al.* 2000; Williamson and Mesquita 2001).

A filter model for the movements of individuals (Gascon *et al.* 1999) predicts a gradual increase in species richness from a fine-pore size matrix (i.e. pasture) to larger-pore sized matrix habitats (i.e. second growth and primary forests). This model accurately applies to frogs in an Amazonian landscape where increments in species richness are associated with decreasing habitat disturbance (Tocher 1998). In highly disturbed matrix habitats (i.e. pasture), fewer species occur than in areas that are in different phases of forest recovery. In addition, a high proportion of all species in each habitat tend to be those that were originally associated with primary forest habitat (Zimmerman and Bierregaard 1986). Consequently, even young, low second growth forests will contain over 65% of the species complement present in adjacent primary forest (Tocher 1998).

There is also a strong correlation between the abundances of species in the matrix habitat and their persistence index in forest fragments (Malcolm 1991; Gascon et al. 1999), suggesting that the nature of the matrix habitat can determine how well fragments will maintain their pool of species in the long term (Gascon and Lovejoy 1998).

A third guideline that may be critical to the viability of many amphibian populations, particularly those restricted to small patches of remaining forest, is that forest edges should be managed to minimize the impact of edge effects. Studies of forest fragmentation have shown that forest edges represent a primary threat for many species (Bierregaard *et al.* 2001). Laurance *et al.* (2002) described alterations in a suite of environmental variables due to edge creation, from increased wind disturbance to lower soil-moisture content. These physical factors may effectively reduce the area of suitable habitat for survival and reproduction of many amphibian species, particularly those that have a completely terrestrial life cycle.

A fourth guideline relevant to the management of landscape processes is the control of three common practices: fire use, introduction of exotic species, and application of toxic chemicals. The combination of fire and chemicals has been used to increase crop production despite many associated health risks. Similarly, exotic plant introductions have resulted in the replacement of many native species (Olden *et al.* 2004). In many cases, these exotic plant species are more resistant to fire and can be favored over native species by repeated use of fire. Accidental and intentional introduction of fish and non-native amphibian species may be a key factor in the spread of the amphibian pathogen chytridiomycosis, which is responsible for local extirpations and probably species extinctions throughout the Andes (Stuart *et al.* 2004).

Fine-scale analysis of single species

Our analysis of site options for the conservation of *Atelopus carbonerensis* provides an example of how a fine-scale examination of locality records and remaining habitat can focus research (i.e. searches for "missing" species) and establish specific priorities for protection and management of sites. We suggest that the broader regional analysis can identify and prioritize which species require such higher resolution studies. This prioritization should result in great savings in both financial resources and time, as well as ensure that the species which are in greatest need of study and conservation are identified as such. As our case example for *Atelopus carbonerensis* illustrates, the small distributions of amphibians, particularly the threatened species, generally means that the scale at which conservation targets are set within landscapes are going to be smaller than for many other taxa. Furthermore, the high beta-diversity and life-history variation among species of amphibians means that specific targets may need to be designed for relatively small species assemblages. We recognize that identification of site-level priorities for single species poses a great challenge to conservation planners. However, we believe that the relative cost of such planning may be minimal relative to the gains achieved by being able to prioritize management efforts in the most important sites for species. Nevertheless, we acknowledge that the number of threatened amphibians in the region calls for broad-scale initiatives that will better target conservation of this group at the landscape scale. Below, we discuss two general areas which deserve study so as to improve the identification of targets for how landscapes should be managed for threatened amphibians.

Generally, demographic and genetic connectivity among populations across a landscape are viewed as processes that promote viability within both local populations and across metapopulations or other ensemble population structures (Gilpin and Soulé 1986). The threat of disease for *Atelopus carbonerensis*, and many other species in the Andes Region, could be argued as a reason to not promote or even inhibit movement of individuals among sites. However, the epidemiology of chytridiomycosis is not yet well understood and, furthermore, genetic and demographic exchange may have actually contributed to the persistence of populations despite the occurrence of the disease. Thus, much may be gained from general epidemiological studies and the testing of specific hypotheses for how some populations, or individuals in some cases, have persisted despite the prevalence of chytridiomycosis.

As with many of the most threatened frogs in the Andes Region, *Atelopus carbonerensis* is dependent on both freshwater and terrestrial habitats. A primary challenge of the landscape-level conservation needs for this species is the maintenance of high quality stream water which can be jeopardized by socio-economic activities far upstream from sites where the species occurs. A goal for conservation of all threatened species that depend on such freshwater resources must be to ensure that site-level actions are accompanied by initiatives that protect the entirety of the upstream habitat. Because stream habitats may become poor breeding grounds if stream siltation occurs, this conservation target may transcend from management of the immediate stream habitat to management of how forests are logged and other activities within large areas of a stream's watershed despite the fact that threatened species may physically utilize a relatively small proportion of the upland habitats. An analysis that identified watersheds associated with the upstream habitats of threatened amphibians would be helpful in setting conservation targets for threatened amphibians in the Andes Region and elsewhere.

It is important to note that several landscape-level targets for amphibian conservation may be amenable to a variety of economic activities. For instance, the aforementioned management of forests in upland habitats upstream from specific conservation sites can probably include sustainable forestry as long as careful attention is paid to regulating these activities such that adverse stream quality does not result. Other economic activities that are probably possible in such areas include farming of shade grown coffee, cacao, and other crops. Indeed, these activities may be possible even within the specific sites in which many threatened species occur, particularly if such activities are conducted within a managed forest mosaic that includes parcels in which the natural understory is allowed to grow. Future conservation efforts would benefit from research that refines how targets could be set to balance economic activities with the biological needs of threatened amphibians.

ACKNOWLEDGEMENTS

We thank Simon Stuart for providing Global Amphibian Assessment data and for sharing information on the status of Andean amphibians.

References

Bierregaard, R. O. Jr., C. Gascon, T. E. Lovejoy and R. Mesquita. 2001. *Lessons from Amazonia: The Ecology and Conservation of a Fragmented Forest.* New Haven, CT: Yale University Press.

Corlett, R. T. 2000. Environmental heterogeneity and species survival in degraded tropical landscapes. Pp. 333–55 in M. J. Hutchings, E. A. John and A. J. A. Stewart (eds.) *The Ecological Consequences of Environmental Heterogeneity.* London: British Ecological Society.

Eken, G., L. Bennun, T. M. Brooks. 2004. Key biodiversity areas as site conservation targets. *BioScience* 54:1110–18.

Fahrig, L. 2003. Effects of habitat fragmentation on biodiversity. *Annual Review of Ecology, Evolution and Systematics* 34:487–515.

Gascon, C. and T. E. Lovejoy. 1998. Ecological impacts of forest fragmentation in central Amazonia. *Zoology, Analysis of Complex Systems* 101:273–80.

Gascon, C., T. E. Lovejoy, R. O. Bierregaard, Jr. *et al.* 1999. Matrix habitat and species persistence in tropical forest remnants. *Biological Conservation* 91:223–30.

Gascon C., G. B. Williamson and G. A. B. Fonseca. 2000. Receding forest edges and vanishing reserves. *Science* 288:1356–8.

Gascon, C., G. A. B. da Fonseca, W. Sechrest, K. A. Billmark and J. Sanderson. 2004. Biodiversity conservation in deforested and fragmented landscapes: an overview. Pp. 15–32 in G. Schroth, G. A. B. da Fonseca, C. A. Harvey *et al.* (eds.) *Agroforestry and Biodiversity Conservation in Tropical Landscapes.* Washington, D.C.: Island Press.

Gilpin, M. E. and M. E. Soulé. 1986. Minimum viable population: processes of species extinction. Pp. 19–34 in M. E. Soulé (ed.) *Conservation Biology: the Science of Scarcity and Diversity.* Sunderland, MA: Sinauer Associates.

La Marca, E., A. Rodríguez and J. E. García-Pérez. 2006. *Atelopus carbonerensis.* In 2006 IUCN *Red List of Threatened Species.*

Laurance, W. F. and M. A. Cochrane. 2001. Synergistic effects in fragmented landscapes. Special section. *Conservation Biology* 15:1488–535.

Laurance, W. F. and C. Gascon. 1997. How to creatively fragment a landscape. *Conservation Biology* 11:577–9.

Laurance, W. F., T. E. Lovejoy, H. L. Vasconcelos *et al.* 2002. Ecosystem decay of Amazonian forest fragments: a 22-year investigation. *Conservation Biology* 16:605–18.

Lima, M. and C. Gascon. 1999. The conservation value of linear forest remnants in central Amazonia. *Biological Conservation* 91:241–7.

Lips, K. R., F. Brem, R. Brenes *et al.* 2006. Emerging infectious disease and the loss of biodiversity in a Neotropical amphibian community. *Proceedings of the National Academy of Sciences of the United States of America* 103:3165–70.

Malcolm, J. R. 1991. The small mammals of Amazonian forest fragments: pattern and process. Ph.D. thesis, University of Florida.

Margules, C. R. and R. L. Pressey. 2000. Systematic conservation planning. *Nature* 405:243–53.

Menges, E. S. 1992. Stochastic modeling of extinction in plant populations. Pp. 253–75 in P. L. Fiedler and S. K. Jain (eds.) *Conservation Biology: The Theory and Practice of Nature Conservation, Preservation and Management.* New York, NY: Chapman and Hall.

Mesquita, R. C. G., P. Delamônica and W. F. Laurance. 1999. Effect of surrounding vegetation on edge-related tree mortality in Amazonian forest fragments. *Biological Conservation* 91:129–34.

Naughton-Treves, L., J. L. Mena, A. Treves, N. Alvarez and V. C. Radeloff. 2002. Wildlife survival beyond park boundaries: the impact of slash-and-burn agriculture and hunting on mammals in Tambopata, Peru. *Conservation Biology* 17:1106–17.

Olden, J. D., N. L. Poff, M. R. Douglas, M. E. Douglas and K. D. Fausch. 2004. Ecological and evolutionary consequences of biotic homogenization. *Trends in Ecology and Evolution* 19:18–24.

Pounds, J. A., M. R. Bustamante, L. A. Coloma *et al.* 2006. Widespread amphibian extinctions from epidemic disease driven by global warming. *Nature* 439:161–7.

Ricketts T. H., E. Dinerstein, T. Boucher *et al.* 2006. Pinpointing and preventing imminent extinctions. *Proceedings of the National Academy of Sciences of the United States of America* 102:18497–501.

Rodrigues, A. S. L., S. J. Andelman, M. I. Bakarr *et al.* 2004. Effectiveness of the global protected area network in representing species diversity. *Nature* 428:640–3.

Rodriguez-Mahecha, J. V., P. Salaman, P. Jorgensen *et al.* 2004. Tropical Andes. Pp. 73–9 in R. A. Mittermeier, P. R. Gill, M. Hoffman *et al.* (eds.) *Hotspots Revisited.* Mexico City: Cemex.

Sanderson, J., G. A. B. da Fonseca, C. Galindo-Leal *et al.* 2006. Escaping the minimalist trap: design and implementation of large-scale biodiversity corridors. Pp. 620–48 in K. R. Crooks and M. Sanjayan (eds.) *Connectivity Conservation.* Cambridge, UK: Cambridge University Press.

Scariot, A. 2001. Effects of landscape fragmentation on palm communities. Pp. 121–35 in R. O. Bierregaard, Jr., C. Gascon, T. E. Lovejoy and R. Mesquita (eds.) *Lessons from Amazonia: The Ecology and Conservation of a Fragmented Forest.* Washington, D.C.: Library of Congress and Smithsonian Institution.

Semlitsch, R. D. 1998. Biological delineation of terrestrial buffer zones for pond breeding salamanders. *Conservation Biology* 12:1113–19.

Stuart, S. N., J. S. Chanson, N. A. Cox *et al.* 2004. Status and trends of amphibian declines and extinctions worldwide. *Science* 306:1783–6.

Tabarelli M., W. Mantovani and C. A. Peres. 1999. Effects of habitat fragmentation on plant guild structure in the montane Atlantic forest of southeastern Brazil. *Biological Conservation* 91:119–27.

Tabarelli, M., J. M. C. Silva and C. Gascon. 2004. Forest fragmentation, synergisms and the impoverishment of neotropical forests. *Biodiversity and Conservation* 13:1419–25.

Tocher, M. 1998. A comunidade de anfíbios da Amazônia central: diferenças na composição específica entre a mata primária e pastagens. Pp. 219–32 in C. Gascon and P. Moutinho (eds.) *Floresta Amazônica: Dinâmica, Regeneração e Manejo.* Manaus: Instituto Nacional de Pesquisas da Amazônia.

Venticinque, E. M. and H. G. Fowler. 2001. Local extinction risks and asynchronies: the evidence for a metapopulation dynamics of a social spider,

Anelosimus eximius (Araneae, Theridiidae). Pp. 187–98 in R. O. Bierregaard, Jr., C. Gascon, T. E. Lovejoy and R. Mesquita (eds.) *Lessons from Amazonia: The Ecology and Conservation of a Fragmented Forest.* Washington D.C.: Library of Congress and Smithsonian Institution.

Williamson, G. B. and R. C. G. Mesquita. 2001. Effects of fire on rainforest regeneration in the Amazon Basin. Pp. 325–34 in R. O. Bierregaard, Jr., C. Gascon, T. E. Lovejoy and R. Mesquita (eds.) *Lessons from Amazonia: the Ecology and Conservation of a Fragmented Forest.* Washington, D.C.: Library of Congress and Smithsonian Institution.

Williamson, G. B., R. Mesquita, K. Ickes and G. Ganade. 1998. Estratégias de árvores pioneiras nos Neotrópicos. Pp. 131–44 in C. Gascon and P. Moutinho (eds.) *Floresta Amazônica: Dinâmica, Regeneração e Manejo.* Manaus: Instituto Nacional de Pesquisas da Amazônia.

Zimmerman, B. L. and R. O. Bierregaard, Jr. 1986. Relevance of the equilibrium theory of island biogeography with an example from Amazonia. *Journal of Biogeography* 13:133–43.

Zuidema, P. A., J. A. Sayer and W. Dijkman. 1996. Forest fragments and biodiversity: the case for intermediate-sized conservation areas. *Environmental Conservation* 23:290–7.

Selecting biodiversity indicators to set conservation targets: species, structures, or processes?

SVEN G. NILSSON

INTRODUCTION

An important goal in sustainable forestry is to maintain biodiversity, i.e. to use the forest but still maintain all the indigenous species and their genetic variation. To do this, it is essential to maintain important structures and processes on which numerous species are dependent. However, how do we know that biodiversity is maintained in managed forest landscapes? How much of the important structures, e.g. large living and dead trees that dominate in old-growth forests (Nilsson *et al.* 2002), is needed? How often and at what intensity should processes such as ecological disturbances by water, wind, fire, large herbivores, insect outbreaks, etc. be allowed/initiated? Obviously, owing to limited knowledge and human resources, it is presently impossible to count all species in a forest, a task that has yet to be achieved in any forest in the world. Large old-growth forests harbor exceedingly rich faunas and floras (Bobiec *et al.* 2005) and numerous species depend on dead wood (Elton 1966; Siitonen 2001). We also have to set some targets for important structures and/or use biodiversity indicators, which can tell us that biodiversity is preserved in managed forest landscapes. There have been several major approaches to this difficult problem of setting conservation targets for the maintenance of biodiversity.

Setting Conservation Targets for Managed Forest Landscapes, ed. M.-A. Villard and B. G. Jonsson. Published by Cambridge University Press.
© Cambridge University Press 2009.

1. **Strict protection strategy to protect remaining natural forest**: set aside 5, 10, 20, or 50% of the forest land for conservation and allocate the rest to management. Carry out management of protected areas, sometimes through the removal of introduced species and/or restoration of managed forests to a more natural state.

2. **Managing structures and processes to conserve natural variation**: maintain a given density of important structures, agents, and processes for biodiversity, such as old trees, dead trees, forest fires, natural water regimes, grazing by large herbivores, etc.

3. **Targets related to presence or frequency of species, i.e. organisms as biodiversity indicators**: monitor the presence and/or density of biodiversity indicators among animals, plants, and/or fungi. Usually, species with large area requirements, specialized habitat demands, and/or low dispersal propensity are suggested as biodiversity indicators.

The first two strategies presume that we know "how much is enough"; the third may be used to evaluate any strategy including adaptive management. These different approaches, singly or combined, all have their advantages and disadvantages, which I review here using examples and evidence mainly from temperate and boreal forests of Europe.

SETTING TARGETS: POLITICS AND SCIENCE

Targets and indicators of sustainable forestry depend on the goals, which are mainly set in a political context. For instance, in Sweden, all parties in the parliament have agreed that all indigenous species should be preserved (Anon. 1991). Should this apply to all species in all regions where they have potential habitat (even if not occurring now)? What about extinct species in the focal country? Is it enough to have a sparse population of individual displaying capercaillies *Tetrao urogallus* (a grouse) or should the goal be to have some large leks with over 10 males, which dominate in pristine landscapes? Such questions are not addressed in the political statement but need to be considered if we want to meet conservation goals through appropriate targets. Further, the occurrence patterns of a lekking species (as single males or in larger leks) may influence the evolution of its characteristics over the long term. So, how we formulate conservation goals is not only a political issue.

Are some species, e.g. keystone species or popular species, more important to preserve regionally than rare species and species that are difficult to see owing to small size or nocturnal habits? For scientists it is important to recognize whether an issue is mainly political or whether it is scientifically important. Obviously, there is an interaction since scientific data can influence policy and vice versa. Statements may be given a scientific appearance but, upon closer inspection, turn out to be without substance. An instructive example was provided by Pykälä (2004) when forest authorities said that forest practices were sustainable but empirical data established rapid decline of rare epiphytic lichens. Thus, in the absence of monitoring of species and their population trends, the concept of sustainable management is diluted. A quantitative approach aiming at maintaining viable populations of target species in the long term is particularly useful.

STRICT PROTECTION STRATEGY

How much of a forest must be set aside from forestry for its biodiversity to be maintained? There have been many suggestions; for example, in the FSC (Forest Stewardship Council) certification system in Sweden, 5% is set aside (Anon. 2000). The international goal is that 10% of all ecosystens should be strictly protected (Anon. 1980). However, scientific evidence indicates that the proportion may be over 50% in some situations (Soulé and Sanjayan 1998; Holland *et al.* 2005; Svancara *et al.* 2005). The amount required for efficient biodiversity conservation certainly differs depending on forest type, forestry practices, and regional forest history. Thus, how the forests surrounding protected areas are managed is crucial for how much protected forest is needed to achieve stated goals.

Species in virgin forests seem to be more sensitive to human impact than species that have lived in forests previously managed in some way. In the latter, the most sensitive species have apparently been extirpated (Balmford 1996). Since an overwhelming majority of the forests of the world have been used over hundreds or thousands of years, virgin forests are rare or absent in most parts of the world, especially in Europe, south of the boreal region (Hannah *et al.* 1995).

In intensively managed regions, a major problem is to identify the original forest vegetation, its natural disturbance regimes, and the resulting indigenous flora and fauna (Nilsson *et al.* 2005). Just leaving to free succession a given proportion of the previously managed forests may be a very inefficient and even unsuccessful way to restore the original forest types and to protect their organisms. For example, in regions subjected to frequent forest fires resulting in an open forest dominated by pine (*Pinus sylvestris*) and oaks (*Quercus* spp.), as was the case in south-eastern Sweden (Niklasson and Drakenberg 2001; Nilsson *et al.* 2001; Lindbladh *et al.* 2003), one should restore a similar disturbance regime with frequent fires. In this region, there are currently no forest reserves that can maintain the original disturbance regime, owing to their small area (Niklasson and Nilsson 2005).

When little natural forest remains, a problem is to allocate conservation resources in space to maximize persistence of species over the long run (e.g. Ovaskainen 2002; Cabeza and Moilanen 2003). A general recommendation is to cluster effort in space with restoration patches near remaining natural forests where threatened species persist (e.g. Hanski 2000; Nilsson *et al.* 2001, 2005; Cabeza and Moilanen 2003; Moilanen and Winthle 2006). Thus, a major problem in this strict protection strategy is that the spatial distribution of protected areas is rarely explicitly addressed. Numerous studies on vertebrates have shown that habitat fragmentation influences the occurrence of many species; recently, evidence has also come from studies of mosses (Snäll *et al.* 2005; Löbel *et al.* 2006) and lichens (Jüriado *et al.* 2006).

MANAGING STRUCTURES

Large living and dead trees

Since a major aim of forestry is to produce timber and, therefore, to remove stems before they get rotten, the largest difference between virgin and managed forests is the density of old living and large dead trees. The difference is especially pronounced for large dimensions, where less than 1% of the original volume remains in many managed forests in Europe (Nilsson *et al.* 2001, 2005; Siitonen 2001; Rouvinen and Kuuvulainen 2005). Recent studies in boreal forests of northern Europe have shown correlations between densities of dead trees and richness of wood beetles (Økland 1996; Martikainen *et al.* 2000; Siitonen *et al.* 2001; Juutinen *et al.* 2006) and wood fungi (Bader *et al.* 1995; Stokland 2001). The incidence per tree of some red-listed beetles dependent on tree hollows also increased with the number of large hollow oaks in a group (Ranius 2002a). Even litter-dwelling beetles are more abundant and species-rich near coarse dead wood, for reasons that are still unknown (Topp *et al.* 2006). These general patterns may hold within a region, but not if forest stands are sampled in different regions with long and short histories of exploitation (Penttilä *et al.* 2006).

Based on general extinction models and a few empirical studies, we have suggested that a target for sustainable forestry is to aim for at least 20% of original densities of large living and dead trees (Nilsson *et al.* 2001), based on reference values in old-growth forests (for Europe, see Jonsson and Kruys

2001; Nilsson *et al.* 2002). This translates to 20–30 m³ ha⁻¹ of dead wood in temperate and southern boreal forests, and there are some indications that this relation holds for at least some groups of organisms. For boreal spruce-dominated old-growth forests in southern Finland, which often contained more than 100 m³ ha⁻¹ of dead wood, dead wood amounts of 20 m³ ha⁻¹ seem to be a lower limit for the persistence of some threatened polypore species (Penttilä *et al.* 2004). Similarly, forest stands with threatened wood beetles in boreonemoral Uppland, Sweden, contained about 30 m³ ha⁻¹ of dead wood, 10–30 times more than in the surrounding managed forest (Jonsson and Kruys 2001; Siitonen *et al.* 2001; Eriksson 2002). More studies are needed to test the validity of the suggestion of a minimum of 20% of original amounts of dead and old trees for biodiversity conservation. Some species may need larger amounts or aggregated substrates, but knowledge is poor on this topic. How large should such a patch with high density of coarse dead wood and old trees be to retain the most sensitive species in the long run? The spatial distribution and quality of these crucial substrates for efficient biodiversity conservation offers important research questions for the future (see Schiegg 2000; Edman *et al.* 2004).

Forest openness

To maximize timber production, a management goal in Europe has been to fill in glades and maintain dense forests. This has eliminated many species dependent on sunlit herbs and dead wood from managed forests, especially in temperate regions (e.g. Warren and Key 1991; Freese *et al.* 2006). Numerous wood-living species benefit from wood exposed to the sun in wind-fall gaps or early-successional stands after fire, in both temperate and boreal forests, e.g. the beetles *Ampedus cinnaberinus*, *Denticollis borealis*, *Grynocharis oblonga*, *Peltis grossa*, *Tragosoma depsarium*, and *Upis ceramboides* (Nilsson and Baranowski 1996, 1997a; Jonsell *et al.* 1998; Similä *et al.* 2006; Bouget and Duelli 2004; Wikars 2004; Bouget 2005; Hyvärinen *et al.* 2005; Wikars and Orrmalm 2005). I have found no suggestion on the appropriate size of openings for these species, but the beetle *Tragosoma depsarium* living in large pine logs exposed to the sun may need a considerable area (Wikars 2004).

Among butterflies, many species have drastically declined in temperate forests owing to an increase in tree density compared with stand structures produced by traditional small-scale management (e.g. Bergman 1999; Freese *et al.* 2006; Van Swaay *et al.* 2006). Among vertebrates, many studies have examined the habitat of the capercaillie (*Tetrao urogallus*) and found that an open coniferous forest with rich ground vegetation with *Vaccinium myrtillus* provides suitable habitat (e.g. Storch 1994; Suter *et al.* 2002). However, the optimal openness for this species is too dense for several of heat-demanding wood-living beetles mentioned above. Thus, a range of forest stands with different degrees of openness are needed to preserve all species, but how can we decide on the optimal combination without studying species? The size and quality of open spaces needed for different species assemblages is also an important question (Bouget and Duelli 2004). Based on the original disturbance regimes (see below), larger open patches are expected to be optimal in boreal compared with temperate forests and also in pine-dominated forests maintained by frequent fires compared with spruce-dominated forests.

Ecotones

Natural forest landscapes were characterized by a high degree of spatial heterogeneity. Forest/wetland edges provided sunlit trees and shrubs. Such ecotones have received little attention but they are believed to be important for many organisms (Sjöberg and Ericson 1997; Esséen 2006). Permanent natural edges between forest and wetlands, and anthropogenic edges between old forest and clearcuts have different effects on species (Siitonen *et al.* 2005 and references therein). The wet microclimate along streams provides habitat for some mosses, for example, which can survive if a zone of forest at least 15 m wide is left along brooks when the managed forest is harvested (Hylander *et al.* 2002). Some insects mainly live in seasonally flooded dead trees, e.g. the click beetle *Ampedus sanguinolentus* (Nilsson and Baranowski 1997b), and the beaver *Castor fiber* may formerly have provided a continuous supply of large decomposing logs partly immersed in water. However, we apparently do not know how much natural ecotones are needed and how they should look like for species preservation at the landscape level.

MANAGING PROCESSES

Knowledge of natural disturbance regimes is of central importance when managing forest reserves and for maintaining species richness in working forests (reviews in Esséen *et al.* 1997; Nilsson and Ericson 1997; Bengtsson *et al.* 2000; Vera 2000; Granström 2001; Nilsson *et al.* 2001, 2005). The extent and intensity of forest fires and grazing by large herbivores can change forest structure, dominant trees, etc. and are therefore key processes (e.g. Zackrisson 1977; Bengtsson *et al.* 2000; Niklasson and Granström 2000; Vera 2000; Niklasson and Drakenberg 2001; Svenning

2002; Lindbladh *et al.* 2003). In northern Europe and elsewhere, there is a large regional variation in the density of lightning-initiated forest fires (Granström 1993; Chapter 7, this volume) and the message to conservation is to follow the natural frequency, disturbance patch size distribution, intensity, and seasonality as much as possible. A major problem in Europe is that forest reserves are small. In the region with the highest fire frequency in south-eastern Sweden, 0.20–0.25 lightning-initiated forest fires per 10,000 ha per year have been recorded (Granström 1993). In a small forest reserve of 100 ha, a typical size in this region, one would have to wait about 1,000 years to see a natural forest fire, if fire control around the reserve remains as intensive as it is now (Niklasson and Nilsson 2005). This calls for active fire management in reserves and managed forests dominated by pine (*Pinus sylvestris*). However, this is complicated when rare species dependent on the new situation (more closed vegetation containing much Norway spruce, *Picea abies*) have colonized reserves (Niklasson and Drakenberg 2001).

Grazing by large herbivores was a prominent factor in most forests over very long periods, even though these most important keystone species have been extinct for 10,000–20,000 years in Europe (Barnosky *et al.* 2004). Later, domestic animals have been important in shaping forest vegetation (Nilsson 1997; Bengtsson *et al.* 2000; Vera 2000; Nilsson *et al.* 2005). Probably for this historical reason, traditional agricultural landscapes where grazing has taken place among old trees and flowering shrubs are among the most species-rich ecosystems in Europe with many threatened species (e.g. Harding and Rose 1986). Bringing back extant large herbivores to forests, such as cattle and horses in temperate Europe, should thus be a high priority, but grazing pressure must not be excessive.

Water regimes in forests have been extensively changed, not least because of the hunting to near-extinction of the European beaver (*Castor fiber*). The sibling species in America, *C. canadensis*, is a keystone species, altering the environment in many ways (e.g. Naiman *et al.* 1988; Bailey and Whitham 2006), which certainly also applies to the European beaver (Rosell *et al.* 2005). Reintroducing this species is thus an efficient way to restore an important ecosystem process, and beavers are an indicator of sustainable forest management within their original distribution range.

In European forests, where Norway spruce is an important species, the bark beetle *Ips typographus* is a keystone species, producing groups of standing and, later, fallen dead trees beneficial to many saproxylic organisms. Furthermore, this bark beetle can open up a dense spruce-dominated forest, favoring reproduction of shade-intolerant tree species such as birches

(*Betula* spp.), aspen (*Populus tremula*), pine (*Pinus sylvestris*) and sallow (*Salix caprea*), and their associated organisms.

In conclusion, to preserve biodiversity at the landscape level, it is crucial to maintain a range of natural disturbance agents, as briefly reviewed here (see also Nilsson and Ericson 1997; Bengtsson *et al.* 2000; Nilsson *et al.* 2005). However, the frequency and intensity of these disturbances are system-specific and, therefore, experiments and evaluations must be performed in each region to arrive at an appropriate and cost-efficient level of disturbance to maintain biodiversity.

WHY DO WE NEED INDICATOR SPECIES?

If there is a close functional correlation between important structures and processes and the diversity and distribution of organisms, we may not have to keep track of all plant and animal species. But how often is this often implicit assumption actually met? The temperate forest of Europe has been dramatically transformed by human activities for several hundred years (Perlin 1988); old-growth forest, in particular, is highly fragmented (highly isolated, small remnant patches) compared with the situation in primeval forest landscapes. Temperate and boreal forests support a diverse fauna and flora, a large part of which is dependent on old trees and dead wood (e.g. Elton 1966; Warren and Key 1991; Kirby and Drake 1993; Siitonen 2001; Berg *et al.* 2002; Bobiec *et al.* 2005). Many lichens are dependent on old trees (e.g. Rose 1976) and some higher plants are also chiefly confined to ancient forests. Do these species track the changing distribution of forest land, old and dead trees on the landscape, or is forest history the most important factor explaining their present distribution? This is a difficult question, mainly because relevant historical data for crucial tests are rarely available (Nilsson *et al.* 2001; Gu *et al.* 2002). Indirect evidence or deductions from current distributions are often the only possibilities to test the assumption of a close correspondence between a temporal continuity of structures (suitable habitat) and species composition.

Many studies of forest plants in temperate forests have shown that the historical distribution of forests determines the current occurrences of species and many species are largely restricted to ancient woodlands. In these studies, woodlands were defined as ancient if continuity of forest land over time was indicated by available historical sources. In Europe, historical sources usually come from maps and descriptions from the sixteenth century onwards (e.g. Rackham 1980; Peterken and Game 1984). Recent secondary woodlands are on former cultivated ground and their origin can be determined from historical sources. Some vascular plants are largely restricted to ancient woodlands (see Chapter 11, this volume) over large parts of Europe, including *Galium odoratum, Hordelymus europaeus, Lamium galeobdolon, Melica uniflora, Milium effusum, Paris quadrifolia,* and *Primula elatior* (e.g. Rackham 1980; Hermy and Stieperaere 1981; Peterken and Game 1984; Dzwonko and Loster 1989, 1992; Wulf 1993; Hermy 1994; Brunet and von Oheimb 1998). In some cases, potential confounding factors such as soil chemistry can be eliminated (Brunet 1993). The restriction of some plant species to small ancient forest patches has a multitude of effects, sometimes resulting in reduced fitness (Honnay *et al.* 2005). However, to my knowledge, this phenomenon has not been documented for vascular plants of the boreal region, suggesting that the dispersal propensity of species in a region is linked to the characteristic disturbance regimes (Nilsson and Ericson 1997). The dominant, large-scale disturbance regimes in boreal forests (e.g. Zackrisson 1977; Niklasson and Granström 2000) may have selected for a generally higher dispersal propensity than for organisms in the temperate forests, where small-scale disturbances dominate (e.g. Falinski 1986; Pontailler *et al.* 1997; Emborg *et al.* 2000). Similar reasoning can be applied to different structures and their dependent species within a region. The species dependent on very old trees or trees in fire refuges may be a special case in boreal forests, since their habitat may have a long-term continuity over time (cf. Siitonen and Saaristo 2000; Gu *et al.* 2002; Penttilä *et al.* 2006).

Some organisms are dependent on resources that are unpredictable in time and space, e.g. recently burnt forest, and these species have over evolutionary time been selected to posess a high dispersal propensity (Southwood 1977). Indeed, there is indirect evidence that some insects dependent on forest fires have a very high dispersal potential (Nilsson *et al.* 2001). At the other end of the scale are habitats that have been highly stable in time and space over evolutionary time, e.g. old hollow trees in temperate forests, predicted to harbor species with a low dispersal propensity (Martin 1989; Nilsson and Baranowski 1994). This prediction has been upheld by tests on beetles dependent on hollow trees in temperate forests, which use patches of old-growth beech forest with different history but all with many suitable hollow trees (Nilsson and Baranowski 1997b). A similar pattern applies to the beetle *Osmoderma eremita* living in old hollow oaks. The latter species was found to fly less than 200 m, although dispersal movements up to 800 m could have been detected by using telemetry, and as many as 85% of the individuals remained in their natal tree all their life (Ranius and Hedin 2001; Hedin *et al.* 2008). In boreal forests of Europe, wet spruce-dominated *Picea abies* forests may be the most stable type and, interestingly, the beetle *Phyto kolwensis* living in recently fallen large spruce logs appears to have a low dispersal propensity. The current distribution of this beetle is most accurately correlated with an occurrence of old, previously suitable, logs of spruce (Siitonen and Saaristo 2000). This correlation suggests that *Phyto kolwensis* is now unable to track habitat availability. A similar situation seems to apply for some threatened polyporous fungi living in spruce logs in boreal forests (Penttilä *et al.* 2006).

Not all fire-dependent or fire-favored organisms can track suitable habitat in burnt forests. The fungi *Daldinia loculata* growing on fire-killed deciduous trees was found to have variable occurrence in recent burns of central Sweden. A high frequency of occurrence coincided with a long history of frequent fires and some rare and red-listed beetles were also restricted to such burns (Wikars 2001). In this case, the fungi *Daldinia loculata* seemed to be an efficient indicator, adding significant historical information to current dead wood structures. Thus, several studies have found that indicator species can add valuable information about forest history and biodiversity not shown by structures alone.

SELECTING INDICATOR SPECIES

When habitats are reduced and fragmented into small patches, the first species to disappear are often specialized ones, those occupying higher trophic levels, or those with large body size (e.g. Nilsson 1986; Dobson *et al.* 2006; Penttilä *et al.* 2006). Thus, such specialized or area-demanding species may be suitable as indicators although other considerations must be included when selecting indicator species (Pearson 1994; Lambeck 1997; Noss 1999; Nordén and Appelqvist 2001; Carignan and Villard 2002). Continued occurrence of these species at the landscape level indicates sufficient environmental concern, although there are several caveats.

Many species can persist in a landscape where their habitat is highly fragmented and ephemeral owing to their high dispersal propensity, e.g. bark beetles living in recently dead trees (Nilsson *et al.* 2001 and references therein). Such species are obviously not suitable as indicators of a preserved biodiversity. Instead, a low dispersal propensity is typical of many efficient indicator species, e.g. for the lichen *Lobaria pulmonaria* growing on old trees (Nilsson *et al.* 1995; Öckinger *et al.* 2005) and the beetle *Osmoderma eremita* living in hollow deciduous trees (Ranius and Hedin 2001; Ranius 2002a; Hedin 2003; Hedin *et al.* 2008). In the lichen *Lobaria pulmonaria*, diaspores can be found far from the trees where the species now occurs

(Werth *et al.* 2006), but this potential for long-distance dispersal does not seem to be realized. Instead, the establishing phase on tree trunks seems to be critical (Hazell and Gustafsson 1999; Hedenås and Ericson 2000; Öckinger *et al.* 2005). In old-growth beech forests, the number of red-listed beetle species was higher in hollow beeches in nearly primeval stands with many rare lichen epiphytes, including *Lobaria pulmonaria*, than in the previously managed but still old beech stands lacking such lichens (Nilsson and Baranowski 1997b). This indicates that some red-listed species have not been able to recolonize hollow trees in previously-managed stands even though they now contain many apparently suitable microhabitats. In wood-living polypores, there seems to be a negative correlation between colonization ability and sensitivity to fragmentation (Penttilä *et al.* 2006). Thus, what is important when selecting useful indicator species is a spatially restricted colonization in the current landscape and not dispersal ability *per se*.

The number of click beetles (Coleoptera, Elateridae) dependent on hollow trees at a site was suggested as a useful indicator of conservation value in temperate forests owing to their low expected dispersal propensity (Nilsson and Baranowski 1994). Note that dispersal propensity is the realized frequency and distance of dispersal in an actual landscape, whereas dispersal ability refers to the maximum extent of dispersal movements. Consistent with this suggestion, sites with several click beetle species correspond very well with the richest sites for other threatened wood-living beetles in Sweden (Nilsson 2001). Thus, it has been suggested that both the number of indicator species and the occurrence of single species can be used when selecting forests of high conservation value.

Another criterion for a suitable indicator species, apart from a low dispersal propensity, is that it should be relatively easy to find, preferably during most of the year. This criterion is met by many lichens, mosses, and most forest beetles (using exit holes in bark or wood) suggested as biodiversity indicators of forest stands and landscapes in Sweden (Rundlöf and Nilsson 1995; Nitare 2000; Nilsson *et al.* 2001; Niklasson and Nilsson 2005; Table 5.1). In hollow trees, insect fragments can also be found all year round. General sampling of insects by using various traps is much more expensive than directly verifying species in the field mainly by using exit holes (as illustrated for northern Europe by Ehnström and Axelsson 2002).

In North America, forest vertebrates dominate among putative biodiversity indicator species (Hunter 1999). Such species may be difficult to detect over long periods of the year, but they also have advantages. An

Table 5.1. *Important structures and processes in forests and suggested indicator species for sufficient amounts in southern Sweden*

Birds and fire-dependent species are suggested as responding to the largest (landscape) scale.

Structures/processes	Suggested indicator species
Structures/processes at landscape scale	
Old deciduous trees	*Dendrocopos minor*
Dead deciduous trees	*Dendrocopos leucotos*
Older coniferous forest	*Tetrao urogallus*
Dead coniferous trees	*Picoides tridactulus*
Young deciduous succession	*Tetrao tetrix*
Burnt deciduous trees	*Daldinia loculata*
	Platyrhinus resinosus
	Denticollis borealis
	Dicerca furcata
Burnt coniferous trees	*Oxypteris acuminata*
Fire-scarred coniferous trees	*Dicerca moesta*
Structures/processes at smaller scale	
Riparian forest and water regime	*Dichelyma capillaceum*
Former grazing pressure and soil status	*Actaea spicata*
	Lathyrus vernus
	Tilia cordata
	Galium odoratum
	Festuca altissima
Old deciduous trees	*Lobaria* spp.
	Cyphelium inquinans (sun-exposed stem)
	Basidia rosella
	Gyalecta ulmi
	Thelotrema lepadinum
Old beech trees	*Pyrenula nitida*
Old oak trees	*Lecanographa amylacea*
	Corticeus fasciatus
Old aspen trees	*Collema* spp.
	Lamellocossus terebra (shaded stem)
	Descarpentriesina variolosa (sun-exposed stem)
Old spruces with sun-exposed stem	*Microbregma emarginata*
Old pines with sun-exposed stem	*Nothorhina punctata*
Continuity of spruce and clean air	*Alectoria sarmentosa*
Hollow oaks	*Gnorimus variabilis*
	Tenebrio opacus
	Allecula morio
Hollow deciduous trees	*Elater ferrugineus*
	Osmoderma eremita
	Liocola marmorata
	Gnorimus nobilis

Table 5.1. *(cont.)*

Structures/processes	Suggested indicator species
	Allecula rhenana
	Prionychus spp.
	Ischnomera spp.
Older coarse wood	*Ceruchus chrysomelinus*
	Platycerus spp.
Large dead oaks	*Lymexylon navale*
	Hypulus quercinus
	Lucanus cervus
	Bostrichus capucinus
Brown-rotten wood	*Peltis grossa* (snags)
	Ostoma ferruginea
	Thymalus limbatus
Large standing broad-leaved trees	*Dorcus parallelepipedus*
Large standing dead beeches	*Anoplodera scutellata*
Coarse deciduous wood	*Ampedus nigroflavus*
	Xylophilus corticalis
	Grynocharis oblonga
Coarse wood of birches and aspen	*Acanthoderes clavipes*
	Necydalis major
	Corticeus unicolor
	Corticeus bicolor
Recently dead aspen trees	*Cucujus cinaberinus*
	Saperda perforata
Trees with *Fomes fomentarius*	*Scardia boletella*
	Oplocephala haemorrhoidalis
Alder snags (sunlit)	*Dicerca alni*
Recently dead coarse wood	*Harminius undulatus*
Old coarse wood (sunlit)	*Lacon* spp.
Dead trees in riparian forest	*Ampedus sanguinolentus*
Old coarse pine wood (sunlit)	*Calitys scabra*
	Tragosoma depsarium
Coarse pine wood (sunlit)	*Ergates faber*
	Buprestis novemmaculata
Recently dead spruces	*Callidium coriaceum*
	Semanotus undatus

Source: From Niklasson and Nilsson (2005).

important one is that vertebrates often have large area requirements and that they integrate features difficult to measure in the forest landscape. In Europe, woodpeckers and grouse species have often been suggested as biodiversity indicators (Angelstam *et al.* 2004; Table 5.1). The white-backed woodpecker (*Dendrocopos leucotos*) is dependent on large patches with many dead deciduous trees where it feeds on wood-living insects. In Finland, many threatened beetles occurred in forests where this woodpecker bred (Martikainen *et al.* 1998). In central Europe, its territory covers at least 100 ha (Wesolowski 1995). Its smaller relative, the lesser spotted wood-pecker (*Dendrocopos minor*), feeds mainly on longhorn beetle larvae in dead branches (Olsson *et al.* 2001) and it requires at least 40 ha of older forest dominated by deciduous trees within at most 200 ha (Wiktander *et al.* 2001). Thus, even if this species were found to fly long distances to feed during a day, food resources must not be too fragmented in space to support a breeding pair. In coniferous forest, the three-toed woodpecker (*Picoides tri-dactylus*) requires at least 100 ha of forest with 15–20 m^3 ha^{-1} of dead wood (Bütler *et al.* 2004). Several woodpecker species seem to perform well as indicators for other bird species in forests (Roberge and Angelstam 2006). Population declines in several woodpecker species have been attributed to forestry (Nilsson *et al.* 1992; Virkkala *et al.* 1993; Niklasson and Nilsson 2005) and may thus indicate a general decline in forest bird populations. In contrast, the black woodpecker (*Dryocopus martius*), a keystone species providing large cavities for other hole-nesting species of large body size (Johnsson *et al.* 1993), is not declining and can breed successfully in highly fragmented forests (Tjernberg *et al.* 1993).

Among grouse species, the capercaillie is a lekking species dependent on a rather open pine-dominated forest. In continuous suitable habitat, the leks are spaced regularly about 2 km apart, but the species only occurs where there are patches of at least 50 ha of suitable habitat. Larger leks with over ten males require about 300 ha of suitable forest (Wegge and Rolstad 1986). Capercaillie leks coincide with the occurrence of other old forest bird species such as three-toed woodpecker, pygmy owl (*Glaucidium passerinum*), and red-breasted flycatcher (*Ficedula parva*) (Pakkala *et al.* 2003; see also Suter *et al.* 2002).

A robust system of indicator species includes species from several tax-onomic groups, since they respond to different spatial scales and habi-tat features. Also within an organism group, several indicator species are preferable to avoid random effects and to cover larger regions, forest types, and successional stages after fire or windfall (Nilsson *et al.* 2001). There are also regional differences (Berg *et al.* 2002): a species may be useful as an indicator in one region but not in others. In naturally dynamic forests, both early- and late-successional stages have distinct species assemblages, both for insects (e.g. Similä *et al.* 2002) and fungi (e.g. Junninen *et al.* 2006). Therefore, species from all successional stages must be represented among biodiversity indicators and not only old-growth species as is often the case.

In summary, useful biodiversity indicators are (1) species with large area requirements, often vertebrates; (2) species with low dispersal propensity in the focal region, often vascular plants or species dependent on stable habitat as old and hollow trees; (3) specialized species restricted to one seral stage or a rare substrate, often insects or cryptogams; (4) species that are relatively easy to find, preferably during most of the year.

COMBINING SPECIES AND SUBSTRATES

It has been argued that the best way forward is to use structures and processes and not species when setting conservation targets for sustainable forest management (e.g. Lindenmayer *et al.* 2000). However, this argument disregards the enormous variation in current knowledge of organisms in different regions and forest types (e.g. Grove 2002). When available, why not use the known occurrences and habitat requirements of species when developing conservation plans? This is especially relevant in temperate Europe, where the distribution and habitat requirement of many forest-dependent organisms are relatively well known. Also, geographical information systems provide an efficient tool to accumulate species information and use it in harvest planning.

The work on old and large-diameter trees in southern Sweden may serve as an example of an approach combining forest species and stand structures. A two-step method for finding the most important sites for conservation of threatened forest organisms was suggested for forests in highly transformed regions of Sweden (Rundlöf and Nilsson 1995; Nilsson *et al.* 2001). First, an inventory of individual large and hollow trees should be performed at the landscape scale, followed by an inventory of indicator species, mainly among lichens and beetles dependent on old and dead trees. The tree inventory locates the oldest trees in the focal landscape, where the most demanding and threatened species can be found. Second, indicator species are surveyed on and in these trees. Tests of the method in some areas revealed that most trees supporting theatened lichens and beetles occurred in agricultural landscapes, mainly in pastures with small tree stands or scattered trees (Nilsson *et al.* 1994). Based on a sample of these trees, most were over 150 years old (Niklasson 2003; Öckinger *et al.* 2005; Mats Niklasson, unpublished data). In southern Sweden, most old trees have been removed from the managed forests, and hot spots for red-listed beetles now mainly occur on wooded pastures on large estates or on very stony grounds unsuitable for agricultural production (Nilsson 2001). The general approach of both mapping large and hollow trees and their dependent species when selecting priority tracts for nature reserves is now generally applied in southern Sweden (Naturvårdsverket 2004). However, when selecting stands for biodiversity conservation on forest lands in this region, reliance on structures alone is still dominating, even though many indicator species among lichens, fungi, and mosses have been proposed (Nitare 2000; Table 5.1).

Data about forest structure, as outlined above, and indicator species are useful when planning for sustainable forest management, especially when forest history is considered. The number of indicator species found in a stand or forest landscape in combination with the number/area of old trees/stands may show how important a high degree of environmental concern is in this particular area. The composition of the indicator species assemblage in a given forest stand or landscape can also point to the most important structures and processes needed in this particular area.

PROBLEMS OF SCALE

Different species respond to factors at different scales and conservation targets are also set at different scales. Targets and conservation efforts differ between countries, but also among regions within a country. There may be a mismatch between the scale over which species respond and the scale over which conservation is planned. For many countries in Europe, this is a problem since many private forest estates are small compared to the species requirements, or species occurring as metapopulations with rapid colonization–extinction dynamics. Examples of the latter may be some fire-dependent species, but the appropriate scales are currently unknown. However, the appropriate scale to manage processes and monitor indicator species in forest landscapes is unlikely to be less than 1,000 ha, and probably should often be much larger. We have suggested that it is considerably larger in boreal than temperate regions, owing to the scale of natural disturbance regimes (Nilsson et al. 2001). Several studies of birds preferring old-growth boreal forests have shown that they have higher densities in larger patches, indicating that these species respond to forest patterns over several thousands of hectares (Virkkala and Rajasärkkä 2006 and references therein). In temperate forest types, dominated by deciduous trees, many bird species with relatively large territories are absent from small forest patches (e.g. Ahlén and Nilsson 1982; Nilsson 1986). The nuthatch (*Sitta europaea*), a species preferring old forests, had 50% higher density in a large forest compared with smaller forest patches, even though the latter were larger than its territory size (Matthysen 1999). Another study did not find any edge effect on density for this species, but a strong negative edge effect on the density of the red-breasted flycatcher (Brazaitis and Angelstam 2004). Beetles, flies, lichens, and fungi dependent on dead/old trees respond at scales of at least several thousand hectares, the largest scale examined until now (Økland 1996; Paltto et al. 2006; Penttilä et al. 2006; Franc et al. 2007). Thus, in temperate forests with many private owners, land use decisions are taken at scales much smaller than those over which many forest species respond.

TAXONOMIC INCONGRUENCE

At large spatial scales within a region, there is a low correlation between species richness in different taxonomic groups (e.g. Pendergast and Eversham 1997; Wolters et al. 2006). However, when selecting sites for conservation, a local scale is often used. In European forests, stands smaller than 100 ha are often assessed. Forest fertility of a site may predict the richness of breeding birds and vascular plants (Nilsson 1979; Similä et al. 2006), but not saproxylic species (Similä et al. 2006). Such taxonomic differences must be dealt with in general monitoring schemes.

As a case study exemplifying these issues, Nilsson et al. (1995) found a very weak association between the number of red-listed lichens growing on trees and the total number of red-listed saproxylic beetles in 14 unmanaged hemiboreal forest stands (updated data with two additional stands in Table 5.2), possibly owing to various types of past management. Dying trees had previously been harvested for firewood in the area and beetles dependent on big dead trees have only persisted on a few sites, often far from the farmsteads. On the other hand, lichens dependent on old living trees have generally persisted on different sites, often on stony or unproductive sites near farmsteads (Nilsson et al. 1994). However, the number of red-listed saproxylic beetles dependent on hollow trees was strongly correlated with the number of red-listed epiphytic lichens (Fig. 5.1). Both these latter organism groups were mainly present in forest stands of the largest estates of the region. The conspicous lichen Lobaria pulmonaria was an efficient indicator of such sites with many red-listed lichens and wood-living beetles living in hollow trees, but not other red-listed wood-living beetles mainly living in big dead trees (Table 5.1). Thus, Lobaria pulmonaria only indicated some of the valuable conservation sites in the region, whereas the rare beetle Ceruchus chrysomelinus living in large downed logs indicated the few sites in Sweden where many such logs have been present over a longer period of time. Interestingly, this beetle is among the most common wood-living beetle species in the large virgin Bialowieza forest in Poland (Nilsson, personal observations), but otherwise very rare in western Europe. Sites

Table 5.2. *Forest stand data on area (ha), recorded number of red-listed (red = all and thr = threatened) lichens (L) and beetles (B)*

Threatened species are all red-listed species except those in category near threatened NT (Gärdenfors 2000). The number of red-listed beetle species mainly living in hollow trees (B h) or elsevhere (B oth) is also given.

Study plot	Area	L red	L thr	B red	B thr	B h	B oth
With *Lobaria pulmonaria:*							
Median:	27	9	2	24	4	8	16
Bjurkärr	50	28	13	62	12	25	37
Agnäs	70	26	10	24	3	8	16
Bokhultet, Växjö	–	9	3	13	2	5	8
Möckelsnäs	27	13	2	22	4	7	15
Siggaboda	8	12	2	35	5	11	24
Djäknabygd-Råshult	16	9	2	34	4	11	23
Taxås	45	4	1	27	1	6	21
Stenbrohult	9	8	3	20	4	8	12
Rönnäs-Agunnaryd	27	2	0	13	0	6	7
Without *Lobaria pulmonaria:*							
Median:	36	1	0	20	2	4	15
Höö	30	12	4	26	6	11	15
Marsholm N	21	2	0	24	1	2	22
Tångarne	53	2	1	13	1	1	12
Stockanäs	30	1	0	34	2	4	30
Marsholm S	29	0	0	34	4	5	29
Byvärma	52	0	0	20	3	4	16
Bölsö	41	1	0	6	0	2	4
Vedåsa	56	1	0	5	1	0	5
Osaby	–	14	4	19	6	9	10

Revised data from Nilsson *et al.* (1995), based on expanded studies and the red list according to Gärdenfors (2000).

where *C. chrysomelinus* occurs support many other red-listed wood-living beetles (Nilsson *et al.* 2000) but most hot spots for threatened wood-living beetles in southern Sweden were found in grazed pastures with very old oaks (Nilsson 2001). For the latter habitat type, the beetle *Osmoderma eremita* is a useful indicator of the presence of other red-listed beetles (Ranius 2002b). Similar to these examples from Sweden, in forests in Norway hotspots for species associated with logs and sites with lichens in the genus *Lobaria* were usually located in different stands (Gjerde *et al.* 2007). Thus, a set of indicator species must contain several species from different taxonomic groups representing all forest types, structures, and successional stages in a region to capture all types of forests important to biodiversity conservation.

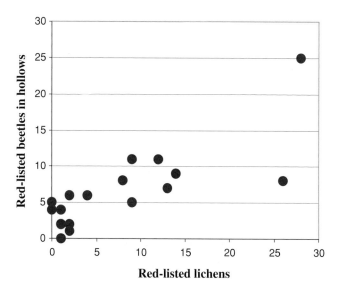

Figure 5.1. Correlation between the number of red-listed epiphytic lichen species in a stand and the number of red-listed beetle species living in hollow trees. It should be noted that there is no correlation between lichens and other wood-living beetles (Table 5.2).

TIME LAGS AND EXTINCTION DEBTS

If the current distribution of species in a forest landscape is a reflection of former management, many occurrences of threatened species may be transient remnants bound for extinction, i.e. representing an extinction debt (Hanski 2000; Berglund and Jonsson 2005; Löbel *et al.* 2006). In such cases, some indicator species may lie, since current habitat extent is unable to support viable populations of focal species in the long run. For forest plants, extinction debts may persist over more than 100 years (Vellend *et al.* 2006). Therefore, it is crucial to know the forest history of a landscape when evaluating the conservation potential and actions needed. Ancient oak trees in Sweden provide an instructive example. They were very abundant in the cultural landscape until about 170 years ago, but shortly after strict protection was lifted in 1830, more than a million old oaks were cut down (Eliasson and Nilsson 1999, 2002). In effect, numerous small groups of very old oaks were strongly isolated from other such groups. Now, about 150 years after this drastic habitat reduction, dependent species like the beetle *Osmoderma eremita* survive in more than 100 widely distributed sites in Sweden (Antonsson *et al.* 2003), but almost all populations are small and probably not viable in the long run. The situation for the species seems to be similar all over Europe (Ranius *et al.* 2005). On the other hand, the middle spotted woodpecker (*Dendrocopos medius*), which also depended on stands with old oaks in Sweden, was widespread 150 years ago, when suitable habitat occurred over large regions. After habitat destruction and isolation, it took over 100 years until the last local population became extinct in 1982 (Pettersson 1985). The difference from *Osmoderma* is that where one pair of the woodpeckers can live, a whole metapopulation of *Osmoderma* can occur, as can be deduced from a study by Ranius (2000). Another difference may be that birds respond relatively fast to habitat changes, as found for two grouse species (Angelstam 2004), while for example some red-listed beetles living in hollow trees can survive at least 50 years in old-growth stands of only a few hectares (Nilsson and Baranowski 1997b). However, the long-term viability of populations restricted to such small relict stands is questionable; fast restoration of surrounding habitat is probably required to prevent the extinction debt to be realized.

In the boreal forest, fragmentation and reduction of old-growth has been dramatic over the past 100 years, and populations in the small remaining patches are unlikely to be viable in the long run (Hanski 2000; Berglund and Jonsson 2005; Löbel *et al.* 2006). Thus, even if biodiversity indicator species and structures are present in a forest stand, this may not show the long-term potential of the stand (Gu *et al.* 2002). A landscape approach is needed when selecting stands for biodiversity conservation (e.g. Cabeza and Moilanen 2003), but historical knowledge of decreasing habitats is also needed to determine what should be restored (Nilsson *et al.* 2001, 2005). The more recently and drastically a habitat has declined, the more urgent and cost-efficient is its restoration. This, of course, presumes that some species dependent on this habitat have persisted.

CONCLUSIONS

From this review it should be obvious that we need to restore natural disturbance processes in forests and also perform measurements of both important structures and sets of indicator species to determine whether targets for forest biodiversity conservation are going to be met. There is a definite need for reliable lists of indicator species of temporal forest continuity, especially the historical occurrence of old trees and large dead trees, a property that may be difficult to deduce from the present forest structure. Indicator species lists have been suggested for vascular plants, lichens, mosses, fungi, and beetles, but validation tests of their performance are still rare. Vascular plants may indicate the former degree of land use, canopy openness, and grazing pressure in a temperate forest, but they say nothing about the species richness of lichens and beetles that are strongly dependent on old trees and dead wood. However, critical tests of assumed correlations between structures and species richness and composition are similarly few. A set of indicator species must contain several species from different taxonomic groups representing all forest types, structures, and successional stages in a region to capture all types of forest important for biodiversity conservation. Monitoring of species must target the critical habitats and also be performed at an appropriate scale. The composition of the indicator species assemblage in a given landscape can point to the most important structures and processes needed in this particular area.

Extinction debts complicate monitoring, but following the temporal changes of both structures and associated species over time and space can reveal such debts. If suitable habitat increases owing to restoration but the dependent species do not respond over the short term, this may imply an extinction debt. Forest history provides evidence of increasing and deceasing natural disturbances and important structure for many species. Restoration efforts are most cost-efficient when they target recently decreasing natural disturbances and structures.

An important research question is to find out whether it is possible to estimate the number and composition of species, especially red-listed species, in a forest from the present structure and condition of the forest, or if forest history and continuity is an overriding factor. If the latter is true, it has important implications for nature conservation. Then, forest continuity should be the prime criterion for the selection of conservation forests since assemblages of forest organisms are not replaceable within a reasonable time. Current evidence points to the greater importance of continuity in temperate than boreal forests, possibly owing to the original scale and intensity of natural disturbances.

ACKNOWLEDGEMENTS

Bengt Gunnar Jonsson and Reed F. Noss provided valuable comments on this review.

References

Ahlén, I. and S. G. Nilsson. 1982. Species richness and area requirements of forest bird species on islands with natural forests in Lake Mälaren and Hjälmaren. *Vår Fågelvärld* 41:161–84.

Angelstam, P. 2004. Habitat threshold and effects of forest landscape change on the distribution and abundance of black grouse and capercaillie. *Ecological Bulletins* 51:173–87.

Angelstam, P. *et al.* 2004. Habitat modelling as a tool for landscape-scale conservation – a review of parameters for focal forest birds. *Ecological Bulletins* 51:427–53.

Anonymous. 1980. *World Conservation Strategy: Living Resource Conservation for Sustainable Development.* Gland, Switzerland: IUCN-UNEP-WWF.

Anonymous. 1991. *Proposition 1990/91:90. En God Livsmiljö.* Stockholm: Swedish Parliament.

Anonymous. 2000. *Svensk FSC-Standard för Certifiering av Skogsbruk.* Uppsala, Sweden: Svenska FSC-rådet.

Antonsson, K., J. Hedin, N. Jansson, S. G. Nilsson and T. Ranius. 2003. Läderbaggens (*Osmoderma eremita*) förekomst i Sverige. *Entomologisk Tidskrift* 124:225–40.

Bader, P., S. Jansson and B. G. Jonsson. 1995. Wood-inhabiting fungi and substratum decline in selectively logged boreal spruce forests. *Biological Conservation* 72:355–62.

Balmford, A. 1996. Extinction filters and current resilience: the significance of past selection pressures for conservation biology. *Trends in Ecology and Evolution* 11:193–6.

Bailey, J. K. and T. G. Whitham. 2006. Interactions between cottonwood and beavers positively affect sawfly abundance. *Ecological Entomology* 31:294–7.

Barnosky, A. *et al.* 2004. Assessing the causes of late Pleistocene extinctions on the continents. *Science* 306:70–5.

Bengtsson, J., S. G. Nilsson, A. Franc and P. Menozzi. 2000. Biodiversity, disturbances, ecosystem function and management of European forests. *Forest Ecology and Management* 132:39–50.

Berg, Å., U. Gärdenfors, T. Hallingbäck and M. Norén. 2002. Habitat preferences of red-listed fungi and bryophytes in woodland key habitats in southern Sweden – analyses of data from a national survey. *Biodiversity and Conservation* 11:1479–503.

Berglund, H. and B. G. Jonsson. 2005. Verifying an extinction debt among lichens and fungi in northern Swedish boreal forests. *Conservation Biology* 19:338–48.

Bergman, K.-O. 1999. Habitat utilization by *Lopinga achine* (Nymphalidae: Satyrinae) larvae and ovipositing females: implication for conservation. *Biological Conservation* 88:69–74.

Bobiec, A. (ed.), J. M. Gutowski, K. Zub, P. Pawlaczyk and F. L. William. 2005. The afterlife of a tree. WWF-Poland, The World Wide Fund for Nature.

Bouget, C. 2005. Short-term effect of windstorm disturbance on saproxylic beetles in broadleaved temperate forests: Part I: Do environmental changes induce a gap effect? *Forest Ecology and Management* 216:1–14.

Bouget, C. and P. Duelli. 2004. The effects of windthrow on forest insect communities: a literature review. *Biological Conservation* 118:281–99.

Brazaitis, G. and P. Angelstam. 2004. Influence of edges between old deciduous forest and clearcuts on the abundance of passerine hole-nesting birds in Lithuania. *Ecological Bulletins* 51:209–17.

Brunet, J. 1993. Environmental and historical factors limiting the distribution of rare forest grasses in south Sweden. *Forest Ecology and Management* 61:263–75.

Brunet, J. and G. von Oheimb. 1998. Migration of vascular plants to secondary woodlands in southern Sweden. *Journal of Ecology* 86:429–38.

Bütler, R., P. Angelstam, P. Ekelund and R. Schlaepfer. 2004. Dead wood threshold values for the three-toed woodpecker presence in boreal and sub-Alpine forest. *Biological Conservation* 119:305–18.

Cabeza, M. and A. Moilanen. 2003. Site-selection algorithms and habitat loss. *Conservation Biology* 17:1402–13.

Carignan, V. and M.-A. Villard. 2002. Selecting indicator species to monitor ecological integrity: a review. *Environmental Monitoring and Assessment* 78:45–61.

Dobson, A. *et al.* 2006. Habitat loss, trophic collapse, and the decline of ecosystem services. *Ecology* 87:1915–24.

Dzwonko, Z. and S. Loster. 1989. Distribution of vascular plant species in small woodlands on the western Carpathian foothills. *Oikos* 56:77–86.

Dzwonko, Z. and S. Loster. 1992. Species richness and seed dispersal to secondary woods in southern Poland. *Journal of Biogeography* 19:195–204.

Edman, M., N. Kruys and B. G. Jonsson. 2004. Local dispersal sources strongly affect colonization patterns of wood-decaying fungi on spruce logs. *Ecological Applications* 14:893–901.

Ehnström, B. and R. Axelsson. 2002. *Insektsgnag i Bark och Ved*. Uppsala, Sweden: ArtDatabanken.

Eliasson, P. and S. G. Nilsson. 1999. [The Swedish oak during the 16th and 17th centuries – quantities, qualities and biodiversity.] *Bebyggelsehistorisk Tidskrift* 37:33–64.

Eliasson, P. and S. G. Nilsson. 2002. 'You Should Hate Young Oaks and Young Noblemen': the environmental history of oaks in eighteenth- and nineteenth-century Sweden. *Environmental History* 7:657–75.

Elton, C. S. 1966. *The Pattern of Animal Communities*. London: Methuen.

Emborg, J., M. Christensen and J. Heilmann-Clausen. 2000. The structural dynamics of Suserup Skov, a near-natural temperate deciduous forest in Denmark. *Forest Ecology and Management* 126:173–89.

Eriksson, P. 2002. [Methods to monitor woodliving insects.] Upplandsstiftelsen och Naturvårdsverket. Stockholm: Naturvårdsverkets Förlag.

Esseén, P.-A. 2006. Edge influence on the old-growth forest indicator lichen *Alectoria sarmentosa* in natural ecotones. *Journal of Vegetation Science* 17:185–94.

Esseén, P.-A., B. Ehnström, L. Ericson and K. Sjöberg. 1997. Boreal forests. *Ecological Bulletins* 46:16–47.

Falinski, J. B. 1986. Vegetation dynamics in temperate lowland primeval forest. Ecological studies in Bialowieza forest. *Geobotany* 8:1–537.

Franc, N., F. Götmark, B. Økland, B. Norden and H. Paltto. 2007. Factors and scales potentially important for saproxylic beetles in temperate mixed oak forest. *Biological Conservation* 135:86–98.

Freese, A., J. Benes, R. Bolz *et al.* 2006. Habitat use of the endangered butterfly *Euphydryas maturna* and forestry in Central Europe. *Animal Conservation* 9:388–97.

Gärdenfors, U. (ed.) 2000. *Rödlistade arter i Sverige 2000 – The 2000 Red List of Swedish Species*. Uppsala, Sweden: ArtDatabanken, SLU.

Gjerde, I., M. Sætersdal and H. H. Blom. 2007. Complementary Hotspot Inventory – a method for identification of important areas for biodiversity at the forest stand level. *Biological Conservation* 137:549–57.

Granström, A. 1993. Spatial and temporal variation in lightning ignitions in Sweden. *Journal of Vegetation Science* 4:737–44.

Granström, A. 2001. Fire management for biodiversity in the European boreal forest. *Scandinavian Journal of Forest Research* Suppl. 3:62–9.

Grove, A. S. 2002. Saproxylic insect ecology and the sustainable management of forest. *Annual Review of Ecology and Systematics* 33:1–23.

Gu, W. D., R. Heikkilä and I. Hanski. 2002. Estimating the consequences of habitat fragmentation on extinction risk in dynamic landscapes. *Landscape Ecology* 17:699–710.

Hannah, L., J. L. Carr and A. Lankerani. 1995. Human disturbance and natural habitat: a biome level analysis of a global data set. *Biodiversity and Conservation* 4:128–55.

Hanski, I. 2000. Extinction debt and species credit in boreal forests: modelling the consequences of different approaches to biodiversity conservation. *Annales Zoologici Fennici* 37:271–80.

Harding. P. T. and F. Rose. 1986. *Pasture-woodlands in Lowland Britain. A Review of their Importance for Wildlife Conservation*. Huntingdon, UK: Institute of Terrestrial Ecology.

Hazell, P. and L. Gustafsson. 1999. Retention of trees at final harvest – evaluation of a conservation technique using epiphytic bryophyte and lichen transplants. *Biological Conservation* 90:133–42.

Hedenås, H. and L. Ericson. 2000. Epiphytic macrolichens as conservation indicators: successional sequence in *Populus tremula* stands. *Biological Conservation* 93:43–53.

Hedin, J. 2003. Metapopulation ecology of *Osmoderna eremita* – dispersal, habitat quality and habitat history. Ph.D thesis, Lund University, Lund, Sweden.

Hedin, J., T. Ranius, S. G. Nilsson and H. G. Smith. 2008. Restricted dispersal in a flying beetle assessed by telemetry. *Biodiversity and Conservation* 17:675–84.

Hermy, M. 1994. Effects of former land use on plant species diversity and pattern in European deciduous woodlands. Pp. 123–43 in T. J. B. Boyle and C. E. B. Boyle (eds.) *Biodiversity, Temperate Ecosystems, and Global Change*. Berlin: Springer.

Hermy, M. and H. Stieperaere. 1981. An indirect gradient analysis of the ecological relationships between ancient and recent riverine wood-lands to the south of Bruges. *Vegetatio* 44:46–9.

Holland, J. D., L. Fahrig and N. Cappucino. 2005. Fecundity determines the extinction threshold in a Canadian assemblage of longhorn beetles (Coleoptera: Cerambycidae). *Journal of Insect Conservation* 9:109–19.

Honnay, O., H. Jacquemyn, B. Bossuyt and M. Hermy. 2005. Forest fragmentation effects on patch occupancy and population viability of herbaceous plant species. *New Phytologist* 166:723–36.

Hunter, M. L. (ed.) 1999. *Maintaining Biodiversity in Forest Ecosystems*. Cambridge, UK: Cambridge University Press.

Hylander, K., B.-G. Jonsson and C. Nilsson. 2002. Evaluating buffer strips along boreal streams using bryophytes as indicators. *Ecological Applications* 12:797–806.

Hyvärinen, E., J. Kouki, P. Martikainen and H. Lappalainen. 2005. Short-term effects of controlled burning and green-tree retention on beetle (Coleoptera) assemblages in managed boreal forests. *Forest Ecology and Management* 212:315–32.

Johnsson, K., S. G. Nilsson and M. Tjernberg. 1993. Characteristics and utilization of old black woodpecker holes by hole-nesting species. *Ibis* 135:410–16.

Jonsson, B. G. and Kruys, N. (eds.) 2001. Ecology of woody debris in boreal forests. *Ecological Bulletins* 49.

Jonsell, M., J. Weslien and B. Ehnström. 1998. Substrate requirements of red-listed saproxylic invertebrates in Sweden. *Biodiversity and Conservation* 7:749–64.

Junninen, K., M. Similä, J. Kouki and H. Kotiranta. 2006. Assemblages of wood-inhabiting fungi along the gradients of succession and naturalness in boreal pine-dominated forests in Fennoscandia. *Ecography* 29:75–83.

Juutinen, A., M. Mönkkönen and A.-L. Sippola. 2006. Cost-efficiency of decaying wood as a surrogate for overall species richness in boreal forests. *Conservation Biology* 20:84–94.

Jüriado, I., A. Suija and J. Liira. 2006. Biogeographical determinants of lichen species diversity on islets in the West-Estonian Archipelago. *Journal of Vegetation Science* 17:125–34.

Kirby, K. J. and C. M. Drake. 1993. *Dead Wood Matters: The Ecology and Conservation of SaproxylicInvertebrates in Britain.* Proceedings of a British Ecological Society Meeting, Dunham Massey Park, 24 April 1992. Peterborough: English Nature.

Lambeck, R. J. 1997. Focal species: a multi-species umbrella for nature conservation. *Conservation Biology* 11:849–56.

Lindbladh, M., M. Niklasson and S. G. Nilsson. 2003. Long-time record of fire and open canopy in a high biodiversity forest in southeast Sweden. *Biological Conservation* 114:231–43.

Lindenmayer, D. B., C. R. Margules and D. B. Botkin. 2000. Indicators of biodiversity for ecologically sustainable forest management. *Conservation Biology* 14:941–50.

Löbel, S., T. Snäll and H. Rydin. 2006. Metapopulation processes in epiphytes inferred from patterns of regional distribution and local abundance in fragmented forest landscapes. *Journal of Ecology* 94:856–68.

Martikainen, P., L. Kaila and Y. Haila. 1998. Threatened beetles in White-backed Woodpecker habitats. *Conservation Biology* 12:293–301.

Martikainen, P., J. Siitonen, L. Kaila, P. Punttila and J. Rauh. 2000. Species richness of Coleoptera in mature managed and old growth boreal forests in southern Finland. *Biological Conservation* 94:199–209.

Martin, O. 1989. Click beetles (Coleoptera, Elateridae) from old deciduous forest in Denmark. *Entomologiske Meddelelser* 57:1–107. (In Danish with English summary.)

Matthysen, E. 1999. Nuthatches (*Sitta europea*: Aves) in forest fragments: Demography of a patchy population. *Oecologia* 119:501–9.

Moilanen, A. and B. A. Winthle. 2006. Uncertainty analysis favours selection of spatially aggregated reserve networks. *Biological Conservation* 129: 427–34.

Naiman, R. J., C. A. Johnston and J. C. Kelly. 1988. Alteration of North-American streams by beaver. *BioScience* 38:753–62.

Niklasson, M. 2003. En undersökning av trädåldrar i halländska skogsreservat. Report 2002:28. Halmstad, Sweden: County Administration of Halland.

Niklasson, M. and B. Drakenberg. 2001. A 600-year tree-ring fire history from Norra Kvills National Park, southern Sweden: implications for conservation strategies in the hemiboreal zone. *Biological Conservation* 101:63–71.

Niklasson, M. and A. Granström. 2000. Numbers and size of fires: long term trends in a Swedish boreal landscape. *Ecology* 81:1484–99.

Niklasson, M. and S. G. Nilsson. 2005. *Skogsdynamik och arters Bevarande – Bevarandebiologi, Skogshistoria, Skogsekologi och deras Tillämpning i Sydsveriges Landskap.* Lund: Studentlitteratur.

Nilsson, S. G. 1979. Density and species richness of some forest bird communities in South Sweden. *Oikos* 33:392–401.

Nilsson, S. G. 1986. Are bird communities in small biotope patches random samples from communities in large patches? *Biological Conservation* 38:179–204.

Nilsson, S. G. 1997. Forests in the temperate-boreal transition: natural and man-made features. *Ecological Bulletins* 46:61–71.

Nilsson, S. G. 2001. The most valuable areas for preservation of biodiversity in southern Sweden – woodliving beetles as guides to hot-spots. *Fauna och Flora* 96:59–70. (In Swedish with English summary.)

Nilsson, S. G., U. Arup, R. Baranowski and S. Ekman. 1994. Tree-dependent lichens and beetles in old-fashioned agricultural landscapes. *Svensk Botanisk Tidskrift* 85:1–12. (In Swedish with English summary.)

Nilsson, S. G. and R. Baranowski. 1994. Indicators of megatree continuity – Swedish distribution of click beetles (Coleoptera: Elateridae) dependent on hollow trees. *Entomologisk Tidskrift* 115:81–97. (In Swedish with English summary.)

Nilsson, S. G. and R. Baranowski. 1996. Changes in the Swedish distribution of click beetles (Elateridae) occurring in the boreal forest. *Entomologisk Tidskrift* 117:87–101. (In Swedish with English summary.)

Nilsson, S. G. and R. Baranowski. 1997a. Changes in the distribution of southern click beetles dependent on dead trees (Coleoptera: Elateridae and Lissomidae) in Sweden. *Entomologisk Tidskrift* 118:73–98. (In Swedish with English summary.)

Nilsson, S. G. and R. Baranowski. 1997b. Habitat predictability and the occurrence of beetles in old growth beech forests. *Ecography* 20:491–8.

Nilsson, S. G., R. Baranowski, B. Ehnström *et al.* 2000. *Ceruchus chrysomelinus* (Coleoptera, Lucanidae), a disappearing virgin forest relict species? *Entomologisk Tidskrift* 121:137–46. (In Swedish with English summary.)

Nilsson, S. G. and L. Ericson. 1997. Conservation of plant and animal populations in theory and practice. *Ecological Bulletins* 46:87–101.

Nilsson, S. G., O. Olsson, S. Svensson and U. Wiktander. 1992. Population trends and fluctuations in Swedish woodpeckers. *Ornis Svecica* 2:13–21.

Nilsson, S. G., U. Arup, R. Baranowski and S. Ekman. 1995. Lichens and beetles as indicators in conservation forests. *Conservation Biology* 9:1208–15.

Nilsson, S. G., J. Hedin and M. Niklasson. 2001. Biodiversity and its assessment in boreal and nemoral forests. *Scandinavian Journal of Forest Research* 16, Suppl. 3:10–26.

Nilsson, S. G., M. Niklasson, J. Hedin *et al.* 2002. Densities of large living and dead trees in old-growth temperate and boreal forests. *Forest Ecology and Management* 161:189–204.

Nilsson, S. G., M. Niklasson, J. Hedin, P. Eliasson and H. Ljungberg. 2005. Biodiversity and sustainable forestry in changing landscapes – principles and southern Sweden as an example. *Journal of Sustainable Forestry* 21:12–42.

Nitare, J. (ed.) 2000. *Signalarter – Indikatorer på Skyddsvärd Skog.* Jönköping: Skogsstyrelsen Förlag.

Nordén, B. and T. Appelqvist. 2001. Conceptual problems of ecological continuity and its bioindicators. *Biodiversity and Conservation* 10:779–91.

Noss, R. F. 1999. Assessing and monitoring forest biodiversity: a suggested framework and indicators. *Forest Ecology and Management* 115:135–46.

Öckinger, E., M. Niklasson and S. G. Nilsson. 2005. Is local distribution of the epiphytic lichen *Lobaria pulmonaria* limited by dispersal capacity or habitat quality? *Biodiversity and Conservation* 14:759–73.

Økland, B. 1996. Unlogged forest: important sites for preservating the diversity of mycetophilids (Diptera: Sciaroidea). *Biological Conservation* 76:297–310.

Olsson, O., U. Wiktander, A. Malmqvist and S. G. Nilsson. 2001. Variability of patch type preferences in relation to resource availability and breeding success in a bird. *Oecologia* 127:435–43.

Ovaskainen, O. 2002. Long-term persistence of species and the SLOSS problem. *Journal of Theoretical Biology* 218:419–33.

Pakkala, T., J. Pellikka and H. Linden. 2003. Capercaillie *Tetrao urogallus* – a good candidate for an umbrella species in taiga forests. *Wildlife Biology* 9:309–16.

Paltto, H., B. Nordén, F. Götmark and N. Franc. 2006. At which spatial and temporal scales does landscape context affect local density of Red Data Book and Indicator species? *Biological Conservation* 133:442–54.

Pearson, D. L. 1994. Selecting indicator taxa for the quantitative assessment of biodiversity. *Philosophical Transactions of the Royal Society of London B* 345:75–9.

Pendergast, J. R. and B. C. Eversham. 1997. Species richness covariance in higher taxa: empirical tests of the biodiversity indicator concept. *Ecography* 20:210–16.

Penttilä, R., J. Siitonen and M. Kuusinen. 2004. Polypore diversity in managed and old-growth boreal *Picea abies* forests in southern Finland. *Biological Conservation* 117:271–83.

Penttilä, R., M. Lindgren, O. Miettinen, H. Rita and I. Hanski. 2006. Consequences of forest fragmentation for polyporous fungi at two spatial scales. *Oikos* 114:225–40.

Perlin, J. 1988. *A Forest Journey. The Role of Wood in the Development of Civilization.* London: W.W. Norton and Company.

Peterken, G. F. and M. Game. 1984. Historical factors affecting the number and distribution of vascular plant species in the woodlands of central Lincolnshire, England. *Journal of Ecology* 72:155–82.

Pettersson, B. 1985. Extinction of an isolated population of the middle spotted woodpecker *Dendrocopos medius* (L.) in Sweden and its relation to general theories on extinction. *Biological Conservation* 32:335–53.

Pontailler, J.-Y., A. Faille and G. Lemée. 1997. Storms drive successional dynamics in natural forests: a case study in Fontainebleau forest (France). *Forest Ecology and Management* 98:1–15.

Pykälä, J. 2004. Effects of new forestry practices on rare epiphytic macrolichens. *Conservation Biology* 18:831–8.

Rackham, O. 1980. *Ancient Woodland*. Norwich: Fletcher and Son.

Ranius, T. 2000. Minimum viable metapopulation size of a beetle, *Osmoderma eremita*, living in tree hollows. *Animal Conservation* 3:37–43.

Ranius, T. 2002a. *Osmoderma eremita* as an indicator of species richness of beetles in tree hollows. *Biodiversity and Conservation* 11:931–41.

Ranius, T. 2002b. Influence of stand size and quality of tree hollows on saproxylic beetles in Sweden. *Biological Conservation* 103:85–91.

Ranius, T. and J. Hedin. 2001. The dispersal rate of a beetle, *Osmoderma eremita*, living in tree hollows. *Oecologia* 126:363–70.

Ranius, T., L. O. Aguado, K. Antonsson *et al.* 2005. *Osmoderma eremita* (Coleoptera, Scarabaeidae, Cetoniinae) in Europe. *Animal Biodiversity and Conservation* 28:1–44.

Roberge, J.-M. and P. Angelstam. 2006. Indicator species among resident forest birds – a cross-regional evaluation in northern Europe. *Biological Conservation* 130:134–47.

Rose, F. 1976. Lichenological indicators of age and environmental continuity in woodlands. Pp. 279–307 in D. H. Brown, D. L. Hawksworth and R. H. Bailey (eds.) *Lichenology. Progress and Problems*. London: Academic Press.

Rosell, F., O. Bozér, P. Collen and H. Parker. 2005. Ecological impact of beavers *Castor fiber* and *Castor canadensis* and their ability to modify ecosystems. *Mammal Review* 35:248–76.

Rouvinen, S. and T. Kuuvulainen. 2005. Tree diameter distributions in natural and managed old *Pinus sylvestris*-dominated forests. *Forest Ecology and Management* 208:45–61.

Rundlöf, U. and S. G. Nilsson. 1995. *Fem Ess Metoden. Spåra skyddsvärd skog i södra Sverige*. Stockholm: Naturskyddsföreningen.

Schiegg, K. 2000. Effects of dead wood volume and connectivity on saproxylic insect species diversity. *Ecoscience* 7:290–8.

Siitonen, J. 2001. Forest management, coarse woody debris and saproxylic organisms: Fennoscandian boreal forests as an example. *Ecological Bulletins* 49:11–41.

Siitonen, J. and L. Saaristo. 2000. Habitat requirements and conservation of *Pytho kolwensis*, a beetle species of old-growth boreal forest. *Biological Conservation* 94:211–20.

Siitonen, J., R. Penttilä and H. Kotiranta. 2001. Coarse woody debris, polyporous fungi and saproxylic insects in an old-growth spruce forest in Vodlozero National Park, Russian Karelia. *Ecological Bulletins* 49:231–42.

Siitonen, P., A. Lehtinen and M. Siitonen. 2005. Effects of forest edges on the distribution, abundance, and regional persistence of wood-rotting fungi. *Conservation Biology* 19:205–60.

Similä, M., J. Kouki, P. Martikainen and A. Uotila. 2002. Conservation of beetles in boreal pine forests: the effects of forestage and naturalness on species assemblages. *Biological Conservation* 106:19–27.

Similä, M., J. Kouki, M. Mönkkönen, A.-L. Sippola and E. Huhta. 2006. Co-variation and indicators of species diversity: can richness of forest-dwelling species be predicted in northern boreal forests? *Ecological Indicators* 6:686–700.

Sjöberg, K. and L. Ericson. 1997. Mosaic boreal landscapes with open and forested wetlands. *Ecological Bulletins* 46:48–60.

Snäll, T., J. Ehrlén and H. Rydin. 2005. Colonization-extinction dynamics of an epiphyte metapopulation in a dynamic landscape. *Ecology* 86:106–15.

Soulé, M. E. and M. A. Sanjayan. 1998. Conservation targets: do they help? *Science* 279:2060–1.

Southwood, T. R. E. 1977. Habitat, the templet for ecological strategies? *Journal of Animal Ecology* 46:337–65.

Stokland, J. N. 2001. The coarse woody debris profile: an archive of recent forest history and an important biodiversity indicator. *Ecological Bulletins* 49:71–83.

Storch, I. 1994. Habitat and survival of capercaillie *Tetrao urogallus* nests and broods in the Bavarian alps. *Biological Conservation* 70:237–43.

Suter, W., R. F. Graf and R. Hess. 2002. Capercaillie (*Tetrao urogallus*) and avian biodiversity: testing the umbrella-species concept. *Conservation Biology* 16:778–88.

Svancara, L. K., R. Brannon, J. M. Scott, R. F. Noss and R. L. Pressey. 2005. Policy-driven versus evidence-based conservation: a review of political targets and biological needs. *BioScience* 55:989–95.

Svenning, J. C. 2002. A review of natural vegetation openness in north-western Europe. *Biological Conservation* 104:133–48.

Tjernberg, M., K. Johnsson and S. G. Nilsson. 1993. Density variation and breeding success of the Black Woodpecker *Dryocopus martius* in relation to forest fragmentation. *Ornis Fennica* 70:155–62.

Topp, W., H. Kappes, J. Kulfan and P. Zach. 2006. Litter-dwelling beetles in primeval forests of Central Europe: does deadwood matter? *Journal of Insect Conservation* 10:229–69.

Van Swaay, C., M. Warren and G. Loïs. 2006. Biotope use and trends of European butterflies. *Journal of Insect Conservation* 10:189–209.

Vellend, M. *et al.* 2006. Extinction debt of forest plants persists for more than a century following habitat fragmentation. *Ecology* 87:542–8.

Vera, F. W. M. 2000. *Grazing Ecology and Forest History*. Wallingford, UK: CABI Publishing.

Virkkala, R., T. Alanko, T. Laine and J. Tiainen. 1993. Population contraction of the white-backed woodpecker *Dendrocopos leucotos* in Finland as a consequence of habitat alteration. *Biological Conservation* 66:47–53.

Virkkala, R. and A. Rajasärkkä. 2006. Spatial variation of bird species in landscapes dominated by old-growth forests in northern boreal Finland. *Biodiversity and Conservation* 15:2143–62.

Warren, M. S. and R. S. Key. 1991. Woodlands: past, present and potential for insects. Pp. 155–212 in N. M. Collins and J. A. Thomas (eds.) *The Conservation of Insects and their Habitats*. London: Academic Press.

Wegge, P. and J. Rolstad. 1986. The spacing of capercaillie leaks in relation to habitat and social organization. *Behavioural Ecology and Sociobiology* **19**:401–8.

Werth, S. *et al.* 2006. Quantifying dispersal and establishment limitation in a population of an epiphytic lichen. *Ecology* **87**:2037–46.

Wesolowski, T. 1995. Value of Bialowieza Forest for the conservation of white-backed woodpecker *Dendrocopos leucotos* in Poland. *Biological Conservation* **71**:69–75.

Wikars, L.-O. 2001. The wood-decaying fungus *Daldinia loculata* (Xyleariacae) as an indicator of fire-dependent insects. *Ecological Bulletins* **49**:263–8.

Wikars, L.-O. 2004. Habitat requirements of the pine wood-living beetle *Tragosoma depsarium* (Coleoptera: Cerambycidae) at log, stand, and landscape scale. *Ecological Bulletins* **51**:287–94.

Wikars, L.-O. and C. Orrmalm. 2005. Större svartbaggen (*Upis ceramboides*) i norra Hälsingland. *Entomologisk Tidskrift* **126**:161–70.

Wiktander, U., O. Olsson and S. G. Nilsson. 2001. Seasonal variation in home-range size, and habitat area requirement of the lesser spotted woodpecker (*Dendrocopos minor*) in southern Sweden. *Biological Conservation* **100**:387–95.

Wolters, V., J. Bengtsson and A. S. Saitzev. 2006. Relationship among the species richness of different taxa. *Ecology* **87**:1886–95.

Wulf, M. 1993. Zur Bedeutung historisch alter Waldflächen für den Pflanzenartenschutz. *Verhandlungen Gesellschaft für Ökologie* **22**:269–72.

Zackrisson, O. 1977. Influence of forest fires on the North Swedish boreal forest. *Oikos* **29**:22–32.

Selecting species to be used as tools in the development of forest conservation targets

JEAN-MICHEL ROBERGE AND PER ANGELSTAM

INTRODUCTION

Habitat loss is considered as one of the greatest threats to biodiversity worldwide (Wilson 1988; Pimm and Raven 2000). Both theoretical and empirical studies indicate that there are critical limits to the amount of habitat that can be lost without reducing the viability of populations (e.g. Fahrig 2001) or disrupting important ecosystem processes (Hobbs 1993). In analogy to the concept of critical load of airborne pollution (Nilsson and Grennfelt 1988), which may lead to the loss of ecological integrity in forest ecosystems, critical loss and fragmentation of habitat may lead to dysfunctional habitat networks (Angelstam *et al.* 2004a,b).

Knowledge about the necessary characteristics, quantity, spatial config- uration, and dynamics of different ecosystem types required to maintain forest biodiversity is a prerequisite for effective conservation and restora- tion planning. Gaining such knowledge requires studies of dose–response, where the dose is the parameter value of a given ecological variable (e.g. amount of a given resource or rate of a key process) and the response can be measured as the status of biodiversity components (e.g. presence of a species, or even better, fitness of individuals in a population). How- ever, the present level of empirical knowledge on that topic is limited, both with respect to which variables are critical at different spatial scales and the parameter values associated with the presence of viable populations or functioning ecosystems (Tear *et al.* 2005). One important reason for that knowledge gap lies in the fact that such an approach requires systematic,

Setting Conservation Targets for Managed Forest Landscapes, ed. M.-A. Villard and B. G. Jonsson. Published by Cambridge University Press.

replicated macroecological empirical studies, which are very costly to implement (Angelstam *et al.* 2004b).

A crucial element in the design of ecological dose–response studies is the selection of relevant response variables. This chapter focuses on the use of species – or, rather, the status of their populations and constituting individuals – as response variables in studies aiming to derive quantitative conservation targets in forest landscapes. As shown by Nilsson (Chapter 5, this volume), an ideal set of response variables should represent the compositional, structural, and functional elements of forest biodiversity. In that context, species as such have traditionally been considered as belonging to the compositional elements of biodiversity. In the present chapter, species are considered in a broader perspective. We argue that selected species and functional groups may – following critical validation – be used to represent important structures and functions in forest ecosystems, and thus guide conservation planning. Although there is an increasing body of knowledge about the importance of specific structures and processes for the conservation of biodiversity in different types of forest ecosystems, the question "How much is enough?" remains largely unanswered. Quantifying the requirements of specialized and demanding species indicating critical structures and processes constitutes a logical first step in answering that central question.

Given the tradeoff between the myriad species with widely different life-history traits present in most forest ecosystems and the limited amounts of resources dedicated to quantitative ecological research, there is a need for careful selection of species to be the focus of dose–response studies in forest landscapes. In this chapter, we aim to propose criteria for the selection of such species, using the Baltic Sea region of northern Europe as a case in point.

SELECTING SPECIALIZED SPECIES AS RESPONSE VARIABLES

Ecological setting and anthropogenic impacts

Obviously, different species (or groups thereof) vary in their utility as response variables for studies aimed at deriving quantitative forest conservation targets. For example, some generalist forest species need little more than the mere presence of trees. Knowledge on the requirements of such species is consequently of little use to the conservation of the broader biodiversity. Rather, it would be sensible to concentrate on species that are specialized on particular forest types or on specific resources whose abundances are influenced by anthropogenic land use or other drivers of biodiversity change. This requires a sound understanding of how natural and anthropogenic disturbances occur in the different types of forests of the focal region (Angelstam 2006; see also Chapters 5, 7, and 17, this volume).

A description of the forests' ecological characteristics requires the identification of the major forest ecosystem types and their natural dynamics (e.g. Angelstam 1998a). This first step is crucial, as conservation targets should ultimately be defined for all of the naturally occurring types of forest environments. Accordingly, the suite of species to be used as response variables should include species specialized on each of those different natural forest types (e.g. Nilsson *et al.* 2001; Angelstam *et al.* 2004c). In addition, knowledge of the natural disturbance dynamics provides insight as to which scales are relevant to conservation planning. Species from different taxonomic groups may prove most useful at different spatial scales: vascular plants, fungi, and lichens may respond well to the availability of structures and to processes taking place at the scales of trees and forest stands, whereas other taxa such as birds and mammals may better reflect processes occurring at the scales of landscapes and ecoregions (Angelstam 1998b; Nilsson *et al.* 2001; Angelstam *et al.* 2005).

Once the ecological setting has been described, there is a need to portray the range of anthropogenic impacts on the biodiversity of the forests (or cultural woodlands, cf. Peterken 1996) of the focal region. This allows identifying the main threats to forest biodiversity and stratifying the region's landscapes according to their degree of ecological integrity (*sensu* Karr 1992) or naturalness (*sensu* Peterken 1996). That stratification is important in the context of identifying appropriate species to be used as response variables, as priority should be given to species specialized on those forest types or resources which are most threatened by anthropogenic activities. Moreover, the stratification according to anthropogenic impact is crucial from a study design perspective. Indeed, dose–response studies should cover a wide enough range of the gradient in anthropogenic impact (i.e. the "dose"), from reference landscapes with high ecological integrity to severely altered landscapes. In regions with a very long history of intensive land use and little forest left in a near-natural state, some of the most specialized species may have become extirpated and therefore cannot be used for such studies, unless the range of forest conditions can be "stretched" by expanding the study area to include less affected forest landscapes. That often requires cross-regional or international collaboration (Angelstam *et al.* 2004b).

The Baltic Sea region of northern Europe provides a useful illustration of how the ecological setting and anthropogenic impacts on the forests can be described. Two main gradients characterize that region at the macroecological scale: a biogeographic gradient from nemoral forests in the south to boreal forests in the north, and a gradient in anthropogenic impact from more intensively managed forests in the west to less intensively managed forests in the east (Angelstam *et al.* 1997). Thus, from the point of view of designing large-scale dose–response studies, this region constitutes a useful landscape-scale laboratory (*sensu* Diamond 1986; Kohler 2002) (Box 6.1).

Forest community representation

In most cases, the ecological communities associated with each of the identified forest types comprise very large numbers of species. Consequently, an approach to target setting considering all species individually is generally impossible. Thus, it is desirable to identify a limited number of species to be used as "representatives" for the associated communities (Kavanagh 1991). The presence and fitness of such species can then be used as response variables in studies aiming to derive quantitative conservation targets for different critical resources or forest ecosystem types at various scales. Such species may be identified based on knowledge about their occurrence patterns and habitat requirements, as well as on the basis of their functional roles in the ecosystem.

Species occurrence patterns

A species will present greater potential as a tool for the conservation of forest biota if it is shown to indicate reliably the presence of many other species dependent on the same forest type or resource (e.g. Suter *et al.* 2002). A simple and straightforward method for identifying species representing species-rich communities is to compare species richness in the presence vs. absence of the potential indicator species. This method, however, tells little about the identity of the species which tend to co-occur with the indicator. Are they mostly common species with generalized requirements, or are rare species (likely to be specialized or threatened) also co-occurring with the indicator? An alternative approach, which accounts more explicitly for the patterns of co-occurrence among species, builds on nestedness analysis (Patterson and Atmar 1986). Species assemblages are said to be nested if rare species are confined to species-rich sites and species-poor sites support only common species. Hence, nestedness is an asset when it comes to identifying reliable indicators of species-rich assemblages including rare species. An overview of a procedure for selecting indicators of species richness based on nested subsets theory – illustrated by an example with forest birds in the Baltic Sea region – is presented in Box 6.2. Here, nestedness

Box 6.1   The Baltic Sea region as a landscape laboratory

Biogeographically, the Baltic Sea region stretches from the nemoral forest zone in the south to the boreal zone in the north (Mayer 1984). In nemoral forests, dominated by broad-leaved deciduous tree species, natural disturbances historically acted over small spatial scales, resulting in gap dynamics. Landscapes with more or less continuous forest and woodland thus used to be common. Large herbivores, first wild and then domestic species, affected tree regeneration and growth and created woodlands of varying openness (Vera 2000). Boreal forest landscapes, on the other hand, were dominated by conifers, although shade-intolerant deciduous tree species occupied higher proportions in early-successional stages. Here, most areas were naturally affected by large-scale disturbances such as fire episodes of varying intensity and extent, with the exception of wet and high-altitude forests, where gap dynamics prevailed (Angelstam 1998b; Pennanen 2002). The transition from nemoral forests in the south to boreal forests in the north is gradual, forming a wide zone called the hemiboreal (or boreonemoral) ecoregion (Nilsson 1997).

The forests and woodlands of the Baltic Sea region have been subjected to human influence for a very long time. In the nemoral and hemiboreal forest regions, most of the landscapes have been severely altered throughout history, and large areas of forest and woodland were gradually cleared for agricultural development over a period of several thousands of years (Mayer 1984; Hannah *et al.* 1995). In the boreal region, only a small proportion of the forests have been cleared for conversion to other land uses, but logging has taken place in most areas. Logging increased as the economies of western Europe developed onwards from the medieval period. For example, as the demand for raw materials increased, most of the oak forests in the Baltic States were affected by logging during the seventeenth and eighteenth centuries (Dzintara 1999). Similarly, during the latter half of the nineteenth century, the industrial revolution in western Europe caused a rapid increase in the harvest of large trees from the still largely naturally dynamic forests in boreal Fennoscandia (Östlund and Zackrisson 2000) and triggered the development of today's very intensive sustained-yield forestry in that area. Logging in western Russia became large scale as the Soviet Union developed its system of economic development, but management has not, yet, become as intensive as in Fennoscandia in that area.

Today, reference landscapes for naturally dynamic forests are mostly confined to regions in the periphery of economic development (Whyte 1998). For the nemoral and hemiboreal regions, the Białowieża Forest in north-eastern Poland and western Belarus is the largest of the few remaining reference areas (Jedrzejewska and Jedrzejewski 1998), while smaller areas in a near-natural state can be found in the Baltic States (Kurlavičius *et al.* 2004). For the boreal forest, small reference areas are found in northern Fennoscandia, whereas large reference landscapes are confined to Russia (Angelstam *et al.* 1997; Yaroshenko *et al.* 2001). Continued trajectories of

(cont.)

economic development such as the gradual expansion of the timber frontier in the boreal forest (Imbeau *et al.* 2001) and the eastwards extension of the European Union contribute to transform landscapes from less to more intensively managed (Mayer *et al.* 2005).

The intensification of forest management has led to major changes in the composition, structure, and function within forest ecosystems (e.g., Esseen *et al.* 1997). In the Baltic Sea region, these alterations include truncated stand age distributions, reduced densities of large trees, changes in tree species composition, and the loss of large intact areas. In particular, dramatic decreases in the amounts of dead wood and in the area covered by older deciduous forest threaten the persistence of many species in the areas characterized by a long history of intensive management (Esseen *et al.* 1997; Nilsson 1997; de Jong 2002).

Box 6.2   Nestedness analysis and indicator species

Among the several approaches used to identify potential species-richness indicators, there has been growing interest in the use of nested subsets theory (Patterson and Atmar 1986; Wright and Reeves 1992; Cutler 1994). Assemblages are said to be nested when species-poor patches support a subset of the species found in species-rich patches. In a perfectly nested system, rare species are confined to species-rich sites. In a non-nested system, on the other hand, a number of rare species will occur in depauperate sites and some common species will be absent from species-rich sites. The data can be presented as a presence–absence matrix, where the columns represent the different species and the rows depict the sites (Fig. 6.1a). If the species are ordered from the most common (left) to the rarest (right) and sites are ranked from the most species-rich (top) to the most species-poor (bottom), a nested pattern will result in all occurrences being concentrated in the top left corner of the matrix. In that situation, the occurrence of the rarest species can be used as an indicator of complete species assemblages. Thus, nestedness is a desirable property if the aim is to identify species that reliably indicate species-rich assemblages (Fleishman *et al.* 2000b; Berglind 2004; Sætersdal *et al.* 2005).

Perfect nestedness is rarely observed in nature. Hence, there is a need to quantify the degree of conformity to nestedness for real-world assemblages. A number of metrics have been proposed for assessing nestedness of species assemblages (for reviews, see Wright and Reeves 1992; Cutler 1994). Generally, statistical significance is assessed by comparing the value of the nestedness metric with a distribution of values for random matrices obtained from Monte-Carlo simulations. In order to avoid detecting nestedness as a simple artifact of passive sampling, the null matrices for the simulations should be built in a way that respects the observed frequencies of the species in the actual assemblages, which is the case in the RANDNEST model proposed by Jonsson (2001) (see also Fischer and Lindenmayer 2002).

To illustrate this approach, we present the results for resident birds of deciduous forest in landscape units of 100 ha in southern Sweden (Roberge and Angelstam 2006). Here, we used the nestedness temperature calculator developed by Atmar and Patterson (1993), whereby the nestedness score is a "temperature" ranging from 0° (perfectly nested) to 100° (totally random). As shown in Fig. 6.1b, the species' occurrences are concentrated in the top left corner of the matrix. The temperature of the matrix is 11°; the pattern is highly significant since none of the 1,000 simulated random matrices generated by using RANDNEST has such a low temperature.

If the assemblages are found to be significantly nested, one can proceed and assess the contribution of individual species to the nested patterns. This can be done by looking at whether the occurrences of each individual species tend to be concentrated in the species-richest sites, using for example Mann–Whitney U-tests on the ranks of the presences in the ordered matrix (Simberloff and Martin 1991; Fleishman and Murphy 1999). In our example with deciduous forest birds in southern Sweden (Fig. 6.1b), 8 of the 12 species conform significantly to nestedness patterns ($p < 0.05$) and two do not (black woodpecker and jay; see caption to Fig. 6.1 for all scientific names), whereas two other species are ubiquitous (great tit and treecreeper). Among the many species showing high conformity to nestedness, some occur so frequently that they could hardly be used as indicators of species-rich communities. Thus, indicator species should not be too common and therefore should be sought in the right-hand side of the ordered presence–absence matrix.

One approach that incorporates both nestedness and frequency of occurrence consists of ranking the species according to two criteria. First, species are ranked from that showing the best conformity to nestedness to that showing the poorest fit. Second, the species are ranked according to their frequency of occurrence from the rarest to the most common. An index of relative indicator value (RIV) can then be calculated for each species as follows:

$$RIV = \frac{[S + 1 - rank(N)] \times [S + 1 - rank(F)]}{S^2}$$

where S is the total number of species, and $rank(N)$ and $rank(F)$ are the ranks of the species according to nestedness and frequency of occurrence, respectively. The possible values of the index range from $1/S^2$ to 1, high values being associated with good conformity to nested patterns and low frequencies (i.e. occurrence restricted to species-rich sites). When applying this procedure to our example with deciduous forest birds, the marsh tit and the lesser spotted woodpecker obtain the highest relative indicator value. We repeated the exercise above using data from three other hemiboreal landscapes of the Baltic Sea region (central Sweden, Lithuania, and north-east Poland) and found a generally high conformity to nestedness as well as high cross-regional consistency in the identity of the best indicator species for birds of deciduous forest. Similar results were found for birds of coniferous forests, although the assemblages were not significantly nested for that forest type in the Swedish study areas (Roberge and Angelstam 2006).

(a)

	Species 1	Species 2	Species 3	Species 4	Species 5	
Site 1	1	1	1	1	1	5
Site 2	1	1	1	1	0	4
Site 3	1	1	1	0	0	3
Site 4	1	1	0	0	0	2
Site 5	1	0	0	0	0	1
	5	4	3	2	1	

(b)

	GRTI	TREE	JAY	BLWO	GSWO	BLTI	LTTI	BULL	NUTH	LSWO	GRWO	MATI	
I	1	1	1	1	1	1	1	1	1	1	1	1	12
AD	1	1	1	1	1	1	1	1	1	1	1	1	12
L	1	1	1	1	1	1	1	1	1	1	1	1	12
H	1	1	1	1	1	1	1	1	1	1	1	1	12
O	1	1	1	1	1	1	1	1	1	1	1	0	11
N	1	1	1	1	1	1	1	0	1	1	1	1	11
M	1	1	1	0	1	1	1	1	1	1	1	1	11
B	1	1	1	1	1	1	1	1	1	1	0	0	10
D	1	1	1	1	1	1	1	1	1	1	0	0	10
AB	1	1	1	1	1	1	1	1	1	0	0	0	9
F	1	1	1	1	1	1	1	0	1	1	0	0	9
C	1	1	1	1	1	1	1	0	1	1	0	0	9
AA	1	1	1	1	1	1	1	1	0	0	0	0	8
Z	1	1	1	1	1	1	1	0	0	1	0	0	8
T	1	1	1	1	1	1	1	0	0	1	0	0	8
J	1	1	0	1	1	1	1	0	1	0	0	1	8
A	1	1	1	1	1	1	1	0	1	0	0	0	8
Y	1	1	1	1	1	1	1	1	0	0	0	0	8
G	1	1	1	1	1	1	1	1	0	0	0	0	8
E	1	1	1	1	1	1	1	0	1	0	0	0	8
X	1	1	1	1	1	0	0	1	1	0	0	0	7
R	1	1	1	1	1	1	0	0	1	0	1	0	7
W	1	1	1	1	1	1	0	0	1	0	0	0	7
V	1	1	1	1	1	0	0	1	0	0	1	0	7
Q	1	1	1	1	1	0	0	1	0	0	1	0	7
P	1	1	1	1	1	0	0	1	0	0	0	0	6
U	1	1	1	1	1	1	0	0	0	0	0	0	6
AC	1	1	1	1	0	1	0	1	0	0	0	0	6
S	1	1	1	1	0	0	1	0	0	0	0	0	5
K	1	1	1	1	1	0	0	0	0	0	0	0	5
	30	30	29	29	28	23	20	18	18	13	11	6	

Figure 6.1. Presence–absence matrices ordered from the most common (leftmost) to the rarest (rightmost) species and from the species-richest (top) to the species-poorest (bottom) site. The symbols 1 and 0 depict presence and absence of a given species, respectively. Row and column totals are given in the margins. (a) Theoretical example of perfectly nested assemblages with five species and five sites. (b) Co-occurrence patterns of resident forest birds of deciduous forests in 30 landscape units of 100 ha (denoted by letter codes on the left) in southern Sweden. GRTI, great tit *Parus major*; TREE, treecreeper *Certhia familiaris*; JAY, jay *Garrulus glandarius*; BLWO, black woodpecker *Dryocopus martius*; GSWO, great spotted woodpecker *Dendrocopos major*; BLTI, blue tit *Cyanistes caeruleus*; LTTI, long-tailed tit *Aegithalos caudatus*; BULL, bullfinch *Pyrrhula pyrrhula*; NUTH, nuthatch *Sitta europaea*; LSWO, lesser spotted woodpecker *Dendrocopos minor*; GRWO, green woodpecker *Picus viridis*; MATI, marsh tit *Poecile palustris*.

analysis is proposed as a tool in the context of selecting potential indicator species that could be the focus of studies aiming to derive quantitative conservation targets. Other applications based on species co-occurrence patterns, such as those related to the selection of sites to be included in reserve networks, may involve different species selection criteria and are treated elsewhere (see, for example, Fleishman *et al.* 2000a).

Several studies have assessed nestedness of species assemblages in forest ecosystems. The vast majority of these have found significantly nested patterns for a variety of taxa including birds (Blake 1991; Simberloff and Martin 1991; Hansson 1998; Jansson 1998; Wethered and Lawes 2005; Roberge and Angelstam 2006), invertebrates (Berglind 2004; Hylander *et al.* 2005), plants (Hansson 1998; Honnay *et al.* 1999; Jonsson 2001; Berglund and Jonsson 2003), and fungi (Berglund and Jonsson 2003). This suggests that there may be good potential for identifying forest species indicating species-rich assemblages with high reliability. Some forest assemblages, however, have been shown to be clearly non-nested (e.g. Jonsson 2001; Sætersdal *et al.* 2005), meaning that nestedness should be demonstrated empirically for the studied taxa and region rather than being assumed *a priori*. It should also be kept in mind that nestedness is not a binary property (i.e. nested or not). Rather, different systems are characterized by varying degrees of nestedness. One's ability to predict local species richness (or sequences of extinction/colonization) in different locations will be positively related to the degree of nestedness.

The use of nestedness analysis, however, presents a number of limitations. First, it does not address the possibility of temporal turnover in species composition at different locations. Moreover, by its very nature, nestedness analysis is based on presence–absence data. Such data are commonly used as they can be collected at low costs over large areas, but their utility is limited. For example, some of the sites supporting the largest numbers of species (as measured from presence–absence data) may actually be sink habitats for some of those species (Salomon *et al.* 2006). Therefore, valuable information could be gained by incorporating data on reproductive success or other fitness indicators for the different species, focusing on those that are of special conservation concern (e.g. red-listed species).

Species requirements

When using indicator species as response variables in ecological dose–response studies, the results will have especially high value for conservation planning if the requirements of the indicators for particular resources are shown to encapsulate those of many other species. If the latter applies, the indicators could act as "umbrella species", i.e. species whose conservation confers protection on large numbers of naturally co-occurring species (Fleishman *et al.* 2000a; Roberge and Angelstam 2004). In that respect, one should validate whether most species respond in the same way as the potential indicator species to variations in the amounts of critical resources. Box 6.3 presents an example of how data on the amounts of particular

Box 6.3   Exploring species requirements

In Box 6.2, an analysis of co-occurrence patterns among deciduous-forest bird species in southern Sweden showed that the studied species tend to occur in a nested (i.e. hierarchical) manner. All of the species treated in that analysis can breed in pure deciduous forests (Roberge and Angelstam 2006). However, the different species have various degrees of specialization in deciduous forest, from coniferous–deciduous generalists, such as the jay, to typical deciduous-forest specialists, such as the marsh tit. To cast light on the possible mechanisms behind the nested patterns of occurrence, we ordered the sites in the matrix as a function of their species richness (cf. rows in Fig. 6.1b). We then explored the relationship between the resulting site ranks and the habitat variable suspected to be limiting to most species in that group, i.e. the amount of deciduous forest within the landscape units. There was a strong positive relationship between site ranks and mean basal area of deciduous trees (Spearman rank correlation; $r_s = 0.78$, $n = 30$, $p < 0.001$). This suggests that the rarest species – whose occurrence often indicated species-rich assemblages (cf. Box 6.2) – tended to occur only in forests with high basal areas of deciduous trees. In particular, the marsh tit seemed to be the most demanding species as it occurred only in landscape units with a mean basal area of deciduous trees (diameter at breast height [DBH] $\geq$ 10 cm) of at least 7 m² ha^{-1}. Thus, management aiming to provide sufficient amounts of deciduous forest for that species may also maintain a whole suite of species dependent on deciduous forest, i.e. the marsh tit is likely to function as an umbrella species. Of course, this exercise only consists in a coarse preliminary check. In fact, at a finer scale, the different species may need different habitat features within deciduous and mixed forest. Nevertheless, while future studies will refine our knowledge of the critical variables for each species, results from such a simple approach may allow us to prioritize the work toward the definition of quantitative management targets by focusing on the requirements of particular species whose conservation is likely to benefit many others.

forest resources can be combined with species co-occurrence patterns to shed light on such possible umbrella effects.

There is growing interest in the development of general and systematic approaches for selecting potential umbrella species based on species' requirements. A major contribution in that field was the "focal species" approach developed by Lambeck (1997). It consists in identifying the main threats to biodiversity and then using the needs of the most sensitive species for each threatening factor as a basis for setting conservation targets. Lambeck (1997) allocated species at risk to four major categories: area-limited, resource-limited, dispersal-limited, or process-limited (Table 6.1). This categorization is consistent with the need to derive conservation targets

Table 6.1. *Examples of threat factors and vulnerable species in forest landscapes of the Baltic Sea region, northern Europe*

Cause of vulnerability[a]	Examples of threats	Examples of vulnerable taxa
Area-limited	Decreased area of older forest	Large-ranging birds and mammals specialized on older forest
Dispersal-limited	Isolation of old forest patches	Foliose and fruticose lichens specialized on older forest
	Anthropogenic barriers to movement in forest watercourses	Fish and amphibians
Resource-limited	Decreased amounts of dead wood	Saproxylic invertebrates and wood-decaying fungi, several woodpecker species
	Lower densities of very large trees	Hollow-using vertebrates and invertebrates, birds building large nests in tree crowns
Process-limited	Reduced incidence of forest fires	Fire-dependent insects and plants
	Browsing by ungulates at unnaturally high densities	Diverse assemblages dependent on tree species preferred by browsers (e.g. aspen *Populus tremula* and rowan *Sorbus aucuparia* in boreal forest)

[a] *Source*: Lambeck (1997).

for habitat features, landscape structure, and ecological processes in addition to population parameters, expressed by Villard and Jonsson in Chapter 1, this volume. Thus, species could be selected to represent not only the range of naturally occurring forest types, but also each of Lambeck's (1997) main threat categories.

The focal species approach has been used at different stages of conservation and restoration planning in Australian (Lambeck 1999; Brooker 2002), European (Bani *et al.* 2002, 2006), and North American (Hess and King 2002; Rubino and Hess 2003; Beazley and Cardinal 2004; Hess *et al.* 2006) landscapes. Although it has been found useful in many cases, the focal species approach is not without shortcomings. For example, identifying the taxa most threatened by each factor may prove extremely difficult as it requires much data (Lindenmayer *et al.* 2002). This would be most problematic in very complex forest ecosystems harboring many little-known or unknown species, such as in tropical forests. However, it would probably be easier to apply in simpler systems such as boreal and northern temperate forests. A possible avenue may be to use expert knowledge as a way to obtain a preliminary list of potential focal species for different threats (see below), and let future dose–response field data improve knowledge about the requirements of the different candidates.

The main underlying assumption of the focal and umbrella species approaches is that landscapes meeting the requirements of the species that seem to be the most demanding or sensitive will be suitable for other taxa sharing similar habitats. There is a need for systematic validation of that hypothesis in actual landscapes. Roberge and Angelstam (2004) and Roberge (2006) reviewed the limited evidence on that topic and concluded that focal and umbrella species may constitute effective conservation tools in some, but by no means all, situations. Testing the hypothesis that species selected as potential focal species in different types of forest landscapes actually indicate what they should – and that conservation planning based on those species' requirements satisfies the needs of the other species – should be a research priority. Long-term monitoring programs are essential in that context.

Functional roles

Another issue of importance in the species selection process is the species' functions in the forest ecosystem. Different species bear a range of functions in ecosystems and can therefore be classified into broad "functional groups". Biodiversity conservation is best achieved if each important functional group of organisms is represented by several ecologically equivalent species (Walker 1995). Thus, a classification into major functional groups, grouping species according to their qualitative habitat requirements, trophic roles, and life-history strategies, could provide an additional systematic basis for the selection of species to be the focus of conservation planning. In that respect, keystone species (Paine 1969) and ecosystem engineers (Jones et al. 1994) should be given priority due to the unique functions they assume in the ecosystem. A function-based approach may also facilitate the work in regions with very high species diversity, where comprehensive species surveys are expensive. Admittedly, grouping species into functional groups can be a challenging task in forest ecosystems where many species still remain unknown to science and where knowledge about critical structures and processes is currently limited. Still, concentrating on a restricted number of species representing the main identified functional groups could provide a systematic foundation for the work toward the development of conservation targets, which could then be improved gradually as better knowledge of species and their functions becomes available.

Measurability and communication value

In addition to the ecological criteria presented above, we envisage two additional species properties that are desirable from a pragmatic point of view: ease of measure and communication value. Given that ecological research is subject to strict budgetary constraints, tradeoffs related to cost-effectiveness are inevitable in the species selection process. The ease with which population status can be measured varies greatly among species as well as among higher taxonomic groups requiring different sampling methodologies (e.g. Juutinen and Mönkkönen 2004; Chapter 16, this volume). Hence, it may be a sensible choice to focus, to begin with, on species whose status is relatively easy to determine in the field, and later proceed by exploring the requirements of more cryptic species or other species relatively challenging to survey.

Research aimed at developing conservation targets is of little use if the results are not communicated effectively to the main actors exercising governance and management in forest landscapes. As those actors have varying degrees of knowledge about forest biodiversity and management, it is crucial to present the scientific results in manners that are easily accessible and understandable. Among the different types of elements of biodiversity, species are probably the one to which people relate most easily. Thus, expressing conservation targets as the requirements for functioning social units or viable populations of particular species would be a sensible approach from a pedagogical point of view. In that context, some well-known species may prove more effective tools than lesser-known taxa for communicating the needs for forest conservation and restoration to the different actors (Uliczka *et al.* 2004). Moreover, when communicating with the latter, it should be made explicit that the selected species are, in most cases, only a way to depict the broader status of the forest structures and processes that they represent. Otherwise, there is a risk that events such as the extinction of a species could be wrongly interpreted as the end of the need for conservation actions for the associated habitat.

Species selection across multiple taxonomic groups

The criteria presented above (summarized in Table 6.2) should aid the selection of species that would be the focus of studies aiming to define conservation targets in forest landscapes. Ideally, the selected species should possess all of these desired properties. In practice, however, it may prove

Table 6.2. *Main characteristics making a species useful for ecological dose–response studies*

1. Specialized on a given forest type or critical resource, or dependent on a specific ecosystem process
2. Reliable indicator of species-rich communities for the focal forest type
3. Highly demanding (focal or umbrella function) or key functional role in the ecosystem
4. Population status easily measurable and habitat requirements expressible as variables with which managers and other stakeholders are familiar

difficult to identify individual species possessing all of these. Thus, different species may be selected based on different properties (e.g. some for their high indicator value and others for their key functional roles) to form complementary suites of species.

As stressed in the preceding sections, making informed decisions when it comes to selecting species to be used in conservation research and planning requires large amounts of knowledge about diverse taxonomic groups. Because of the need to act quickly, there is a growing demand for efficient screening methods in the species selection process, which optimize the use of available information. Systematic methods to gather and manage expert knowledge are increasingly used for that purpose. For example, Hess and King (2002) used a Delphi survey approach to identify species to be used as tools for conservation planning in the Triangle region of North Carolina, USA. The approach involved asking questions about species and threats to panelists in structured, written communication, and reporting the summarized responses back to the panelists, who could subsequently refine or revise their contributions, until consensus was reached. The participating panelists included 28 wildlife-habitat experts from the region, working for a range of organizations. Using three rounds of surveys, a list of landscape types was generated, and candidate species were identified among birds, mammals, reptiles, and amphibians, based on their potential role as umbrella or focal species, or their function in the ecosystem. Similarly, for forests of Nova Scotia (Canada) and Maine (USA), Beazley and Cardinal (2004) used a survey approach to identify potential focal species – including those with potential keystone, umbrella, flagship (i.e. communication), or indicator roles – among mammals, birds, reptiles, amphibians, and freshwater fish. In south-eastern Australia, Kavanagh *et al.* (2004) used expert knowledge to categorize functional groups of forest species among vertebrates and plants in terms of their sensitivity to logging. Expert judgment was then used in combination with data to categorize over 500 individual species of vertebrate according to their degree of exposure to logging and to the shape of their response to logging over the time of one rotation. Such systematic knowledge on the relative sensitivity of different forest species to a particular threat offers a useful basis for the preliminary selection of species which could become the focus of more detailed studies aiming to derive conservation targets.

As a result of an uneven level of knowledge about species belonging to different higher taxa, most past attempts to identify sensitive or functionally important species in forest landscapes have suffered from a lack of taxonomic representativeness. Hence, one way to improve such assessments in the future would be to gradually include species or functional groups from all main higher taxa, including fungi, plants, and invertebrates, as knowledge about their requirements improves. Finally, it should be stressed that the lists of candidate species obtained in such assessments are only preliminary and should be subject to empirical validation.

CONCLUSIONS

Species represent important compositional elements of forest biodiversity. Moreover, through their requirements or function, many species integrate key structures and processes in forest ecosystems (Hansson and Larsson 1997; Thompson and Angelstam 1999). Studying the requirements of ecologically specialized species will undoubtedly contribute to improving the knowledge base required to answer the question "How much is enough?". Moreover, expressing conservation targets as a function of the requirements of functioning social units or viable populations of wisely selected species is expected to facilitate communication with land managers, policy-makers, and the public. Although this chapter focused on species and their requirements, it should be kept in mind that species-oriented approaches are not a panacea. Ecosystem approaches, adopting a holistic view of the systems considering, among other things, energy and mineral flows, disturbance regimes, and heterogeneity (Hansson and Larsson 1997) represent complementary avenues which should also be considered in the development of conservation targets (Franklin 1993).

ACKNOWLEDGEMENTS

We thank NSERC, FORMAS, FQRNT, the Lennart Hjelm Foundation, Mistra, the Helge Axson Johnson Foundation, the Swedish Environmental

Protection Agency, and the Wallenberg Foundation for financial support of our work on forest conservation planning and indicators.

References

Angelstam, P. 1998a. Maintaining and restoring biodiversity by developing natural disturbance regimes in European boreal forest. *Journal of Vegetation Science* 9:593–602.

Angelstam, P. 1998b. Towards a logic for assessing biodiversity in boreal forest. Pp. 301–13 in P. Bachmann, M. Köhl and R. Päivinen (eds.) *Assessment of Biodiversity for Improved Forest Planning*. Dordrecht, The Netherlands: Kluwer Academic Publishers.

Angelstam, P. 2006. Maintaining cultural and natural biodiversity in Europe's economic centre and periphery. Pp. 125–43 in M. Agnoletti (ed.) *The Conservation of Cultural Landscapes*. Oxford, UK: CABI International.

Angelstam, P., V. Anufriev, L. Balciauskas *et al*. 1997. Biodiversity and sustainable forestry in European forests – how west and east can learn from each other. *Wildlife Society Bulletin* 25:38–48.

Angelstam, P., M. Dönz-Breuss and J.-M. Roberge (eds). 2004a. Targets and tools for the maintenance of forest biodiversity – an introduction. *Ecological Bulletins* 51:11–24.

Angelstam, P., S. Boutin, F. Schmiegelow *et al*. 2004b. Targets for boreal forest biodiversity conservation – a rationale for macroecological research and adaptive management. *Ecological Bulletins* 51:487–509.

Angelstam, P., J.-M. Roberge, A. Lõhmus *et al*. 2004c. Habitat modelling as a tool for landscape-scale conservation – a review of parameters for focal forest birds. *Ecological Bulletins* 51:427–53.

Angelstam, P., J.-M. Roberge, T. Ek and L. Laestadius. 2005. Data and tools for conservation, management, and restoration of forest ecosystems at multiple scales. Pp. 269–83 in J. A. Stanturf and P. Madsen (eds.) *Restoration of Boreal and Temperate Forests*. Boca Raton, FL: CRC Press.

Atmar, W. and B. D. Patterson. 1993. The measure of order and disorder in the distribution of species in fragmented habitat. *Oecologia* 96:373–82.

Bani, L., M. Baietto, L. Bottoni and R. Massa. 2002. The use of focal species in designing a habitat network for a lowland area of Lombardy, Italy. *Conservation Biology* 16:826–31.

Bani, L., D. Massimino, L. Bottoni and R. Massa. 2006. A multiscale method for selecting indicator species and priority conservation areas: a case study for broadleaved forests in Lombardy, Italy. *Conservation Biology* 20:512–26.

Beazley, K. and N. Cardinal. 2004. A systematic approach for selecting focal species for conservation in the forests of Nova Scotia and Maine. *Environmental Conservation* 31:91–101.

Berglind, S.-Å. 2004. Area-sensitivity of the sand lizard and spider wasps in sandy pine heath forests – umbrella species for early successional biodiversity conservation? *Ecological Bulletins* 51:189–207.

Berglund, H. and B. G. Jonsson. 2003. Nested plant and fungal communities; the importance of area and habitat quality in maximizing species capture in boreal old-growth forests. *Biological Conservation* 112:319–28.

Blake, J. G. 1991. Nested subsets and the distribution of birds on isolated woodlots. *Conservation Biology* 5:58–66.

Brooker, L. 2002. The application of focal species knowledge to landscape design in agricultural lands using the ecological neighbourhood as a template. *Landscape and Urban Planning* 60:185–210.

Cutler, A. H. 1994. Nested biotas and biological conservation: metrics, mechanisms, and meaning of nestedness. *Landscape and Urban Planning* 28:73–82.

de Jong, J. 2002. *Populationsförändringar hos Skogslevande Arter i Relation till Landskapets Utveckling*. Uppsala, Sweden: Centrum för Biologisk Mångfald. (In Swedish.)

Diamond J. 1986. Overview: laboratory experiments, field experiments, and natural experiments. Pp. 3–22 in J. M. Diamond and T. J. Case (eds.) *Community Ecology*. New York, NY: Harper and Row.

Dzintara, A. (ed.) 1999. *Latvijas Mezu Vesture lidz 1940 Gadam*. Riga, Latvia: World Wildlife Fund. (In Latvian.)

Esseen, P.-A., B. Ehnström, L. Ericson and K. Sjöberg. 1997. Boreal forests. *Ecological Bulletins* 46:16–47.

Fahrig, L. 2001. How much habitat is enough? *Biological Conservation* 100:65–74.

Fischer, J. and D. B. Lindenmayer. 2002. Treating the nestedness temperature calculator as a "black box" can lead to false conclusions. *Oikos* 99:193–9.

Fleishman, E. and D. D. Murphy. 1999. Patterns and processes of nestedness in a Great Basin butterfly community. *Oecologia* 119:133–9.

Fleishman, E., D. D. Murphy and P. F. Brussard. 2000a. A new method for selection of umbrella species for conservation planning. *Ecological Applications* 10:569–79.

Fleishman, E., B. G. Jonsson and P. Sjögren-Gulve. 2000b. Focal species modeling for biodiversity conservation. *Ecological Bulletins* 48:85–99.

Franklin, J. F. 1993. Preserving biodiversity: species, ecosystems, or landscapes? *Ecological Applications* 3:202–5.

Hannah, L., J. L. Carr and A. Lankerani. 1995. Human disturbance and natural habitat: a biome level analysis of a global data set. *Biodiversity and Conservation* 4:128–55.

Hansson, L. 1998. Nestedness as a conservation tool: plants and birds of oak-hazel woodland in Sweden. *Ecology Letters* 1:142–5.

Hansson, L. and T.-B. Larsson. 1997. Conservation of boreal environments: a completed research program and a new paradigm. *Ecological Bulletins* 46:9–15.

Hess, G. R. and T. J. King. 2002. Planning open spaces for wildlife. I. Selecting focal species using a Delphi survey approach. *Landscape and Urban Planning* 58:25–40.

Hess, G. R., F. H. Koch, M. J. Rubino *et al.* 2006. Comparing the potential effectiveness of conservation planning approaches in central North Carolina, USA. *Biological Conservation* 128:358–68.

Hobbs, R. J. 1993. Effects of landscape fragmentation on ecosystem processes in the Western Australian wheatbelt. *Biological Conservation* 64:193–201.

Honnay, O., M. Hermy and P. Coppin. 1999. Nested plant communities in deciduous forest fragments: species relaxation or nested habitats? *Oikos* 84:119–29.

Hylander, K., C. Nilsson, B. G. Jonsson and T. Göthner. 2005. Differences in habitat quality explains nestedness in a land snail meta-community. *Oikos* **108**:351–61.

Imbeau, L., M. Mönkkönen and A. Desrochers. 2001. Long-term effects of forestry on birds of the Eastern Canadian boreal forests: a comparison with Fennoscandia. *Conservation Biology* **15**:1151–62.

Jansson, G. 1998. Guild indicator species on a landscape scale – an example with four avian habitat specialists. *Ornis Fennica* **75**:119–27.

Jedrzejewska, B. and W. Jedrzejewski. 1998. *Predation in Vertebrate Communities.* Berlin: Springer-Verlag.

Jones, C. G., J. H. Lawton and M. Shachak. 1994. Organisms as ecosystem engineers. *Oikos* **69**:373–86.

Jonsson, B. G. 2001. A null model for randomization tests of nestedness in species assemblages. *Oecologia* **127**:309–13.

Juutinen, A. and M. Mönkkönen. 2004. Testing alternative indicators for biodiversity conservation in old-growth boreal forests: ecology and economics. *Ecological Economics* **50**:35–48.

Karr, J. R. 1992. Ecological integrity: protecting Earth's life support systems. Pp. 223–36 in R. Costanza, B. G. Norton and B. D. Haskell (eds.) *New Goals for Environmental Management.* Washington, D.C.: Island Press.

Kavanagh, R. P. 1991. The target species approach to wildlife management: gliders and owls in the forests of southeastern New South Wales. Pp. 377–83 in D. Lunney (ed.) *Conservation of Australia's Forest Fauna.* Sydney, Australia: Royal Zoological Society of New South Wales.

Kavanagh, R. P., R. H. Loyn, G. C. Smith, R. J. Taylor and P. C. Catling. 2004. Which species should be monitored to indicate ecological sustainability in Australian forest management? Pp. 959–87 in D. Lunney (ed.) *Conservation of Australia's Forest Fauna* (2nd edn). Mosman, NSW, Australia: Royal Zoological Society of New South Wales.

Kohler, R. E. 2002. *Landscapes and Labscapes – Exploring the Lab-Field Border in Biology.* Chicago, IL: University of Chicago Press.

Kurlavičius, P., R. Kuuba, M. Lūkins *et al.* 2004. Identifying high conservation value forests in the Baltic States from forest databases. *Ecological Bulletins* **51**:351–66.

Lambeck, R. J. 1997. Focal species: a multi-species umbrella for nature conservation. *Conservation Biology* **11**:849–56.

Lambeck, R. J. 1999. *Landscape Planning for Biodiversity Conservation in Agricultural Regions: A Case Study from the Wheatbelt of Western Australia.* Environment Australia, Biodiversity Technical Paper 2. Canberra, Australia.

Lindenmayer, D. B., A. D. Manning, P. L. Smith *et al.* 2002. The focal-species approach and landscape restoration: a critique. *Conservation Biology* **16**:338–45.

Mayer, A. L., P. E. Kauppi, P. K. Angelstam, Y. Zhang and P. M. Tikka. 2005. Importing timber, exporting ecological impact. *Science* **308**:359–60.

Mayer, H. 1984. *Die Wälder Europas.* Stuttgart: Gustav Fischer Verlag. (In German.)

Nilsson, J. and P. Grennfelt. (eds.) 1988. *Critical Loads for Sulphur and Nitrogen.* Copenhagen, Denmark: Nordic Council of Ministers.

Nilsson, S. G. 1997. Forests in the temperate-boreal transition: natural and man-made features. *Ecological Bulletins* 46:61–71.

Nilsson, S. G., J. Hedin and M. Niklasson. 2001. Biodiversity and its assessment in boreal and nemoral forests. *Scandinavian Journal of Forest Research* Suppl. 3:10–26.

Östlund, L. and O. Zackrisson. 2000. The history of the boreal forest in Sweden: a multidisciplinary approach. Pp. 119–28 in M. Agnoletti and S. Anderson (eds.) *Methods and Approaches in Forest History*. Wallingford, UK: CABI Publishing.

Paine, R. T. 1969. A note on trophic complexity and community stability. *American Naturalist* 103:91–3.

Patterson, B. D. and W. Atmar. 1986. Nested subsets and the structure of insular mammalian faunas and archipelagos. *Biological Journal of the Linnean Society* 28:65–82.

Pennanen, J. 2002. Forest age distribution under mixed-severity fire regimes – a simulation-based analysis for middle boreal Fennoscandia. *Silva Fennica* 36:213–31.

Peterken, G. F. 1996. *Natural Woodland: Ecology and Conservation in Northern Temperate Regions*. Cambridge, UK: Cambridge University Press.

Pimm, S. L. and P. Raven. 2000. Extinction by numbers. *Nature* 403:843–5.

Roberge, J.-M. 2006. Umbrella species as a conservation planning tool – an assessment using resident birds in hemiboreal and boreal forests. Doctoral thesis, Swedish University of Agricultural Sciences (SLU), Uppsala, Sweden.

Roberge, J.-M. and P. Angelstam. 2004. Usefulness of the umbrella species concept as a conservation tool. *Conservation Biology* 18:76–85.

Roberge, J.-M. and P. Angelstam. 2006. Indicator species among resident forest birds – a cross-regional evaluation in northern Europe. *Biological Conservation* 130:134–47.

Rubino, M. J. and G. R. Hess. 2003. Planning open spaces for wildlife 2: modeling and verifying focal species habitat. *Landscape and Urban Planning* 64:89–104.

Sætersdal, M., I. Gjerde and H. H. Blom. 2005. Indicator species and the problem of spatial inconsistency in nestedness patterns. *Biological Conservation* 122:305–16.

Salomon, A. K., J. L. Ruesink and R. E. DeWreede. 2006. Population viability, ecological processes and biodiversity: valuing sites for reserve selection. *Biological Conservation* 128:79–92.

Simberloff, D. and J.-L. Martin. 1991. Nestedness of insular avifaunas: simple summary statistics masking complex species patterns. *Ornis Fennica* 68:178–92.

Suter, W., R. F. Graf and R. Hess. 2002. Capercaillie (*Tetrao urogallus*) and avian biodiversity: testing the umbrella-species concept. *Conservation Biology* 16:778–88.

Tear, T. H., P. Kareiva, P. L. Angermeier *et al.* 2005. How much is enough? The recurrent problem of setting measurable objectives in conservation. *BioScience* 55:835–49.

Thompson, I. D. and P. Angelstam. 1999. Special species. Pp. 434–59 in M. L. Hunter (ed.) *Maintaining Biodiversity in Forest Ecosystems*. Cambridge, UK: Cambridge University Press.

Uliczka, H., P. Angelstam and J.-M. Roberge. 2004. Indicator species and biodiversity monitoring systems for non-industrial private forest owners – is there a communication problem? *Ecological Bulletins* 51:379–84.

Vera, F. W. M. 2000. *Grazing Ecology and Forest History*. Wallingford, UK: CABI Publishing.

Walker, B. 1995. Conserving biological diversity through ecosystem resilience. *Conservation Biology* 9:747–52.

Wethered, R. and M. J. Lawes. 2005. Nestedness of bird assemblages in fragmented Afromontane forest: the effect of plantation forestry in the matrix. *Biological Conservation* 123:125–37.

Whyte, I. D. 1998. Rural Europe since 1500: areas of retardation and tradition. Pp. 243–58 in R. A. Butlin and R. A. Dodgshon (eds.) *An Historical Geography of Europe*. Oxford, UK: Oxford University Press.

Wilson, E. O. (ed.) 1988. *Biodiversity*. Washington, D.C.: National Academy Press.

Wright, D. H. and J. H. Reeves. 1992. On the meaning and measurement of nestedness of species assemblages. *Oecologia* 92:416–28.

Yaroshenko, A. Yu., P. V. Potapov and S. A. Turubanova. 2001. *The Intact Forest Landscapes of Northern European Russia*. Moscow, Russia: Greenpeace Russia and Global Forest Watch.

Bridging ecosystem and multiple species approaches for setting conservation targets in managed boreal landscapes

PIERRE DRAPEAU, ALAIN LEDUC, AND YVES BERGERON

INTRODUCTION

Over the past three decades, conservation biology has shown quite clearly that the maintenance of biodiversity cannot by itself be achieved solely with networks of protected areas, no matter how functional those may be (Janzen 1983; Boersma and Parrish 1999; Gaston *et al.* 2002; Rodriguez *et al.* 2004). The managed matrix into which such protected areas are embedded greatly matters. Approaches to ensure the retention of native habitats outside protected areas and within managed landscapes is of paramount importance for fulfilling the long-term maintenance of biodiversity. Traditionally, wildlife management has tackled issues of biological conservation by using single-species habitat requirements approaches focused on game species, endangered species, or indicator species (Rosene 1969; Severinghaus 1981; Bart 1995; Block *et al.* 1995). Incorporating the conservation of all native species in managed landscapes raises concerns about the appropriateness of single-species approaches or even conservation shortcuts such as flagship, keystone, or umbrella species (Caro and O'Doherty 1999; Caro 2003; Roberge and Angelstam 2004; Huggett 2005; Lindenmayer *et al.* 2005).

Another conservation planning approach has increasingly been proposed as an alternative to species-oriented conservation: ecosystem-oriented conservation planning, also referred to as coarse-filter strategies (Noss 1987;

Setting Conservation Targets for Managed Forest Landscapes, ed. M.-A. Villard and B. G. Jonsson. Published by Cambridge University Press.
© Cambridge University Press 2009.

Hunter *et al.* 1988). The coarse-filter approach implies that at landscape and regional scales, an adequate representation (distribution and abundance) of forest cover types should be maintained. The implicit assumption underlying this approach is that a coarse filter will simultaneously supply habitat needed by a majority of species and maintain essential ecological functions in managed ecosystems (Hunter *et al.* 1988; Welsh 1988; Franklin 1993; Hunter 1993; Bunnell 1995; Gauthier *et al.* 1996; Landres *et al.* 1999; Seymour and Hunter 1999). This, in turn, raises the question of what benchmark conditions should determine an "adequate" representation of forest cover types. In northern (boreal, hemiboreal) and coastal forests, several studies have proposed that natural disturbance regimes should provide such benchmark conditions by determining the natural range of variation in the amount of different forest cover types to be maintained in managed landscapes (De Long and Tanner 1996; Bergeron and Harvey 1997; Angelstam 1998; Bergeron *et al.* 1999, 2002; Harvey *et al.* 2002). In the boreal forest of North America, the recent improvement of our knowledge on fire regimes has provided insight into natural disturbance dynamics (Payette *et al.* 1989; Bergeron 1991; Johnson and Wowchuck 1993; Larsen 1997; Johnson *et al.* 1998; Bergeron *et al.* 2001, 2004a,b). This knowledge has been used to develop targets with regards to the proportion of different forest cover types (early-, mid-, and late-seral stages) that should be maintained in managed landscapes (Bergeron *et al.* 1999; Harvey *et al.* 2002; Bergeron 2004).

Whereas ecosystem-oriented approaches may seem like a promising first step in conservation planning for biodiversity maintenance in landscapes managed for timber harvesting, their efficiency to do so should be assessed through direct monitoring of biodiversity (Block *et al.* 1995). This, in turn, re-emphasizes the challenge of selecting organisms on which the coarse-filter strategy could be tested. Several authors have, however, suggested that organisms associated with habitats of concern may provide a target group of species on which such evaluation could be conducted (Lambeck 1997; Roberge and Angelstam 2004; Huggett 2005; Chapter 6, this volume). Such a multiple species approach may indeed better assess the scope and limitations of ecosystem-oriented management approaches given that it may improve our understanding of the relationships between species and their environment while encapsulating many species simultaneously.

Boreal ecosystems are mainly under even-aged management, which results in increases in the proportion of early-seral habitats and concurrent decreases in late-seral habitats (Spies *et al.* 1994; Gauthier *et al.* 1996; Drapeau *et al.* 2000; Bergeron *et al.* 2002; MacLean *et al.* 2005). Organisms that are associated with late-seral forests can thus be candidates to assess the potential of ecosystem-oriented approaches for conservation planning.

In this chapter, we present a conceptual framework for setting biodiversity conservation targets in managed forest landscapes that is based on the complementarities (*sensu* Lindenmayer *et al.* 2007) of ecosystem and species-oriented approaches. We draw on empirical work conducted on the effects of natural disturbances on both the forest cover (ecosystems) and the avifauna (species) at the transition zone between mixedwood and conifer-dominated forests in Québec, Canada. We first summarize current knowledge on natural fire regimes and current forest management in this part of the boreal ecosystem. We then use empirical dendroecological data on the size and the frequency of wildfires in eastern Canada to simulate the age-class distribution of forest cover types and estimate their historical variability at a regional scale ($>15,000$ km^2). The range of variation in the proportion of forest cover types, in particular late-seral habitats (>100 years), provides natural disturbance-based management (NDBM) targets. Third, we assess the efficiency of these targets to maintain songbird species through comparisons of single species tolerance to loss of late-seral forest at the landscape scale. Finally, we discuss how bridging natural disturbance-based knowledge and species knowledge to habitat loss and fragmentation can improve the process of setting conservation targets for biodiversity maintenance in managed boreal ecosystems.

NATURAL DISTURBANCES AND CURRENT FOREST MANAGEMENT IN THE EASTERN CANADIAN BOREAL FOREST

The eastern Canadian boreal forest is affected by many natural disturbance agents including fire (Bergeron 1991; Payette 1992; Bergeron *et al.* 2001, 2004a, 2006), insect outbreaks (Jardon *et al.* 2003; McKinnon and MacLean 2003; MacLean *et al.* 2005; Taylor and MacLean 2005), and windthrow (Ruel 1995; Ruel *et al.* 2001; Taylor and MacLean 2005). However, as it is the case elsewhere in the boreal forest, fire is the natural disturbance that has the most widespread influence in structuring the amount and distribution of forest cover types at regional scales (Johnson 1992; Payette 1992; Angelstam 1998; Bergeron *et al.* 2004a). Forest fire regimes, defined by frequency, size, intensity, seasonality, fire type, and severity (Flannigan 1993; Weber and Flannigan 1997) have a significant influence on boreal forest attributes, including age-structure of landscape mosaics and structural and compositional attributes of stands (Bergeron *et al.* 2002; Harper *et al.* 2002;

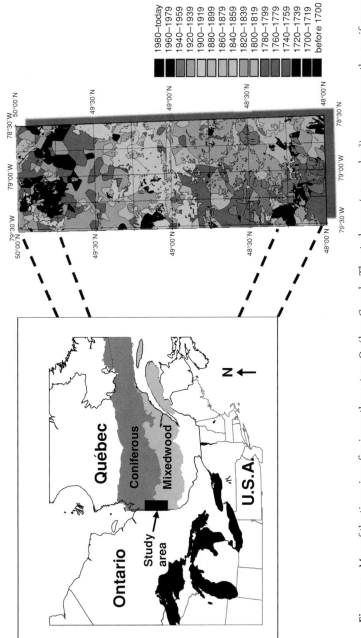

Figure 7.1. Map of the time since fire in north-western Québec, Canada. The study area (15,000 km²) encompasses the coniferous and the mixedwood boreal zones. Fire history reconstruction is based on dendroecological records from 315 sites (137 in the coniferous zone and 178 in the mixedwood zone) for an average of one sample per 50 km². Disks or increment cores were collected at each site, preferably from pioneer tree species, to reconstruct past fire events of the past 300 years (see Bergeron *et al.* 2004a for details).

Drapeau *et al.* 2003). Considerable amplitude may exist on each fire regime axis, and this can vary from region to region (Bergeron *et al.* 2004b). The risk of a fire occurring is such that one site may burn two years in a row whereas another site may be spared for several hundred years. Similarly, the area burned by a fire can vary from less than one hectare to hundreds or several thousands of square kilometers. Finally, whereas certain surface fires may only affect ground vegetation, an intense crown fire will kill virtually all trees in its path and may consume the forest humus layer down to the mineral soil. Apart from the variability imposed by permanent site features, which influence thermal, moisture, and nutritional regimes, the disturbance regime is by itself an important driver responsible for the variety of forest habitats that occur in a region.

Studies of natural fire history reconstruction at the transition zone between mixedwood and conifer-dominated forests in north-western Québec, Canada (Fig. 7.1) show that the natural forest mosaic contains a large proportion of stands that have not burned for more than 100 years (Bergeron *et al.* 2004a). Figure 7.2 illustrates the proportion of the different stand types according to time since the last fire in north-western Québec, documented in Bergeron *et al.* (2001, 2004a). Naturally disturbed forest landscapes in this portion of the boreal ecosystem are thus mainly composed of late-seral forests and historically represented a major part of the forested landscape in these regions, at least during the past 300 years (Bergeron *et al.* 2001, 2004a; Harper *et al.* 2003). Forest cover types range from mixed woods on upland sites with balsam fir (*Abies balsamea*), trembling aspen (*Populus tremuloides*), paper birch (*Betula papyrifera*), jack pine (*Pinus banksiana*), and white spruce (*Picea glauca*) to stands dominated by black spruce (*P. mariana*) on lowland sites (Bergeron and Dubuc 1989; Harper *et al.* 2003; Gauthier *et al.* 2004).

The increased importance of industrial timber harvesting since the late 1940s has, however, considerably transformed the landscape. In our study area an even-aged management system with clearcutting practices has been extensively used over the entire managed area. This has truncated the age-class distribution of stands by reducing the regional importance of late-seral forests to the expanse of early and mid-seral stages as is shown for an extensive portion (45,000 km^2) of north-western Québec within which our study area lies (Fig. 7.3). Contrary to fire, which exerts no selection on stand age (Johnson 1992; Johnson *et al.* 1998), forest harvesting is systematic and does not spare any forest that exceeds rotation age. Hence, in north-western Québec, whereas the average fire cycle (the time needed to burn a total area equivalent to the size (15,000 km^2) of the study area) is 139 years (Bergeron

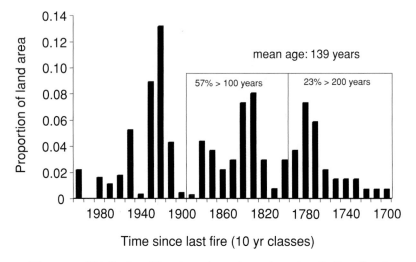

Time since last fire (10 yr classes)

Figure 7.2. Distribution of forest age-classes in north-western Québec, Canada. Overall mean fire cycle is 139 years. The proportion of the land area that has not burned in 100 years or 200 years is presented.

et al. 2004a), the use of a 100 years harvest rotation is likely to cause a major shift in the age-class distribution of this part of the boreal forest (Fig. 7.4).

NATURAL DISTURBANCE-BASED ECOSYSTEM TARGETS

Setting ecosystem targets requires knowledge not only of natural disturbance regimes but also of their historical variability (Landres *et al.* 1999). Dendroecological studies can provide data on size, frequency, and severity of fire disturbances, but the temporal extent of these studies is limited as they provide a single average in time with a range of variation in the proportions of forest age-classes over a short period (less than 300 years). Paleoecological studies such as that of Carcaillet *et al.* (2001) report that large tracts of black spruce (*Picea mariana*) forests have not burned for thousands of years, suggesting that past landscape mosaics were also dominated by late-seral forests in north-western Québec (Canada). However, such information is limited in terms of how it can be generalized over larger spatial scales. Better assessment of the variability of forest age-classes is thus necessary to set management targets that encompass the range of possibilities provided by historic conditions generated by natural disturbance regimes. Spatially explicit models with simulation routines that incorporate empirical data

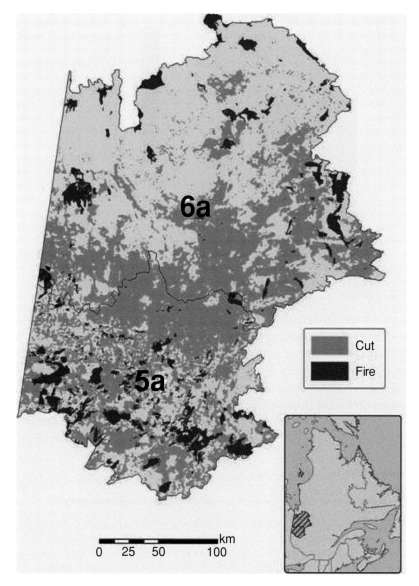

Figure 7.3. Areas affected by industrial timber harvesting (light gray) and wildfires (dark gray) from 1940 to 2005 in north-western Québec. Numbers refer to Québec's ecoregional classification (5a: balsam fir – white birch; 6a: black spruce – feathermoss) as defined by Saucier *et al.* (1998).

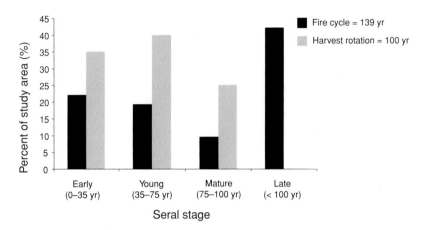

Figure 7.4. Comparisons between the natural fire cycle and the current timber management rotation in north-western Québec for the proportions of forest cover types (defined by age-class) in the landscape.

from retrospective studies on fire history and forest dynamics can be used to estimate the historical variability in forest conditions at the landscape level. Such information provides the range of variation under which managers can maintain the different forest cover types (early, mid, late-seral forest) within forest management units (FMU) that cover several thousands of square kilometers in our study area. Using a stochastic simulation approach (see Box 7.1), we documented the historical variability in the amount of late-seral forests (>100 years) in the eastern portion of the Canadian

---

Box 7.1   Simulations of late-seral forests in Québec's boreal landscapes

In order to explore the long-term variability in proportions of late-seral forests (> 100 years) under different fire regimes, we ran simulations using a stochastic approach similar to the one used by Wimberly et al. (2000) to estimate the historical variability of old forests in the Oregon Coast Range. Simulations were conducted using SELES (Spatially Explicit Landscape Event Simulator) modeling environment (Fall and Fall 2001) as in Belleau et al. (2007). Since the objective was to establish the range of historical variability of late-seral forests (>100 years) in naturally disturbed landscapes, our model was based on two key fire regime parameters: length of fire cycle and mean fire size. These parameters are recognized in the literature to describe fire regimes reasonably at the landscape scale.

Simulations were conducted on a territory for which the extent is set to 50 times the mean fire size used in the simulations to limit scale and boundary effects (Shugart and West 1981). In northern boreal forests this could correspond to a land unit of over 7,500 km². This has been found to be large enough to capture the maximum size that can be reached by a fire event with any reasonable likelihood, and to limit the influence of large fire events on overall stand age structure. Each cell represents a homogenous 10-ha area of the landscape; stands emerge as adjacent cells with the same characteristics. One hundred replicates of each fire cycle scenario were simulated for a period of 2,000 years to ensure mean stand age stabilization (at least twice the fire cycle length; Baker 1995). To limit effects of stand age legacy, each simulation was initiated setting stands at age zero. Since we assumed independence between stand ages and burning vulnerability, we considered that setting the landscape at age zero did not affect the effective fire size distribution, burned area dispersion, or long-term stand age structure. Finally, we used the past 1,000 years to characterize the historical variability in the proportion of late-seral forest stands.

The model operated in a two-step procedure. First, based on the simulated territory size (extent, see above), and on the fire cycle (100–500 years) simulated during the run, the number of fire events by year was randomly chosen from a Poisson distribution (Baker et al. 1991; Boychuk et al. 1997; Wimberly et al. 2000) where the annual average fire occurrence is given by:

Fire occurrence = extent (ha)/mean fire size (ha) × fire cycle (yr).

Second, the size of each fire event was randomly selected from a negative exponential distribution based on the mean fire size. Although other distributions could potentially fit the empirical fire size distribution (e.g. lognormal), the negative exponential was preferred because it is largely accepted in the boreal forest and has been recently used elsewhere (Baker et al. 1991; Boychuk et al. 1997; Wimberly et al. 2000; Bergeron et al. 2002; Belleau et al. 2007), and it only required a single parameter to estimate. Given that natural regeneration of most of the forest mosaic in the eastern boreal forest was linked to fires that exceed 1,000 ha (Bergeron et al. 2002), simulations were run on fires >1,000 ha with mean fire size ranging from 3,000 to 15,000 ha (see Bergeron et al. 2004a). Based on Van Wagner's (1978) assumption that stands burn independently of their age, ignition locations of fires were randomly chosen over the entire grid (whole territory). Once initiated, a modeled fire randomly spreads to one or two of the eight neighboring cells that have not burnt during the event time step. A fire will spread until the chosen fire event size is reached. The shape of the fire was not directly controlled, but the alternate spreading to one or two cells of the neighbors avoids the creation of a circular shape. Compared with empirical data, simulated fire shapes were realistic. Finally, simulations were conducted for severe stand-replacing fires. We recognize that this is an oversimplification of fire effects on vegetation given the variation in severity of wildfires both between and within fire events (Bergeron et al. 2002, 2004a). Hence, our model may underestimate the proportion of late-seral forest cover for the different fire regimes simulated.

Table 7.1. *Fire regime characteristics of representative regions of the eastern Canadian boreal forest that were used for simulations of variability in the fire cycle*
Depending on the study region, fire history was conducted for different time periods ranging from 1740 to 1998.

Region	Source	Study area (km²)	Mean fire size[a] (ha)	Fire cycle
North-eastern Ontario	Lefort *et al.* (2003)	8,245	1,224	172
North-western Québec, coniferous portion	Bergeron *et al.* (2001, 2004a)	7,500	17,567	135
North-western Québec, mixedwood portion	Bergeron *et al.* (2001, 2004a)	7,500	969	111
Central Québec[b]	Lesieur *et al.* (2002)	3,844	—	123
Southern Labrador	Foster (1983)	48,500	20,289	500

[a] Mean fire sizes were estimated from the Canadian large fire database or from the provincial database when available (Québec). Fires < 200 ha were not included in the computations.

[b] Evaluation of mean fire size was not possible in this region owing to the limited number of fire events in the past 80 years.

boreal forest. Simulation models were parameterized by using not only fire history reconstructions conducted in our study area but all empirical fire event published data available for eastern Canada, so as to have a wider array of fire regimes to simulate (Table 7.1).

Simulation results indicate that the mean amount of late-seral forests varied from a low of 37% to a high of 75% as fire risk decreased from 100 year fire cycles to cycles of over 400 years (Fig. 7.5). The temporal variation (such as described by standard deviation (SD) upper and lower bounds for simulation runs of 1,000 years) in the mean proportion of late-seral forests was highly similar across fire cycles, with a slightly wider variation in long fire cycles (>250 years). Overall, this curve and its range of variation provides benchmarks for setting management target zones of the amount of late-seral forests at the FMU level with respect to a region's fire cycle. For instance, in our study area for an estimated fire cycle of 139 years (Bergeron *et al.* 2001), the amount of forests older than 100 years to be maintained should be between 39% and 54% (Fig. 7.5). This becomes our NDBM management target for the maintenance of late-seral forests at the scale of an FMU.

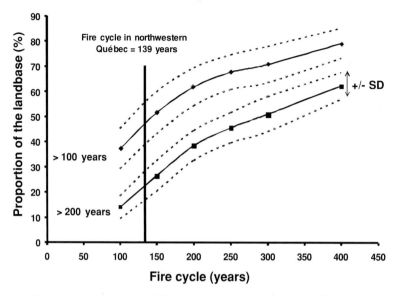

Figure 7.5. Simulated variability in the mean proportions (%) of late-seral forests (>100 years) for a gradient of fire cycles ranging from 100 to 500 years.

RESPONSE OF ORGANISMS TO THE AMOUNT OF LATE-SERAL FOREST

The rationale that management favoring composition and structure of the forest cover within the range of natural ecosystems should maintain biodiversity and essential ecological functions needs to be challenged (Franklin 1993; Hunter 1999). The direct response of organisms to these landscape patterns, particularly species that are associated with habitats of concern such as late-seral forests, is one way to assess the efficiency of natural disturbance-based targets in maintaining species in managed forests. Using a multiple-species approach centered on specific threats such as loss or fragmentation of habitat to make such assessments may enhance the value of the exercise (Block et al. 1995; Lambeck 1997), particularly if they show threshold responses (Imbeau et al. 2001; Radford et al. 2005; Guénette and Villard 2005; Chapter 8, this volume). Here, we examine the efficiency of the proportion of late-seral forests based on natural disturbances (NDBM targets) in providing adequate conditions for bird species associated with these habitats in our study area. This is done by superimposing the NDBM target zone defined in Fig. 7.5 to individual species' response curves to changes in the amount of older forests at the landscape scale in north-western Québec (Box 7.2). Our intent is not to set conservation targets

Box 7.2   Forest bird response to reduction in older forest cover

Data were obtained from an ongoing research program on bird response to habitat loss and fragmentation in north-western Québec, within the 15,000 km² area where fire regimes where determined (see Bergeron *et al.* 2004a). Forest birds were surveyed in 1,239 sampling stations in both upland and lowland sites along the successional gradient of seral stages that ranges from early post-fire or post-harvest stands to old-growth stands (>200 years). Prior knowledge of fire history reconstruction (Bergeron 1991; Bergeron *et al.* 2001, 2004b) facilitated the stratification of our sampling scheme. Censuses were conducted by using fixed-radius (100 m) point counts from early June to early July for 15 or 20 min; each count point was visited twice during the breeding season (see Drapeau *et al.* 2000, 2003 for more details on methods).

   To measure the rate of old forest occupancy by single bird species we used a subset of 360 count points surveyed in late-seral forest stands (>100 years) sampled in landscapes of post-fire origin that range from one year after fire to 290 years. Late-seral forest habitat surrounding these count points within a 1 km radius ranged from 3% to 95%. Along this gradient in the amount of late-seral forests we used a moving window procedure to compute the proportion of count points where a given species was present for a fixed range of 20% forest cover values (±10% from the median value) along our gradient. Computations were done for each 1% increment by moving the window iteratively along the habitat amount gradient. Results were then plotted and adjusted by using polynomial regression models. All computations were conducted on an Excel spreadsheet. Here, we represent unadjusted computed rates of occupancy for Swainson's thrush (*Catharus ustulatus*) and its fitted moving average curve in the boreal mixedwood portion of our study area.

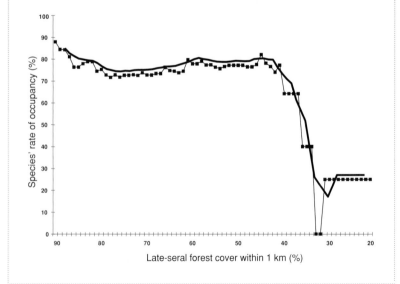

from these species but rather to determine how ecosystem-based targets of late-seral forests can support populations at levels that do not compromise their persistence if applied in a managed landbase. The shape of species' response curves (point type, zone-type threshold, or no threshold, *sensu* Huggett 2005) can provide warning signals as to how organisms are likely or not to persist when forest management exceeds the natural range of variation for a given forest cover type.

Previous work in this portion of the boreal forest provided baseline information on species associations with forest cover types (Imbeau *et al.* 1999, 2001, 2003; Drapeau *et al.* 2000, 2002, 2003). These studies have shown that late-seral forest habitats do not harbor unique bird species but that many forest species reach their abundance peak in these cover types (Schieck *et al.* 1995; Imbeau *et al.* 1999). Using an approach that ranks species according to their sensitivity to different threats, Imbeau *et al.* (2001) compared Fenno-Scandian boreal forests with boreal forests of eastern North America. They found that species most at threat were mainly composed of residents in both regions and that many of them were associated with deadwood. Among the most highly sensitive species with regards to habitat alteration of late-seral stages induced by forest management we find boreal woodpeckers, nuthatches, creepers, and chickadees (Imbeau *et al.* 2001). In our studies, brown creeper (*Certhia americana*), red-breasted nuthatch (*Sitta canadensis*), and, at much lower abundance, the American three-toed woopecker (*Picoides dorsalis*) were also associated with older forest types (Drapeau *et al.* 2002, 2003). Migratory species such as Swainson's thrush (*Catharus ustulatus*), ovenbird (*Seiurus aurocapilla*), and golden-crown kinglet (*Regulus satrapa*) were also strongly associated with late-seral stands (>100 years) in either mixedwood or black spruce forest cover types (Drapeau *et al.* 2000, 2003).

Figure 7.6 depicts three types of habitat occupancy pattern that characterize species sensitive to loss of late-seral cover types in boreal forests of north-western Québec, Canada. The shape of fitted (moving average) response curves varies from a sharp point-type threshold (*sensu* Huggett 2005) for Swainson's thrush to a zone-type threshold (Huggett 2005) for the ovenbird, and a gradual decline (no threshold) across most of the habitat amount gradient for the brown creeper (Fig. 7.6). Clearly, even though numerous late-seral bird species are sensitive to the reduction in amount of older forest in the landscape, not all species respond in a point-type threshold fashion. However, species such as Swainson's thrush that do show a sharp threshold response are likely to represent key monitors for detection of shifts in forest conditions that can compromise species persistence

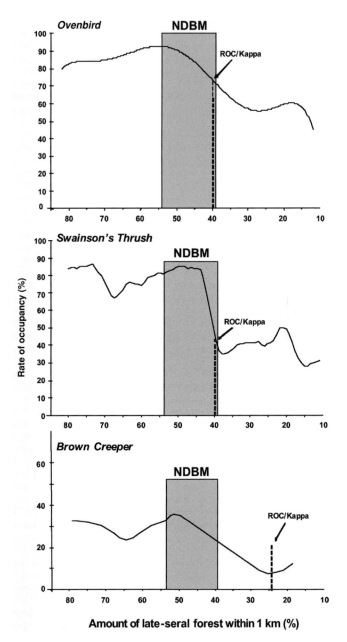

Figure 7.6. Rate of occupancy curves of three species sensitive to loss of older forests in natural boreal landscapes of north-western Québec, Canada. Gray shaded areas represent the natural disturbance-based management target zone (39%–54%) of forests older than 100 years for the fire cycle (139 years) of the study area. Dashed lines indicate ROC (receiver-operating characteristic) and Kappa analyses cut-off values of older forest where species' probability of presence is significantly affected.

at the FMU level. Knowledge of the shape of species' responses to habitat loss is thus informative for understanding and managing the tradeoffs between socially and economically acceptable timber yield and biodiversity conservation (see also Radford *et al.* 2005).

Overlays of the NDBM target zone for our study area on species curves provide a direct measure of how effective management of late-seral forest structure and composition at the scale of FMUs could be for late-seral forest birds (Fig. 7.6). The high rates of habitat occupancy of species within the NDBM target zone is suggestive that large populations of these species could be maintained in such a management scheme since rates of occupancy are correlated with population size (Blondel *et al.* 1981; Bibby *et al.* 1992; Gibbons *et al.* 1993). However, the rate of occupancy of all species becomes weak (indicating smaller population size) when the neighboring amount of older forests falls under 30%, a value that has often been identified as an ecological threshold below which population persistence is jeopardized (Andrén 1994; Andrén *et al.* 1997; Fahrig 1998; Jansson and Angelstam 1999; Radford and Bennett 2004; Radford *et al.* 2005). Maintaining across several thousands of square kilometers (FMU level) a proportion of the landscape under a forest cover that has structural and compositional attributes of late-seral forests thus offers a promising perspective from the standpoint of forest bird conservation.

Finally, cut-off values (dotted lines) are presented for the amount of late-seral forest under which the probability of predicting the presence of individual species is optimized (Fig. 7.6). These values are derived from logistic regression models of individual species' presence–absence in response to late-seral forest cover using receiver-operating characteristic (ROC) analysis (Manel *et al.* 2001) and Cohen's Kappa statistic (Fielding and Bell 1997). These quantitative approaches determine cut-off values at which the contrast between presence and absence is highest, thus providing a quantitative measure of the breakpoint at which discrimination between presence and absence is at its best for a given explanatory variable (in our case amount of older forest habitat). Beyond that point prediction of species occurrence becomes more risky. Guénette and Villard (2005) recently used ROC analysis to detect habitat alteration thresholds in bird species occurrence patterns in hemiboreal forest landscapes of New Brunswick, Canada. For each of the three species in Fig. 7.6, cut-off values derived from either ROC or Cohen's Kappa statistic were similar. The amount of late-seral forest habitat at which the contrast between presence and absence was highest differed, however, among species. These values were within the lower limit of the NDBM target zone for Swainson's thrush and ovenbird (Fig. 7.6).

The brown creeper cut-off value was far from the NDBM target zone given the gradual shape of its response to older forest habitat reduction (Fig. 7.6). Species that show a steep decline in population size, such as Swainson's thrush, for which the rate of occupancy is reduced by 50% compared with the rate detected within the NDBM target zone, the prediction of species occurrence becomes difficult.

ECOLOGICAL THRESHOLDS AND MANAGEMENT TARGETS

In recent years the concept of ecological thresholds has gained interest both in theoretical ecology (With and Crist 1995; Fahrig 1998, 2001, 2002) and in resource management and conservation planning (Mönkkönen and Reunanen 1999; Rempel et al. 2004; Guénette and Villard 2005; Huggett 2005; Lindenmayer and Luck 2005; Ranius and Fahrig 2006). The idea that abrupt changes in organisms abundance or occupancy response to habitat alteration could provide targets at which forest management should aim is appealing for resources managers. However, as noted by Radford et al. (2005) setting conservation targets within managed landscapes at the level of these ecological thresholds is risky given that they often represent points of instability for which primary demographic processes (mortality, productivity, birth) may be altered before species reach these thresholds. Lindenmayer et al. (2005) criticized the threshold concept on the grounds of its limited application in landscape management due to the high variability in responses of individual species to habitat alteration and the fact that for several species responses were more in the form of a gradient than a sharp breakpoint. In this chapter, management targets can rely on knowledge of both the natural dynamics of the forest and multiple-species response patterns to changes in native late-seral forest cover. Whereas our management targets are not necessarily based on ecological threshold relationships, some species can respond to loss of late-seral forests in a threshold fashion. The NDBM target zone was consistently above the level at which rates of occupancy of species decline, suggesting that managing FMUs within the historical range of late-seral forest conditions is likely to maintain populations of associated species. The lower limit of the NDBM target zone was, however, within single species ecological threshold responses both for species that show a sharp decline in rate of occupancy and for species that have a zone-type decline. Hence, maintaining the amount of late-seral forest at this lower limit increases the risk of affecting those demanding species. We thus reiterate that ecological thresholds should be viewed as unacceptable levels of habitat alteration, rather then being used as maximum levels of habitat retention in managed areas (Lindenmayer and Luck 2005; Radford *et al.* 2005; Ranius and Fahrig 2006). Setting management or conservation targets at the level of such thresholds is likely to further generate a collapse in species populations. Ecological thresholds should thus be viewed as warning signals instead of management targets to be implemented.

LINKAGES BETWEEN ECOSYSTEM AND SPECIES-BASED MANAGEMENT APPROACHES

Ecosystem and species-based management approaches have respectively been defined as coarse-filter and fine-filter management strategies (*sensu* Hunter 1990). They are often presented as complementary on the basis that maintenance of habitat conditions will first adequately maintain the majority of species and functions without the need for species-specific guidelines whereas in a second step additional management considerations will be developed for species that are not covered by coarse filters. With this perspective, these approaches are at best sequential and do not assume a feedback on one another. Moreover, whereas it is often said that fine filters are used for species whose habitat requirements are not met by coarse-filter strategies, we consider that species-specific management approaches have rarely resulted from a preliminary evaluation of coarse-filter adequacy but are rather independent initiatives given their traditional use in wildlife management (Block *et al.* 1995). Here, we argue that the simultaneous determination of a NDBM target zone (coarse-filter) and multiple-species response curves to habitat alteration of late-seral forests (fine-filters) provide a more direct interaction between these approaches. First, it allows evaluation of the efficiency of ecosystem-based planned forest conditions (late-seral stages) in maintaining populations of sensitive species at levels that are potentially adequate for long-term viability. Second, instead of providing single conservation targets, our approach supplies an array of targets (NDBM, ROC and Kappa cut-offs, shapes of individual species response curves) that may be viewed as a set of warning signals that are of different significance for species population's sensitivity but that enable managers to assess over a wider range of information the risks and tradeoffs between economic and species maintenance in managed landscapes. Third, using both approaches simultaneously attenuates recent criticism of the value of species-based biodiversity surrogate schemes for science-based conservation planning and management of forest ecosystems (Caro and O'Doherty 1999; Roberge and Angelstam 2004; Huggett 2005;

Lindenmayer *et al.* 2005). The use of multiple species downsizes this problem given that species are examined individually but patterns are determined for more than one species at a time, providing a broader spectrum of responses that increases our ability to pinpoint the most sensitive species for which we need to monitor more closely.

Throughout this chapter we used songbirds as a focal group for our multiple species-level approach. In the boreal forest, habitat requirements of other taxonomic groups ranging from epiphytic lichens (Esseen and Renhorn 1998; Rheault *et al.* 2003) to saproxylic insects (Martikainen 2001; Saint-Germain *et al.* 2007a) or to large ungulates like woodland caribou (Schaefer 2003; Courtois *et al.* 2004) could be used as a means to guide forest management with regards to conservation of biodiversity. Moreover, these species or groups of species could be used along a hierarchy of scales (tree, stand, forest mosaic, forest landscape). They should be selected on the basis of their sensitivity to the main threats (discussed above) of current even-aged forest management but also with regard to how knowledge of their habitat requirements can be used to develop specific forest conditions to be preserved when conducting landscape planning for biodiversity conservation. Focus on the most demanding species may be a strategic approach in such conservation planning (Lambeck 1997; Ranius and Fahrig 2006).

IMPLEMENTING FOREST MANAGEMENT SYSTEMS TO MAINTAIN LATE-SERAL SPECIES DIVERSITY

The alteration in the supply of late-seral stages and their related habitat features across currently managed forest landscapes has led the scientific community to propose alternatives to current even-aged management that are based on natural disturbance dynamics (Attiwill 1994; Bergeron and Harvey 1997; Angelstam 1998; De Long 2002). Use of rotations of variable length in proportions similar to those observed in the natural fire regime is a possible alternative (Burton *et al.* 1999; Seymour and Hunter 1999) to maintain late-seral forests. However, the approach may be applicable only in ecosystems where tree species are long-lived and can thus support longer rotations. In boreal forests composed of relatively short-lived tree species this approach is likely to lead to fiber loss and a decrease in allowable cut. Alternatively, Bergeron *et al.* (1999) suggested varying silvicultural practices in managed landscapes to maintain structural and compositional attributes of all age-classes present in naturally disturbed forest landscapes including late-seral stages. It would thus be possible to treat a given proportion of the landbase by clearcutting followed by seeding or planting incorporating, however, more permanent retention (*sensu* Franklin *et al.* 2002) of unharvested patches and clumps of live and dead trees within cutover agglomerations (an adapted even-aged system with biological legacies). Another proportion of the forest cover would be managed with an uneven-aged system with partial cuts and selection cuts which approach the natural development and irregular structure of late-seral stands, including small canopy openings that could resemble gap replacement disturbances such as windthrow and insect outbreaks (see Belle-Isle and Kneeshaw 2007).

Gauthier *et al.* (2004) illustrate the development and initial implementation of a natural disturbance-based management approach that relies on diversification of silvicultural practices in a pilot study conducted in the black spruce–feathermoss ecoregion (Saucier *et al.* 1998) of north-western Québec. The management strategy used relies on both an even-aged system with clearcutting to initiate stand regeneration in one portion of the landbase and an uneven-aged system that uses partial harvesting techniques (partial cutting or selective cutting) to maintain or establish the structural and compositional characteristics of late-seral stages. Based on natural disturbance knowledge, they defined (1) landscape-level objectives for the proportion of the landbase to be treated by each forest management system, (2) patterns of harvesting that define the spatial and temporal distribution of harvesting activities, and (3) silvicultural guides that will be used by forest managers to establish the appropriate silvicultural prescription for a given stand. Finally, they compared the natural disturbance-based approach with a conventional even-aged management system used across the entire landbase and found that the annual allowable cut is only slightly affected, indicating that in boreal regions such an approach could maintain habitat diversity with low economic compromises with regard to merchantable volumes. Gauthier *et al.* (2004) specify that the proportion of stands submitted to each of these treatments will vary depending on the natural disturbance cycle and maximum harvest age and thus should not be uniform from one region to another across the boreal forest.

Maintaining a high proportion of late-seral forests at the FMU level such as suggested by our NDBM targets will require implementing uneven-aged management (partial cutting practices) over large portions of FMUs (McComb *et al.* 1993; Franklin *et al.* 2002; Bergeron 2004; Bergeron *et al.* 1999, 2002, 2004b). Moreover, such practices should aim at maintaining compositional and structural biological legacies (*sensu* Franklin *et al.* 2000) of late-seral forests. Levels of timber removal and correspondingly forest retention (in terms of both quantity and quality of structural and compositional attributes) can be determined through benchmark information from late-seral forest structure and compositional patterns (Franklin *et al.* 2002; Harper *et al.* 2003, 2005; Gauthier *et al.* 2004). This first step in landscape planning should, however, be followed by a refinement of management targets of these attributes using late-seral species habitat requirements. For instance, epiphytic lichens are sensitive to microclimatic conditions (increased solar radiation, higher wind velocity, and lower air humidity) that occur at or near canopy openings in the forest cover. The level of forest cover removal and its spatial distribution in partial cuts could affect the composition and abundance of epiphytic lichen communities through reduced dispersal of propagules of individual species (Dettki *et al.* 2000; Sillett *et al.* 2000). Hence, knowledge of these organisms' critical distance for dispersal could refine the spatial pattern of tree retention to be set at the stand level. Recent studies on the responses of late-seral species to partial cutting at different levels of timber removal are also likely to provide baseline information on appropriate levels of canopy removal for maintenance of late-seral species (Chambers *et al.* 1999; Simon *et al.* 2000; Leupin *et al.* 2004; Guénette and Villard 2005; Harrison *et al.* 2005). These studies have, however, mainly been conducted on species that are sensitive to the "green" tree component of stands. Deadwood associates and their response to partial cutting have received far less attention (but see Jonsson *et al.* 2005 for a review) even though deadwood is a key habitat attribute for a wide range of species associated with late-seral forests including saproxylic insects, fungi, birds, and mammals that use cavities (Harmon *et al.* 1986; Martin and Eadie 1999; Grove 2002; Saint-Germain *et al.* 2007b). Species-oriented research on habitat requirements of these organisms within the context of partial cuts is thus greatly needed to produce a more integrated set of management guidelines for organisms associated with live and dead trees. Approaches such as the one developed by Guénette and Villard (2005) for setting stand-level quantitative targets for structural features to be maintained within retained patches should be helpful in this regard.

Because natural disturbance regimes in boreal forests generate large-scale fragmentation of the forest cover, natural disturbance-based management will continue to rely in part on even-aged management (Bergeron *et al.* 2002; Gauthier *et al.* 2004). Spatial patterning of cutover areas and intervening forest tracts (late-seral forests) in the landbase is thus also critical for maintaining adequate forest conditions for biodiversity, particularly since persistence in the fragmented portions of the landscape often relies on multiple populations and their capacity to interact (Opdam 1991; Hanski *et al.* 1996; Bennett 2003). Knowledge of the size, shape, and spatial arrangement of green forest patches left within wildfires can provide ecosystem-based guidelines for the design of remnant forests in even-aged managed forests (Kafka *et al.* 2001; Perron 2003). In a study of habitat type distribution in a wildfire in north-western Québec, Kafka *et al.* (2001) provide detailed information on the spatial configuration of retention areas and found that unburned patches averaged 52 ha in size and were frequently surrounded by lightly burned zones, suggesting a high degree of connectivity between the burned matrix and unburned vegetation.

The other source of information for providing management guidelines for late-seral habitat retention in cutover areas should come from species' responses to the availability of remnant habitats in recently burned landscapes (Schieck and Hobson 2000; Morissette *et al.* 2002; Hannon and Drapeau 2005). In naturally disturbed landscapes it is assumed that forest-dependent species are tolerant of these landscape-scale changes (Niemi *et al.* 1998; Drapeau *et al.* 2000; Schmiegelow and Mönkkönen 2002). Regional populations may vary with the amount of available habitat and become abundant in areas where forest conditions are dominant but more limited in areas characterized by recent burns. Comparisons between organisms' responses to habitat alteration induced by logging and by wildfires could also provide key information on species' sensitivity to natural fragmentation of late-seral forest habitat vs. human-induced fragmentation. Management targets could thus be based on the tolerance of organisms to forest removal following both natural and human-induced disturbances, allowing a measure of the capacity of remnant habitats to achieve sustainable landscape functions (refuges, dispersal channels, or both for late-seral species) in fragmented landscapes that are part of FMUs. For instance, response patterns of late-seral bird species to distance from unharvested large tracts (Kouki and Väänänen 2000; Leboeuf 2004) could provide management guidelines for the critical isolation of remnant habitats at which these species are likely to persist during the regeneration of the forest matrix. This should mitigate the cumulative negative impacts on biodiversity (Kouki and Väänänen 2000; Smith *et al.* 2001) that often result from current forest management where the spatial extent of harvested areas (Fig. 7.3) is in excess of the range of natural forest fragmentation.

Habitat loss of late-seral forest through harvesting can also lead to habitat degradation, whereas remnant habitats are often those that are left aside once more productive sites are exploited (Scott *et al.* 2001). Indeed, structural and compositional elements can be lost or at least become much less variable in habitat remnants of cutover areas (Angelstam 1996; Mascaruá Lopéz *et al.* 2006; Vaillancourt 2007). Consequently, retention of forest patches within even-aged managed areas must also incorporate in the planning process structural elements that make up the biological legacies (*sensu* Franklin *et al.* 2000, 2002) that Hunter (2005) recently described as mesofilters. Deadwood (in terms of both volume and variety of decay stages) is among those key elements that may likely upgrade the quality of remnant habitats for biodiversity conservation in managed forest landscapes (Jonsson *et al.* 2005; Ranius and Fahrig 2006). Here again, species-oriented approaches are likely to provide direct knowledge of habitat associations for many wood-dependent species (Saint-Germain *et al.* 2007b).

For boreal regions that have not been harvested or that are in the early stage of harvesting natural forests (the northern portion of Canada and some regions in Russia), a management framework based on knowledge of both ecosystem and species' responses to natural disturbances can be implemented, provided there is adequate scientific knowledge. Such regions are, however, becoming rare as second-growth forest landscapes gain in overall importance throughout boreal environments (Yaroshenko *et al.* 2001; Lee *et al.* 2003). For landscapes that result from a first timber rotation, natural disturbance-based management targets could be set forth in the next harvesting round in order to move the managed landscape towards desired future conditions that are within the historical range of the forest (Nonaka and Spies 2005). In current managed landscapes, which are often out of bound as for the amount of habitats of concern, relying on NDBM targets is difficult, and knowledge of species' responses to changes in sensitive habitats becomes critical for providing managers and planners with guidelines to biodiversity conservation in these altered systems. Finally, forest conditions projected by NDBM may not be reached entirely, owing to constraints imposed by social and economical considerations linked with timber production. The NDBM management scheme may thus be partly implemented, i.e. implemented at levels below those initially proposed. Here again multi-species approaches based on the response functions of organisms to habitat alteration (Lambeck 1997; Imbeau *et al.* 2001) become critical for evaluating how far management targets are from species' critical habitat requirements that may compromise their persistence.

CONCLUSION

An important finding from our current knowledge of natural disturbance regimes in the eastern Canadian boreal forest is that forest cover older than the current timber harvesting rotation age (>100 years) was not historically a marginal but rather a dominant component of the landbase (Bergeron *et al.* 2006). Hence, even though organisms may be adapted to varying habitat loss and fragmentation in time and space through large-scale natural disturbances, the systematic shift in the proportion of early vs. late-seral forests that even-aged management has generated in the past decades throughout the eastern boreal forest of North America (Bergeron *et al.* 2002; Harper *et al.* 2002) raises concerns about the capacity of such conventional forestry to maintain biodiversity in managed landscapes. The resulting loss and fragmentation of late-seral forests may exert a pressure on biodiversity that is above its tolerance under natural disturbance regimes. It is thus important to implement at the regional scale retention strategies within FMUs that reduce the gap between current even-aged harvested landscapes and naturally disturbed landscapes both within (late-seral forest patches) and between (late-seral forest tracts) cutover areas. This should be a high priority for resource managers and conservation planners, given the rate at which natural forests are converted to cutover landscapes in the boreal forest throughout Canada (Lee *et al.* 2003).

Setting management targets for the conservation of biodiversity will require that an integrated strategy be set where the proportion of the landbase to be maintained in late-seral forest cover types and the spatial patterning of harvest for both clearcuts and partial cuts are viewed as complementary elements. This calls for more synergies between species and ecosystem-oriented approaches. In this chapter, we have illustrated how multi-species responses to changes in surrounding late-seral forest cover can assess the effectiveness of our NDBM target zone in maintaining species of concern. Within this perspective, ecosystem knowledge sets forest conditions and species become evaluative indicators (Kneeshaw *et al.* 2000; Rempel *et al.* 2004) that test the management approach. The complementarities between species and ecosystem approaches may, however, evolve one step further if knowledge of species' habitat requirements (seral stage, stand-level structural attributes, patch size, or connectedness) is used to set forest conditions in combination with those patterned by natural disturbances. In an adaptive management context, guidelines developed from natural disturbance regimes (NDBM targets) could benefit from a more in-depth understanding of species–habitat relationships.

Finally, improving the capacity of the managed matrix to maintain biodiversity is likely to consolidate protected areas, particularly if they are integrated into a larger regional planning framework (Gaston *et al.* 2002; Noss *et al.* 2002). Spatial patterns of harvesting could be designed within the managed matrix to provide linkages in the landscape between protected areas (Bennett 2003). Likewise, managed forest landscapes that result from strategies aimed at maintaining stand and landscape compositions and structures similar to those that characterize natural ecosystems require benchmarks such as protected areas to assess their effectiveness in achieving conservation of biological diversity.

ACKNOWLEDGEMENTS

This contribution was supported by grants from the Sustainable Forest Management Network of Centres of Excellence (SFMN), the Natural Science and Engineering Research Council of Canada (NSERC), le Fonds Québecois de la recherche sur la nature et la technologie (FQRNT), and la chaire industrielle CRSNG UQAT-UQAM en aménagement forestier durable à P. Drapeau, Y. Bergeron, and A. Leduc. We thank S. Gauthier, M. Flannigan, P. Lefort, V. Kafka, M. Leboeuf, L. Imbeau, A. Nappi, and D. Kneeshaw, who discussed with us many of the ideas presented in this chapter. We thank all colleagues and graduate students who have worked on the different projects related to this chapter. Finally, we thank the two anonymous reviewers who provided insightful comments and greatly improved the final version of this chapter.

References

Attiwill, P. M. 1994. The disturbance of forest ecosystems: the ecological basis for conservative management. *Forest Ecology and Management* 63:247–300.

Andrén, H. 1994. Effects of forest fragmentation on birds and mammals in landscapes with different proportions of suitable habitat: a review. *Oikos* 71:355–66.

Andrén, H., A. Delin and A. Seiler. 1997. Population response to landscape changes depends on specialization to different landscape elements. *Oikos* 80:193–6.

Angelstam, P. 1996. The ghost of forest past – natural disturbance ergimes as a basis for reconstruction for biologically diverse forests in Europe. Pp. 287–337 in R. M. DeGraaf and R. I. Miller (eds.) *Conservation of Faunal Diversity in Forested Landscapes.* London: Chapman and Hall.

Angelstam, P. 1998. Maintaining and restoring biodiversity in European boreal forests by developing natural disturbance regimes. *Journal of Vegetation Science* 9:593–602.

Baker, W. L. 1995. Long term response of disturbance landscapes to human intervention and global change. *Landscape Ecology* 10:143–59.

Baker, W. L., S. L. Egbert and G. F. Frazier. 1991. A spatial model for studying the effects of climatic change on the structure of landscapes subject to large disturbances. *Ecological Modeling* 56:109–25.

Bart, J. 1995. Amount of suitable habitat and viability of northern spotted owls. *Conservation Biology* 9:943–6.

Belleau, A., Y. Bergeron, A. Leduc, S. Gauthier and A. Fall. 2007. Using spatially explicit simulations to explore size distribution and spacing of regenerating areas produced by wildfires: recommendations for designing harvest agglomerations for the Canadian boreal forest. *Forestry Chronicle* **83**:72–83.

Belle-Isle, J. and D. Kneeshaw. 2007. A stand and landscape comparison of the effects of a spruce budworm (*Chrositoneura fumiferana* (Clem.)) outbreak to the combined effects of harvesting and thinning on forest structure. *Forest Ecology and Management* **246**:163–74.

Bennett, A. F. 2003. *Linkages in the Landscape: The Role of Corridors and Connectivity in Wildlife Conservation*. Gland, Switzerland: IUCN.

Bergeron, Y. 1991. The influence of island and mainland lakeshore landscapes on boreal forest fire regimes. *Ecology* **72**:1980–92.

Bergeron, Y. 2000. Species and stand dynamics in the mixed woods of Quebec's southern boreal forest. *Ecology* **81**:1500–16.

Bergeron, Y. 2004. Is regulated even-aged management the right strategy for the Canadian boreal forest? *Forestry Chronicle* **80**:458–62.

Bergeron, Y. and M. Dubuc. 1989. Succession in the southern part of the Canadian boreal forest. *Vegetatio* **79**:51–63.

Bergeron, Y. and B. Harvey. 1997. Basing silviculture on natural ecosystem dynamics: an approach applied to the southern boreal mixedwood forest of Quebec. *Forest Ecology and Management* **92**:235–42.

Bergeron, Y., B. Harvey, A. Leduc and S. Gauthier. 1999. Forest management guidelines based on natural disturbance dynamics: stand- and forest-level considerations. *Forestry Chronicle* **75**:49–54.

Bergeron, Y., S. Gauthier, V. Kafka, P. Lefort and D. Lesieur. 2001. Natural fire frequency for the eastern Canadian boreal forest: consequences for sustainable forestry. *Canadian Journal of Forest Research* **31**:384–91.

Bergeron, Y., S. Gauthier, A. Leduc and B. Harvey. 2002. Natural fire regime: a guide for sustainable management of the Canadian boreal forest. *Silva Fennica* **36**:81–95.

Bergeron, Y., S. Gauthier, M. Flannigan and V. Kafka. 2004a. Fire regimes at the transition between mixedwood and coniferous boreal forest in northwestern Québec. *Ecology* **85**:1916–32.

Bergeron, Y., M. Flannigan, S. Gauthier, A. Leduc and P. Lefort. 2004b. Past, current and future fire frequency in the Canadian boreal forest: implications for sustainable forest management. *Ambio* **33**:356–60.

Bergeron, Y., D. Cyr, C. R. Drever *et al.* 2006. Past, current, and future fire frequencies in Québec's commercial forests: implications for the cumulative effects of harvesting and fire on age-class structure and natural disturbance-based management. *Canadian Journal of Forest Research* **36**:2737–44.

Bibby, C. J., N. D. Burgess and D. A. Hill. 1992. *Bird Census Techniques*. San Diego, CA: Academic Press.

Block, W. M., D. M. Finch and L. A. Brennan. 1995. Single species vs. multiple species approaches for management. Pp. 461–76 in T. E. Martin and D. M. Finch (eds.) *Ecology and Management of Neotropical Migratory Birds: A Synthesis and Review of Critical Issues*. New York, NY: Oxford University Press.

Blondel, J., C. Ferry and B. Frochot. 1981. Point counts with unlimited distance. *Studies in Avian Biology* 6:414–20.

Boychuk, D., A. H. Perera, M. T. Ter-Mikaelian, D. L. Martell and C. Li. 1997. Modelling the effect of spatial scale and correlated fire disturbances on forest age distribution. *Ecological Modeling* 95:145–64.

Bunnell, F. 1995. Forest-dwelling vertebrate faunas and natural fire regimes in British Columbia: patterns and implications for conservation. *Conservation Biology* 9:636–44.

Burton, P. J., D. D Kneeshaw and K. D. Coates. 1999. Managing forest harvesting to maintain old growth in boreal and sub-boreal forests. *Forestry Chronicle* 75:623–31.

Carcaillet, C., Y. Bergeron, P. J. H. Richard *et al.* 2001. Change of fire frequency in the eastern Canadian boreal forests during the Holocene: does vegetation composition or climate trigger the fire regime? *Journal of Ecology* 89:930–46.

Caro, T. M. 2003. Umbrella species: critique and lessons form East Africa. *Animal Conservation* 6:171–81.

Caro, T. M. and G. O'Doherty. 1999. On the use of surrogate species in conservation biology. *Conservation Biology* 13:805–14.

Chambers, C. L., W. C. McComb and J. C. I. Tappeiner III. 1999. Breeding bird responses to three sylvicultural treatments on the Oregon Coast Range. *Ecological Applications* 9:171–85.

Courtois, R., J.-P. Ouellet, C. Dussault and A. Gingras. 2004. Forest management guidelines for forest-dwelling caribou in Québec. *Forestry Chronicle* 80: 601–7.

Boersma, P. D. and J. K. Parrish. 1999. Limiting abuse : marine protected areas, a limited solution. *Ecological Economics* 31:287–304.

De Long, S. C. 2002. Using nature's template to best advantage in the Canadian boreal forest. *Silva Fennica* 36:401–8.

De Long, S. C. and D. Tanner. 1996. Managing the pattern of forest harvest: lessons from wildfire. *Biodiversity and Conservation* 5:1191–205.

Dettki, H., P. Klintberg and P.-A. Esseen. 2000. Are epiphytic lichens in young forests limited by local dispersal? *Ecoscience* 7:317–25.

Drapeau, P., A. Leduc, J.-F. Giroux, J.-P. L. Savard, Y. Bergeron and W. L. Vickery. 2000. Landscape-scale disturbances and changes in bird communities of boreal mixed-wood forests. *Ecological Monographs* 70:423–44.

Drapeau, P., A. Nappi , J.-F. Giroux, A. Leduc and J.-P. Savard. 2002. Distribution patterns of birds associated with snags in natural and managed eastern boreal forests. Pp. 193–205 in W. F. Laudenslayer, P. J. Shea, B. E. Valentine, C. P. Weatherspoon and T. E. Lisle (eds.) 2002. USDA Forest Service General Technical Report PSW-GTR 181. Albany, CA: USDA Forest Service Pacific Southwest Research Station.

Drapeau, P., A. Leduc, Y. Bergeron, S. Gauthier and J.-P. Savard. 2003. Les communautés d'oiseaux des vieilles forêts de la pessière à mousses de la ceinture d'argile: problèmes et solutions face à l'aménagement forestier. *Forestry Chronicle* 79:531–40.

Esseen, P.-A. and K.-E. Renhorn. 1998. Edge effects on an epiphytic lichen in fragmented forests. *Conservation Biology* 12:1307–17.

Fahrig, L. 1998. When does fragmentation of breeding habitat affect population survival? *Ecological Modeling* **105**:273–92.

Fahrig, L. 2001. How much habitat is enough? *Biological Conservation* **100**: 65–74.

Fahrig, L. 2002. Effect of habitat fragmentation on the extinction threshold: a synthesis. *Ecological Applications* **12**:346–53.

Fall, A. and J. Fall. 2001. A domain-specific language for models of landscape dynamics. *Ecological Modeling* **141**:1–18.

Flannigan, M. D. 1993. Fire regime and the abundance of red pine. *International Journal of Wildland Fire* **3**:241–7.

Flannigan, M. D., K. A. Logan, B. D. Amiro, W. R. Skinner and B. J. Stocks. 2005. Future area burned in Canada. *Climatic Change* **72**:1–16.

Fielding, A. H. and J. F. Bell. 1997. A review of methods for the assessment of prediction errors in conservation presence/absence models. *Environmental Conservation* **24**:38–49.

Foster, D. R. 1983. The history and pattern of fire in the boreal forest of southeastern Labrador. *Canadian Journal of Botany* **61**:2459–71.

Franklin, J. 1993. Preserving biodiversity: species, ecosystems or landscapes? *Ecological Applications* **3**:202–5.

Franklin, J. F., D. Lindenmayer, J. A. MacMahon *et al.* 2000. Threads of continuity. *Conservation Biology in Practice* **1**:9–16.

Franklin, J. F., T. A. Spies, R. Van Pelta *et al.* 2002. Disturbances and structural development of natural forest ecosystems with silvicultural implications, using Douglas-fir forests as an example. *Forest Ecology and Management* **155**: 399–423.

Gaston, K. J., R. L. Pressey and C. R. Margules. 2002. Persistence and vulnerability: retaining biodiversity in the landscape and in protected areas. *BioScience* (Suppl. 2) **27**: 361–84.

Gauthier, S., A. Leduc and Y. Bergeron. 1996. Forest dynamics modelling under a natural fire cycle: a tool to define natural mosaic diversity in forest management. *Environmental Monitoring Assessment* **39**:417–34.

Gauthier, S., T. Nguyen, Y. Bergeron *et al.* 2004. Developing forest management strategies based on fire regimes in northwestern Quebec, Canada. Pp. 219–29 in A. H. Perera, L. J. Buse and M. G. Weber (eds.) *Emulating Natural Forest Landscape Disturbances: Concepts and Applications*. New York, NY: Columbia University Press.

Gibbons, D. W., J. B. Reid and R. A. Chapman. 1993. *The New Atlas of Breeding Birds in Britain and Ireland: 1988–1991*. London: T. & A. D. Poyser.

Guénette, J.-S. and M.-A. Villard. 2005. Thresholds in forest bird response to habitat alteration as quantitative targets for conservation. *Conservation Biology* **19**:1168–80.

Grove, S. J. 2002. Saproxylic insect ecology and the sustainable management of forests. *Annual Review of Ecology and Systematics* **33**:1–23.

Hannon, S. J. and P. Drapeau. 2005. Bird responses to burning and logging in the boreal forest of Canada. *Studies in Avian Biology* **30**:97–115.

Hanski, I., A. Moilanen and M. Gyllenberg. 1996. Minimum viable metapopulation size. *American Naturalist* **147**:527–41.

Harmon, M. E., J. F. Franklin, F. J. Swanson *et al.* 1986. Ecology of coarse woody debris in temperate ecosystems. *Advances in Ecological Research* 15:133–302.

Harrison, R. B., F. K. A. Schmiegelow and R. Naidoo. 2005. Stand-level response of breeding forest songbirds to multiple levels of partial-cut harvest in four boreal forest types. *Canadian Journal of Forest Research* 35:1553–67.

Harper, K. A., Y. Bergeron, S. Gauthier and P. Drapeau. 2002. Structural development of black spruce forests following fire in Abitibi, Québec: a landscape scale investigation. *Silva Fennica* 36:249–63.

Harper, K. A., C. Boudreault, L. De Grandpré *et al.* 2003. Structure, composition and diversity of old-growth black spruce boreal forest of the Clay Belt region in Québec and Ontario. *Environmental Review* 11:S79–S98.

Harper, K. A., Y. Bergeron, P. Drapeau, S. Gauthier and L. De Grandpré. 2005. Structural development following fire in black spruce boreal forest. *Forest Ecology and Management* 206:293–306.

Harvey, B. D., A. Leduc, S. Gauthier and Y. Bergeron. 2002. Stand-landscape integration in natural disturbance-based management of the southern boreal forest. *Forest Ecology and Management* 155:369–85.

Huggett, A. J. 2005. The concept and utility of ecological thresholds in biodiversity conservation. *Biological Conservation* 124:301–10.

Hunter, M. L. Jr. 1990. *Wildlife, Forests, and Forestry: Principles of Managing Forests for Biological Diversity.* Englewood Cliffs, NJ: Prentice-Hall.

Hunter, M. L. Jr. 1993. Natural fire regimes as spatial models for managing boreal forests. *Biological Conservation* 65:115–20.

Hunter, M. L. Jr. 1999. *Maintaining Biodiversity in Forest Ecosystems.* Cambridge, UK: Cambridge University Press.

Hunter, M. L. Jr. 2005. A mesofilter conservation strategy to complement fine and coarse filters. *Conservation Biology* 19:1025–9.

Hunter, M. L. Jr., G. L. Jacobson and T. Webb III. 1988. Paleoecology and the coarse filter approach to maintaining biological diversity. *Conservation Biology* 2:375–85.

Imbeau, L., J.-P. L. Savard and R. Gagnon. 1999. Comparing bird assemblages in successional black spruce stands originating from fire and logging. *Canadian Jounal of Zoology* 77:1850–60.

Imbeau, L., M. Mönkkönen and A. Desrochers. 2001. Long-term effects of forestry on birds of the eastern Canadian boreal forests: a comparison with Fennoscandia. *Conservation Biology* 15:1151–62.

Imbeau, L., P. Drapeau and M. Mönkkönen. 2003. Edge species in forest patches within agricultural landscapes: are we confusing response to edges and successional status? *Ecography* 26:514–20.

Janzen, D. H. 1983. No park is an island: increase in interference from outside as park size decreases. *Oikos* 41:402–10.

Jansson, G. and P. Angelstam. 1999. Threshold levels of habitat composition for the presence of the long-tailed tit (*Aegithalos caudatus*) in a boreal landscape. *Landscape Ecology* 14:283–90.

Jardon, Y., H. Morin and P. Dutilleul. 2003. Périodicité et synchronisme des épidémies de la tordeuse des bourgeons de l'épinette au Québec. *Canadian Journal of Forest Research* 33:1947–61.

Johnson, E. A. 1992. *Fire and Vegetation Dynamics: Studies from the North American Boreal Forest.* Cambridge, UK: Cambridge University Press.

Johnson, E. A. and D. R. Wowchuk. 1993. Wildfires in the southern Canadian Rocky Mountains and their relationship to mid-tropospheric anomalies. *Canadian Journal of Forest Research* 23:1213–22.

Johnson, E. A., K. Miyanishi and J. M. H. Weir. 1998. Wildfires in the western Canadian boreal forest: landscape patterns and ecosystem management. *Journal of Vegetation Science* 9:603–10.

Jonsson, B. J., N. Kruys and T. Ranius. 2005. Ecology of species living on dead wood – lessons for dead wood management. *Silva Fennica* 39:289–309.

Kafka, V., S. Gauthier and Y. Bergeron. 2001. Fire impacts and crowning in the boreal forest: study of a large wildfire in western Quebec. *International Journal of Wildland Fire* 10:119–27.

Kouki, J. and A. Väänänen. 2000. Impoverishment of resident old-growth forest bird assemblages along an isolation gradient of protected areas in eastern Finland. *Ornis Fennica* 77:145–54.

Kuuluvainen, T. 2002. Natural variability of forests as a reference for restoring and managing biological diversity in boreal Fennoscandia. *Silva Fennica* 36:97–125.

Lambeck, R. J. 1997. Focal species: a multi-species umbrella for nature conservation. *Conservation Biology* 11:849–56.

Landres, P. B., P. Morgan and F. J. Swanson. 1999. Overview of the use of natural variability concepts in managing ecological systems. *Ecological Applications* 9:1179–88.

Larsen, C. P. S. 1997. Spatial and temporal variations in boreal forest fire frequency in northern Alberta. *Journal of Biogeography* 24:663–73.

Leboeuf, M. 2004. Effets de la fragmentation générée par les coupes en pessière noire à mousses sur huit espèces d'oiseaux de forêt mature. M.Sc. thesis. Montreal, Canada: Université du Québec à Montréal.

Lee, P., D. Aksenov, L. Laestadius, R. Nogueron and W. Smith. 2003. *Canada's Large Intact Forest Landscapes.* Edmonton, Alberta: Global Forest Watch Canada.

Lefort, P., S. Gauthier and Y. Bergeron. 2003. The influence of fire weather and land use on the fire activity of the Lake Abitibi area, Eastern Canada. *Forest Science* 49:509–21.

Lesieur, D., S. Gauthier and Y. Bergeron. 2002. Fire frequency and vegetation dynamics for the south-central boreal forest of Quebec, Canada. *Canadian Journal of Forest Research* 32:1996–2009.

Leupin, E. E., T. E. Dickinson and K. Martin. 2004. Resistance of forest songbirds to habitat perforation in a high-elevation conifer forest. *Canadian Journal of Forest Research* 34:1919–28.

Lindenmayer, D. B. and G. Luck. 2005. Synthesis: thresholds in conservation and management. *Biological Conservation* 124:351–4.

Lindenmayer, D. B., S. McIntyre and J. Fischer. 2003. Birds in eucalypt and pine forests: landscape alteration and its implications for research models of faunal habitat use. *Biological Conservation* 110:45–53.

Lindenmayer, D. B., J. Fischer and R. B. Cunningham. 2005. Native vegetation cover thresholds associated with species responses. *Biological Conservation* 124:311–16.

Lindenmayer, D. B., J. Fischer, A. Felton *et al.* 2007. The complementarity of single-species and ecosystem-oriented research in conservation research. *Conservation Biology* 116:1220–6.

MacLean, D. A., D. A. Etheridge, R. G. Wagner and J. S. Wilson. 2005. Changes in landscape composition and stand structure from 1945–2002 on an industrial forest in New Brunswick, Canada. *Canadian Journal of Forest Research* 35:1965–77.

Manel, S., H. C. Williams and S. J. Ormerod. 2001 Evaluating presence–absence models in ecology: the need to account for prevalence. *Journal of Applied Ecology* 38:921–31.

McKinnon, W. E. and D. A. MacLean. 2003. The influence of forest and stand conditions on spruce budworm defoliation in New Brunswick, Canada. *Forest Science* 49:657–67.

Mascarúa López, L., K. Harper and P. Drapeau. 2006. Edge influence on forest structure in large forest remnants, cutblock separators and riparian buffers in managed black spruce forests *Ecoscience* 13:226–33.

Martikainen, P. 2001. Conservation of threatened saproxylic beetles: significance of retained aspen *Populus tremula* on clearcut areas. *Ecological Bulletin* 49:205–18.

Martin, K. and J. M. Eadie. 1999. Nest webs: a community-wide approach to the management and conservation of cavity-nesting birds. *Forest Ecology and Management* 115:243–57.

McComb, W. C., T. A. Spies and W. H. Emmingham. 1993. Douglas-fir forests: managing for timber and mature-forest habitat. *Journal of Forestry* 91:31–42.

Mönkkönen, M. and P. Reunanen. 1999. On critical thresholds in landscape connectivity: a management perspective. *Oikos* 84:302–6.

Morissette, J. L., T. P. Cobb, R. M. Brigham and P. C. James. 2002. The response of boreal forest songbird communities to fire and post-fire harvesting. *Canadian Journal of Forest Research* 32:2169–83.

Niemi, G., J. Hanowski, P. Helle *et al.* 1998. Ecological sustainability of birds in boreal forests. *Conservation Ecology* 2:1–27.

Nonaka, E. and T. A. Spies. 2005. Historical range of variability in landscape structure: a simulation study in Oregon, USA. *Ecological Applications* 15:1727–46.

Noss, R. F. 1987. From plant communities to landscapes in conservation inventories: a look at The Nature Conservancy (USA). *Biological Conservation* 41:11–37.

Opdam, P. 1991. Metapopulation theory and habitat fragmentation: a review of holarctic breeding bird studies. *Landscape Ecology* 5:93–106.

Payette, S. 1992. Fire as a controlling process in the North American boreal forest. Pp. 144–69 in H. H. Shugart, R. Leemans and G. B. Bonan (eds.) *A Systems Analysis of the Global Boreal Forest*. Cambridge, UK: Cambridge University Press.

Payette, S., C. Morneau, L. Sirois and M. Desponts. 1989. Recent fire history of the northern Québec biomes. *Ecology* 70:656–73.

Perron, N. 2003. Peut-on et doit-on s'inspirer de la variabilité naturelle des feux pour élaborer une stratégie écosystémique de répartition des coupes à l'échelle du paysage? le cas de la pessière noire à mousse de l'Ouest au Lac-Saint-Jean. Ph.D. thesis, Université Laval, Québec: Presses de l'Université Laval.

Radford, J. Q. and A. F. Bennett. 2004. Thresholds in landscape parameters: occurrence of the white-browed treecreeper *Climacteris affinis* in Victoria, Australia. *Biological Conservation* 117:375–91.

Radford, J. Q., A. F. Bennett and G. J. Cheers. 2005. Landscape-level thresholds of habitat cover for woodland-dependent birds. *Biological Conservation* 124:317–37.

Ranius, T. and L. Fahrig. 2006. Targets for maintenance of dead wood for biodiversity conservation based on extinction thresholds. *Scandinavian Journal of Forest Research* 21:201–8.

Rempel, R. S., D. W. Andison and S. J. Hannon. 2004. Guiding principles for developing an indicator and monitoring framework. *Forestry Chronicle* 80:82–90.

Rheault, H., P. Drapeau, Y. Bergeron and P.-A. Esseen. 2003. Edge effects on epiphytic lichens in managed black spruce forests of eastern North America. *Canadian Journal of Forest Research* 33:23–32.

Roberge, J.-M. and P. Angelstam. 2004. Usefulness of the umbrella species concept as a conservation tool. *Conservation Biology* 18: 76–85.

Rodriguez, A. S. L., S. J. Andelman, M. I. Bakarr *et al.* 2004. Effectiveness of the global protected area network in representing species diversity. *Nature* 428:640–3.

Rosene, W. 1969. *The Bobwhite Quail, its Life and Management*. Hartwell, GA: The Sun Press.

Ruel, J.-C. 1995. Understanding windthrow: silvicultural implications. *Forestry Chronicle* 71:434–45.

Ruel, J.-C., D. Pin and K. Cooper. 2001. Windthrow in riparian buffer strips: effect of wind exposure, thinning and strip width. *Forest Ecology and Management.* 143:105–13.

Saint-Germain, M., C. M. Buddle and P. Drapeau. 2007a. Primary attraction and random landing in host-selection by wood-feeding insects: a matter of scale? *Agricultural and Forest Entomology* 9:227–35.

Saint-Germain, M., P. Drapeau and C. Buddle. 2007b. Host-use patterns of saproxylic wood-feeding Coleoptera adults and larvae along the decay gradient in standing dead black spruce and aspen. *Ecography* 30:737–48.

Saucier, J.-P., J.-F. Bergeron, P. Grondin and A. Robitaille. 1998. The land regions of southern Québec (3rd version): one element in the hierarchical land classification system developed by the Ministère des Ressources Naturelles du Québec. Ministère des Ressources Naturelles du Québec, Quebec City, Québec, Canada. Internal Report.

Schaefer, J. A. 2003. Long-term range recession and the persistence of caribou in the taiga. *Conservation Biology* 17:1435–9.

Schieck, J. and K. A. Hobson. 2000. Bird communities associated with live residual tree patches within cut blocks and burned habitat in mixedwood boreal forests. *Canadian Journal of Forest Research* 30:1281–95.

Schieck, J., M. Nietfeld and J. B. Stelfox. 1995. Differences in bird species richness and abundance among three successional stages of aspen dominated boreal forests. *Canadian Journal of Zoology* **73**:1417–31.

Schmiegelow, F. K. A. and M. Mönkkönen. 2002. Habitat loss and fragmentation in dynamic landscapes: avian perspectives from the boreal forest. *Ecological Applications* **12**:375–89.

Severinghaus, W. D. 1981. Guild theory development as a mechanism for assessing environmental impact. *Environmental Management* **5**:187–90.

Seymour, R. and M. Hunter Jr. 1999. Principles of ecological forestry. Pp. 22–61 in M. L. Hunter Jr. (ed.) *Maintaining Biodiversity in Forest Ecosystems.* Cambridge, UK: Cambridge University Press.

Shugart, H. H. and D. C. West. 1981. Long term dynamics of forest ecosystems. *American Scientist* **69**:647–52.

Simon, N. P. P., F. E. Schwab and A. W. Diamond. 2000. Patterns of breeding bird abundance in relation to logging in western Labrador. *Canadian Journal of Forest Research* **30**:257–63.

Sillett, S. C., B. McCune, J. E. Peck, T. R. Rambo and A. Ruchty. 2000. Dispersal limitations of epiphytic lichens result in species dependent on old-growth forests. *Ecological Applications* **10**:789–99.

Spies, T. A., W. J. Ripple and G. A. Bradshaw. 1994. Dynamics and pattern of a managed coniferous forest landscape in Oregon. *Ecological Applications* **4**:555–68.

Taylor, S. L. and D. A. MacLean. 2005. Rate and causes of decline of mature and overmature balsam fir and spruce stands in New Brunswick, Canada. *Canadian Journal of Forest Research* **35**:2479–90.

Vaillancourt, M.-A. 2007. Caractérisation de la disponibilité des arbres potentiels à la nidification du Garrot d'Islande dans la forêt boréale de l'est du Québec. M.Sc. thesis. Montreal, Canada: Université du Québec à Montréal.

Van Wagner, C. E. 1978. Age-class distribution and the forest fire cycle. *Canadian Journal of Forest Research* **8**:220–7.

Vincent, J. S. and L. Hardy. 1977. L'Évolution et l'extension des lacs glaciaires Barlow et Ojibway en territoire québécois. *Géographie Physique du Quaternaire* **31**:357–72.

Weber, M. G. and M. D. Flannigan. 1997. Canadian boreal forest ecosystem structure and function in a changing climate: impact on fire regime. *Environmental Review* **5**:145–66.

Welsh, D. A. 1988. Meeting the needs of non-game forest wildlife. *Forestry Chronicle* **64**:262–6.

With, K. A. and T. O. Crist. 1995. Critical thresholds in species' responses to landscape structure. *Ecology* **76**:2446–59.

Wimberly, M. C., T. A. Spies, C. J. Long and C. Whitlock. 2000. Simulating historical variability in the amount of old forest in the Oregon Coast Range. *Conservation Biology* **14**:167–80.

Yaroshenko, A. Y., P. V. Potapov and S. A. Turubanova. 2001. *The Last Intact Forest Landscapes of Northern European Russia.* Moscow: Greenpeace Russia.

Thresholds, incidence functions, and species-specific cues: responses of woodland birds to landscape structure in south-eastern Australia

ANDREW F. BENNETT AND JAMES Q. RADFORD

INTRODUCTION

Looking out from a vantage point across a large tract of forest gives a superficial impression of uniformity; the crowns of canopy trees follow the folds and contours of the landscape to provide a continuous cover of wooded vegetation. But this visual appearance belies the truth: forested landscapes are far from uniform. On closer examination, they comprise a complex mosaic of different vegetation types and stands of different age-classes, differing structural features, and modified to varying extent by human land-uses. Forests have a critical role in the conservation of biodiversity throughout the world (Peterken 1996; Laurance and Bierregard 1997; Lindenmayer and Franklin 2002), and a key feature contributing to their conservation value is the response of forest biota to the heterogeneity inherent in forested landscapes (Lindenmayer et al. 2006). Consequently, an understanding of the implications of landscape structure for the maintenance of species and ecological processes is an important foundation for forest management and biodiversity conservation.

How do forest biota respond to landscape structure?

Conservation of biodiversity in forested landscapes requires a multi-scaled approach to management, including measures at regional, landscape, and

Setting Conservation Targets for Managed Forest Landscapes, ed. M.-A. Villard and B. G. Jonsson. Published by Cambridge University Press.

stand scales (Lindenmayer and Franklin 2002). Our focus here is the landscape scale and the opportunity to enhance conservation outcomes by managing and manipulating landscape structure. This spatial scale is important for several reasons. First, the landscape scale is that at which most land managers must operate and make decisions: for example, management decisions relating to the extent and spatial arrangement of logging areas; the location and extent of areas to be burned to reduce the risk of wildfire; the siting of recreation facilities to minimize adverse impacts; and the most effective location for restoration actions in modified landscapes. Second, a landscape perspective is necessary to understand the conservation requirements of many species. For example, large tracts of habitat may be necessary to maintain viable populations of species; numerous species move between complementary elements in the landscape on a daily or seasonal basis (Law and Dickman 1998) and for many forest-dependent species it is essential to understand the impacts associated with modified or novel land uses adjacent to forest remnants (Laurance and Vasconcelos 2004).

A central issue, therefore, is to understand how plants and animals respond to landscape structure and to the changes in structure brought about by human land uses. Which aspects of landscape structure are associated with a more sustainable forest ecosystem and which are detrimental? Are there particular components of forest landscapes that enhance biodiversity? Is it necessary to have a minimum proportional cover in the forest landscape of a particular vegetation type and stand structural type, or post-fire seral stage? Are there spatial patterns of landscape elements that are likely to be more or less effective in achieving biodiversity conservation?

In recent decades, much progress has been made in gaining a better understanding of forested landscapes, both in continuous forests and fragmented forest landscapes. Many studies have obtained empirical data on the relative values of different kinds of elements in forested landscapes: for example, riparian buffer strips (Darveau *et al.* 1995; Palmer and Bennett 2006; Chapter 3, this volume); forest stands at different stages of post-logging regeneration (Loyn 1985; Smith 1985); plantation forests (Renjifo 2001; Lindenmayer *et al.* 2002); and forest blocks of different sizes and management histories (Suckling 1982; Newmark 1991). Such studies have provided many valuable insights but the data relate primarily to the use of, or conservation value of, single types of landscape components; they do not provide comparative data on combinations of elements that make up a forest mosaic.

Other studies have explicitly measured the structure of the landscape around survey sites or forest stands, and related the occurrence of species or assemblages to the attributes of the surrounding landscape (Drolet *et al.* 1999; Jansson and Angelstam 1999; Mazerolle and Villard 1999; McAlpine *et al.* 2006). For example, Loyn *et al.* (2001) modeled the factors influencing the presence of forest owls in extensive forests of the highlands of south-eastern Australia and found that mapped variables representing forest composition and structure surrounding survey sites explained more variation in the occurrence of owl species than could be predicted by the forest habitat at the survey site. However, although such studies provide further insights for forest managers, particularly the capacity to test for influences at multiple spatial scales, they do not directly compare forest mosaics. The response variable (e.g. occurrence of a species) is measured at a single site or patch, and the measures of composition or spatial configuration of the forest mosaic represent the context for that site or patch.

In order to make quantitative comparison of the conservation values of different forest landscapes, it is necessary to make direct comparisons between the status of species or assemblages in a series of "whole mosaics" or "landscape units" that have different properties. That is, the forest mosaic becomes the unit of study, and the response variable must represent the status of species or assemblages in the mosaic as a whole, rather than in one component. There are a small number of studies where such an approach has been taken, in which forest biota have been measured to represent heterogeneous forest mosaics within continuous forest (McGarigal and McComb 1995; Jokimäki and Huhta 1996; Mitchell *et al.* 2006), or where forests occur in modified landscapes (Andrén 1992; Trzcinski *et al.* 1999; Villard *et al.* 1999; Boulinier *et al.* 2001). For example, Gjerde *et al.* (2005) recorded the abundance of woodpeckers in 100 ha forest mosaics in western Norway along a gradient of conversion of pine forests to spruce plantations. The number of woodpecker species per mosaic peaked between 20% and 40% cover of spruce plantation; with greater proportional cover, the richness of woodpeckers declined.

The primary thesis of this chapter is that conservation of forest biota and ecosystems will be enhanced by a better understanding of how the properties of forested landscapes influence the biota; particularly by identifying quantitative relationships between components of landscape structure and the status of forest biota. We first outline four kinds of properties of land mosaics that influence the status of fauna in forested landscapes. We then present a case study from south-eastern Australia, describing an investigation of the influence of landscape structure on woodland birds in a region where forests persist amongst agricultural lands. Finally, we discuss how insights from this type of research approach can assist in setting goals for practical conservation management.

Properties of mosaics

Land mosaics have properties that differ from those of their individual components. These properties are a product of the numbers, types, and spatial arrangement of the elements or land uses that occur within it (Forman 1995; Wiens 1995; Bennett *et al.* 2006). There are four main types of property, each of which can be represented by different measures or variables.

(a) The total *extent* of habitat refers to the total area of all vegetation patches or land uses that provide habitat for a particular taxon, regardless of the size, shape, or location of each patch in the mosaic.

(b) *Composition* of a mosaic refers to the types of different elements present (e.g. vegetation types, age classes, land uses) and their relative proportions. It may be measured by the number (richness) of different types of elements, by diversity indices (e.g. Shannon–Wiener index, evenness), or by the use of multivariate statistics based on the proportions of different elements.

(c) *Configuration* refers to the spatial arrangement of elements in a land mosaic. A large number of measures have been proposed to quantify aspects of configuration (e.g. Turner *et al.* 2001). Several distinct components of spatial configuration include the degree to which habitat for a taxon is aggregated (cf. dispersed) in the mosaic; the extent of subdivision (i.e. the number of habitat patches for a given amount of habitat), and the relative shape of patches (Bennett *et al.* 2006).

(d) *Environmental variation* refers to the relative variation in physical aspects of the environment within each mosaic, such as elevation, rainfall, or geological substrates. The geographic location of a landscape is also an important factor; it may influence the physical environment, and the likelihood of occurrence of species in relation to their geographic ranges.

These types of property can be measured for all land mosaics. In continuous forests, emphasis will be given to within-forest structural variation. For example, composition of the forest mosaic may be based on parameters such as the proportions of post-logging regrowth (McGarigal and McComb 1995; Chapin *et al.* 1998), or of different forest types (Jansson and Angelstam 1999; Gjerde *et al.* 2005). In fragmented forest landscapes, emphasis is usually given to the pattern of remnant forests. Extent of habitat is measured as the total amount of forest, composed of numerous patches amongst other land uses (Andrén 1992; Trczinski *et al.* 1999; Villard *et al.* 1999). Composition of the mosaic may be measured by gradients in the proportions of different land uses (e.g. arable land, grazing, forests, human settlement) (Bennett *et al.* 2004; Radford *et al.* 2005), or by indices based on diversity of land uses (Pino *et al.* 2000; Atauri and de Lucio 2001; Luoto *et al.* 2004).

A cautionary note is required concerning the level of intercorrelation that often exists between variables representing landscape structure. For example, measures of the extent of a habitat and its spatial configuration are often strongly correlated (Fahrig 2003), making it difficult to pinpoint true causal relationships. Forest management will be more effective if it is known which landscape properties have the strongest and most direct influences on biota, so that they can be given priority for conservation management or manipulation. The effects of different landscape properties can be identified by careful study design and the use of statistical procedures to disentangle the independent effects of correlated measures (e.g. McGarigal and McComb 1995; Villard *et al.* 1999; Mac Nally 2000).

FOREST AND WOODLAND BIRDS IN SOUTHERN AUSTRALIA

There is much concern about population decline and deteriorating conservation status of birds typically associated with the dry open eucalypt forests and woodlands of southern Australia (Robinson and Traill 1996; Reid 1999; Ford *et al.* 2001). Ford *et al.* (2001) outlined a number of hypotheses for the decline of woodland birds and identified potential causal processes associated with habitat loss, habitat fragmentation, and habitat degradation. A fundamental issue is the rate and extent of loss of forest and woodland vegetation across temperate southern Australia. In many regions, up to 90% or more of the native vegetation has been cleared in 150 years of European settlement (i.e. less than the lifespan of a single tree!), to be replaced by cereal crops and pastures of exotic grasses (Saunders 1989; Robinson and Traill 1996; Lunt and Bennett 2000).

In addition to the impacts on native flora and fauna, excessive loss of indigenous vegetation has other effects on the environment, including changes to hydrological regimes, groundwater levels, terrestrial microclimates, soil structural properties, and increased erosion (Hobbs 1993; Vesk and Mac Nally 2006). National programs to reverse the detrimental effects of vegetation loss are underway, including protection of existing forests and revegetation to increase the amount of wooded vegetation in the landscape. Many issues that land management agencies seek to address by restoration relate to landscape-level properties of the environment. For example, how much forest is sufficient to ensure that existing native biota will persist? What is the most suitable pattern of forested vegetation to achieve an effective habitat network for forest-dependent species?

These are the kinds of questions that stimulated this case study. We used "whole mosaics" as the unit of study, in order to relate the status of the avifauna to the properties of forest mosaics at a scale relevant to land management.

Study design

We surveyed forest and woodland-dependent birds (hereafter woodland birds) in 24 "landscapes", each 10 km × 10 km in size (100 km²) in north-central Victoria, Australia (Radford *et al.* 2005). This size was chosen because it is large relative to the daily movements of most woodland birds, includes several types of forest vegetation, and is at a scale relevant to land management. In this region, >80% of the original eucalypt forest and woodland has been cleared, with >90% removed in most local areas (ECC 1997). Disproportionate loss of vegetation has occurred on the most fertile soils. The remaining forests occur on both public and private land, ranging from small patches (<10 ha) and linear strips along roads and streams, to large tracts of up to 30,000 ha (Fig. 8.1). Forests are subject to a range of land uses. Some are reserved and managed as national parks, flora and fauna reserves, and historic reserves; others are used for timber production (mostly for firewood and fence posts), gold mining, eucalyptus oil extraction, honey production, and outdoor recreation (ECC 1997). Forests on private land are mostly grazed by stock.

The 24 study landscapes were selected to represent variation in two parameters: first, a gradient of decreasing extent of remnant forest cover, from 60% to less than 2%; and second, to contrast landscapes in which forest cover was aggregated in one or a few larger blocks with those in which it was dispersed among many smaller patches (Fig. 8.2). Birds were surveyed at ten sites in each landscape with each site surveyed four times, twice each in the breeding and non-breeding season. Survey sites were located in five types of wooded element (large blocks >40 ha, small blocks <40 ha, streamside vegetation, roadside strips, and scattered trees among farmland), based on the relative proportions of each type in the landscape (see Radford *et al.* 2005 for details). Thus, in each landscape, birds were

Figure 8.1. An aerial view of part of the study region in northern Victoria, illustrating forest blocks dispersed amongst agricultural lands. Grazing of sheep for wool production is the main agricultural enterprise in this landscape.

sampled from the same total area of wooded cover. The data were collated to provide two measures of the status of woodland birds in each landscape:

- the richness of woodland bird species (i.e. the total number of species pooled across all sites in the landscape);
- the incidence of individual species of birds, where incidence refers to the proportion of surveys in each landscape ($n = 40$) in which a species was recorded.

Variables measured to describe each landscape represented the four types of property (see Radford *et al.* 2005; Radford and Bennett 2007):

(a) extent of forest vegetation (total tree cover, measured by remote sensing);
(b) configuration of forest vegetation (e.g. number of forest patches, patch shape index);
(c) composition of the landscape (e.g. diversity of vegetation types, gradients of land use in the non-forested part of the landscape);
(d) environmental variation and geographic location (e.g. range in elevation, easting).

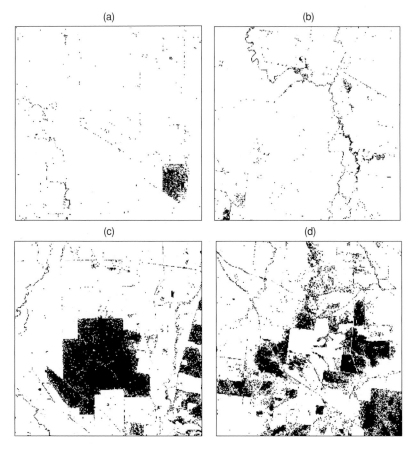

Figure 8.2. Examples of study landscapes (each 100 km²) illustrating aggregated (a, c) and dispersed (b, d) patterns of forest vegetation (shown in black) for approximately 2% (a, b) and 20% (c, d) forest cover, respectively.

How do woodland birds respond to landscape structure?

A total of 156 species of land bird were recorded, of which 80 species are regarded as typical of the region and woodland-dependent; they form the basis for subsequent discussion.

Species richness

Species richness of woodland birds in each landscape ranged from 12 to 53 with a mean of 38.4 species (± 10.5 s.d). What determines the richness of birds at the landscape level? A multiple regression model identified four variables that together accounted for 75% of the variation in richness between landscapes (Radford *et al.* 2005). The number of woodland bird species was predicted to increase with:

(a) increasing forest cover in the landscape;
(b) decreasing regularity in the average shape of forest patches;
(c) increasing topographic relief in the landscape, and
(d) the position of the landscape along an eastward geographic gradient.

Notably, the extent of forest cover was the variable of greatest importance, accounting for some 55% of the variance in species richness. That is, the number of woodland species is primarily driven by the total amount of eucalypt forest and woodland in the landscape. To explore this relationship further, we examined univariate relationships between species richness and forest cover by fitting a number of alternate models. The "best fit" models were those that showed a gradual decline in species richness at higher levels of forest cover, and a rapid loss of species below 10% cover, with a marked discontinuity around the 10% level. A "broken stick" model, consisting of two regression lines that join at a breakpoint of 10% cover (Fig. 8.3; see Toms and Lesperance 2003, for further information on "piecewise" regression) was the best fit to the data as indicated by Akaike's Information Criterion, highlighting the marked change that occurs around this level.

This relationship provides strong evidence for the concept of a threshold response by woodland birds to landscape structure. An ecological threshold refers to a point or zone in a relationship at which a small change in an explanatory variable has a marked effect on the response variable (Wiens *et al.* 2002; Huggett 2005). In this study, there appears to be a threshold in forest cover at around 10% of the landscape, below which there is a disproportionately rapid decline in the species richness of woodland birds (Radford *et al.* 2005).

Does this mean that 10% forest cover across the landscape is an appropriate target for the conservation of woodland birds? Our response is an emphatic "NO". This threshold represents a position along the gradient of landscape change at which species richness crashes. Multiple local extinction events occur and the woodland bird community rapidly collapses. However, local extinction of a species does not just "suddenly occur", but is the end point of a process of population decline. In many landscapes, species were recorded as present, and thus added to the species richness tally, but may have been represented by a dwindling overall population, a single localized group, or even a single individual. The long-term persistence of woodland birds at the landscape level depends on the presence of a

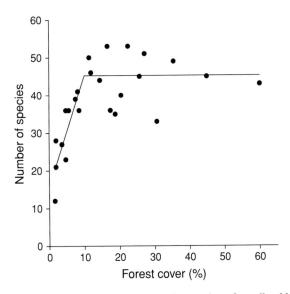

Figure 8.3. Relationship between the number of woodland bird species and percent forest cover in 24 study landscapes in northern Victoria. The solid line represents a "broken stick" regression with breakpoint at 10% cover, and the dotted line indicates the 10% threshold in forest cover at which there is a dramatic change in species richness. See text for conservation implications of this threshold.

sustainable breeding population. Thus, the management target must be well on the "safe" side of the threshold, at a level at which most species' populations are not vulnerable to decline. But how far from the threshold is "safe"?

Incidence of individual species

Species richness is an assemblage-level response in which all species are grouped together. However, although all species were assessed *a priori* to be woodland-dependent, they differ in the use of forest resources such as food types and microhabitat requirements for foraging and breeding, and in their scale of movement through the landscape.

We modeled the incidence of woodland birds in the 24 landscapes to identify those properties of the land mosaic of greatest influence on each species. Two analytical approaches were used (see Radford and Bennett 2007, for detailed explanation). First, hierarchical partitioning (HP) is a method that can be used to identify the "independent" and "joint" contributions that each predictor variable makes to explaining variation in a response variable (Chevan and Sutherland 1991; Mac Nally 2000). Second, Bayesian variable selection (BVS), a multivariate modeling procedure, was used to identify the most credible set of explanatory variables for each species. Analyses were carried out for 58 of the 80 woodland species: those that occurred in five or more of the 24 landscapes.

There was wide variation in species' responses, demonstrating that although all are woodland-dependent, different species respond to different landscape properties (Fig. 8.4) (Radford and Bennett 2007). Key findings from these analyses for individual species include the following.

(a) Extent of forest cover in the landscape was the single most important variable explaining the incidence of woodland birds, based on the number of species for which forest cover made a substantial independent contribution to explaining variance (HP), and for which it was included in the most credible set of explanatory variables (BVS) (Fig. 8.4). Incidence of these species at wooded sites in the landscape increased with increasing overall extent of forest cover.

(b) Numerous species were influenced by variables representing landscape composition, most notably by a gradient in agricultural land use in the region (from primarily cropping to primarily grazing), and by the average condition of the vegetation at each survey site.

(c) Variables representing the configuration of forest cover were important for many fewer species than was the amount of forest cover but, where important, they indicated negative effects of forest fragmentation. For example, a number of species occur at a higher incidence in landscapes in which forest cover is aggregated (for a given extent of forest cover) than where it is dispersed (Fig. 8.4).

(d) A subset of 19 species was influenced by the geographic position of the landscape. Species associated with mesic forests of the Great Dividing Range (e.g. pied currawong *Strepera graculina*, scarlet robin *Petroica multicolor*) were more likely to occur in the east, whereas others were more likely in the west of the region (e.g. white-plumed honeyeater *Lichenostomus penicillatus*).

Several specific examples illustrate the variation in response of woodland birds to landscape structure. For the eastern yellow robin *Eopsaltria australis* and rufous whistler *Pachycephala rufiventris*, forest cover was the only variable included in the most probable set of explanatory variables. For the crested bellbird *Oreoica gutturalis* and white-browed babbler

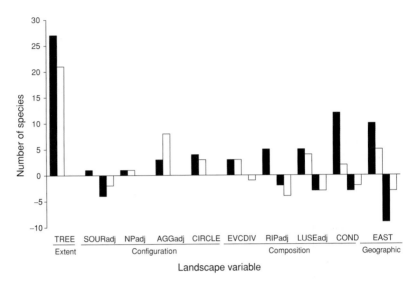

Figure 8.4. Relative importance of different kinds of landscape variable in explaining the incidence of woodland birds in study landscapes based on the number of species for each landscape variable for which:

(a) the independent contribution in hierarchical partitioning was significant (■) and;
(b) the probability of a non-zero coefficient in Bayesian variable selection was >0.9 (□).

The direction of the bar indicates the number of species for which the relationship was positive or negative for each variable.

TREE, extent of forest cover; $SOUR_{adj}$, distance to a large (>10,000 ha) forest; NP_{adj}, number of discrete forest patches; AGG_{adj}, degree of aggregation of forest patches; CIRCLE, index of patch shape complexity; EVCDIV, diversity of vegetation types; RIP_{adj}, extent of streamside vegetation; $LUSE_{adj}$, PCA ordination factor describing a gradient in agricultural land use from primarily cropping to primarily grazing; COND, index of vegetation condition and disturbance; EAST, geographic location. Subscript $_{adj}$ denotes that the original variable was regressed against TREE and the residuals used as an adjusted measure.

From Radford and Bennett (2007), *Journal of Applied Ecology*; with permission from Blackwell Publishing.

Pomatostomus superciliosus, it was forest cover together with distance to the nearest continuous forest of >10,000 ha. Thus, each of these species is primarily responding (positively) to the total amount of forest within or close to the landscape. Other species such as the grey shrike-thrush *Colluricincla harmonica* and spotted pardalote *Pardalotus punctatus* responded to both the amount of wooded cover and its spatial configuration; they occurred in higher incidence in landscapes with more forest cover and where that cover was aggregated into larger blocks. The incidence of the brown treecreeper *Climacteris picumnis* was most strongly related to the diversity of forest vegetation types and the condition of the vegetation at each site, whereas for the white-plumed honeyeater *Lichenostomus penicillatus* the diversity of vegetation types and geographic location (greater incidence to the west) were of greatest influence.

The importance of total extent of forest cover in explaining the incidence of individual species suggested that this relationship was worthy of closer attention. Univariate relationships between species' incidence and tree cover were examined by fitting a range of models to identify the "best" shape, or form, of this relationship. Examples of two contrasting types of response shape (or incidence function) are illustrated in Fig. 8.5.

First, a non-significant relationship (i.e. slope not different from zero) was found for the white-winged chough (Fig. 8.5a). There is no change in the incidence of this species as the amount of forest cover in the landscape decreases. That is, even though the extent of its forest habitat decreased, it was recorded with a similar frequency of occurrence in surveys in the wooded elements in each landscape. However, because forest cover in the landscape is lost and the species cannot persist in cleared farmland that replaces it, this relationship implies that the overall population size of the white-winged chough will decrease in direct proportion to the rate of forest loss. This pattern of population change as forest cover declined was shown by approximately one-third of woodland species (for which adequate data were available).

Second, for the eastern yellow robin (and numerous other species) there was a curvilinear response (Fig. 8.5b). As the amount of forest cover in the landscape decreased, there was a decline in the species' incidence, at first gradual and then accelerating. This response shape suggests that as forest cover is lost, not only is there a reduction in overall population size due to loss of habitat alone, but the species' incidence in remaining wooded elements also declines, further compounding overall population reduction. For these types of species, the process of population decline speeds up as forest cover decreases. Of critical importance is that this process of compounded decline commences at levels of forest cover well above the 10% threshold at which species richness crashes.

Managing landscape structure to achieve conservation goals

How can this type of research approach, based on collecting empirical data at the landscape level, be used to set quantitative goals for biodiversity

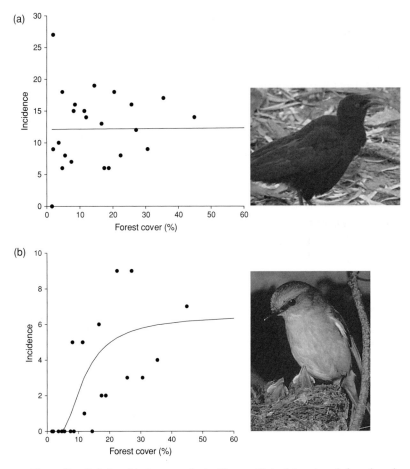

Figure 8.5. Relationship between the incidence of (a) white-winged chough and (b) eastern yellow robin and the percentage cover of forest vegetation in 24 study landscapes in northern Victoria. (Photos: McCann collection, DSE.)

conservation in forested landscapes? We outline below five points relating to the role of landscape structure, and illustrate them with reference to this case study.

Setting conservation targets depends on knowledge of the particular system

Scientific research seeks generality in understanding, such that new insights are relevant and applicable in as many circumstances as possible. However, although principles can often be extrapolated among different ecosystems, the variation in biota and idiosyncratic features of different ecosystems mean that caution must be exercised in extrapolating specific targets or goals. For example, in a number of studies in land mosaics (including this case study), variation in species richness or in the occurrence of biota is influenced by the geographic location of the mosaic, as well as properties relating to its habitat features (Boulinier *et al.* 2001; Smith *et al.* 2001; Radford *et al.* 2005).

Outcomes and conservation goals arising from this work in north-central Victoria are most relevant to other dry forests and woodlands on the inland slopes of the Great Dividing Range of south-eastern Australia that have similar forest types, land-use history, and avifauna. None the less, the concepts identified here, including a threshold response of species richness to forest cover, species-specific cues to landscape structure, and different response shapes for species' incidence in relation to forest cover, are likely to be relevant to other regions in Australia and other countries.

Setting targets for landscape structure depends on the conservation goal

Managing or manipulating the structure of forested landscapes is likely to be inefficient unless the conservation goals are clearly defined. Different conservation outcomes are often related to different aspects of landscape structure. For example, the total species richness of a faunal group is frequently related to the heterogeneity of the landscape (Bohning-Gaese 1997; Atauri and de Lucio 2001; Luoto *et al.* 2004), whereas the richness of a subset of species, or occurrence of a single species, is generally most strongly influenced by the total extent of its habitat in the landscape (Trzcinski *et al.* 1999; Bailey *et al.* 2002).

Our results show that if the goal is to maximize the species richness of woodland birds, then particular attention should be given to maintaining or increasing the total extent of forest cover in the landscape. In contrast, if the goal is to enhance the status of a particular species (e.g. a threatened species) or subset of species, then attention should be given to the specific features of the forest landscape that elicit the strongest response. This may be an attribute such as the amount of riparian vegetation, the degree to which forests are aggregated into larger blocks, or the condition of the vegetation.

To address a primary conservation goal of maintaining rich assemblages of woodland birds in highly modified landscapes in northern Victoria, we provided advice to land managers that emphasized the importance of the total amount of forest cover (Radford *et al.* 2004). We recommended a target of around 30% forest cover to have a high likelihood of sustaining diverse communities of woodland birds. This was based on:

- a threshold response at 10% cover, below which bird communities rapidly collapse
- the need to be well on the safe side of this level to account for the process of decline and potential for time-lag effects
- the form of the relationship between species' incidence and forest cover for selected species, in which population decline accelerates at levels of forest cover of 20% or more (Fig. 8.5).

It is important to note the context for this target. Forest cover across the region is presently much less than 30% and in many districts there is less than 10% cover. This target sets a challenging goal that requires not only protection and management of remaining forests but a long-term restoration process. Of course, this single target is not necessarily adequate to meet the conservation requirements of every species. Rare species that were seldom detected, such as the threatened regent honeyeater *Xanthomyza phrygia*, may be more sensitive to landscape change and disappear at levels of forest cover much greater than 30%, or their status may depend on other processes such as competition or predation.

Identify the critical properties of landscape structure

Landscape-level management of forest mosaics to achieve conservation outcomes depends on knowing the most appropriate parameters to manipulate. This means it is first necessary to recognize the different kinds of properties of forest mosaics, measure variables that represent each of these properties, and analyse the influence of each on the response variable of interest. It is also important to recognize that the variables describing landscape properties are often strongly correlated to each other and that we must take appropriate steps to determine the independent influence of each property. Otherwise, there is a risk of attributing the effects of landscape structure to a factor of indirect influence, and implementing management actions that are less effective than they could be.

A key outcome from this case study is the identification of the relative influence on woodland birds of all four main types of landscape property. This gives insight into the *kinds* of target to set in relation to landscape structure. Here, the total extent of forest cover emerged as a key attribute of landscapes in northern Victoria that influences both the richness of woodland birds and the incidence of many individual species. Configuration of forests was generally much less important for woodland birds than forest extent, at this landscape scale. However, a notable finding was the influence of the aggregation of forest cover for a number of species. This suggests that restoration actions that increase the extent of forest cover by consolidating large blocks of forest will be beneficial for forest-dependent species.

A limitation of our approach is that we used a single fixed size (100 km²) for a "landscape", when it is likely that many species respond to landscape structure at different scales. It would be valuable to know whether assemblages and species respond to landscape structure in different ways at different spatial scales, and what kinds of changes occur across scales.

Expect non-linear ecological responses to landscape change

Understanding the manner in which species, assemblages, or ecological processes respond to landscape change is fundamental to effective land management. Many ecological relationships are not linear; the change in the response of the biota is not consistent across the spectrum of landscape change (see Chapter 9, this volume). Curvilinear responses (Fig. 8.5b) and threshold responses mean that at particular stages of landscape change there is a disproportionate rate of change in the biota, sometimes with quite abrupt responses that herald a shift in the state of the system. Wiens *et al.* (2002: 30) noted that "Nature is full of thresholds layered upon thresholds". From a management perspective, it is critical to know where along the gradient of environmental change species are most sensitive and where precipitous declines may occur. It is also relevant for landscape restoration to know where the greatest return for effort invested is likely to be achieved and where little response may occur (Fig. 8.6).

This study found strong evidence for a threshold response in the species richness of woodland birds to landscape forest cover (Fig. 8.3). The marked decline at around 10% forest cover provides a danger signal for managers; landscapes at or below this level are likely to be experiencing drastic loss of the woodland fauna. However, as mentioned previously, many species individually show declining trends in their incidence well above 10% forest cover. Finally, relationships between the incidence of individual species and landscape forest cover displayed a range of response shapes (Fig. 8.5), highlighting the diverse ways in which species respond to change.

Set management goals at different spatial scales

The approach outlined in this chapter, based on "whole mosaics" as the unit of study, is an effective way to identify the relative importance to biota of

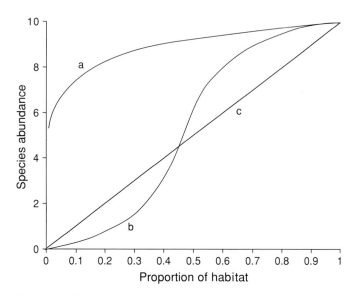

Figure 8.6. The form of the relationship between species abundance and the proportion of forest cover in the landscape has great relevance for practical landscape management. For hypothetical species (a), protection or restoration of forest cover in landscapes with <10% cover is likely to have marked conservation benefits. In contrast, for species (b) there will be limited benefit from restoration or revegetation of such landscapes; the most effective actions are likely to be in landscapes with some 40–50% forest cover. For species (c), the linear response suggests that conservation benefits will accrue from restoration in landscapes at all levels of forest cover.

different kinds of landscape property. However, organisms respond to environmental cues at multiple scales. Consequently, landscape-scale targets must also be integrated with site-level targets that ensure that the habitat is of sufficient quality to meet the local resource requirements of individuals or subpopulations for food, shelter, and reproduction (e.g. Lindenmayer 2000; Bütler et al. 2004).

The white-browed babbler provides a relevant example in this study. At the landscape level, the incidence of this colonial, insectivorous species was most strongly related to total forest cover in the landscape (positive relationship) and the distance to the nearest source area of >10,000 ha (negative relationship); thus it depends on extensive forest within and close to the landscape. However, at a local scale, this species requires dense patches of shrubby vegetation (1–3 m tall) in the forest understorey in which it builds its nests and day-roosts.

Box 8.1 Management scenarios for woodland birds in different landscapes

There is no "correct" or universal answer to the question of how much native vegetation is enough for woodland birds to thrive in modified landscapes. By outlining the consequences of realistic scenarios, we can gain an understanding of what is likely to happen to the fauna in *this* landscape if we manage it in *this* way. These scenarios relate to woodland birds and forest cover in northern Victoria (Radford *et al.* 2004).

(a) *Landscape with 5% forest cover, mainly along streams and roadsides and in small remnants.*
 The native fauna in this landscape is in trouble: it is highly modified and dominated by farmland species (such as Australian magpie *Gymnorhina tibicen*, galah *Cacatua roseicapilla*, crested pigeon *Ocyphaps lophotes*), although woodland-associated species such as eastern rosella *Platycercus eximius* and laughing kookaburra *Dacelo novaeguineae* occur along roadsides and creeks, in small remnants, and among scattered trees. Even in very low-cover landscapes, some woodland-dependent species persist. Some may be widespread (e.g. musk lorikeet *Glossopsitta concinna*, grey shrike-thrush) but most occur in small and dwindling numbers (e.g. sacred kingfisher *Todiramphus sanctus*, weebill *Smicrornis brevirostris*). Five percent forest cover is not enough to support viable populations of most species or to sustain ecological processes.

(b) *Landscape with 10%–15% cover, including linear strips and a range of forest patch sizes.* The prospects for native wildlife are brighter in this scenario. Woodland-dependent species are likely to occur here in greater diversity and abundance, and birds such as the brown treecreeper and black-chinned honeyeater *Melithreptus gularis* are more prevalent. The abundance of patch edges and range of patch sizes creates a varied landscape, one favored by species such as the jacky winter *Microeca fascinans* and mistletoebird *Dicaeum hirundinaceum*. Some species sensitive to landscape change occur but in smaller populations than in less modified landscapes (e.g. hooded robin *Melanodryas cucullata*, white-browed babbler). This landscape is likely to support a high diversity of native species but they may not persist in the long term.

(c) *Landscape with 30%–35% forest cover, including large connected forest blocks.* Landscapes with 30%–35% forest cover support resilient faunal populations more capable of withstanding environmental fluctuations. Ecological processes (e.g. predator–prey relationships, tree regeneration, provision of specialist habitats, mistletoe dispersal) are more robust, and woodland species are expected to outnumber farmland and woodland-associated species. Many species uncommon in low-cover landscapes (such as eastern yellow robin, Gilbert's whistler *Pachycephala inornata*, swift parrot *Lathamus discolor*) occur in larger numbers, greatly improving their chances of long-term survival. Large blocks of forest, a key feature of landscapes with >30% cover, harbor area-sensitive species such as the crested bellbird and speckled warbler *Chthonicola sagittata*, which are unlikely to occur in landscapes with less native

(cont.)

vegetation. The conservation values of high-cover landscapes depend largely on the integrity of the large forest blocks, which must be preserved from degrading land uses (e.g. excessive firewood removal, grazing by domestic stock) or fragmentation into smaller blocks.

Scenarios as a tool for assisting decision-making

Land managers often seek specific targets for management, but scientists often are reluctant to commit to specific quantitative targets. This reluctance can be because conservation goals are often poorly defined, different conservation goals require different targets, there is never a single "correct" answer for all contingencies or locations, and because nature is inherently variable.

An alternative to proposing specific targets for landscape structure is to approach the issue in a different way. Rather than asking "What target should we aim for to achieve a particular conservation goal?", a useful question is "What will happen in *this landscape* if we manage it in *this way?*" This can lead to the delineation of a set of scenarios that reflect the choices available to land managers, and that illustrate the likely outcomes of different decisions. Such scenarios can be quantitative in nature when they are based on empirical research.

When communicating research outcomes from this study to land managers, we used a scenario approach as a complement to recommending a specific target for landscape structure (Radford *et al.* 2004). The three scenarios were descriptive (see Box 8.1), but the examples presented were based on quantitative analysis of empirical data from the study landscapes. By selecting and referring to species that are most likely to be known to land managers (rather than rare or threatened species, for example), the message is likely to be more effective.

ACKNOWLEDGEMENTS

We thank Marc-André Villard for his invitation to contribute this chapter. Funding for our research was provided by Land and Water Australia (Native Vegetation Program, Project DUV6), the Departments of Sustainability and Environment, and Primary Industries, respectively, and the Australian Research Council (LP0560309). The work was carried out in accordance with permits from the Department of Sustainability and Environment (No. 10003782). We thank J. Thomson and R. Mac Nally (Monash University) for statistical advice, and M.-A. Villard, H. Possingham, and an anonymous referee for their comments on the manuscript.

References

Andrén, H. 1992. Corvid density and nest predation in relation to forest fragmentation: a landscape perspective. *Ecology* **73**:794–804.

Atauri, J. A. and J. V. de Lucio. 2001. The role of landscape structure in species richness distribution of birds, amphibians, reptiles and lepidopterans in Mediterranean landscapes. *Landscape Ecology* **16**:147–59.

Bailey, S.-A., R. H. Haines-Young and C. Watkins. 2002. Species presence in fragmented landscapes: modelling of species requirements at the national level. *Biological Conservation* **108**:307–16.

Bennett, A. F., S. A. Hinsley, P. E. Bellamy, R. Swetnam and R. Mac Nally. 2004. Do regional gradients in land use influence richness, composition and turnover of bird assemblages in woods? *Biological Conservation* **119**:191–206.

Bennett, A. F., J. Q. Radford and A. Haslem. 2006. Properties of land mosaics: implications for nature conservation in agricultural environments. *Biological Conservation* **133**:250–64.

Bohning-Gaese, K. 1997. Determinants of avian species richness at different spatial scales. *Journal of Biogeography* **24**:49–60.

Boulinier, T., J. D. Nichols, J. E. Hines *et al.* 2001. Forest fragmentation and bird community dynamics: inference at regional scales. *Ecology* **82**:1159–69.

Bütler, R., P. Angelstam, P. Ekelund and R. Schlaepfer. 2004. Dead wood threshold values for the three-toed woodpecker presence in boreal and sub-Alpine forest. *Biological Conservation* **119**:305–18.

Chapin, T. G., D. J. Harrison and D. D. Katnik. 1998. Influence of landscape pattern on habitat use by American marten in an industrial forest. *Conservation Biology* **12**:1327–37.

Chevan, A. and M. Sutherland. 1991. Hierarchical partitioning. *American Statistician* **45**:90–6.

Darveau, M., P. Beauchesne, L. Bélanger, J. Huot and P. Larue. 1995. Riparian forest strips as habitat for breeding birds in boreal forest. *Journal of Wildlife Management* **59**:67–78.

Drolet, B., A. Desrochers and M.-J. Fortin. 1999. Effects of landscape structure on nesting songbird distribution in a harvested boreal forest. *Condor* **101**:699–704.

Environment Conservation Council. 1997. *Box-Ironbark Forests and Woodlands Investigation. Resources and Issues Report*. Victoria, Australia: Environment Conservation Council.

Fahrig, L. 2003. Effects of habitat fragmentation on biodiversity. *Annual Review of Ecology, Evolution and Systematics* **34**:487–515.

Ford, H. A., G. W. Barrett, D. A. Saunders and H. F. Recher. 2001. Why have birds in the woodlands of Southern Australia declined? *Biological Conservation* **97**:71–88.

Forman, R. T. T. 1995. *Land Mosaics. The Ecology of Landscapes and Regions*. Cambridge, UK: Cambridge University Press.

Gjerde, I., M. Saetersdal and T. Nilsen. 2005. Abundance of two threatened woodpecker species in relation to the proportion of spruce plantations in native pine forests of western Norway. *Biodiversity and Conservation* **14**:377–93.

Hobbs, R. J. 1993. Effects of landscape fragmentation on ecosystem processes in the Western Australian wheatbelt. *Biological Conservation* **64**:193–201.

Huggett, A. J. 2005. The concept and utility of "ecological thresholds" in biodiversity conservation. *Biological Conservation* **124**:301–10.

Jansson, G. and P. Angelstam. 1999. Threshold levels of habitat composition for the presence of the long-tailed tit (*Aegithalos caudatus*) in a boreal landscape. *Landscape Ecology* **14**:283–90.

Jokimäki, J. and E. Huhta. 1996. Effects of landscape matrix and habitat structure on a bird community in northern Finland: a multi-scale approach. *Ornis Fennica* **73**:97–113.

Laurance, W. F. and R. O. Bierregard (eds.) 1997. *Tropical Forest Remnants: Ecology, Management, and Conservation of Fragmented Communities*. Chicago, IL: University of Chicago Press.

Laurance, W. F. and H. L. Vasconcelos. 2004. Ecological effects of habitat fragmentation in the tropics. Pp. 33–49 in G. Schroth, G. A. B. da Fonseca, C. A. Harvey *et al.* (eds.) *Agroforestry and Biodiversity Conservation in Tropical Landscapes*. Washington, D.C.: Island Press.

Law, B. S. and C. R. Dickman. 1998. The use of habitat mosaics by terrestrial vertebrate fauna: implications for conservation and management. *Biodiversity and Conservation* **7**:323–33.

Lindenmayer, D. B. 2000. Factors at multiple scales affecting distribution patterns and its implications for animal conservation – Leadbeater's possum as a case study. *Biodiversity and Conservation* **9**:15–35.

Lindenmayer, D. B. and J. F. Franklin. 2002. *Conserving Forest Biodiversity: A Comprehensive Multiscaled Approach*. Washington, D.C.: Island Press.

Lindenmayer, D. B., R. B. Cunningham, C. F. Donnelly, H. Nix and B. D. Lindenmayer. 2002. Effects of forest fragmentation on bird assemblages in a novel landscape context. *Ecological Monographs* **72**:1–18.

Lindenmayer, D. B., J. F. Franklin and J. Fischer. 2006. General management principles and a checklist of strategies to guide forest biodiversity conservation. *Biological Conservation* **131**:433–45.

Loyn, R. H. 1985. Bird populations in successional forests of Mountain Ash *Eucalypt regnans* in central Victoria. *Emu* **85**:213–30.

Loyn, R. H., E. G. McNabb, L. Volodina and R. Willig. 2001. Modelling landscape distributions of large forest owls as applied to managing forests in north-east Victoria, Australia. *Biological Conservation* **97**:361–76.

Lunt, I. and A. F. Bennett. 2000. Temperate woodlands in Victoria: distribution, composition and conservation. Pp. 17–31 in J. Hobbs and C. J. Yates (eds.) *Temperate Eucalypt Woodlands in Australia: Biology, Conservation, Management and Restoration*. Chipping Norton, NSW: Surrey Beatty & Sons.

Luoto, M., R. Virkkala, R. K. Heikkinen and K. Rainio. 2004. Predicting bird species richness using remote sensing in boreal agricultural-forest mosaics. *Ecological Applications* **14**:1946–62.

Mac Nally, R. 2000. Regression and model building in conservation biology, biogeography and ecology: the distinction between – and reconciliation of – "predictive" and "explanatory" models. *Biodiversity and Conservation* **9**:655–71.

Mazerolle, M. J. and M.-A. Villard. 1999. Patch characteristics and landscape context as predictors of species presence and abundance: a review. *Ecoscience* **6**:117–24.

McAlpine, C. A., J. R. Rhodes, J. G. Callaghan *et al.* 2006. The importance of forest area and configuration relative to local habitat factors for conserving forest mammals: a case study of koalas in Queensland, Australia. *Biological Conservation* **132**:153–65.

McGarigal, K. and W. C. McComb. 1995. Relationships between landscape structure and breeding birds in the Oregon Coast Range. *Ecological Monographs* **65**:235–60.

Mitchell, M. S., S. H. Rutzmoser, T. B. Wigley *et al.* 2006. Relationships between avian richness and landscape structure at multiple scales using multiple landscapes. *Forest Ecology and Management* **221**:155–69.

Newmark, W. D. 1991. Tropical forest fragmentation and the local extinction of understorey birds in the Eastern Usambara Mountains, Tanzania. *Conservation Biology* **5**:67–78.

Palmer, G. C. and A. F. Bennett. 2006. Riparian zones provide for distinct bird assemblages in forest mosaics of southeast Australia. *Biological Conservation* **130**:447–57.

Peterken, G. F. 1996. *Natural Woodland. Ecology and Conservation in Northern Temperate Regions.* Cambridge, UK: Cambridge University Press.

Pino, J., F. Roda, J. Ribas and X. Pons. 2000. Landscape structure and bird species richness: implications for conservation in rural areas between natural parks. *Landscape and Urban Planning* **49**:35–48.

Radford, J. Q. and A. F. Bennett. 2007. The relative importance of landscape properties for woodland birds in agricultural environments. *Journal of Applied Ecology* **44**:737–47.

Radford, J. Q., A. F. Bennett and L. McRaild. 2004. *How Much Habitat is Enough? Planning for Wildlife Conservation in Rural Landscapes.* Burwood, Victoria, Australia: Deakin University.

Radford, J. Q., A. F. Bennett and G. J. Cheers. 2005. Landscape-level thresholds of habitat cover for woodland-dependent birds. *Biological Conservation* **124**:317–37.

Reid, J. R. W. 1999. *Threatened and Declining Birds in the New South Wales Sheep-Wheat Belt. 1. Diagnosis, Characteristics and Management.* Consultancy report to NSW National Parks and Wildlife Service. Canberra: CSIRO Wildlife and Ecology.

Renjifo, L. M. 2001. Effect of natural and anthropogenic landscape matrices on the abundance of subandean bird species. *Ecological Applications* **11**:14–31.

Robinson, D. and B. J. Traill. 1996. Conserving woodland birds in the wheat and sheep belts of southern Australia. *RAOU Conservation Statement* (Supplement to *Wingspan* Vol. 6 No. 2) **10**:1–16.

Saunders, D. A. 1989. Changes in the avifauna of a region, district and remnant as a result of fragmentation of native vegetation: the wheatbelt of Western Australia. A case study. *Biological Conservation* **50**:99–135.

Smith, A. A., S. M. Redpath, S. T. Campbell and S. J. Thirgood. 2001. Meadow pipits, red grouse and the habitat characteristics of managed grouse moors. *Journal of Applied Ecology* **38**:390–400.

Smith, P. 1985. Effects of intensive logging on birds in eucalypt forest near Bega, New South Wales. *Emu* **85**:15–21.

Suckling, G. C. 1982. Value of preserved habitat for mammal conservation in plantations. *Australian Forestry* **45**:19–27.

Toms, J. D. and M. L. Lesperance. 2003. Piecewise regression: a tool for identifying ecological thresholds. *Ecology* **84**:2034–41.

Trzcinski, M. K., L. Fahrig and G. Merriam. 1999. Independent effects of forest cover and fragmentation on the distribution of forest breeding birds. *Ecological Applications* **9**:586–93.

Turner, M. G., R. H. Gardner and R. V. O'Neill. 2001. *Landscape Ecology in Theory and Practice.* New York, NY: Springer-Verlag.

Vesk, P. A. and R. Mac Nally. 2006. The clock is ticking – revegetation and habitat for birds and arboreal mammals in rural landscapes of southern Australia. *Agriculture, Ecosystems and Environment* **112**:356–66.

Villard, M.-A., M. K. Trzcinski and G. Merriam. 1999. Fragmentation effects on forest birds: relative influence of woodland cover and configuration on landscape occupancy. *Conservation Biology* **13**:774–83.

Wiens, J. A. 1995. Landscape mosaics and ecological theory. Pp. 1–26 in L. Hansson, L. Fahrig and G. Merriam (eds.) *Mosaic Landscapes and Ecological Processes.* London: Chapman and Hall.

Wiens, J. A., B. Van Horne and B. R. Noon. 2002. Integrating landscape structure and scale into natural resource management. Pp. 23–67 in J. Liu and W. W. Taylor (eds.) *Integrating Landscape Ecology into Natural Resource Management.* Cambridge, UK: Cambridge University Press.

Landscape thresholds in species occurrence as quantitative targets in forest management: generality in space and time?

MATTHEW G. BETTS AND MARC-ANDRÉ VILLARD

INTRODUCTION

Simulation models predict that habitat loss may reach a threshold level below which ecological processes change abruptly (Fahrig 1998; With and King 1999; Flather and Bevers 2002). Effects of fragmentation *sensu stricto* are then detected, whereby increasing distances among patches and matrix resistance reduce the likelihood of recolonization after local extinctions (Lande 1987; With and King 1999). By definition, models simplify reality; therefore, they do not always represent appropriate metaphors for real landscapes because they tend to assume sharply contrasted habitat mosaics. None the less, different species perceive the same landscape differently and those specializing on habitat types dramatically altered by management may exhibit actual fragmentation effects and species-specific thresholds.

Surprisingly few studies have examined the landscape-scale effects of forest management on animals and plants. Previous landscape-scale studies have mainly examined species response to different landscape contexts or landscape structures in forests fragmented by agriculture (see Chapter 8, this volume, for a review). Managed forest landscapes are thought to be more permeable to the movements of vertebrate forest animals because contrasts among forest stands are generally softer than between forests and cropfields or pastures, for example. Indeed, fragmentation effects have mainly been detected in forests fragmented by agriculture or in island archipelagoes

Setting Conservation Targets for Managed Forest Landscapes, ed. M.-A. Villard and B. G. Jonsson. Published by Cambridge University Press.

(Mönkkönen and Reunanen 1999). Clearcuts may become relatively permeable to forest bird movements as soon as the regeneration provides some cover (Sieving *et al.* 1996), although juveniles may not move across them as readily as adults. Indeed, Robichaud *et al.* (2002) compared mist net capture rates before and after experimental harvesting in a boreal mixedwood forest and found that capture rates of juveniles in mist nets placed in a riparian buffer strip increased in the first year after harvesting of adjacent forest and remained higher than pre-harvest capture rates four years post-harvest. However, only four of 21 woodland-nesting bird species had not been observed or captured in the adjacent regenerating clearcut four years after harvesting.

Landscape thresholds, if they exist, would provide major insights for conservation planning and forest management because they represent points (or ranges) in habitat loss where rates of population decline or species loss may accelerate (Huggett 2005). At such threshold levels, small increases in habitat amount managed for conservation may have large payoffs for species persistence (Fig. 9.2) or the conservation of species-rich assemblages. However, as we show in this chapter, the position of an empirical threshold does not necessarily coincide with the management targets necessary to achieve a conservation goal (see also Chapter 8, this volume). Here, the goal is to ensure the long-term persistence of a given species or species assemblage. We will return to this important issue in the Discussion, below.

To study species response to landscape management, researchers should be able to map or predict the distribution of focal species and, ideally, some parameter of fitness or population growth reflecting habitat quality. Depending on the type of organism considered, the technical difficulty involved in collecting such data may turn landscape surveys into a prohibitive endeavor. In contrast, presence–absence or at least presence data exist for substantially more species because they are relatively easy to collect. With the existence of approaches for estimating detectability (Schieck 1997; Kéry and Schmid 2005), such data may be used over longer time periods to estimate demographic processes (e.g. metapopulation dynamics) (MacKenzie *et al.* 2003).

Nevertheless, few tests of landscape-scale thresholds in either species demography or occurrence have been performed in the field. This may reflect the paucity of formal statistical approaches for threshold detection rather than the rarity of actual threshold relationships. Methods for identifying thresholds in occurrence (binomial) data appear to have lagged behind those appropriate for continuous data (e.g. Toms and Lesperance 2003). This is problematic because presence–absence data are commonly used in ecology to predict species distributions (Guisan and Thuiller 2005).

A second potential stumbling block to detection of landscape thresholds in forest mosaics is the coarseness of the predictor variables generally available (e.g. "forest", "developed land"). It is important to accurately define the distribution of habitat for species under consideration to ensure that landscape metrics are relevant to the species at hand (Vos *et al.* 2001; Betts *et al.* 2007). On the other hand, it is not always possible to develop species-specific models for all species of concern. Ideally, conservation targets should be defined based on the requirements of the focal region's most sensitive species (e.g. Guénette and Villard 2005).

A few studies have tested for threshold (non-linear) relationships in species occurrence as a function of landscape structure (e.g. Homan *et al.* 2004; Betts *et al.* 2007; Denoël and Ficetola 2007; Chapter 7, this volume). These studies tend to recommend conservation targets that are on or above threshold values. However, if landscape-scale thresholds are to be applied beyond the boundaries of a given study area, it is critical for conservation planners to know about the robustness of such conservation targets (Chapter 7, this volume). The generality of habitat studies to broader spatial extents and longer time periods is often assumed in the development of conservation policy, but rarely tested (Wallington *et al.* 2005).

In this chapter, we test for thresholds in the occurrence of forest songbirds in relation to landscape structure by using two different statistical techniques: receiver-operating characteristic (ROC) analysis and segmented logistic regression (Muggeo 2003). We examine the strengths and weaknesses of both of these approaches to species distribution modeling and conservation planning. Using data from three geographically discrete study areas each located within *c.* 250 km radius, we determine to what extent the thresholds obtained can be generalized (a) across space; (b) over time; (c) across spatial extents; and (d) across species. Each of these comparisons also provides an opportunity to compare the behavior of threshold detection methods. Species-specific thresholds are examined using the proportion of mature forest in the landscape as a common currency, and more complex landscape metrics derived from spatially explicit, species-specific distribution models (the "organism-based" or "species-centered" approach) (Betts *et al.* 2006b).

METHODS

We used data from three different study areas located in the province of New Brunswick, Canada. Two of these (Black Brook, 47°23′N, 67°40′W; Riley Brook, 47°11′N, 67°13′W) are located in north-western New Brunswick whereas the third is located *c.* 250 km away, in south-eastern New Brunswick (Greater Fundy Ecosystem, 46°05′–45°28′N; 66°05′–64°57′W, hereafter 'Fundy'). All study areas are characterized by broadly similar forest types and harvest systems, although north-western landscapes were characterized by a higher proportion of conifer plantations than the south-eastern landscape surveyed. In each study area, birds were surveyed by using the point count method, in which observers record all individuals seen or heard within either a 50 m radius (Riley Brook, Fundy) or 100 m radius (Black Brook) (see Guénette and Villard 2005; Betts *et al.* 2006a). Differences in point count radii among studies should result in higher overall probability of detection for the same species in Black Brook than in the other two study areas. However, all other things being equal, the shape of the response of individual species to landscape structure should remain the same. Nevertheless, we acknowledge that methodological differences undoubtedly decreased the likelihood of finding similarities in threshold values among study areas. Hence, our results should be considered conservative. Protocols also varied slightly with respect to habitat sampling and characterization of landscape structure. Therefore, we conducted pairwise comparisons between these study areas depending on the compatibility of the habitat and landscape data sets.

Among the bird species surveyed, we selected five wood warbler species (family Parulidae) that are known to be associated with mature (>60 years) forest (Blackburnian warbler *Dendroica fusca*; black-throated blue warbler *D. caerulescens*; black-throated green warbler *D. virens*; northern parula *Parula americana*; and ovenbird *Seiurus aurocapilla*). In New Brunswick, mature forests are the stand age classes declining at the fastest rate (Betts *et al.* 2003, 2007a). The five species represent a variety of ecological niches: the ovenbird nests and forages on the ground; the black-throated blue warbler nests and forages in the shrub layer; the three other species nest and forage in the subcanopy and canopy (Poole 2005).

In a separate study we developed spatially explicit models for the distribution of 21 bird species based on local scale variables derived from a geographic information system GIS) as predictor variables (e.g. age class, stand composition, canopy cover, elevation; Betts *et al.* 2006a). The GIS land-cover data originated from the New Brunswick Forest Inventory (NBDNR 1993), which are based on interpreted and digitized aerial photographs taken in 1993 (1:12 500 scale, color) and updated to 2000 with satellite imagery (30 m^2 resolution; Betts *et al.* 2003). None of these initial models relied on landscape-scale data. We developed habitat-suitability maps (30 m^2 resolution) for each species by mapping the fitted values of GIS habitat models

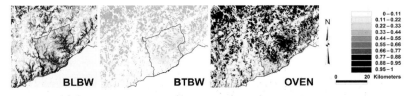

Figure 9.1. Quantitative habitat suitability maps in the Greater Fundy Ecosystem for three songbirds that were used as a basis for testing for thresholds in species occurrence. Darker shading indicates higher probability of occurrence. Solid outline indicates boundaries of Fundy National Park (BLBW, Blackburnian warbler; BTBW, black-throated blue warbler; OVEN, ovenbird) (adapted from Betts *et al.* 2007a).

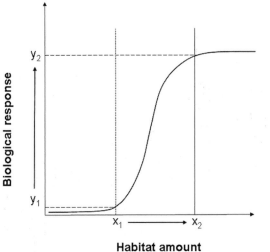

Habitat amount

Figure 9.2. Hypothetical example of the insight thresholds may provide when setting management targets. A small increase in amount of habitat from x_1 to x_2 results in a relatively large gain in conservation value (e.g. population size, species occurrence, species density).

(Fig. 9.1). To obtain a measure of habitat amount, we summed the estimated probability of occurrence surrounding each sample point at two spatial extents: 1,000 and 2,000 m (after Betts *et al.* 2007a). This method constitutes the "organism-based" approach to modeling the effects of landscape structure on species occurrence. Rather than relying on generic cover-type descriptors of landscape structure (e.g. "mature forest"), it relies on quantitative species-specific definitions of habitat amount and landscape pattern at landscape scales.

Box 9.1 Statistical methods to detect thresholds in binary data

Ecologists frequently collect data from a large number of locations and it is not always possible or even appropriate to estimate the abundance of each species precisely. In such cases, data can be collected on the presence or absence of each species, if absences can be properly validated (see Guénette and Villard 2005). Otherwise, the species is either present or undetected. In this chapter, we wanted to determine whether species exhibited thresholds in their response to varying amounts of habitat in the landscape. Using data from three study areas, we compared the threshold values indicated by two different statistical methods: receiver-operating chacteristic (ROC) analysis and segmented logistic regression.

Both methods detect thresholds by using an iterative procedure, i.e. an operation is repeated until an optimum value is obtained. In the case of ROC analysis, we selected thresholds corresponding to the value on the x-axis (here, habitat amount) minimizing the sum of false positives and false negatives. A false positive is a case where an event is observed (e.g. presence of species X) even though the logistic regression model predicted no event (here, absence of species X). A false negative is the opposite. A cut-off value corresponding to the lowest sum of false positives and false negatives is then identified on the y-axis. The ROC threshold is calculated by isolating the corresponding x value (labeled x_t) in the logistic equation as follows:

$$x_t = [\ln(1/c - 1) + \beta_0]/_-\beta_1$$

where c is the cut-off value, β_1 is the logistic regression coefficient, and β_0 is the intercept. The behavior of ROC thresholds is closely examined in Chapter 3 (this volume) by using a numerical simulation.

Segmented logistic regression uses maximum likelihood estimation to find the best fit of a model to the data. The user specifies the response variable (species presence or absence; y-axis), predictor variables (e.g. amount of forest; x-axis), and the number of breakpoints (thresholds) to be tested. The segmented logistic regression is specified as:

$$p = \exp(\beta_0 + \beta_1 x + \beta_2(x - \psi)_+)/1 + \exp(\beta_0 + \beta_1 x + \beta_2(x - \psi)_+)$$

where p is the probability of species occurrence, x is the independent variable, ψ is the breakpoint (threshold), and $(x - \psi)_+ = (x - \psi) \chi I (x > \psi)$ being $I(A) = 1$ if A is true, β_0 is the intercept, β_1 is the slope of the left line segment (that is, for $x \geq \psi$), and β_2 is the difference-in-slopes parameter. Thus, $(\beta_1 + \beta_2)$ is the slope of the right line segment $(x > \psi)$. Segmented logistic regression relies on an iterative fitting process to estimate ψ, β_0, $\beta_1 \ldots \beta_i$ (Muggeo 2003). Multiple $\hat{\psi}$ and $\hat{\beta}$ are fitted repeatedly until estimates converge at the maximum likelihood estimate. Thus, maximum likelihood "searches" for the breakpoint(s) and slopes of regression lines to optimize model fit. An information theoretic (e.g. AIC, BIC) approach can then be used to test whether threshold models fit the data better than non-threshold (linear) models. Information theoretic approaches encourage model parsimony; the best models are those with the best fit but with the fewest parameters (see Muggeo 2003; Betts *et al.* 2007 for more details).

Vegetation plot data were used to account for local habitat suitability (see Guénette and Villard 2005; Betts et al. 2006b). We modeled bird–habitat relationships by using logistic regression. Thresholds in either (a) mature forest or (b) amount of habitat (defined above) were detected either by using ROC analysis (Guénette and Villard 2005) or segmented logistic regression (Muggeo 2003; Betts et al. 2007a). These statistical threshold-detection methods are explained in Box 9.1. We used locally weighted regression splines (loess) plots to show the smoothed distribution of raw presences and absences in relation to amount of mature forest and habitat amount (e.g. Fig. 9.3a).

First, we compared thresholds detected for a given species in two different study areas. Depending on the need for detailed stand-level or landscape-level data, we compared the Fundy study area with either the Black Brook or the Riley Brook (north-western New Brunswick) study area. Then, we compared thresholds detected for a given species over three successive years. A third comparison pertained to variations in thresholds detected for the same species across spatial extents (150 m – 2 km surrounding each sample point). We also compared threshold responses (or lack thereof) among forest bird species at a given location and year. Finally, we examined whether landscape metrics defined from an "organism-based perspective" (i.e. spatially explicit habitat models developed for individual species) improve the consistency in thresholds (a) among species, (b) between study areas (Riley Brook and Fundy), and (c) between statistical techniques. This final test could only be conducted for three species because GIS models did not have adequate prediction success for the other species in both regions. In all cases of threshold detection, we controlled for the effects of both spatial autocorrelation and variation introduced by differences in local variation (Box 9.2; see Guénette and Villard 2005; Betts et al. 2007b).

RESULTS

We found statistical support for segmented thresholds in amount of mature forest in at least one study area for two of five species (black-throated blue warbler, Blackburnian warbler; Table 9.1). Thresholds were supported for all three species in at least one study area as a function of habitat amount (Table 9.2). However, in both cases segmented thresholds tended to have less support when we statistically controlled for local habitat variation (Tables 9.1 and 9.2; see Box 9.2). We estimated ROC thresholds for all species in all study areas. Both threshold methods showed varying

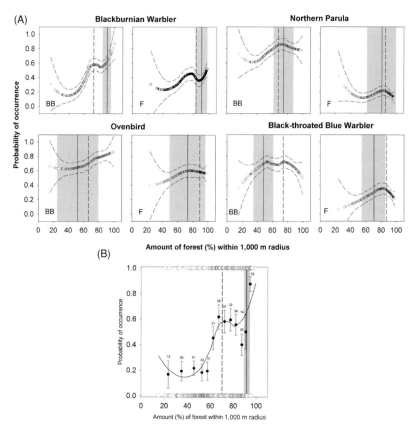

Figure 9.3. (A) Relationships between species occurrence and percent forest cover within a 1 km radius (314 ha) in Black Brook (BB) and Fundy (F) study areas for four wood warbler species. Dashed lines show ROC thresholds. Segmented thresholds are shown as solid black vertical lines (gray shading, 95% CI). Note that segmented threshold models were not supported in the majority of these cases (see Table 9.1); (B) detailed graph for Blackburnian warbler in the Black Brook study area, showing estimated probability of presence (black dots ± SE), actual presence–absence data points (white dots), and a locally weighted regression line. Numbers above error bars indicate sample sizes.

consistency among study areas, methods, and species, and over time. We discuss each of these aspects below.

Geographical consistency in thresholds

Consistency in thresholds as a function of mature forest within a 1,000 m radius obtained from segmented logistic regression was high only

Box 9.2 Statistical methods to control for spatial autocorrelation and local variation

Forests tend to have high variation in site-level quality, even in stands that fall within the same coarse categorizations (e.g. hardwood forest, mature forest). This high variation, which may reflect site-specific variability in productivity, understory density, etc., can mask the influence of landscape structure on animal occurrence. We statistically controlled for this variation by including important local variables in landscape models. Conversely, lack of independence among sample points that are close together (spatial autocorrelation) may amplify apparent effects of landscape structure by artificially increasing the number of sample points with similar ecological responses (see Lichstein *et al.* 2002). Thus, it is important to statistically control for both local variation and spatial autocorrelation when testing for landscape thresholds. This is accomplished by including both site-level variables that are known to influence the distribution of the species in question, and "spatial autocovariates" in occurrence models. Spatial autocovariates are calculated by summing the number of species presences at neighboring points within different radii (called "lags") surrounding each sample point. By using such variables as covariates in habitat use models, it is possible to account for potential lack of independence among points that are close together.

for the Blackburnian warbler (Table 9.1; Fig. 9.3). For this species, the segmented threshold value we found was nearly identical between the Fundy and Black Brook study areas. However, this non-linear relationship did not receive consistent statistical support in both study areas. A threshold in Blackburnian warbler occurrence was strongly supported in Black Brook, but received only moderate support in Fundy (Δ AIC 2.63 from the linear model). The segmented model that controlled for local variation did not even converge in Fundy (Table 9.1). Similarly, thresholds for black-throated blue warbler were roughly similar (*c.* 11% difference); 95% confidence intervals ($1.96 \times$ s.e.) of the estimated thresholds in each study area overlapped. However, the strength of the Fundy model was equivocal (segmented model Δ AIC 0.04 from linear model). Ovenbird and black-throated green warbler showed greater variation in threshold values between study areas (*c.* 20%), irrespective of the threshold detection method used. However, for these species, thresholds in species occurrence as a function of mature forest did not receive much support (Table 9.1).

Our comparison of thresholds in species occurrence as a function of (species-specific) habitat amount did not show any greater consistency between study areas (Table 9.2; Fig. 9.4). Thresholds were strongly

Table 9.1. *Thresholds (ROC and segmented: see Box 9.1) in probability of occurrence of five species of wood warbler in relation to the percent of mature forest within a 1 km radius landscape in two study areas of New Brunswick, Canada*

Note that negative Δ AIC values indicate low or no support for segmented threshold models. Rows in bold indicate statistical support for segmented thresholds in either models including only landscape terms or models controlling for local variation (full models).

Location	AUC (AUC full model)[a]	ROC threshold	Segmented threshold (SE)	Segmented threshold full model (SE)[a]	Δ AIC to linear model (full model)[c]
Blackburnian					
Fundy	0.60 (0.69)	83.26	92.67 (5.56)	NA[b]	−2.63
Black Brook	**0.70 (0.86)**	**68.12**	**92.57 (2.32)**	**92.96 (1.18)**	**8.09 (3.13)**
Ovenbird					
Fundy	0.52 (0.75)	85.15	76.09 (15.46)	71.2 (15.95)	−1.63 (−1.63)
Black Brook	0.61 (0.88)	64.29	53.30 (14.74)	NA[b]	−2.45
Black-throated green					
Fundy	0.54 (0.58)	86.21	88.33 (12.81)	NA[b]	−3.30 (−0.24)
Black Brook	0.62 (0.89)	62.80	NA[b]	95.27 (8.52)	
Black-throated blue					
Fundy	**0.51 (0.72)**	**85.01**	**69.91 (7.00)**	**70.45 (9.50)**	**1.50 (−0.04)**
Black Brook	**0.50 (0.87)**	**67.15**	**45.01 (6.43)**	**81.67 (11.52)**	**3.02 (0.81)**
Northern parula					
Fundy	0.50 (0.70)	84.72	81.10 (10.65)	77.76 (22.44)	−1.83 (−3.19)
Black Brook	0.60 (0.82)	64.03	76.64 (9.11)	73.34 (12.76)	0.80 (−2.05)

[a] Full model includes autocovariates, local, and landscape variables.

[b] No model convergence.

[c] AIC values in brackets correspond to models that include landscape and local variables as well as spatial autocovariates.

Table 9.2. *Thresholds (ROC and segmented: see Box 9.1) in probability of occurrence of forest birds as a function of the percent of habitat in a 1 km (Blackburnian warbler) or 2 km radius landscape (black-throated blue warbler, ovenbird) in two study areas of New Brunswick (Greater Fundy Ecosystem, Riley Brook)*

Note that negative Δ AIC values indicate low or no support for segmented threshold models. Rows in bold indicate statistical support for segmented thresholds in either models including only landscape terms or models controlling for local variation (full models).

Location	AUC (AUC full model)[a]	ROC threshold	Segmented threshold (SE)	Segmented threshold full model (SE)[b]	Δ AIC to linear model (full model)[c]
Blackburnian					
Fundy	0.59 (0.66)	29.67	**16.74 (3.18)**	**14.73 (2.93)**	**0.1 (1.34)**
Riley Brook	0.61 (0.81)	25.90	33.76 (8.04)	15.74 (2.07)	−3.42 (−2.05)
Ovenbird					
Fundy	0.56 (0.74)	38.71	**29.88 (3.48)**	**28.20 (5.08)**	**8.29 (3.19)**
Riley Brook	0.72 (0.78)	20.11	NA[b]	**19.79 (6.87)**	NA (−2.34)
Black-throated blue					
Fundy	0.61 (0.75)	15.60	**8.83 (0.62)**	**8.63 (0.70)**	**13.77 (5.0)**
Riley Brook	0.68 (0.72)	19.65	NA[b]	NA[b]	NA[b]

[a] Full model includes autocovariates, local, and landscape variables.

[b] No model convergence.

[c] AIC values in brackets are from models that include landscape and local variables as well as spatial autocovariates.

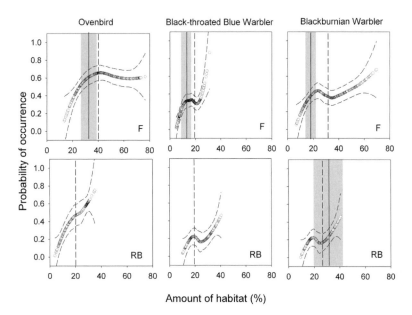

Figure 9.4. Occurrence of three species in relation to the amount of habitat in a landscape in Fundy (F) and Riley Brook (RB) (Blackburnian warbler, 1 km radius; other species, 2 km radius). Dashed lines show ROC thresholds. Segmented thresholds are shown as solid black vertical lines (gray shading, 95% CI).

supported in Fundy for both ovenbird and black-throated blue warbler but received weak (ovenbird) or no support (black-throated blue) in Riley Brook. Although segmented thresholds were similar for Blackburnian warbler when we controlled for local variation, they did not receive strong support in either study area (Table 9.2).

ROC thresholds as a function of mature forest amount showed important differences (>20%) between study areas (Table 9.1). However, when considering habitat amount, they tended to be more similar, particularly for ovenbird and black-throated blue warbler (<5%) (Table 9.2).

Temporal consistency in thresholds

Using both segmented and ROC methods, there appeared to be some consistency in threshold values obtained for individual species in the Fundy study area over three successive years (Fig. 9.5). It should be noted that although surveys took place in the same study area, birds were sampled at different study plots in 2001 than in 2002 and 2003. The occurrence of one species, the black-throated blue warbler, exhibited segmented thresholds that were largely robust to changes in time and space, at least within a local

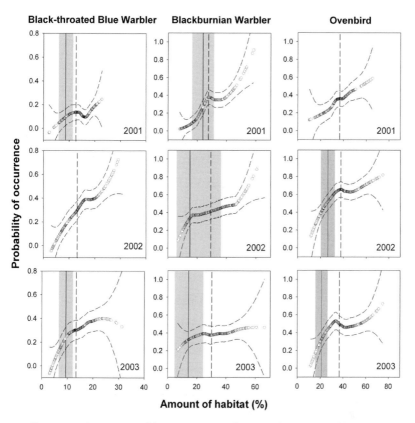

Figure 9.5. Occurrence of three species in relation to the amount of habitat within a 1 km radius (Blackburnian warbler) or 2 km radius (black-throated blue warbler, ovenbird) over three years. Samples were collected in different spatial locations in 2001 than in 2002 and 2003. Dashed lines indicate ROC threshold. Black solid line indicates segmented threshold (gray shading, 95% CI). The presence of segmented thresholds in the figure does not indicate that a threshold model was the most parsimonious (see Tables 9.1 and 9.2).

study region. The ROC approach identified thresholds that were remarkably consistent over the three years of the study (Fig. 9.5). The main difference in threshold values observed in Fig. 9.5 pertains to the threshold detection method we used rather than to the study year (see Discussion).

Consistency in thresholds across spatial extents
Thresholds in habitat amount associated with particular species decreased as spatial extent increased in two of the three species considered (Fig. 9.6). For the black-throated blue warbler, threshold values were

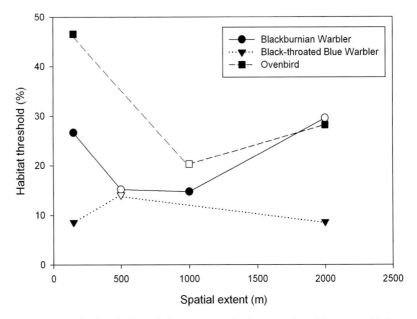

Figure 9.6. Thresholds in habitat amount for three species of forest songbirds in relation to spatial extent considered. Empty symbols indicate no statistical support for a threshold at a particular extent. Thresholds were not calculated if habitat amount data at multiple spatial extents were too highly correlated to allow for comparison.

remarkably consistent, at *c*. 10% suitable habitat within the radius considered. For the ovenbird, however, the shift in threshold amount of habitat was more substantial (from 46% to 25%, when comparing 150 m and 2,000 m extents, respectively).

Variation in thresholds across species

As reported elsewhere (Chapter 7, this volume), there were species-specific variations in threshold values in response to both forest cover and habitat amount in the landscape. Different species appear to decline at different points along the forest or habitat loss gradient (With and Crist 1995). In Black Brook, the Blackburnian warbler exhibited the highest threshold in relation to mature forest (93%). This model was strongly supported. The threshold for the black-throated blue warbler was lower in the same study area (82%). Interestingly, thresholds in mature forest as detected by ROC were surprisingly consistent across species. In Fundy, thresholds ranged from 83% (Blackburnian warbler) to 86% (ovenbird). In Black Brook the range was from 62% (black-throated green warbler) to 68% (Blackburnian warbler). Thresholds in habitat amount varied from 9% (Fundy, black-throated blue warbler) to 28% (Fundy, ovenbird). It is important to note that this substantial range is partly an artifact of the way in which "habitat" was quantified for each species. By definition, rare species have lower probabilities of occurrence. When species-specific habitat suitability is summed at landscape scales (as we have done), the range in habitat amount is lower for rare species. When correcting for this issue by recalculating the proportion of habitat in fully contiguous landscapes to sum to 100%, the black-throated blue warbler and ovenbird models were more similar (23.07% and 30.65%, respectively). Confidence intervals for both adjusted segmented thresholds overlapped (see Betts *et al.* 2007a).

Influence of landscape variable(s) considered

Another source of variation in the threshold values obtained is the actual variable or set of variables used to characterize habitat at the landscape scale. By definition, habitats are species-specific. Hence, one may potentially improve the quality of models predicting the presence of a species by using spatial models incorporating the habitat variables influencing the distribution of a given species (Fig. 9.1; Betts *et al.* 2006b, 2007a). The thresholds we detected by using this species-centered approach tended to be more marked: segmented threshold models for both ovenbird and black-throated blue warbler were strongly supported. However, because we only considered three species with the species-centered approach, it is difficult to draw firm conclusions. The thresholds we detected by using this approach were fairly consistent: across study areas and among species, both segmented and ROC thresholds tended to range from 9% to 30%. Not surprisingly, species-centered thresholds were substantially lower than mature forest thresholds (Tables 9.1 and 9.2).

DISCUSSION

Do threshold responses to landscape structure provide robust conservation targets? Answering this question is critical if we are to use "landscape thresholds" to guide forest management and conservation planning. We expected threshold responses to be species-specific, but we did not know what to expect with regards to their consistency across space, time, or the spatial extents considered. Finally, we wanted to determine to what extent thresholds might vary as a function of the statistical method or analytical approach used.

Geographic consistency in landscape thresholds

A first insight from our analyses is that thresholds do exist for some species in managed forest landscapes, even though boundaries among landscape elements are fuzzier than in many other managed landscape types (e.g. farmland, urbanized landscapes). The threshold values obtained also showed a high degree of consistency through time for a given study area. However, there was fairly high variability in threshold values among study areas. This feature of the thresholds we detected implies that managers need to exhibit considerable caution when extrapolating thresholds from one region to another.

Given the relatively short distances between the study areas we examined, within-region variation in segmented thresholds as a function of both mature forest and habitat amount was somewhat surprising. There are several possible explanations for such variation. First, thresholds in response to mature forest may have varied between Black Brook and Fundy simply because the composition of mature forest varied; mature forest in each case contained different proportions of habitat for each species. For this to be the main cause of variation, we would expect the species-centered approach to exhibit more geographical consistency. Based on the ROC threshold approach, this was true. However, when we used the segmented approach, organism-based thresholds did not appear to be much more robust to geographic location.

A second explanation for lack of geographic consistency relates to differences in sampling design among study areas. This may have influenced statistical power to detect effects. For instance, in Fundy most sampling points were located in mature forest ($n = 505$) whereas in Riley Brook, sampling points were systematically distributed, resulting in $<1/3$ of the samples in the mature forest age class ($n = 90$). In support of this explanation, locally weighted regression splines (loess) plots showed surprising consistency in shape between study areas, even though segmented thresholds were not consistently detected in Riley Brook (Fig. 9.4). A second aspect of this explanation relates to the *range* of sampling. For instance, it would have been impossible to detect the same organism-based threshold for ovenbird in Riley Brook and Fundy because very few landscapes containing more than 30% habitat (the Fundy threshold) were actually sampled in Riley Brook ($n = 7$). Interestingly, the slope of the sub-threshold relationship in both study areas was remarkably similar (Fig. 9.4). A third potential reason for differences in threshold values between study areas is the distinct radii used for sampling birds in Black Brook vs. Fundy (see Methods). Because the detection radius used in Black Brook was greater, we might have expected systematically lower thresholds. We did not find this to be the case. Finally, differences in the thresholds observed could be due to within-region variation in species sensitivity to landscape structure. This seems highly unlikely as only *c.* 250 km separates north-western and south-eastern study areas.

Threshold variation among species

Not surprisingly, thresholds in mature forest amount tended to vary considerably among species. Such variations may be due to differences in each species' particular life-history characteristics. None the less, differences such as the ones observed here indicate that conservation planners and forest managers should consider the requirements of the most demanding species in a region, e.g. the Blackburnian warbler. Guénette and Villard (2005) also found that this species was among the most demanding with respect to structures associated with older forest stands.

Controlling for local habitat variation, organism-based thresholds ranged from 9% to 28%. Although this is substantial variation, as noted in the Results, part of this probably reflects variation in species prevalence. Interestingly, organism-based thresholds fell within the range (10%–30%) predicted by previous quantitative (Andrén 1994) and modeling studies (Fahrig 1998).

Thresholds in mature forest vs. habitat amount

We considered thresholds as a function of both mature forest and species-specific "habitat". Thresholds according to the organism-based approach tended to be much lower. This is likely because habitat for each species is a subset of the total amount of mature forest. There is some evidence that organism-based thresholds were more consistent over time and geographic space. However, as we only considered a small number of species, this question requires further research. It is important to note that, for some species, using an organism-based approach is important for detecting effects of landscape structure. For instance, we did not detect a strong influence of mature forest at the landscape scale on either ovenbird or black-throated blue warbler (Fig. 9.3a). In contrast, in Fundy at least, both species were strongly influenced by habitat amount in the landscape and exhibited strongly-supported thresholds (Table 9.2). If managers had considered only the single variable "mature forest", these sensitivities would have been missed.

On the other hand, using a "generic" land cover variable such as percentage of mature forest makes it possible to compare the responses of different species to the same landscapes. This latter approach may be more appropriate for use in some instances by conservation planners, particularly if the land cover variable of interest is strongly influenced by forest management (e.g. mature forest). By examining relationships between organism-based and generic landscape variables, it might be possible to reconcile these approaches when developing conservation targets. In this study, "generic" mature forest could play important ecological roles beyond acting as breeding habitat. For example, it may represent a highly permeable matrix for the species considered (Robichaud *et al.* 2002). Whether species are responding solely to habitat amount, matrix permeability, or interactions between these components remains an important question for future work.

Just as habitats are species-specific, spatial scales of importance also varied among species. For instance, the amount of habitat at 1 km was the best variable to predict Blackburnian warbler occurrence, whereas habitat amount at 2 km radius best explained ovenbird presence (Betts *et al.* 2007). We hypothesize that such variation likely relates to the scale of dispersal (Bowman 2003) or extra-territorial movements of each species (Norris and Stutchbury 2001). These results highlight the importance of spatial scale in forest ecology and management; conclusions may vary depending on the spatial scale of analysis.

ROC vs. segmented logistic regression

The development of threshold detection methods is relatively recent. Ecologists are just starting to explore their robustness to various characteristics of data sets (e.g. Guénette and Villard 2004; Betts *et al.* 2007). Here, we contrasted the performance of two methods. In the absence of an "absolute" threshold beyond which a species is always present or absent (e.g. Radford and Bennett 2004), one cannot actually test the ability of a method to detect true thresholds. To do so, simulations can be applied to realistic data sets to examine the influence of various threshold types/characteristics (e.g. Guénette and Villard 2004; Chapter 3, this volume; Betts *et al.*, in preparation). In the meantime, we can examine patterns in our results to derive some basic observations on the behavior of each threshold detection method.

We observed systematic differences in the threshold values indicated by the two methods we used. This reflects the fact that segmented logistic regression uses maximum likelihood to "search" for the best breakpoint to explain non-linearity in the relationship between species presence–absence and habitat amount, whereas ROC provides the optimal cut-off point for predicting presence vs. absence (Box 9.1). This means that in some cases, segmented logistic regression identifies non-asymptotic breakpoints (e.g. Fig. 9.3a, b, Blackburnian warbler). In other words, some breaks occur at habitat amount values below a rapid *increase* in probability of occurrence; that is, thresholds exhibit a "hockey stick" pattern rather than an asymptote (e.g. Fig. 9.3b). Although this may be of interest from the standpoint of understanding ecological processes, it is less useful from a management perspective. Managers should set targets for the amount of habitat above which there is a minimal increase in probability of species occurrence (asymptotes). However, a precautionary approach must be applied when using empirical thresholds as guides to define management targets. Thresholds in species richness as a function of habitat amount must also be interpreted with caution because species start declining in abundance at habitat amounts far above the actual threshold value (Chapter 8, this volume).

A key difference between the two threshold detection techniques is that the segmented approach will only calculate a threshold in the instance of a non-linear relationship between the predictor and response variables. It is important to note that we did not detect thresholds for several species in each study area. However, lack of a non-linear relationship does not imply lack of an effect. In the absence of a strongly non-linear response, managers must still rely on an objective approach to establish a conservation target. In such cases, the ROC approach seems highly appropriate. The simulation presented by Villard (Chapter 3, this volume) clearly illustrates this type of situation.

Nevertheless, it is critical to test for non-linear relationships even when using the ROC approach. In several instances, strong relationships between landscape structure and species occurrence could be masked by such non-linearities (Betts *et al.* 2007); very sharp thresholds are poorly modeled by linear models to the extent that important variables can be missed as a result of considering only linear relationships. Incorporating non-linear relationships also improves model calibration (Vaughan and Ormerod 2005); predicted and observed values are more closely matched.

In the case of both threshold detection methods, it is important to note that the thresholds correspond to the *detection* of a species at sampling points. If species detection is imperfect, threshold estimates may be prone to error or bias. In the current study, all species were characterized by reasonably high detection probability (75%–90%) (Farnsworth *et al.* 2002). The risk of bias obviously becomes greater with decreases in detectability (MacKenzie *et al.* 2003). Further research needs to be undertaken on accounting for detectability in statistical threshold tests.

The thresholds we report should not be considered as amounts of habitat below which a population will not persist. Such thresholds should be viewed as "pre-extinction" levels in habitat amount. If landscapes are managed to prevent habitat amount from declining below the threshold in species occurrence, it is unlikely that the entire population will become extinct (Betts *et al.* 2007a). Nevertheless, future studies should test whether thresholds in detection correspond to thresholds in demographic variables (i.e. survival, reproduction; Lampilä *et al.* 2005). The hypothesis to test is that thresholds in species occurrence are positively correlated with thresholds in demographic variables (Bock and Jones 2004). However, the few studies addressing this issue suggest that habitat requirements for lekking (Angelstam 2004) or nesting (Poulin *et al.* 2008) are higher than those associated with species occurrence. Hence, thresholds in the probability of occurrence of individual species should be viewed as what they are: minimum requirements for a species' presence at a given location. Management targets for establishing "conservation blocks" within managed forest landscapes should err on the side of caution until monitoring data confirm that the requirements of species being managed are actually met.

ACKNOWLEDGEMENTS

This research was supported by grants from the Fundy Model Forest, the New Brunswick Environmental Trust Fund, and Parks Canada to MGB, and by a NSERC Discovery Grant and a grant from the Sustainable Forest Management Network to MAV. The manuscript was improved by the comments of Jim Radford and one anonymous reviewer.

References

Andrén, H. 1994. Effects of habitat fragmentation on birds and mammals in landscapes with different proportions of suitable habitat: a review. *Oikos* 71:355–66.

Angelstam, P. 2004. Habitat thresholds and effects of forest landscape change on the distribution and abundance of black grouse and capercaillie. *Ecological Bulletins* 51:173–87.

Betts, M. G., S. E. Franklin and R. G. Taylor. 2003. Interpretation of landscape pattern and habitat change for local indicator species using satellite imagery and geographical information system data in New Brunswick, Canada. *Canadian Journal of Forest Research* 33:1821–31.

Betts, M. G., A. W. Diamond, G. J. Forbes, M.-A. Villard and J. S. Gunn. 2006a. The importance of spatial autocorrelation, extent and resolution in predicting forest bird occurrence. *Ecological Modelling* 191:197–224.

Betts, M. G., G. J. Forbes, A. W. Diamond and P. D. Taylor. 2006b. Independent effects of fragmentation on forest songbirds: an organism-based approach. *Ecological Applications* 16:1076–89.

Betts, M. G., G. J. Forbes and A. W. Diamond. 2007a. Thresholds in songbird occurrence in relation to landscape structure. *Conservation Biology* 21:1046–58.

Betts, M. G., D. Mitchell, A. W. Diamond and J. Bêty. 2007b. Uneven rates of wildlife change as a source of bias in roadside wildlife surveys. *Journal of Wildlife Management* 71:2266–73.

Bock, C. E. and Z. F. Jones. 2004. Avian habitat evaluation: should counting birds count? *Frontiers in Ecology and the Environment* 2:403–10.

Bowman, J. 2003. Is dispersal distance of birds proportional to territory size? *Canadian Journal of Zoology* 81:195–202.

Denoël, M. and G. F. Ficetola. 2007. Landscape-level thresholds and newt conservation. *Ecological Applications* 17:302–9.

Farnsworth, G. L., K. H. Pollock, J. D. Nichols *et al.* 2002. A removal model for estimating detection probabilities from point-count surveys. *Auk* 119:414–25.

Fahrig, L. 1998. When does fragmentation of breeding habitat affect population survival? *Ecological Modelling* 105:273–92.

Flather, C. H. and M. Bevers. 2002. Patchy reaction-diffusion and population abundance: the relative importance of habitat amount and arrangement. *American Naturalist* 159:40–56.

Guénette, J.-S. and M.-A. Villard. 2005. Thresholds in forest bird response to habitat alteration as quantitative targets for conservation. *Conservation Biology* 19:1168–80.

Guénette, J.-S. and M.-A. Villard. 2004. Do empirical thresholds truly reflect species tolerance to habitat alteration? *Ecological Bulletins* 51:163–71.

Guisan, A. and W. Thuiller. 2005. Predicting species distribution: offering more than simple habitat models. *Ecology Letters* 8:993–1009.

Homan, R. N., B. S. Windmiller and J. M. Reed. 2004. Critical thresholds associated with habitat loss for two vernal pool-breeding amphibians. *Ecological Applications* 14:1547–53.

Huggett, A. J. 2005. The concept and utility of ecological thresholds in biodiversity conservation. *Biological Conservation* 124:301–10.

Kéry, M. and H. Schmid 2005. Monitoring programs need to take into account imperfect species detectability. *Basic and Applied Ecology* 5:65–73.

Lampilä, P., M. Mönkkönen and A. Desrochers. 2005. Demographic responses by birds to forest fragmentation. *Conservation Biology* 19:1537–46.

Lande, R. 1987. Extinction thresholds in demographic models of territorial populations. *American Naturalist* 130:624–35.

Lichstein, J. W., T. R. Simonds, S. A. Shrinter and K. E. Franzreb. 2002. Spatial autocorrelation and autoregressive models in ecology. *Ecological Monographs* 72:445–63.

MacKenzie, D. I., J. D. Nichols, J. E. Hines, M. G. Knutson and A. D. Franklin. 2003. Estimating site occupancy, colonization and local extinction when a species is detected imperfectly. *Ecology* 84:2200–7.

Mönkkönen, M. and P. Reunanen. 1999. On critical thresholds in landscape connectivity: a management perspective. *Oikos* 84:302–5.

Muggeo, V. M. R. 2003. Estimating regression models with unknown break points. *Statistics in Medicine* 22:3055–71.

Norris, D. R. and B. J. M. Stutchbury. 2001. Extraterritorial movements of a forest songbird in a fragmented landscape. *Conservation Biology* 15:729–36.

Poole, A. (ed.) 2005. *The Birds of North America Online*. http://bna.birds.cornell.edu.bnaproxy.birds.cornell.edu/BNA/. Ithaca, NY: Cornell Laboratory of Ornithology.

Poulin, J.-F., M.-A. Villard, M. Edman, P. Goulet and A.-M. Eriksson. 2008. Thresholds in nesting habitat requirements of an old forest specialist, the Brown Creeper (*Certhia americana*), as conservation targets. *Biological Conservation* 141:1129–37.

Radford, J. Q. and A. F. Bennett. 2004. Thresholds in landscape parameters: occurrence of the white-browed treecreeper *Climacteris affinis* in Victoria, Australia. *Biological Conservation* 117:375–91.

Robichaud, I., M.-A. Villard and C. S. Machtans. 2002. Effects of forest regeneration on songbird movements in a managed forest landscape of Alberta, Canada. *Landscape Ecology* 17:247–62.

Schieck, J. 1997. Biased detection of bird vocalizations affects comparisons of bird abundance among forested habitats. *Condor* 99:179–90.

Sieving, K. E., M. F. Willson and T. L. De Santo. 1996. Habitat barriers to movement of understory birds in fragmented south-temperate rainforest. *Auk* 113:944–8.

Toms, J. D. and M. L. Lesperance. 2003. Piecewise regression: a tool for identifying ecological thresholds. *Ecology* 84:2034–41.

Vaughan, I. P. and S. J. Ormerod. 2005. The continuing challenges of testing species distribution models. *Journal of Applied Ecology* 42:720–30.

Vos, C. C., J. Verboom, P. F. M. Opdam and C. J. F. ter Braak. 2001. Toward ecologically scaled landscape indices. *American Naturalist* 157:24–41.

Wallington, T. J., R. J. Hobbs and S. A. Moore. 2005. Implications of current ecological thinking for biodiversity conservation: a review of the salient issues. *Ecology and Society* 10:15. Available online at www.ecologyandsociety.org/vol10/iss1/art15.

With, K. A. and T. O. Crist. 1995. Critical thresholds in species' responses to landscape structure. *Ecology* 76:2446–59.

With, K. A. and A. W. King. 1999. Extinction thresholds for species in fractal landscapes. *Conservation Biology* 13:314–26.

The temporal and spatial challenges of target setting for dynamic habitats: the case of dead wood and saproxylic species in boreal forests

BENGT GUNNAR JONSSON AND THOMAS RANIUS

INTRODUCTION

Habitats for species vary substantially in their stability, whether temporally or spatially. Some habitats, such as rocks and lakes, may be present for centuries and only subject to changes in climate, whereas others, such as dung patches or carcasses, may be available only for a single season or even shorter. This variation in predictability constitutes an important selective force for associated species. It has been suggested that the habitat is the template for ecological strategies (Southwood 1977). In this sense, individuals of a species are confronted with the challenge of determining whether reproduction is best achieved "here" or "somewhere else" as well as "now" or "sometime in the future". By addressing these tradeoffs, the successful reproductive strategy will represent the life history of the species. Species adapted to long-lasting, predictable habitats are expected to generally be more sedentary; for them, the spatial distribution of the habitat is particularly important. This is a basic ecological starting point for appreciating the need to include time and space to a greater extent in forest conservation management. If only total habitat amount is considered, but the temporal and spatial distribution is ignored, important factors influencing the long-term viability of focal species will be missed and thus, at least for some species, the risk of decline and extinction will be severely underestimated.

Setting Conservation Targets for Managed Forest Landscapes, ed. M.-A. Villard and B. G. Jonsson. Published by Cambridge University Press.

A frequent approach to model population dynamics spatially is to apply the metapopulation concept. Here, the species are considered to be distributed in discrete patches in space (e.g. meadows, forest stands, ponds, single trees, etc.), themselves united by dispersal events. Extinction and recolonization are the events that drive the dynamics (Hanski 1999). In its classical form, metapopulation theory addressed sites that remained permanent over time. However, recent developments include a growing appreciation that habitat patches may come and go. The occurrence of "patch tracking populations" has been discussed, as well as the implications of the dynamics in patch persistence (Thomas 1994; Keymer et al. 2000). These approaches have recently been expanded to include empirical evaluation in forest ecosystems (Akçakaya et al. 2004, 2005; Snäll et al. 2005; Schroeder et al. 2007).

In forests, many species are associated with habitat elements and substrates that are discrete in space and have a limited longevity. This is particularly true for species associated with tree trunks and dead wood (e.g. Hagan and Grove 1999; Dahlberg and Stokland 2004). It is evident that trees eventually die and subsequently undergo decay, which finally leads to their incorporation in the soil. This implies that both epiphytic and saproxylic (dead wood-dependent) species depend on a habitat with a limited persistence. Deterministic local extinction events as habitat deteriorates must be compensated by the colonization of new tree trunks, snags, or logs.

In this chapter, we focus on the challenges of setting conservation targets for species living on dead wood. Dead wood is important as a focal habitat element for biodiversity in many forest ecosystems, but our discussion should also be viewed as an example of how to approach the conservation of species dependent on dynamic habitats. We refer mostly to our experience from boreal forests in Fennoscandia, but assume that the situation is similar in many forest types. Our approach includes both coarse-filter and fine-filter components (cf. Schultze et al. 2006) as it addresses the availability of dead wood and utilizes the dynamics of particular species.

HOW TO REACH A CERTAIN VOLUME

The volume of dead wood in an unmanaged forest stand is a result of site productivity, tree mortality, and decay. Both the formation and decay of dead wood can be readily modeled. Over longer time periods and large spatial domains in natural forests, the average levels can be set by assuming a balance between stand productivity and average decay rate (e.g. Ranius et al. 2004). However, at a stand scale (single to a few tenths of hectares), the variation around this mean can be substantial (Jonsson 2000; Edman *et al.* 2007). Thus, owing to stochastic variability, it is not possible to predict the exact amount of dead wood within a limited area at a certain moment. In managed forests and forests experiencing frequent fires, standing tree volume and tree mortality change over the rotation period, complicating the prediction of dead wood volumes. Furthermore, the destruction and removal of dead wood during forest operations must be taken into account.

Mortality rates

Tree mortality rates are caused by a multitude of factors, e.g. tree species, stand age, site conditions, and disturbance agents. Managed forests tend to have lower tree mortality than unmanaged stands, which is reasonable since one of the main aims of forest management is to produce stands where growth is directed to healthy trees and natural mortality during stand development, except for early, self-thinning stages after clearcutting, is kept at a minimum. For instance, average annual mortality rates from Fennoscandian managed forests range from 0.07% to slightly more than 1% of trees (Stokland *et al.* 2003). The variation is mainly associated with tree size (trees of intermediate size have lower mortality), tree species (broad-leaf species have higher mortality), stand age (young stands have higher mortality), and site productivity (highly productive sites have higher mortality). Mortality translates into an annual input of dead trees ranging from only 0.1 to 0.3 m^3 ha^{-1} in the region's managed forests, which is consistently less than in old-growth forests.

In order to predict the distribution of dead wood in the forest landscape, average values of tree mortality based on resampling of dead wood with long intervals do not always provide sufficient spatial and temporal resolution. Unfortunately, very limited data on the interannual variation in tree mortality in managed forests are available. Further, it is considered difficult to accurately model natural mortality across larger areas in managed forests (Dobbertin and Biging 1998). In an attempt to use the extensive data from Swedish managed forests, Fridman and Ståhl (2001) methodologically explored the predictive options and developed a functional approach. Their results indicate that although regional models can be developed to mimic the stochastic aspects of mortality, they require extensive data sets to be properly parameterized.

An extreme temporal variation in mortality occurs in forests dominated by large-scale disturbances, such as forest fires. In fire-prone forests, an average mortality rate is basically irrelevant. Here the actual fire regime and fire characteristics will determine a large part of the tree mortality for extended periods of time (Siitonen 2001; Chapter 7, this volume).

Decay approaches

A thorough discussion of general approaches to modeling the decay of dead trees is given by Yin (1999). In most cases, biomass loss is described by a negative exponential function (e.g. Harmon *et al.* 1986; Siitonen 2001).

$$Y_t = Y_0 e^{kt} \tag{1}$$

where Y_t is the mass at time t, Y_0 the initial mass, and k the decay rate constant. The decay rate constant has been analysed and described for various forest types (see, for example, Siitonen 2001 for a review on boreal forests). The decay rate constant ranges between 0.03 and 0.05, which corresponds to a loss of 90% of the biomass over periods of 45–75 years (Krankina and Harmon 1995; Naesset 1999; Tarasov and Birdsey 2001). The variation in decay rates is related to tree species but also to climate and canopy cover. Decay is performed mainly by fungi, and their relation to climate is complex. The actual decay rate is mainly set by the combined effects of temperature and moisture (Yin 1999). When describing decay, the losses of volume, density, and mass behave quite differently. As biomass may be lost without significant change in observable volume, the amount of habitat is lost differently for a species that utilizes the volume as habitat in comparison to a species using the dead tree as a carbon source. In the first case, volume losses are critical; in the latter case, the mass loss is the key. Also complicating the decay process is the loss through fragmentation of the substrate, which may be substantial during later stages of decay.

An alternative approach to describing decay is to follow the transition between defined decay stages (Kruys *et al.* 2002). This could be done using stage transition matrices (see Box 10.1), or by parameterizing a model of decay with a mean and standard deviation for the time a dead wood unit remains in each decay stage (Ranius *et al.* 2003). Although it requires species- and site-specific data, this approach has the benefit of separating the "population" of logs into different decay stages and could thus provide decay stage distributions over time. When predicting habitat suitability for individual species, this is far superior to crude estimates of dead wood volumes, as the majority of species are associated with certain decay stages (Stokland *et al.* 2004).

Box 10.1

Matrix models were developed as a mean to predict dynamics of populations structured into age- or stage classes (Caswell 2000). This approach can also be used to model the dynamics of logs in different decay stages (Kruys *et al.* 2002). Then it is assumed that over a set time interval (e.g. 5 years) each log has a given probability of remaining at the same stage or transiting to later stages of decay. Combined with a function that provides input of fresh dead trees, such a model is able to predict the future composition of dead wood. This includes both quantitative estimates (volumes or numbers) and qualitative estimates (decay stages). Further, if the model is parameterized for logs of varying size, the distribution into different size classes can also be predicted (Edman *et al.* 2007).

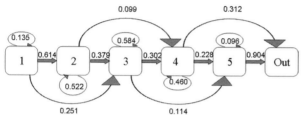

Figure A. Schematic depiction of the model of transition rates between decay classes. For each 5 yr period in the model, a tree may either remain in the same decay class, or move one or two classes. "Out" represents the dead trees that are classified as having left the system. Numbers indicate the probability for each transition based on a parameterization for Norway spruce in northern Sweden (Kruys *et al.* 2002). The number of decay classes and transition possibilities will vary depending on the classification system used, tree species, region, and other factors influencing decay rate.

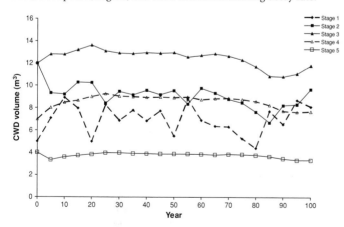

Figure B. Predicted development of dead wood volume in different decay stages based on random mortality (i.e. dead wood input) drawn for a normal distribution with a 5 year average of 6 m^3 ha^{-1}, and a standard deviation of 1.5. Transition rates are those presented in Figure A.

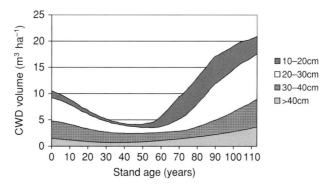

Figure 10.1. Amount of dead wood divided into different diameter classes based on a simulation model predicting dead wood volumes in managed forests. Parameter values are typical for biodiversity-oriented forestry, which implies that some trees are retained at final harvest. (From Ranius *et al.* 2003.)

Synthesizing into stand models

With mechanistic knowledge on stand development, tree mortality, decay of dead wood, and destruction of dead wood during forestry operations, the availability of dead wood substrates can be modeled and thus guide silvicultural management (Franklin *et al.* 2002). Such models are emerging (Ranius *et al.* 2003; Ranius and Kindvall 2004; Andersson *et al.* 2005; Montes and Canellas 2006) and open up the possibility to provide spatially explicit predictions of dead wood volumes and qualities over the landscape scale. This is a significant achievement for analysing habitat availability for saproxylic species under various forest management scenarios (Fig. 10.1). For instance, a full-scale application of current forest certification criteria in Sweden (Forest Stewardship Council 2005) was shown to increase dead wood volumes up to twice the current average in managed forests (Ranius *et al.* 2003). This approach has been further developed by incorporating the financial cost of different management scenarios and taking into account the habitat requirements of saproxylic organisms (Jonsson *et al.* 2006). Clearly, these models can also serve to explore management options allowing to meet predefined targets of dead wood availability.

EXTINCTION THRESHOLDS

Field studies show that at least some saproxylic organisms only occur when a certain amount of habitat is exceeded (reviewed by Ranius and Fahrig 2006; see also Mellen *et al.* 2002 for a practical application of DecAID). This suggests that, for these species, there are extinction thresholds that should be exceeded to allow for local population persistence. For instance, in a study by Holland et al. (2005), 12 longhorn beetle species were absent when the area covered by forest land was below a certain percentage, which differed widely between species (4.8%–99%). Økland et al. (1996) reported that some beetle species were absent when the amount of dead wood within 1 or 4 km² was below a certain level (for five species, a level of total volume of dead wood, and for three species, a certain number of large logs). Ranius (2002) studied beetles associated with hollow trees and found that for several species, especially those that were thought to have a limited dispersal propensity (Ranius 2006), tree-level occupancy was lower in smaller stands (see also Box 10.2). Woodpecker studies have demonstrated that a forest should maintain a certain amount of dead wood, or snags, to become suitable as a breeding habitat (Roberge 2006; three-toed woodpecker: Bütler et al. 2004). Landscape-level thresholds in habitat amount have also been shown for several forest bird species (Chapter 9, this volume, and references therein).

The fact that there are thresholds in the occurrence or reproduction of individual species does not necessarily mean that there are thresholds in the relationship between habitat amount and species richness (but see Chapter 8, this volume). On the contrary, the relationship between species richness of saproxylic species and the amount of dead wood per forest stand has been described by the following function:

$$N = k + m \log V$$

where N is the number of species and V the volume of dead wood (Martikainen et al. 2000; Grove 2002). This is one variety of the species–area functions frequently used, for instance, in island biogeography. The function implies that the species richness increases smoothly with habitat availability, i.e. there is no threshold. The reason why clear thresholds are absent may be that wood-dependent species vary widely in their degree of habitat specialization and dispersal ability. For that reason, they respond to the availability of different kinds of dead wood, and their responses are expressed over different spatial scales.

For saproxylic species, current occurrence patterns reflect not only current habitat availability at the stand level, but they are also affected by the history of individual stands and the occurrence of dispersal sources in neighboring stands (e.g. Gu et al. 2002; Schroeder et al. 2007). All studies presented above represent static snapshots of observed patterns; the spatial and temporal context has rarely been taken into consideration. From

Box 10.2

In a study of beetles associated with hollow oaks (Ranius 2002), some species exhibited lower occupancy per tree in smaller stands compared to larger ones. This suggests that larger stands are necessary for long-term persistence of these species. Based on such observations it is possible to estimate the needs for biodiversity conservation, and here the basic principles of such an estimation is presented (see also Bergman 2003). *Elater ferrugineus* is used as a model species, as it was the most demanding species among the species that occurred frequently enough to allow for statistical analysis; only in a wooded pasture with about 100 hollow trees did it occur more frequently, with an occupancy per tree of about 31% (Ranius 2002). The occupancy could probably be used as a proxy of the proportion of trees that are suitable for the species. Other studies have indicated that 15–20 suitable habitat patches might be necessary for long-term persistence of a species (Thomas and Hanski 1997). If we assume that 20 suitable trees are necessary, the total number of trees with large enough hollows should be 65 in a continuous area. It could be assumed that cavities of that size first develop at an age of 300 years. If the mortality is 0.8% for all oaks that are <500 years old, while for simplicity all remaining trees are assumed to die at an age of 500, this means that in an oak population with a stable age distribution, 7% are older than 300 years and thus potentially suitable for *Elater ferrugineus*. Therefore, to obtain 65 hollow trees, the total number of oaks should be about 930. If each tree is assumed to require an area of 0.02 ha, the minimum area of an oak pasture would be 19 ha. This presupposes that the management is directed solely towards this species. However, to make preservation of all biodiversity possible, the area of a pasture woodland should for several reasons be considerably larger.

(a) The oak pasture should also host species with other requirements.
(b) Within 19 ha, the average number of suitable trees over time may be enough for persistence, but the area desired is rather at the level where the minimum number of suitable trees is sufficient over a longer period. However, to predict that level requires data on temporal variability in recruitment, formation of tree hollows, and tree mortality that is not available.
(c) There are other species in hollow trees that are much rarer than *E. ferrugineus*. Their rarity implies, at least for some species, that they require larger area than *E. ferrugineus* for long-term persistence.
(d) These calculations are based on the fact that *E. ferrugineus* has been found to be relatively frequent in a stand with about 100 hollow trees, but the extinction risk in such a stand has not been estimated, and may be significant.

Thus, when requirements of certain species are analysed as above, the area demanded for biodiversity conservation tends to be underestimated. An alternative approach is to consider the logic of island biogeography, and regard all hollow trees in a stand as one habitat island. If the island has decreased recently, future extinctions will be more frequent than the colonizations, i.e. there is an extinction debt that has to be paid. Extinctions could be avoided by restoring the "island" of hollow oaks, i.e. increasing the number of hollow trees to a historical level. An advantage with this approach is that no knowledge about individual species is necessary, while a disadvantage is that it is difficult to determine which baseline should be used. Oaks decreased severely in Sweden at the beginning of the nineteenth century (Eliasson and Nilsson 2002), and probably the baseline should be set to the situation before that time.

Figure C. Adult of the click beetle *Elater ferrugineus*. (Photo: Vincent Vignon.)

snapshot data it is difficult to interpret extinction thresholds correctly. For instance, if a species is present only in unmanaged forests with a high amount of dead wood, it is impossible to determine whether this species would be able to use a managed forest in which the amount of dead wood was increased to that level during a limited time of the rotation period, or whether that is unlikely because such a habitat patch is too isolated in space and time to be colonized.

MODELING DYNAMIC POPULATIONS

Stand scale

Studies of the dynamics of single populations, ignoring immigration and emigration, have a long tradition in population ecology, starting with the original work by Lotka and Volterra in the early twentieth century. Despite being a standard approach, very few studies of the dynamics of single and isolated populations of wood-dependent species have been performed (but see Gustafsson 2002 for an example). The scarcity of empirical studies most likely reflects the difficulty of following individuals with at least part of their life cycle hidden within dead wood or with some stage composed of minute dispersal propagules.

In recent attempts to model populations at a forest stand scale, the discrete nature of the substrate has been utilized, and a metapopulation view applied, with single trees regarded as local habitat patches (Snäll *et al.* 2003; Ranius 2007). For epiphytic cryptogams it was found that population extinctions (at the tree level) was mostly deterministic (Snäll *et al.* 2003). Thus the model strongly focuses on the colonization phase. When modeling the metapopulation dynamics of *Osmoderma eremita*, it was important to take into account the wide variability in the number of individuals inhabiting the trees, which also causes large variability in local extinction risk (Ranius 2007).

The landscape scale

Theoretical developments over the past two decades in population modeling at the landscape scale hold the promise of a more dynamic, quantitative, and predictive approach to species conservation. A number of recent attempts to quantitatively model saproxylic species have been performed.

With an extensive knowledge of forest history, Gu *et al.* (2002) modeled the occurrence of a set of old-growth saproxylic fungi in central Finland. Besides their significant conclusion that current distribution is strongly affected by past landscape structure, they also showed that relevant models may be developed without extensive knowledge of all aspects of the species' biology or stand development models. Schroeder *et al.* (2007) used a similar approach. However, their study species (a beetle, *Harminius undulatus*) occurred not only in unmanaged forests, but also in managed forests older than 60 years and up to 10 years after harvesting. They found that the prediction from a habitat-dynamic metapopulation model corresponded better to field data than the prediction from a habitat-static model. This emphasizes the importance of a dynamic approach to understand species occurrence in managed forest landscapes. The approach in these studies has been useful in predicting which stands are occupied, but to predict the extinction risk in the future, given different management scenarios, requires more data, especially on colonization ability, and variability (also stochastic) in habitat quality historically and in the future.

Ranius and Kindvall (2006) have predicted extinction risks for model species, taking into consideration both habitat (dead spruce) and metapopulation dynamics. Opportunities to test such predictions also exist for a limited set of real species, where ongoing studies should provide much of this empirical background. Theoretical models (e.g. Hanski 2000) strongly suggest that aggregation of habitats increases population viability. However, at what spatial scale habitat aggregation is desirable is unclear, because for most species the dispersal range is not known. Nevertheless, this implies that the conservation value of an individual stand is influenced by its position in the landscape. This calls for extended landscape planning as a means to improve conservation efficiency. An even distribution of a fixed volume of retained dead wood is likely to be a very inefficient use of a resource valuable for both biodiversity and forest production.

ROADMAP TO QUANTITATIVE TARGETS

In the sections above, we have tried to show the challenges and problems associated with a more quantitative and analytical approach to species in temporary habitats and specifically addressing species using dead wood. However, conservation planning needs a stronger quantitative basis. Because biodiversity in forest ecosystems is connected to a large degree to the trees themselves, there is an inevitable tradeoff between extraction of forest products and biodiversity. In many forest landscapes, there is a distinction between conservation concern taken as a part of regular forest management (green tree retention, buffer zones, woodland key habitats, etc.) and larger sites set aside as protected areas. Together with the occurrence of intensive tree farms, this represents the triad approach (see Chapter 14, this volume). In the next section we will discuss the potential to set targets for dead wood availability in managed forest landscapes (approach I) and for the size of protected areas (approach II). We consider the potential for wood-dependent species very limited in tree farms.

Models for target species in dynamic landscapes

For a limited number of target species, models simulating persistence at a landscape scale could be developed by applying the metapopulation concept. Such models are especially useful for species in habitats that are highly variable over space and time, such as forests affected by management or repeated fires. This is because, for such species, we should expect a large deviation between conclusions drawn from dynamic models in comparison with simple correlations obtained from snapshot data. The outcome from the models may serve as conservation guidelines and exemplify the main options to be considered within the managed landscapes. In practice, we are confined to modeling the dynamics of species suitable for quantitative studies. This unfortunately excludes many of the rarest and most endangered species. These tend to have populations too small to provide sufficient data for model parameterization. This restriction will make it difficult to find study species that are perfect umbrella species (*sensu* Roberge and Angelstam 2003), whose protection implies that a large number of other species belonging to the same community are also protected at the same time. Furthermore, species responses may be largely individual, limiting the possibility of using focal species as representatives of the biota (cf. Lindenmayer *et al.* 2002). For that reason it is desirable that many target species are used, rather than only a very few (cf. Lambeck 1997).

In order to develop a species-specific model for persistence at a landscape level, the following data are needed (see also Box 10.2):

- Preferably, the current occurrences in the landscape and its surroundings are known. This provides the starting point for any simulation of population development. Alternatively, some model could provide spatially explicit predictions of the species' occurrence that also could serve as a starting point.
- Knowledge about which substrate qualities the species utilizes are required.
- For each habitat patch (which could be a forest stand, or a pixel if a grid-based approach is applied) in the landscape, a relevant measure of habitat quality is needed. This measure should come from empirical data on species – habitat associations. In its crudest sense, it should divide the landscape into suitable and unsuitable habitat. In reality, few landscapes are purely "black and white" from the species perspective and a more detailed distinction of relative habitat suitability provides a stronger basis for the model.
- Because a dynamic landscape is assumed, models that describe the change of habitat quality over time must be available. For dead wood, the approaches described above, together with other stand characteristics important for the species (e.g. basal area, tree species composition) could be applied.
- A crucial but unfortunately often lacking component is information on dispersal rate and distances. In many cases, the absence of empirical data implies that a range of realistic dispersal values must be explored.

Also important, and often neglected, is the extent to which dispersal varies over time and among different sections of the landscape. For some species, dispersal implies a great risk and, thus, mortality during dispersal is an issue.

- The probability for local persistence is positively related with the amount of habitat (because much habitat implies a large population size and a low extinction risk due to demographic and environmental stochasticity) and the number of immigrants from neighboring stands. For some species, it may be assumed that the local extinction risk is negligible as long as there is any habitat available at all, while for other species more complicated functions between local extinction risk, habitat availability, and dispersal must be constructed.
- The occurrence of time lags must be addressed. After colonization there may be a time lag before reproduction is possible. Furthermore, survival and continued dispersal may occur even when a patch no longer is suitable for colonization. For long-lived species, these aspects may have a profound role in the dynamics at the landscape scale.

Obviously, this is a data-demanding approach, but nevertheless a tractable way to provide scenario analysis of the persistence of species at the landscape scale. Such scenarios may be balanced by economic analysis to find optimal management alternatives (see Chapter 15, this volume).

Size of protected areas needed for species incompatible with commercial forestry

Models of metapopulations inhabiting a dynamic habitat require so much empirical data and modeling work that they can only be used for a limited number of species. Moreover, the requirements of some species are so high that their conservation is incompatible with commercial forestry. For these species, protected areas may be the only tractable form of protection. A critical question then becomes the area requirements of these species: how large do forest patches have to be to maintain a viable population within one limited reserve (see Box 10.3 for an example)?

This approach also has specific data requirements, as follows.

- *Species-substrate relationships, i.e. frequencies of species on substrates of varying quality.* Based on extensive field inventories, the habitat requirements for larger assemblages of species can be obtained. This should provide frequency estimates of species on particular dead wood qualities. Target

Box 10.3

Phlebia centrifuga is a wood-decaying fungus confined to larger spruce logs in early to intermediate decay stages. In Fennoscandia, it has decreased in both abundance and distribution and its viability in fragmented landscapes may be influenced by its currently small population size (Edman *et al.* 2004a). Based on several data sets collected in northern Sweden, the species' frequency of occurrence varied with diameter class: 0.2% (<20 cm), 1.2% (20–30 cm), and 7.2% (>30 cm). In old-growth forests within the study region, a rough estimate of logs per hectare in different diameter classes gives around 15 logs with diameter 20–30 cm and 35 logs in both classes <20 cm and >30 cm. Recalculating these log data and frequencies suggest that in an old-growth forest of 10 ha, around 25 occurrences of the species is reasonable. In an applied sense, these occurrences could be viewed as "individuals". The number of individuals that represent a viable population is not known, but based on the fairly narrow temporal window of occurrence on single logs (Berglund *et al.* 2005), the known dispersal limitation (Edman *et al.* 2004b), the dynamics of dead wood in old-growth spruce forests (Edman *et al.* 2007), and the risks of genetic drift in small populations it is unlikely that sites of less than 50 ha would support a population that is viable over extended time periods. This represents a projected area demand for a single species and should not be taken as a general figure for wood-decaying fungi. Despite its declining populations, *Phlebia centrifuga* is still a fairly frequent species given sufficient logs of the right quality. In general, the community of wood-decaying fungi is composed of mostly rare and low-abundance species (e.g. Berglund and Jonsson 2001) for which significantly larger areas may be required.

Figure D. The wood fungus *Phlebia centrifuga* growing on Norway spruce logs. (Photo: Jogeir Stokland.)

levels for the number of occurrences (e.g. logs colonized) of the species could be set and used for an analysis of size demands. Here, a critical stage is of course to define the population size (e.g. number of occurrences) for a "viable population". Relevant issues are known population fluctuations, risk of genetic drift, and likelihood of immigration from surrounding sites.

- *Habitat dynamics.* This approach requires models that provide temporal predictions on dead wood availability. Given that the natural variation in mortality and decay rates is known (Ranius *et al.* 2003; Edman *et al.* 2007), the frequency and severity of bottleneck periods can be analysed. It is of significant importance that such bottleneck periods are included in the analysis, as well as an evaluation of areas to protect.

- *Predictions of dead wood quantity and quality over time.* As described above, it is possible to predict availability of dead wood over time with relatively high resolution. Dead wood variables relevant for the substrates used (often tree species, diameter and decay stages) may be included in the models. Such predictions will represent a significant improvement over simplified volume estimates, and they will be of obvious importance when targeting saproxylic species richness and composition (cf. Berglund and Jonsson 2001).

- *Large-scale disturbances.* A complicating factor is the occurrence of large-scale disturbances in otherwise relatively stable forest types. A forest fire may completely alter the structure and successional stage of fairly large protected forest sites. This calls for redundancy in the reserve selection system. Large-scale disturbances may also be a prerequisite for saproxylic species. Here, individual stand models may be of less interest compared with the mosaic of successional stages that occur within larger landscapes. However, this only moves the temporal and spatial extent of the planning to larger scales. The approach could basically be the same: to maintain enough substrates for viable populations based on anticipated number of occurrences.

This approach has limitations. The availability of sites to be set aside may limit the degree to which predicted area requirements can be met. In many regions (e.g. boreal Fennoscandia), the magnitude of forestry is such that old-growth and primeval forests of sufficient size are no longer available. However, this emphasizes the need for restoration and the approach may be used to guide restoration activities also. It should be noted that some species are very sparse in terms of number of individuals or in frequency of log occupancy. These species might end up being "hope-for-the-best-species".

As an example, Lindhe and Lindelöw (2004) collected 47,038 individuals of 316 beetle species by enclosing 130 high stumps, i.e. with a method that means that all beetles had to some extent utilized the stumps. Of these, 64 species were represented by a single individual. This clearly suggests that some species, owing to their rarity, may never be considered in the planning process.

CONCLUSION

Single prescriptions on dead wood volumes are likely to fail to ensure saproxylic species persistence. Variations in dispersal ability, habitat, and area requirements are too extensive to include all species within a single conservation approach. We argue for two main conservation approaches; it should be possible to derive quantitative guidelines to maintain viable populations of particular species within managed forest landscapes. For species with very high habitat specialization or low colonization ability, it is very difficult or even impossible to ensure their persistence within managed forest landscapes. Such species require large reserves. Our suggested approaches to estimating the requirements for persistence (Boxes 10.2 and 10.3), given sufficient empirical data, allow area demands for these species to be addressed and can thus provide a quantitative estimate of required reserve sizes.

The rich and fascinating biota associated with dead wood faces an ever increasing risk of extinction given the growing demand for wood products. Saproxylic species provide a central ecosystem function in forests as they perform the decay of organic matter. In order to support a resilient forest landscape, able to restructure itself after disturbances (forestry, wind, or fire), it is important to maintain viable populations of native species: not only for preserving biodiversity but also for maintaining ecosystem function. Recent studies suggest that the decay ability of species varies substantially depending on site conditions (e.g. canopy cover; Yin 1999; Edman et al. 2006) as well as tree growth rate (Edman et al. 2006). Thus, changes in forest management may cause not only extinction of certain species but also long-term changes in the ecosystem services they provide.

ACKNOWLEDGEMENTS

We sincerely thank Jogeir Stokland, Marc-André Villard, and an anonymous reviewer for constructive criticism on earlier versions of this chapter. Support to this work was given to BGJ by the Baltic Forest EU-Interreg III project and to TR by the project "Prediciting extinction risks for threatened wood-living insects in dynamic landscapes" financed by Formas.

References

Akçakaya, H. R., V. C. Radeloff, D. J. Mladenoff and H. S. He. 2004. Integrating landscape and metapopulation modeling approaches: viability of the sharp-tailed grouse in a dynamic landscape. *Conservation Biology* 18:526–37.

Akçakaya, H. R., J. Franklin, A. D. Syphard and J. R. Stephenson. 2005. Viability of Bell's sage sparrow (*Amphispiza belli* ssp. *belli*): altered fire regimes. *Ecological Applications* 15:521–31.

Andersson, M., B. Dahlin and M. Mossberg. 2005. The forest time machine – a multi-purpose forest management decision-support system. *Computers and Electronics in Agriculture* 49:114–28.

Berglund, H. and B. G. Jonsson. 2001. Predictability of plant and fungi species richness in relation to area, isolation and stand structure of old-growth forest islands. *Journal of Vegetation Science* 12:857–66.

Berglund, H., M. Edman and L. Ericson. 2005. Temporal variation of wood-fungi diversity in boreal old-growth forests: implications for monitoring. *Ecological Applications* 15:970–82.

Bergman, K.-O. 2003. *Bedömning avlångsiktig överlevnad för hotade arter knutna till ekar på Händelö i Norrköpings kommun.* Norrköping, Sweden: Gatu- och parkkontoret [In Swedish.]

Bütler, R., P. Angelstam and R. Schlaepfer. 2004. Quantitative targets for the three-toed woodpecker *Picoides tridactylus*. *Ecological Bulletins* 51:219–32.

Caswell, H. 2000. *Matrix Population Models: Construction, Analysis and Interpretation*, 2nd edn. Sunderland, MA: Sinauer Associates.

Dahlberg, A. and J. Stokland. 2004. *Vedlevande arters krav på substrat – en sammanställning och analys av 3600 arter.* Skogsstyrelsen, Jönköping. [In Swedish.]

Dobbertin, M. and G. S. Biging. 1998. Using the non-parametric classifier CART to model forest tree mortality. *Forest Science* 44:507–16.

Edman, M., N. Kruys and B. G. Jonsson. 2004a. Local dispersal sources strongly affect colonisation patterns of wood-decaying fungi on experimental logs. *Ecological Applications* 14:893–901.

Edman, M., M. Gustafsson, J. Stenlid and L. Ericson. 2004b. Abundance and viability of fungal spores along a forestry gradient – responses to habitat loss and isolation? *Oikos* 104:35–42.

Edman, M., R. Möller and L. Ericson. 2006. Effects of enhanced tree growth rate on the decay capacities of three saprotrophic wood-fungi. *Forest Ecology and Management* 232:12–18.

Edman, M., M. Jönsson and B. G. Jonsson. 2007. Small-scale fungal- and wind-mediated disturbances strongly influence the temporal availability of logs in an old-growth *Picea abies* forest. *Ecological Applications* 17:482–90.

Eliasson, P. and S. G. Nilsson. 2002. "You should hate young oaks and young noblemen". The environmental history of oaks in eighteenth- and nineteenth-century Sweden. *Environmental History* 7:659–77.

Franklin, J. F., T. A. Spies, R. Van Pelt *et al.* 2002. Disturbances and structural development of natural forest ecosystems with silvicultural implications, using Douglas-fir forests as an example. *Forest Ecology and Management* 155:399–423.

Fridman, J. and G. Ståhl. 2001. A three-step approach for modeling tree mortality in Swedish forests. *Scandinavian Journal of Forest Research* 16:455–66.

Grove, S. J. 2002. Saproxylic insect ecology and the sustainable management of forests. *Annual Review of Ecology and Systematics* **33**:1–23.

Gu, W., R. Heikkilä and I. Hanski. 2002. Estimating the consequences of habitat fragmentation on extinction risk in dynamic landscape. *Landscape Ecology* **17**: 699–710.

Gustafsson, M. H. 2002. Distribution and dispersal of wood-decaying fungi occurring on Norway spruce logs. Doctoral thesis, Swedish University of Agricultural Sciences, Silvestria 246, Uppsala, Sweden.

Hagan, J. M. and S. L. Grove. 1999. Coarse woody debris: humans and nature competing for trees. *Journal of Forestry* **97**:6–11.

Hanski, I. 1999. *Metapopulation Ecology.* Oxford, UK: Oxford University Press.

Hanski, I. 2000. Extinction debt and species credit in boreal forests: modelling the consequences of different approaches to biodiversity conservation. *Annales Zoologici Fennici* **37**:271–80.

Harmon, M. E. *et al.* 1986. Ecology of coarse woody debris in temperate ecosystems. *Advances in Ecological Research* **15**:133–302.

Holland, J. D., L. Fahrig and N. Cappuccino. 2005. Body size affects the spatial scale of habitat-beetle interactions. *Oikos* **110**:101–8.

Jonsson, B. G. 2000. Availability of coarse woody debris in an old-growth boreal spruce forest landscape. *Journal of Vegetation Science* **11**:51–6.

Jonsson, M., T. Ranius, H. Ekvall *et al.* 2006. Cost-effectiveness of silvicultural measures to increase substrate availability for red-listed wood-living organisms in Norway spruce forests. *Biological Conservation* **127**:443–62.

Keymer, J. E., P. A. Marquet, J. X. Velasco-Hernández and S. A. Levin. 2000. Extinction thresholds and metapopulation persistence in dynamic landscapes. *American Naturalist* **156**:478–94.

Krankina, O. N. and M. E. Harmon. 1995. Dynamics of the dead wood carbon pool in northwestern Russian boreal forests. *Water, Air and Soil Pollution* **82**:227–38.

Kruys, N., B. G. Jonsson and G. Ståhl. 2002. A stage-based matrix model for decomposition dynamics of woody debris. *Ecological Applications* **12**:773–81.

Lambeck, R. J. 1997. Focal-species: a multi-species umbrella for nature conservation. *Conservation Biology* **11**:849–56.

Lindenmayer, D. B., A. D. Manning, P. L. Smith *et al.* 2002 The focal-species approach and landscape restoration: a critique. *Conservation Biology* **16**:338–45.

Lindhe, A. and Å. Lindelöw. 2004. Cut high stumps of spruce, birch, aspen and oak as breeding substrates for saproxylic beetles. *Forest Ecology and Management* **203**:1–20.

Martikainen, P., J. Siitonen, P. Punttila, L. Kaila and J. Rauh. 2000. Species richness of Coleoptera in mature managed and old-growth boreal forests in southern Finland. *Biological Conservation* **94**:199–209.

Mellen, K., B. G. Marcot, J. L. Ohmann *et al.* 2002. DecAID: A Decaying Wood Advisory Model for Oregon and Washington. *USDA Forest Service Gen. Tech. Rep.* PSW-GTR-181:527–33.

Montes, F. and I. Canellas. 2006. Modelling coarse woody debris dynamics in even-aged Scots pine forests. *Forest Ecology and Management* **221**:220–32.

Naesset, E. 1999. Decomposition rate constants of *Picea abies* logs in southeastern Norway. *Canadian Journal of Forest Research* **29**:372–81.

Økland B., A. Bakke, S. Hågvar and T. Kvamme. 1996. What factors influence the diversity of saproxylic beetles? A multiscaled study from a spruce forest in southern Norway. *Biodiversity and Conservation* 7:75–100.

Ranius, T. 2002. Influence of stand size and quality of tree hollows on saproxylic beetles in Sweden. *Biological Conservation* 103:85–91.

Ranius, T. 2006. Measuring the dispersal of saproxylic insects: a key characteristic for their conservation. *Population Ecology* 48:177–88.

Ranius, T. and L. Fahrig. 2006. Targets for maintenance of dead wood for biodiversity conservation based on extinction thresholds. *Scandinavian Journal of Forest Research* 21:201–8.

Ranius, T. 2007. Extinction risks in metapopulations of a beetle inhabiting hollow trees predicted from time series. *Ecography* 30:716–26.

Ranius, T. and O. Kindvall. 2004. Modelling the amount of coarse woody debris produced by the new biodiversity-oriented silvicultural practices in Sweden. *Biological Conservation* 119:51–9.

Ranius, T. and O. Kindvall. 2006. Extinction risk of wood-living model species in forest landscapes as related to forest history and conservation strategy. *Landscape Ecology* 21: 687–98.

Ranius, T., O. Kindvall, N. Kruys and B. G. Jonsson. 2003. Modelling dead wood in Norway spruce stands subject to different management regimes. *Forest Ecology and Management* 182:13–29.

Ranius, T., N. Kruys and B. G. Jonsson. 2004. Estimation of woody debris quantity in European natural boreal forests – a modeling approach. *Canadian Journal of Forest Research* 34:1025–34.

Roberge, J.-M. 2006. Umbrella species as a conservation planning tool. An assessment using resident birds in hemiboreal and boreal forests. Ph.D. thesis, Department of Conservation Biology, Swedish University of Agricultural Sciences, Uppsala, Sweden.

Roberge, J.-M. and P. Angelstam. 2003. Usefulness of the umbrella species concept as a conservation tool. *Conservation Biology* 18:76–85.

Schroeder, L. M., T. Ranius, B. Ekbom and S. Larsson. 2007. Spatial occurrence in a habitat-tracking metapopulation of a saproxylic beetle inhabiting a managed forest landscape. *Ecological Applications* 17:900–9.

Schultze, L. A., R. J. Mitchell, M. L. Hunter *et al.* 2006. Evaluating the conceptual tools for forest biodiversity conservation and their implementation in the US. *Forest Ecology and Management* 232:1–11.

Siitonen, J. 2001. Forest management, coarse woody debris and saproxylic organisms: Fennoscandian boreal forests as an example. *Ecological Bulletins* 49:11–42.

Snäll, T. P. J. Ribeiro Jr. and H. Rydin. 2003. Spatial occurrence and colonisations in patch-tracking metapopulations: local conditions versus dispersal. *Oikos* 103:566–78.

Snäll, T., J. Pennanen, L. Kivistö and I. Hanski. 2005. Modelling epiphyte metapopulation dynamics in a dynamic forest landscape. *Oikos* 109:209–22.

Southwood, T. R. E. 1977. Habitat, the templet for ecological strategies? *Journal of Animal Ecology* 46:337–65.

Stokland, J. N., R. Eriksen, S. M. Tomter *et al.* 2003. Forest biodiversity indicators in the Nordic countries. *TemaNord* 2003: **514**. Copenhagen, Denmark: Nordic Council of Ministers.

Stokland, J. N., S. M. Tomter and U. Söderberg. 2004. Development of dead wood indicators for biodiversity monitoring: experiences from Scandinavia. Pp. 205–26 in M. Marchetti (ed.) *Monitoring and Indicators of Forest Biodiversity in Europe – from Ideas to Operationality.* EFI proceedings no. 51. Joensuu, Finland: European Forest Institute.

Tarasov, M. E. and R. A. Birdsey. 2001. Decay rate and potential storage of coarse woody debris in the Leningrad region. *Ecological Bulletins* **49**:137–48.

Thomas, C. D. 1994. Extinction, colonization, and metapopulations: environmental tracking by rare species. *Conservation Biology* **8**:373–8.

Thomas, C. D. and I. Hanski. 1997. Butterfly metapopulations. Pp. 359–86 in I. Hanski and M.-E. Gilpin (eds.) *Metapopulation Biology: Ecology, Genetics, and Evolution.* San Diego, CA: Academic Press.

Yin, X. W. 1999. The decay of forest woody debris: numerical modeling and implications based on some 300 data cases from North America. *Oecologia* **121**:81–98.

Opportunities and constraints of using understory plants to set forest restoration and conservation priorities

OLIVIER HONNAY, BRUNO HÉRAULT,
AND BEATRIJS BOSSUYT

INTRODUCTION

Ecological restoration of natural forests on former agricultural land or on sites formerly planted with non-indigenous tree species has become a central component of sustainable forest management in many parts of the world (Angelstam *et al.* 2004; Hérault *et al.* 2005). To become operational at the stand or the landscape level, the principles of sustainable forest management need to be broken down into objectives and in indicators to monitor.

To define the ecological objectives of restoration efforts, a reference or target system is essential. This information generally consists of contemporary ecological data from a reference site (Bakker *et al.* 2000). In the case of forest restoration, the reference may consist of ancient forests (Honnay *et al.* 2002). Ancient forest sites are commonly defined as sites that have been continuously wooded since a reference date in the past, and it is generally accepted that this continuity has not been broken by forest management practices such as coppicing but only by an alternative land use such as cultivation or pasture (Peterken 1996). The reference date varies between regions and countries and, very pragmatically, reflects the availability of the first detailed land-use maps (e.g. 1600, Peterken (1974); 1700, Rackham (1980); 1789, Lawesson *et al.* (1998); 1850, Grashof-Bokdam (1997)).

Setting Conservation Targets for Managed Forest Landscapes, ed. M.-A. Villard and B. G. Jonsson. Published by Cambridge University Press.
© Cambridge University Press 2009.

After setting the objectives, indicators can be measured repeatedly to examine whether they directionally change towards the objectives and to evaluate to what extent the objectives have been reached. Herbaceous plant species can be expected to be well suited as indicators to infer the restoration status of a forest. They are rather easy to identify in the field and it has extensively been demonstrated that some species only colonize newly established forests after a long time period, whereas others are able to recolonize relatively quickly (e.g. Matlack 1994; Wulf 1997; Bossuyt et al. 1999). This results in slow recovery rates of the understory during the restoration process, so that its species composition can be considered to be a valuable indicator of the restoration status. Moreover, species-specific plant life-history traits such as those related to dispersal capacity may provide the necessary insights into the site-specific bottlenecks hampering forest restoration (Verheyen et al. 2003).

Broadly speaking, two types of bottleneck may hamper the recolonization of recently restored forests by herbaceous plant species. The first relates to the inability of a species' diaspores to disperse to a restored forest stand. This is referred to as dispersal limitation. Logically, the importance of dispersal limitation increases as forests become more isolated within the landscape (Jacquemyn et al. 2001). The second bottleneck relates to the inability of successfully dispersed diaspores to germinate and grow into mature, reproductive plants. This is generally referred to as recruitment limitation. Especially in forests restored on former arable land, the latter may be an important colonization constraint because most forest plants lack the ability to compete successfully with species that grow fast on nutrient-rich soils (Verheyen et al. 2003).

The restoration status or conservation value of a forest stand can be assumed to increase asymptotically as a function of time since re-establishment (Jacquemyn et al. 2001) although considerable variance for a certain age class is expected, owing to site-specific constraints related to the two types of colonization bottleneck. The variability in restoration status between forests can be expected to be low just after re-establishment (no forest species present), to increase for intermediate age classes when differences in recruitment and dispersal limitation between sites are fully playing, and to decrease again finally when even the poor colonizers persist in all forest sites (Fig. 11.1).

In this chapter, we explore the opportunities and constraints of using understory species to evaluate the degree to which forest restoration sites have developed towards their ecological reference, and hence to evaluate their conservation value. We distinguish between three approaches, each

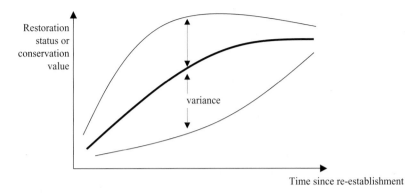

Figure 11.1. Expected evolution of the restoration status or conservation value of recently established forest stands as a function of time. Variance in the restoration status or conservation value is the result of site-specific bottlenecks related to dispersal and recruitment limitation and is expected to be highest at intermediate age classes.

reflecting a certain component of the understory species composition: (i) using ancient-forest indicator species, (ii) comparing species richness and community measures between sites, and (iii) using functional groups based on plant life-history traits. We tested the general performance of these three approaches on a data set of 153 riverine deciduous forests located throughout the Grand-duché de Luxembourg in central-western Europe (details in Hérault and Honnay 2005). The selected forests were established on former fields or open grazed lands and showed no evidence of former plantation events or forestry management practices. Forest stands were grouped into four age classes, pragmatically defined by the available historical maps and reflecting the time since re-establishment (<50 years ($n = 55$), 51–100 years ($n = 46$), 101–225 years ($n = 29$), and >225 years ($n = 23$)). The oldest age class is regarded as the ecological restoration objective. Species abundance in each stand was surveyed in three cover classes: <10%, 10%–50%, and >50%. Reliable indicators for the restoration status of a forest stand should fulfill at least two requirements (Fig. 11.1): (i) their values should covary with time since forest re-establishment, and (ii) although variation of the indicator value within a certain age class can be expected owing to site-specific colonization bottlenecks, variance should be low enough to discriminate statistically between different stand age classes. Additionally, the indicators should ideally offer insights into the ecological processes behind the ecological restoration. This means that when the time since re-establishment of the stands to restore is known, differences in indicator values among stands of similar age can be explained in terms of the colonization bottlenecks. The latter may allow forest managers to lift colonization constraints (e.g. by introducing seeds or removing competitive species such as *Rubus* sp.), or to adapt conservation priorities.

INDICATOR SPECIES

An indicator species has been defined as an organism whose characteristics (presence or absence, population density, dispersal or reproductive success) are used as an index of attributes too difficult, inconvenient, or expensive to measure for other species or environmental conditions of interest (Landres *et al.* 1988). Indicator species have, for example, been used as short cuts to detect environmental pollution, to assess biodiversity, and also to infer forest continuity (e.g. Peterken 1974, Wulf 1997). In the latter case, the presence or absence of a suite of indicator species (generally referred to as "ancient-forest species") in recently established forest stands allows the assessment of the age of the forest land use, which is often difficult to infer from ancient land-use maps. This approach has been criticized for many different reasons, mainly because it is based on correlative assumptions and because ancient forest indicators have been identified without knowing why they are found only (or primarily) in the oldest stands (Norden and Appelqvist 2001; Rolstad *et al.* 2002). Forest stands established hundreds of years ago may, for example, lack certain indicator species simply because they are too isolated from species sources, hampering their colonization.

Here, we are aiming at assessing not forest continuity but rather the ecological status of the restored site in relation to the reference community. The idea is that the abundance of species with a significant affinity for ancient stands can be used as an indicator to infer the restoration status of a forest. Indicator species for ancient forest can be identified by using simple measures of categorical association such as the χ^2 test, or using more complex methods, for example combining a species' relative abundance with its relative frequency in various forest age classes (Dufrêne and Legendre 1997). Many lists of ancient-forest plant species have been derived (e.g. Peterken 1974; Wulf 1997; Hermy *et al.* 1999). Here we used the one compiled for western and central Belgium by Honnay *et al.* (1998) (based on a χ^2 test), and we calculated the average number of ancient forest indicator species in each of the four forest age classes.

The advantages of the indicator species approach are obvious. Starting from an existing indicator species list, only a survey of the presence or absence of the listed species at the restoration sites is required. In our case

Table 11.1. *Average values of the different variables used to asses the restoration status of 153 deciduous forest stands of four age classes*

Different letters indicate a significant difference at the 0.05 level according to Tukey pairwise comparisons. *F*-values are from a one way ANOVA with four age classes. Symbols: ***$p < 0.001$; **$0.001 = < p < 0.01$; *$0.01 = < p < 0.05$.

	< 50 yr (n = 55)	51–100 yr (n = 46)	101–225 yr (n = 29)	> 225 yr (n = 23)	F-statistic
Indicator species	9.6a	12.6b	13.9b	14.0b	11.5***
Species richness	34.0a	39.6b	38.5ab	40.8b	5.6 **
Species diversity	3.26a	3.41b	3.39ab	3.48b	6.5***
Species evenness	0.929a	0.936ab	0.935ab	0.941b	2.9*
DCA axis 1	1.53a	1.92b	2.31c	2.32c	22.6***
DCA axis 2	1.50a	1.61ab	1.69ab	1.92b	4.6**
Barochoreous perennials	5.4a	7.3b	9.1c	9.1c	21.1***
Small geophytes	4.1a	5.6b	5.6b	7.6c	15.2***

study, however, the approach only allowed us to distinguish between the youngest and the three other age classes (Table 11.1). The variability in the number of indicator species within each age class is very high, and even very recently restored forest patches may contain up to 16 indicator species, whereas at least one ancient forest only contains 8 (see Fig. 11.2). The main reason for the low resolution of ancient forest indicator species is related to problems regarding the generalization of these lists across regions. The composition of the species pools between regions is often different. More-over, the species' ecological behavior may vary between biogeographical regions and between forest types (Rolstad *et al.* 2002). For example, *Mercurialis perennis*, often mentioned as an ancient forest indicator, colonizes new forest stands more easily on calcareous than on acidic soils (Peterken and Game 1981). Moreover, it is very problematic to infer why certain ancient forest plant species are present in a specific restoration site but absent from others of the same age. Indeed, the indicator species approach fails to offer any insight into the site-specific constraints related to species dispersal or recruitment limitation locally hampering the restoration process. For all these reasons, indicator species lists can be expected to perform poorly in comparing the status of restoration sites.

SPECIES DIVERSITY AND COMMUNITY MEASURES

Species richness or alpha diversity is the simplest way to describe community diversity (Gotelli and Colwell 2001) and has been used as an indicator

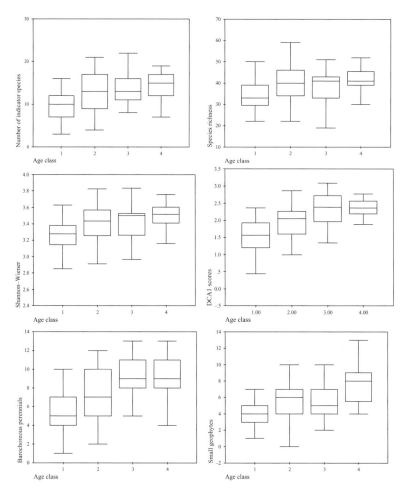

Figure 11.2. Box plots reflecting the median, range, and quartiles of the different variables used to assess the restoration status of 153 deciduous forest stands of four age classes: 1, <50 years ($n = 55$); 2, 51–100 years ($n = 46$); 3, 101–225 years ($n = 29$); 4, >225 years ($n = 23$).

for the restoration status of forest stands before (Pitkänen 1998). The number of plant species in the understory has also been proven to increase with decreasing level of forest disturbance (Aubert *et al.* 2003; Onaindia *et al.* 2004) or with increasing level of forest continuity (Dumortier *et al.* 2002; Graae *et al.* 2003). Other studies, however, have not been able to demonstrate a univocal relationship between the level of forest disturbance or forest continuity on the one hand and species richness on the other (Graae and

Heskjaer 1997; Bossuyt and Hermy 2000; Verheyen *et al.* 2003). Species richness may be more related to habitat diversity within the stand (Dzwonko and Loster 1992; Honnay *et al.* 1999; Dumortier *et al.* 2002) than to the restoration status of the forest. Moreover, several non-specific forest species may be present in the understory layer of recently established forest owing to high soil nutrient and light penetration levels, inflating the species numbers in these stands (Bossuyt and Hermy 2000).

In contrast to species number, species diversity and evenness measures also incorporate patterns of species abundance (Washington 1984; Pitkänen 1998). High evenness indicates that the occurring species are of equal abundance and suggests the absence of dominant species. Evenness is known to increase with succession (McCook 1994) and with decreasing disturbance (Onaindia *et al.* 2004). Evenness can be expected to be higher in restoration sites that are more similar to the reference forest since there is less dominance by competitive species, owing to lower soil nutrient contents and light penetration levels, increasing the competitive advantage of stress-tolerant forest species (Honnay *et al.* 1999; Graae *et al.* 2003).

Species richness and diversity and evenness measures, however, have also been shown to vary with the type of data, the level of observation, and the spatial resolution, resulting in a high intrinsic variability (Huston 1994; Keeley and Fotheringham 2005). Moreover, a given species richness or diversity may result from different ecological mechanisms of species coexistence (Nakashizuka 2001). Therefore, indicators based on species diversity may not be very useful for conservation purposes as they do not provide clues to the mechanisms of species coexistence (Aubert *et al.* 2003).

The reliability of community-based indicators may be improved by using indicators based on the similarity in species composition between the site being evaluated and the reference site, because they take also the identity of the occurring species into account (Onaindia *et al.* 2004). To simplify the similarity matrix, multivariate techniques such as Detrended Correspondence Analysis (DCA) (Hill and Gauch 1980) or non-linear multidimensional scaling (Clarke 1993), ordering vegetation survey plots in a multidimensional space, can be used to describe the main sources of variation in species composition. Plot scores on the axes reflect the species composition in the survey plots, and comparison of plot scores on the multivariate axes allows determining the (dis)similarity in species composition between the plots (e.g. Strandberg *et al.* 2005; Uotila and Kouki 2005).

We calculated average species richness, species diversity and evenness, and DCA scores for each of the four forest age classes (Table 11.1). The

DCA was performed with Canoco for Windows 4.5 (ter Braak and Šmilauer 2002). Because species abundance was surveyed in only three abundance classes, the species diversity and evenness metrics are relatively rough estimates and should be cautiously interpreted against the values of other age classes. Species number, species diversity, and evenness increased with increasing forest age (Table 11.1; Fig. 11.2). Based on these measures, however, only the youngest age class can be distinguished from the other three categories. Variance of the metrics within each age class is very high. Species richness, for example, varies between 22 and 50 species within the most recently established forests, whereas it varies between 30 and 52 species in the reference community (Fig. 11.2). This implies that even recently established forests may be very rich in species. The plant species recorded, however, are generalist species, occurring under high light penetration levels on disturbed, nutrient-enriched soils (Hérault and Honnay 2005). The conservation value of these forests is relatively low. As with the indicator species, all metrics based on diversity have in common that they fail to provide a reliable estimation of the restoration status of the forest. Moreover, no insight into the underlying ecological mechanisms behind the variance within an age class is provided.

Compared to the other community-based indicators, the DCA scores, and in particular those on the first DCA axis, best discriminate the stand age classes (Table 11.1). Additionally, multivariate techniques offer the opportunity to incorporate environmental variables in the analysis, so that the potential determining factors of the differences in species composition can be identified (Graae and Heskjaer 1997). This increases the insight in the underlying ecological processes. However, although multivariate techniques may relate site-specific abiotic conditions to differences in species composition, they do not offer insight into species-specific constraints related to dispersal or recruitment limitation hampering the restoration process. Therefore, indicators taking into account specific life-history traits of the occurring species may still perform much better.

FUNCTIONAL GROUPS

The concept of plant functional groups dates back to the beginning of the nineteenth century, when Von Humboldt (1806) drew up the first recognized classification of physiognomic plant types from South America. The first modern functional classification, however, was the life-form system of Raunkiaer (1934), which is still commonly used today. During the past decades, functional classifications of plants have received renewed attention as a useful tool to predict the effects of human disturbance on biodiversity on the one hand (Pimm *et al.* 1995) and to understand the role of the species diversity on ecosystem functioning on the other (Hooper *et al.* 2005). Therefore, plant functional groups were commonly defined as indicators of response to various types of disturbance, such as fire (Keith and Bradstock 1994), grazing management (McIntyre *et al.* 1995), or global climate change (Johnson *et al.* 1993). More recently, the functional group concept has been applied to habitat fragmentation studies (e.g. Médail *et al.* 1998). In managed forest landscapes, influential works were the one of Metzger (2000) in the tropics and the one of Verheyen *et al.* (2003) in temperate areas. Both studies showed that the functional group approach provides valuable insights into the ecological processes underlying plant species assembly in restored fragmented forests. The use of functional groups as a selection criterion for forest restoration and/or conversion purposes (Gondard *et al.* 2003; Hérault *et al.* 2005) or as a tool for the evaluation of forest management practices (Gondard and Deconchat 2003), however, still remains in its infancy.

A functional group can be defined as a set of species that have similar morphological, physiological, and phenological life-history trait combinations (Lavorel *et al.* 1997). In other words, members of a plant functional group share similar life-history traits, with differences between members within one group being smaller than those among groups (Duckworth *et al.* 2000). It is thus expected that species from a functional group have convergent ecological and evolutionary strategies. However, a consensual definition of plant functional group is still lacking in the scientific community (Wilson 1999). Indeed, some researchers advocate functional groups based on plant response to disturbance (Gitay and Noble 1997) whereas others prefer a definition based on resource use (Hooper and Vitousek 1998). In an attempt at reconciling these views, Lavorel and Garnier (2002) argued that the nature of a functional group remains clearly dependent on the scientific aim of the study.

In a restoration context, it is necessary first to define the specific key requirements for a given herbaceous plant species to survive in a typically fragmented forest landscape consisting of different-aged forest stands. This plant has to persist in the forest stands already colonized and disperse to and establish in the restoration sites. A functional classification of herbaceous plants therefore acknowledges life-history traits involved in persistence, dispersal, and establishment (see Table 11.2 and Weiher *et al.* 1999). Persistence is enhanced by many life-history traits, but the most common ones are related to life-span (e.g. life-form, age at first flowering),

Table 11.2. *Selected plant life-history traits for the functional group approach*

Dispersal-related traits
Clonal propagation
Dispersal type
Seed longevity
Seed production
Seed shape
Seed size

Establishment-related traits
Germination requirements
Relative growth rate
Seed mass

Persistence-related traits
Age at first flowering
Life-forms
Mean shoot height
Onset of flowering
Pollination vector
Potential mycorrhizas

competitive ability (e.g. seed mass, plant height), and to strategy of resource acquisition (e.g. onset of flowering). The latter is very important in temperate forests, where numerous spring ephemerals are specifically adapted to capture resources before canopy closure (Lapointe 2001). Dispersal has a spatial and a temporal dimension (Weiher *et al.* 1999). Dispersal in time can be assessed by measuring the seed longevity (Thompson *et al.* 1998). Dispersal in space is obviously associated with seed mass (i.e. wind-dispersed seeds are lighter, see Leishman *et al.* 1995) but also with seed dispersal mode (anemochory, zoochory, unassisted). Finally, establishment first depends on the germination requirements of the seeds. Indeed, some seeds have the ability to immediately germinate after falling, whereas others need chilling, drying, light, or even scarification (Baskin and Baskin 2001). Second, the seedling size is also commonly considered to be critical for successful establishment. Seedling size is often viewed as a combination of both seed size and relative growth rate (Weiher *et al.* 1999), life-history traits which are easier to measure.

The first step in the delineation of the functional groups is to compile the life-history trait information for the plant species of interest from the existing literature. In Europe, several databases are already available (e.g. Grime *et al.* 1988; Hodgson *et al.* 1995; Julve 1998; Kleyer 1995; Thompson *et al.* 1997); other more ambitious ones should be available in the near future (Knevel *et al.* 2003). Next, a similarity matrix between plant species is calculated based on the life-history trait values of the individual species. At this stage, a similarity coefficient has to be chosen taking into account the specific properties of the data. Life-history trait data are often of mixed nature (qualitative, quantitative, and ordinal trait values) and incomplete. Few similarity coefficients can deal with such data properties (Legendre and Legendre 1998). The Gower coefficient (Gower 1971) is one of them and was used here. The resulting similarity matrix is then used to cluster the species into functional groups by applying a cluster method (here, we used Ward's method). The cut-off level for delineating the functional groups is determined graphically from visual screening of the obtained dendrogram. At this stage, common goals are both not to inflate the number of functional groups and to obtain ecologically meaningful functional groups. This emphasizes the subjective role of the expert's knowledge. Alternatively, an objective criterion such as the Bayesian information criterion can be used (Kolb and Diekmann 2005). To obtain the characteristic life-traits for each functional group, Pearson χ^2 tests (qualitative life-history traits) and Kruskal–Wallis statistics (ordinal and quantitative life-history traits) can be used *a posteriori* to compare the trait values between the identified functional groups (Hérault and Honnay 2005). Next, functional groups can be named according to the life-history traits that drove the clustering procedure.

Seven functional groups were delineated from the studied flora (details in Hérault and Honnay 2005). The product of the presence–absence matrix [site by species] with the binary coded matrix of functional group membership [species by functional group] provides the frequencies of each functional group in each forest stand. These frequencies were tested for their association with the forest age classes to identify which functional groups are good indicators of the restoration status. The abundance of two functional groups strongly increased with forest age and can be considered reliable indicators for the restoration status of the stands (Table 11.1): the barochoreous perennials and the small geophytes.

Barochoreous perennials (e.g. *Stellaria nemorum*, *Glechoma hederacea*, and *Aegopodium podagraria*) encompass plants with unassisted dispersal, unlike all the other groups. They are often hemicryptophytes. Small geophytes (e.g. *Adoxa moschatellina*, *Arum maculatum*, and *Ranunculus ficaria*), on the other hand, are herbaceous plants with perennating tissue (bulbs, corms, rhizomes, stem or root tubers) below the soil surface. They are also characterized by their low stature (<30 cm). Both functional groups flower after one or two years, and preferentially in spring. Both groups also have big and heavy seeds, which are produced in very small numbers. These seeds typically persist less than one year in the topsoil. Moreover, barochoreous perennials and small geophytes exhibit specific life-history traits, such as their vernal phenology, which reflects their successful adaptation to and their restricted distribution in forest habitats (Bierzychudek 1982). Owing to these particular properties, the conservation of populations of barochoreous perennials and small geophytes is of high relevance in temperate forests (Keddy and Drummond 1996; Hermy *et al.* 1999).

Why do these two functional groups fail to quickly colonize recently restored forest stands? First, the newly established forest stands were predominantly located on former meadows or arable land. Both barochoreous perennials and small geophytes do not form a persistent seed bank. Therefore, it can be assumed that these functional groups have colonized the plantation from the surroundings whereas plants from other functional groups could have survived deforestation periods through their seed banks. Second, most barochoreous perennials have extremely low seed dispersal rates (Brunet and Von Oheimb 1998; Bossuyt *et al.* 1999; Dzwonko 2001) because of the combination of large and rare seeds and the lack of dispersal adaptations. Therefore, the strong decrease of barochoreous perennials in newly established forests is very likely dispersal-dependent. Third, small geophytes were under-represented in all restored forests (Table 11.1, Fig. 11.1). Unlike the barochoreous perennials, seeds of small geophytes encompass all dispersal types. Their typical life-history traits are recalcitrant germination and their extremely low stature. Both traits may reflect establishment limitation. Indeed, low germination rates and low stature may result in a strong competitive disadvantage in nutrient-rich, recently restored forests.

In a nutshell, our results suggest that the distribution and abundance of the two derived functional groups are good indicators to infer the restoration status of a forest stand, as shown by the high F-statistics (Table 11.1). Although variance within each age class remains relatively high (Fig. 11.1), their combined use allows to discriminate all age classes. Moreover, the abundance of both of the functional groups in a certain age class provides valuable insights into the ecological mechanisms driving the restoration. Barochoreous perennials will more rapidly colonize a recently established forest located close to an ancient stand than an isolated forest. The absence of small geophytes rather reflects recruitment limitation due to high soil nutrient levels or low canopy closure. These results may provide useful management guidelines for foresters.

Table 11.3. *Comparison of the three different methods used to assess the restoration status of a forest stand*

	Indicator species	Community measures	Functional groups
Reliability	low	medium	high
Time/cost-efficiency	high	medium	medium
Required statistical skills	low	medium	medium/high
Insights in ecological process	low	low	high
Extrapolation potential to other regions	low	low	high
Applicability by forest managers	high	medium	medium

The disadvantages of the approach presented mainly relate to the rather complicated statistical analyses, at least when deriving functional groups from scratch. A strong background in functional ecology is required and this may hamper the application by field practitioners in everyday work. On the other hand, the advantages of using the functional groups when defining and monitoring the restoration status are clear. First of all, studying life-history traits offers valuable insights into the ecological processes underlying the species' distribution patterns, which in turn can support management decisions. At a site scale, this allows the forest managers to understand the biological mechanisms locally hampering or speeding up the restoration process. Additionally, transgressing the species concept substantially increases the predictive and applied power of the obtained results. Although species-centered approaches have led to locally interesting findings and have largely inspired conservation policies, conclusions cannot easily be extrapolated to other biogeographical regions. This seems permitted when using functional groups and allows forest managers to discuss with colleagues from other regions using a common language despite different species pools.

References
Angelstam, P., M. Donz-Breuss and J.-M. Roberge (eds.) 2004. Targets and tools for the maintenance of forest biodiversity. *Ecological Bulletins* **51**.
Aubert M., D. Alard and F. Bureau. 2003. Diversity of plant assemblages in managed temperate forests: a case study in Normandy (France). *Forest Ecology and Management* **175**:321–37.
Bakker J. P., A. P. Grootjans, M. Hermy and P. Poschlod. 2000. How to define targets for ecological restoration? *Applied Vegetation Science* **3**:3–7.
Baskin, C. C. and J. M. Baskin. 2001. *Seeds: Ecology, Biogeography, and Evolution of Dormancy and Germination.* San Diego, CA: Academic Press.

Bierzychudek, P. 1982. Life histories and demography of shade-tolerant temperate forest herbs: a review. *New Phytologist* 90:757–76.

Bossuyt, B. and M. Hermy. 2000. Restoration of the understorey layer of recent forest bordering ancient forest. *Applied Vegetation Science* 3:43–50.

Bossuyt, B., M. Hermy and J. Deckers. 1999. Migration of herbaceous plant species across ancient-recent forest ecotones in central Belgium. *Journal of Ecology* 87:628–38.

Brunet, J. and G. Von Oheimb. 1998. Migration of vascular plants to secondary woodlands in southern Sweden. *Journal of Ecology* 86:429–38.

Clarke, K. R. 1993. Non-parametric multivariate analyses of changes in community structure. *Australian Journal of Ecology* 18:117–43.

Duckworth, J. C., M. Kent and P. M. Ramsay. 2000. Plant functional types: an alternative to taxonomic plant community description in biogeography? *Progress in Physical Geography* 24:515–42.

Dufrêne, M. and P. Legendre. 1997. Species assemblages and indicator species: the need for a flexible asymmetrical approach. *Ecological Monographs* 67:345–66.

Dumortier, M., J. Butaye, H. Jacquemyn *et al.* 2002. Predicting vascular plant species richness of fragmented forests in agricultural landscapes in central Belgium. *Forest Ecology and Management* 158:85–102.

Dzwonko, Z. 2001. Migration of vascular plant species to a recent wood adjoining ancient woodland. *Acta Societatis Botanicorum Poloniae* 70:71–7.

Dzwonko, Z. and S. Loster. 1992. Species richness and seed dispersal to secondary woods in southern Poland. *Journal of Biogeography* 19:195–204.

Gitay, H. and I. R. Noble. 1997. What are functional types and how should we seek them? Pp. 3–19 in T. M. Smith, H. H. Shugart and F. I. Woodward (eds.) *Plant Functional Types: Their Relevance to Ecosystem Properties and Global Change.* Cambridge, UK: Cambridge University Press.

Gondard, H. and M. Deconchat. 2003. Effects of soil surface disturbances after logging on plant functional types. *Annals of Forest Science* 60:725–32.

Gondard, H., J. Sandrine, J. Aronson and S. Lavorel. 2003. Plant functional types: a promising tool for management and restoration of degraded lands. *Applied Vegetation Science* 6:223–34.

Gotelli N. J. and R. K. Colwell. 2001. Quantifying biodiversity: procedures and pitfalls in the measurement and comparison of species richness. *Ecology Letters* 4:379–91.

Gower, J. C. 1971. A general coefficient of similarity and some of its properties. *Biometrics* 27:857–74.

Graae, B. J. and V. S. Heskjaer. 1997. A comparison of understorey vegetation between untouched and managed deciduous forest in Denmark. *Forest Ecology and Management* 96:111–23.

Graae, B. J., P. B. Sunde and B. Fritzbøger. 2003. Vegetation and soil differences in ancient opposed to new forests. *Forest Ecology and Management* 177:179–90.

Grashof-Bokdam, C. J. 1997. Forest plants in an agricultural landscape in the Netherlands: effects of habitat fragmentation. *Journal of Vegetation Science* 8: 21–8.

Grime, J. P., J. G. Hodgson and R. Hunt. 1988. *Comparative Plant Ecology: A Functional Approach to Common British Species.* London: Allen & Unwin.

Hérault, B. and O. Honnay. 2005. The relative importance of local, regional and historical factors determining the distribution of plants in fragmented riverine forests – an emergent group approach. *Journal of Biogeography* 32:2069–81.

Hérault, B., O. Honnay and D. Thoen. 2005. Evaluation of the ecological restoration potential of plant communities in Norway spruce plantations using a life-trait based approach. *Journal of Applied Ecology* 42:536–45.

Hermy, M., O. Honnay, L. Firbank, C. Grashof-Bokdam and J. E. Lawesson. 1999. An ecological comparison between ancient and other forest plant species of Europe, and the implications for forest conservation. *Biological Conservation* 91:9–22.

Hill, M. O. and H. G. Gauch. 1980. Detrended correspondence analysis: an improved ordination technique. *Vegetatio* 42:47–58.

Hodgson, J. G., J. P. Grime, R. Hunt and K. Thompson. 1995. *The Electronic Comparative Plant Ecology.* London: Chapman & Hall.

Honnay, O., B. Degroote and M. Hermy. 1998. Ancient-forest plant species in Western Belgium: a species list and possible ecological mechanisms. *Belgian Journal of Botany* 130:139–54.

Honnay, O., M. Hermy and P. Coppin. 1999. Effects of area, habitat diversity and age of forest patches on plant species richness in Belgium, and consequences for conservation and reforestation. *Biological Conservation* 87:73–84.

Honnay O., B. Bossuyt, K. Verheyen *et al.* 2002. Ecological perspectives for the restoration of plant communities in temperate forests. *Biodiversity and Conservation* 11:213–42.

Hooper, D. U. and P. M. Vitousek. 1998. Effects of plant composition and diversity on nutrient cycling. *Ecological Monographs* 68:121–49.

Hooper, D. U., F. S. Chapin, J. J. Ewel *et al.* 2005. Effects of biodiversity on ecosystem functioning: a consensus of current knowledge. *Ecological Monographs* 75:3–35.

Huston, M. A. 1994. *Biological Diversity: The Coexistence of Species on Changing Landscapes.* New York, NY: Cambridge University Press.

Jacquemyn, H., B. Butaye and M. Hermy. 2001. Forest plant species richness in small, fragmented mixed deciduous forest patches: the role of area, time and dispersal limitation. *Journal of Biogeography* 28:801–12.

Johnson, H. B., H. W. Polley and H. S. Mayeux. 1993. Increasing CO_2 and plant-plant interactions – effects on natural vegetation. *Vegetatio* 104:157–70.

Julve, P. 1998. *Baseflor. Index Botanique, Écologique et Chorologique de la Flore de France.* Lille, France: Institut Catholique de Lille.

Keddy, P. A. and C. G. Drummond. 1996. Ecological properties for the evaluation, management, and restoration of temperate deciduous forest ecosystems. *Ecological Applications* 6:748–62.

Keeley, J. E. and C. J. Fotheringham. 2005. Plot shape effects on species diversity measures. *Journal of Vegetation Science* 16:249–56.

Keith, D. A. and R. A. Bradstock. 1994. Fire and competition in Australian heath – a conceptual-model and field investigations. *Journal of Vegetation Science* 5:347–54.

Kleyer, M. 1995. *Biological Traits of Vascular Plants.* Stuttgart: Arbeitsberichte Institut für Landschaftsplanung und Ökologie.

Knevel, I. C., R. M. Bekker, J. P Bakker and M. Kleyer. 2003. Life-history traits of the Northwest European flora: the LEDA database. *Journal of Vegetation Science* **14**:611–14.

Kolb, A. and M. Diekmann. 2005. Effects of life-history traits on responses of plant species to forest fragmentation. *Conservation Biology* **19**:929–38.

Landres, P. B., J. Verner and J. W. Thomas. 1988. Ecological use of vertebrate indicator species: a critique. *Conservation Biology* **2**:316–28.

Lapointe, L. 2001. How phenology influences physiology in deciduous forest spring ephemerals? *Physiologia Plantarum* **113**:151–7.

Lavorel, S. and E. Garnier. 2002. Predicting changes in community composition and ecosystem functioning from plant traits: revisiting the Holy Grail. *Functional Ecology* **16**:545–56.

Lavorel, S., S. McIntyre, J. Landsberg and T. D. A. Forbes. 1997. Plant functional classifications: from general groups to specific groups based on response to disturbance. *Trends in Ecology and Evolution* **12**:474–8.

Lawesson, J. E., G. De Blust, C. Grashof *et al.* 1998. Species diversity and area-relationships in Danish beech forests (*Fagion sylvaticae*). *Forest Ecology and Management* **106**:35–243.

Legendre, P. and L. Legendre. 1998. *Numerical Ecology*, 2nd edn. Amsterdam, The Netherlands: Elsevier.

Leishman, M. R., M. Westoby and E. Jurado. 1995. Correlates of seed size variation: a comparison among five temperate floras. *Journal of Ecology* **83**:517–30.

Matlack, G. R. 1994. Plant species migration in a mixed-history forest landscape in eastern North America. *Ecology* **75**:1491–502.

McCook, L. J. 1994. Understanding ecological community succession: causal models and theories: a review. *Vegetatio* **110**:115–47.

McIntyre, S., S. Lavorel and R. M. Tremont. 1995. Plant life-history attributes – their relationship to disturbance responses in herbaceous vegetation. *Journal of Ecology* **83**:31–44.

Médail, F., P. Roche and T. Tatoni. 1998. Functional groups in phytoecology: an application to the study of isolated plant communities in Mediterranean France. *Acta Oecologica* **19**:263–74.

Metzger, J. P. 2000. Tree functional group richness and landscape structure in a Brazilian tropical fragmented landscape. *Ecological Applications* **10**:1147–61.

Nakashizuka, T. 2001. Species coexistence in temperate mixed deciduous forests. *Trends in Ecology and Evolution* **16**:205–10.

Norden, B. and T. Appelqvist. 2001. Conceptual problems of ecological continuity and its bioindicators. *Biodiversity and Conservation* **10**:779–91.

Onaindia, M., I. Dominguez, I. Albizu, C. Garbisu and I. Amezaga. 2004. Vegetation diversity and vertical structure as indicators of forest disturbance. *Forest Ecology and Management* **195**:341–54.

Peterken, G. F. 1974. A method of assessing woodland flora for conservation using indicator species. *Biological Conservation* **6**:239–45.

Peterken, G. F. 1996. *Natural Woodland. Ecology and Conservation in Northern Temperate Regions*. Cambridge, UK: Cambridge University Press.

Peterken, G. F. and M. Game. 1981. Historical factors affecting the distribution of *Mercurialis perennis* in Central Lincolnshire. *Journal of Ecology* **69**:781–96.

Pimm, S. L., G. J. Russell, J. L. Gittleman and T. M. Brooks. 1995. The future of biodiversity. *Science* **269**:347–50.

Pitkänen, S. 1998. The use of diversity indices to assess the diversity of vegetation in managed boreal forests. *Forest Ecology and Management* **112**:121–37.

Rackham, O. 1980. *Ancient Woodland*. London: Arnold.

Raunkiaer, C. 1934. *The Life Forms of Plants and Statistical Plant Geography*. Oxford, UK: Clarendon Press.

Rolstad, J., I. Gjerde, V. S. Gunderse and M. Saetersdal. 2002. Use of indicator species to assess forest continuity: a critique. *Conservation Biology* **16**:253–7.

Strandberg, B., S. M. Kristiansen and K. Tybirk. 2005. Dynamic oak-scrub to forest succession: effects of management on understorey vegetation, humus forms and soils. *Forest Ecology and Management* **211**:318–28.

ter Braak, C. J. F. and P. Šmilauer. 2002. *CANOCO Reference Manual and CanoDraw for Windows User's Guide: Software for Canonical Community Ordination (version 4.5)*. Ithaca, NY: Microcomputer Power.

Thompson, K., J. Bakker and R. Bekker. 1997. *The Soil Seed Banks of North West Europe: Methodology, Density and Longevity*. Cambridge, UK: Cambridge University Press.

Thompson, K., J. P. Bakker, R. M. Bekker and J. G. Hodgson. 1998. Ecological correlates of seed persistence in soil in the north-west European flora. *Journal of Ecology* **86**: 163–9.

Uotila, A. and J. Kouki. 2005. Understorey vegetation in spruce-dominated forests in eastern Finland and Russian Karelia: successional patterns after anthropogenic and natural disturbances. *Forest Ecology and Management* **215**:113–37.

Verheyen, K., O. Honnay, G. Motzkin, M. Hermy and D. R. Foster. 2003. Response of forest plant species to land-use change: a life-history trait-based approach. *Journal of Ecology* **91**:563–77.

Von Humboldt, A. 1806. *Ideen zu einer Physiognomik der Gewächse*. Tübingen.

Washington, H. G. 1984. Diversity, biotic and similarity indices. *Water Research* **18**:653–94.

Weiher, E., A. van der Werf, K. Thompson *et al*. 1999. Challenging Theophrastus: a common core list of plant traits for functional ecology. *Journal of Vegetation Science* **10**:609–20.

Wilson, J. B. 1999. Guilds, functional types and ecological groups. *Oikos* **86**:507–22.

Wulf, M. 1997. Plant species as ancient woodland indicators in north-western Germany. *Journal of Vegetation Science* **8**:635–42.

Setting conservation targets for freshwater ecosystems in forested catchments

JOHN S. RICHARDSON AND ROSS M. THOMPSON

INTRODUCTION

Surface waters are the receiving environment for all activities within a catchment, and integrate processes across temporal and spatial scales. Estimates suggest that the rate of loss of freshwater species is five times that of species in temperate terrestrial environments, and rivals the rate found in tropical forests (Revenga *et al.* 2005). Threats to aquatic ecosystems come from a wide variety of land uses, including agriculture, urbanization, mining, forestry, impoundment, and others. Efforts to protect important characteristics of freshwater environments focus on physical and chemical aspects, such as water quality, temperature, channel bedforms, and instream flow needs. The conservation of fish (with a predominant focus on salmonids in northern temperate regions) and protection of aquatic biodiversity in general are often assumed to be served by this focus on the abiotic subsystem.

In forested ecosystems, sustainability of aquatic ecosystem values has been the subject of an enormous effort to determine what land-use practices most affect these systems, and how those impacts might be mitigated (Bormann *et al.* 1974; McEachern *et al.* 2006; Prepas *et al.* 2006; Richardson 2008). The specific mechanisms by which land uses, such as forestry, affect catchments often interact with each other along multiple pathways, for instance concomitant changes in light regimes, temperature, wood and organic matter inputs, etc. (Richardson and Danehy 2007; Thompson *et al.* 2008). Measures to conserve biodiversity and other ecosystem services need to consider the non-independence of these multiple processes. There

Setting Conservation Targets for Managed Forest Landscapes, ed. M.-A. Villard and B. G. Jonsson. Published by Cambridge University Press.

are rules that are commonly applied, such as the proportion of catchments in a particular seral stage, and the maintenance of vegetated reserves or buffers (usually mature trees) along the margins of some freshwaters (Lee *et al.* 2004). We will discuss these rules further, but it is important to determine whether they effectively address all of the conservation objectives. In the general framework of setting general management goals based on the collective values of stakeholders, the critical second step is to set out and clearly define quantitative targets. Unfortunately, quantitative targets flowing from management goals are often vaguely stated, which makes it difficult to assess and monitor the effectiveness or efficiency of management actions. However, without explicit definition of objectives, and measurable targets, it is not possible to determine whether conservation practices have been successful.

In this chapter, we consider the objectives for conservation of freshwaters in landscapes with managed forests in order to appraise the ways in which these objectives or targets have been established and met. Many of the examples we provide may apply to other land-use transformations as well, particularly in the case of agricultural lands. Urbanized landscapes are more permanently transformed and should be treated separately from landscapes with more extensive vegetative cover. We will address how well these objectives fit with our more general concepts of conservation biology, in terms of natural variation on different spatial and temporal scales, and for processes sometimes assumed to be covered under the umbrella of other objectives. One of the most widely applied methods to protect the biodiversity of freshwater ecosystems is the maintenance of riparian reserves (or buffers) along streamsides. What targets should we use to determine whether these actions have been successful at meeting our objectives?

Characterizing forest streams

Forest streams are tightly connected to the surrounding forest via reciprocal flows of nutrients and materials, which strongly influence patterns of both aquatic and terrestrial biodiversity (Baxter *et al.* 2005; Marczak *et al.* 2007) (Fig. 12.1). Riparian vegetation reduces light inputs to smaller streams, moderating temperature variation and limiting algal productivity (Gregory *et al.* 1991; Kiffney *et al.* 2003; Moore *et al.* 2005). Organic matter falling into streams, or carried in dissolved form via groundwater inflows, forms the bioenergetic basis of food webs of the majority of smaller streams (Thompson and Townsend 2004; Richardson *et al.* 2005a,b), and contributes greatly to downstream ecosystems (Wipfli *et al.* 2007). Live vegetation on stream banks and large wood falling into streams provide geomorphologic

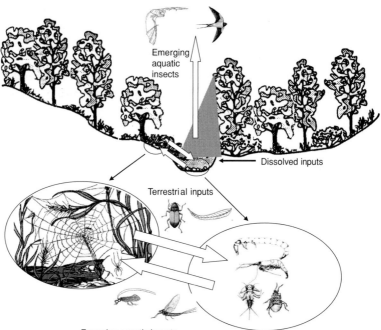

Figure 12.1. Diagrammatic representation of stream–riparian interactions in a typical forested stream, illustrating some of the predominant flows of materials and organisms between aquatic and terrestrial environments in a typical forested stream.

structure and stability, as well as cover and food for various invertebrate and fish species (Benke and Wallace 1997; Davies-Colley 1997).

The combination of habitat variables associated with forested streams results in characteristic patterns of both aquatic and terrestrial biodiversity (Gomi *et al.* 2002; Sabo *et al.* 2005; Richardson and Danehy 2007). Stream fauna in forested streams are dominated by species able to utilize organic inputs from terrestrial settings. This includes species feeding directly on terrestrially derived matter ("shredders") and species which feed further down organic matter processing chains ("collectors"). Key to the transfer of materials and energy from terrestrial matter into aquatic biomass are aquatic fungi and bacteria, which condition and modify recalcitrant materials. Dependence on these processes generates food webs which have a distinctive structure, with abundant weak trophic links to the detrital pool and a high degree of generalization in primary consumers (Thompson and Townsend 2004). In the terrestrial realm, forested streams are also associated with distinctive assemblages of species that either have an aquatic life stage or depend on aquatic invertebrates emerging from streams (Sabo *et al.* 2005).

In this chapter, we will concentrate on forested, temperate streams, although there is an increasing body of work in tropical regions (Flecker *et al.* 2002; Dudgeon 2006; Dudgeon and Smith 2006). We will also largely discuss streams in natural forests, rather than grassland streams that have been subject to afforestation (Weatherley *et al.* 1993; Thompson and Townsend 2004). Although our emphasis will be on reviewing and identifying conservation targets for temperate regions, these may also apply to exotic plantation forests or tropical systems.

Threats and challenges

Identifying conservation targets for freshwater organisms requires a clear identification of threats and an assessment of the sensitivities of various indicators. Conservation values of forest streams are subject to threats from land-use conversion of surrounding lands, diversion and abstraction of flows, and forestry activities in riparian zones.

Conversion to pasture

Primary among the threats to aquatic ecosystems in forest landscapes is permanent forest clearance for pasture creation. Between 2000 and 2005, 7.3 million hectares of forest were cleared every year across the world, mainly in tropical regions for conversion to pasture (FAO 2005). Conversion of forest to pasture has pervasive effects on stream water quality, ecosystem processes, and biota. Pasture streams are typified by increased fine sediment loads, greater nutrient availability, and higher in-stream temperatures (Neill *et al.* 2001; Townsend *et al.* 1997). These physicochemical changes result in aquatic food webs that are based on high algal productivity and are typified by grazer diversity and complex food webs with long food chains (Thompson and Townsend 2004). Higher water temperatures and sedimentation rates, combined with reductions of inputs of large woody material, act to reduce habitat quality for many fish species (Richmond and Fausch 1995; Shaw and Richardson 2001).

Disconnection of flood plains

Changes in hydrological regimes due to human activities such as abstraction and impoundments may strongly influence aquatic systems both directly, due to changes in in-stream habitat, and indirectly, via influences on riparian vegetation. Floodplain forests in many parts of the world rely on periodic inundation to maintain forest health and to provide access for aquatic fauna to terrestrial resources and breeding habitats (Forsberg *et al.* 1993; Bunn and Arthington 2002). Loss of those connections due to water abstraction and flow management can have profound effects on patterns of aquatic biodiversity and ecosystem function.

Forestry

Riparian harvesting of trees can dramatically affect aquatic ecosystems by altering physical environment and biological processes (Broadmeadow and Nisbet 2004; Thompson *et al.* 2008). Clearcutting of riparian margins alters channel bedforms and sediment supply (Beschta 1978; Boothroyd *et al.* 2004). Changes in catchment hydrology following timber harvesting or road building (e.g. reduced transpiration by vegetation, reduced capture of moisture from the air, altered routing of flowpaths) may impact on streams (Moore and Wondzell 2005). Changes in the timing and peaks of flows can alter storage of organic matter and intensify flood peaks, leading to channel reworking or even reduced groundwater inputs during dry seasons (Swank *et al.* 2001; Stott and Mount 2004). Riparian harvesting supplies large amounts of organic matter to the streambed, providing a food source for shredding stream invertebrates, either directly or via incorporation into fungal and bacterial biomass (Bilby and Ward 1991; Tank and Dodds 2003). An opening of the canopy above streams increases light intensity and, thus, algal productivity and the representation of grazing species (Stone and Wallace 1998; Boothroyd *et al.* 2004; Thompson and Townsend 2004). It can also have dramatic impacts on the local thermal regime through an increase in incident solar radiation (Moore *et al.* 2005).

Conservation targets: current and historical approaches

The relationships between forest management practices and integrity of stream ecosystems have been extensively studied and there is a vast literature on the topic. Applications of this information to the conservation of freshwater biodiversity has resulted in the establishment of a wide range of targets, from conservation of particular taxa to strict habitat-based approaches. Here, we summarize some of the general types of measures that have been proposed, along with corresponding targets.

Water quality

The use of fixed water quality guidelines for managing aquatic systems is well established, although it has been more widely applied in agricultural, industrial, and urban streams than in forest systems. This is in part due to the fact that in non-forested drainage basins there are clear water quality impacts from land use: increased release of nitrogen and phosphorus from agricultural lands, and heightened levels of heavy metals and other toxicants from industrial and urban land uses. In forested catchments, the relationships between disturbance and water quality have been less well described, and so the use of strict water quality guidelines is less widely applied for conservation purposes. Some jurisdictions have established guidelines on water temperature for forested catchments. For instance, the British Columbia (Canada) provincial guidelines stipulate that when the fish distribution is unknown in a stream, the mean weekly maximum temperature should not exceed 18 °C (British Columbia Approved Water Quality Guidelines, 2006 Edition, www.env.gov.bc.ca). There is also clear evidence of forestry impacting on water pH (Ormerod *et al.* 1989), and this has been used to guide conservation strategies (Ormerod *et al.* 2006). Although it is known that forestry activities increase concentrations of nitrogen and phosphorus in streams, with effects that may last many years (Likens *et al.* 1969; Neal *et al.* 2004), we are unaware of any creation of specific nutrient targets for the conservation of stream fauna in forest lands. Nor do we suggest that such an approach would be fruitful. Water quality relationships in forested streams are influenced by a range of factors including light availability, absorption by organic matter, and the nature of the stream substrate, among others (Likens *et al.* 1969). Water quality sampling of the scale most usually applied for monitoring (grab sampling from a single location at widely spaced time intervals) is unlikely to adequately encapsulate the effects of forestry activities such that meaningful targets could be established for conservation outcomes.

Managing for endangered species

Freshwater species are generally considered to be at higher risk of future extinction than those of most terrestrial ecosystems, except for tropical rainforests (Revenga *et al.* 2005). The management of a number of endangered species has been the focus of conservation targets for aquatic systems. For instance, conservation strategies for populations of coastal giant salamanders (*Dicamptodon tenebrosus*), coastal tailed frogs (*Ascaphus truei*), and torrent salamanders (*Rhyacotriton* spp.) have resulted in changes to forest management in the Pacific North-west of North America (Stoddard and Hayes 2005). Given the challenges associated with the accurate estimation of populations of these species, especially the wide natural variations in numbers, conservation targets for these species have remained very general, mostly at the level of contrasting frequency of presence versus absence (not detected).

Managing for fish

Given the strong interest in commercial and game fish populations through-out the world, this taxon has often been used as the sentinel for conservation of aquatic habitat. One example of this is the Canadian Government's policy of No Net Loss (NNL) of fish habitat. This policy is based on the maintenance of a quantity of fish habitat often by replacement of habitat lost to development projects. Such projects are meant to be accompanied by appropriate monitoring to assess whether the NNL objective has been met, and the monitoring may include physical, chemical, and/or biological measures (Quigley and Harper 2006a). However, the monitoring require-ments of local agency offices may be vaguely stated, such that measurable outcomes from which to judge success are limited (Quigley and Harper 2006a). In the case of major dam projects, the prescribed goal of no net loss of fish habitat is often verified using in-stream flow assessment tech-niques. In some jurisdictions, in-stream flow targets have been prescribed. In the province of Québec (Canada), the in-stream flow policy enunciates that minimum flow requirements must be estimated using certain low flow statistics that vary between regions and seasons, in order to accommodate for the needs of certain sentinel fish species in each area. Any derogation from this minimum flow requirement requires evidence that a lower flow will not result in net loss of fish habitat. In such cases, an in-stream flow incremental method (IFIM, Bovee *et al.* 1998) is often used to quantify habitat availability for various flow scenarios.

Biomonitoring

The use of invertebrates, algae, and fish communities as proxies for overall aquatic ecosystem health has a long history, and is considered to provide an integrated appraisal of water and overall environmental quality (Hynes 1960). A wealth of indices have been developed which seek to quantify changes in invertebrate communities. In general, these indices fall into two groups. Absolute indices give each taxon in a community a score based on its tolerance to particular environmental impacts. By summing these scores (from either presence–absence or abundance), site scores can be calculated. These can provide a measure of current ecological status or they can be used to monitor changes in environmental condition through time. More commonly, however, relative indices are used to compare site scores to scores from reference sites considered to be in good ecological condition.

Box 12.1 The reference condition

Many quantitative indices of aquatic ecosystem health are based on comparisons of study sites to a reference site which is considered to represent a desired endpoint. Many biomonitoring tools predict what aquatic community is expected at a location, based on an unimpacted reference site in the same biogeographic region. For a given site, the degree of impairment is calculated as how different the community is from that predicted by the reference condition (Bailey *et al.* 2004).

These approaches have been widely applied, but are also open to criticism. In many habitats (particularly lowland streams and large rivers), there are no undisturbed habitats that can act as a reference. Further, in waterways located in production landscapes (e.g. agricultural land and forestry blocks), it may be unrealistic to express stream condition relative to pristine sites. In these landscapes, it may be more useful to define an acceptable level of impairment relative to production benefits, rather than adopting a viewpoint that any impairment is unacceptable.

In North America, this approach was developed as the Index of Biotic Integrity (IBI) (Karr 1981). In Britain (and ultimately in Europe), RIVPACS (River Invertebrate Prediction and Classification System) developed these approaches further by using advanced multivariate techniques to compare degraded and reference sites (Armitage 1989). In several countries, these methods were further developed by including a range of habitat measures as well as data on invertebrates considered as indicators (e.g. AUSRIVAS in Australia [Turak *et al.* 1999] and BEAST in Canada [Reynoldson *et al.* 1995]). Detailed methods for the application and interpretation of these measures have come to be known as the reference condition approach (Bailey *et al.* 2004; see Box 12.1). These approaches have been widely adopted as a core element of state of the environment monitoring, and have been used to establish quantitative conservation and restoration targets.

Managing for functional measures as targets

Emerging from the widespread approach of community biomonitoring and water quality was an awareness that such measures failed to encapsulate ecosystem functions such as primary productivity and organic matter processing. These processes can be thought of as the "engine room" which provides energy to aquatic food webs. Such functional measures have been proposed as a supplement to existing measures of community composition (Bunn 1995; Brooks *et al.* 2002), and leaf litter decomposition rates (Gessner and Chauvet 2002), and ecosystem metabolism (the combination of algal productivity and ecosystem respiration) (Bunn *et al.* 1999), have been suggested as functional measures of system integrity. Forest harvesting in stream catchments generally decreases leaf processing rates over the short term (Webster and Waide 1982), but increases leaf processing rates over the longer term (Griffith and Perry 1991; Hutchens and Benfield 2000; Benfield *et al.* 2001), likely because nutrient availability is increased. Gessner and Chauvet (2002) have proposed a framework for assessing functional stream integrity using leaf litter processing rates, by comparison with reference sites and the use of absolute values. Either approach requires detailed information on the nature of leaf litter entering the stream. Although functional measures have considerable potential, they remain as yet a comparative tool (Lecerf *et al.* 2006).

Habitat-based protection

The costs and difficulties associated with the use of direct measures of biodiversity have led many management agencies to focus on physical habitat as a proxy measure, based on the assumption that amount and productivity of habitat might suffice (Minns and Moore 2003; Harper and Quigley 2005). Initially, physical habitat measures were limited to water quality, but habitat assessment has increased in sophistication with developments in multivariate analysis and modeling. In forest management, habitat protection has been based on two key approaches: maintenance of riparian buffers of various widths, and reintroduction of woody debris into streams. As outlined above, the majority of these approaches have been based on creating fish habitat. However, as pointed out by Quigley and Harper (2006b), success at compliance with guidelines is not equivalent to ecological success. In most cases where habitat protection studies were evaluated, lack of pre-impact data was a serious impediment to evaluation of compliance (Quigley and Harper 2006b).

Moving forward: conservation and restoration

How quantitative are we?

Aquatic ecology is perhaps the area of ecology where quantitative measures of ecosystem health have been applied most widely. Yet Bernhardt *et al.* (2005) documented that over 20% of river restoration projects in the USA had no stated goals. Those projects that had goals were often general and without quantitative targets, such as to enhance water quality, to manage riparian zones, and to improve in-stream habitat (Bernhardt *et al.* 2005). Surprisingly few of the huge variety of indices available have been used to monitor streams in managed forests. Quantitative indices derived from biomonitoring have been widely adopted by managers and policy-makers. However, the establishment and achievement of targets have been made more difficult by the high degree of environmental variability inherent in these systems. To establish the degree of variation in any index of health in an aquatic system requires long time series of data both before and after any activity. The quantitative targets that do exist often have difficulties taking into account natural variance, and detecting effects of management against this environmental "noise". In water quality guidelines for drinking water, there are explicit considerations of safety factors in setting allowable concentrations (e.g. ANZECC 2000). These water quality criteria often have explicit limits on the numbers of consecutive days on which allowable concentrations can be exceeded. Conservation targets for freshwaters require an understanding of natural variance and should include thresholds based on the probability that a measured parameter exceeds absolute target values. The notion of event duration is also key to the establishment of useful targets for aquatic habitat.

The limitation of the reference condition

The use of relative indices to define conservation targets is appealing because it offers a clear trajectory for restoring aquatic systems to a reference condition. However, for many systems, there are no appropriate reference sites to provide a basis of comparison. Even where reference streams exist, these systems vary over many temporal scales. In most cases, we lack long-term data from reference systems which would allow determining a natural range of variation based on long-term background trends such as climate change. In many cases, it is difficult to identify what is the appropriate benchmark or reference because all systems have been heavily modified (Brinson and Rheinhardt 1996). In production landscapes in particular, it may be considered unrealistic to measure condition relative to pristine reference sites. For example, streams that have been subjected to forest harvesting in the riparian zone by using best management practices may be indistinguishable from those harvested by using other means, simply because both are considered degraded relative to the undisturbed condition. The reference condition may provide a useful benchmark to define conservation targets in situations where relatively undisturbed sites exist, and where preservation (protection without further activities) is possible in a stream catchment. For production forests, however, there is an immediate need to carry out surveys of streams under best management scenarios, which will be useful to set reasonable management objectives based on the best compromise between production and aquatic values. The establishment of reasonable management objectives within a production context can then be used as a baseline for seeking improvements in target values through improved management practices.

Restoration

Restoration ecology is now a well-developed science in aquatic systems, but continues to perform poorly in terms of clearly establishing targets and assessing outcomes. A feature of many large-scale river restoration efforts has been poor or absent data prior to undertaking restoration, inadequate assessment of long-term outcomes, and a failure to institute appropriate controls (Roni et al. 2002). Bernhardt et al. (2005) estimate that <10% of river restoration projects in the USA were assessed at all. In general, attempts to remedy degradation from past forestry practices by reintroduction of woody structure into streams have been carried out following the "if you build it they will come" principle. Incorporating restoration studies into broader landscape studies is a necessary step to understanding how factors such as dispersal limitation may determine restoration outcomes. However, recent efforts to focus and define targets in river restoration have explicitly set out criteria for assessment of effectiveness and efficiency (e.g. Palmer et al. 2005). It may be that quantifiable end-points are more easily defined by going from a seriously degraded condition to a more desired state. Nevertheless, criteria-setting for stream restoration, such as population targets for fish populations, may provide a useful starting point for the development of targets for sustainable forest management around streams.

Setting and assessing targets

Biological diversity is an elusive parameter to measure in most systems, as it is a dynamic, adaptive entity, and it rarely persists unaltered for any length of time (Woodward et al. 2002). Select biological measures are used, often as proxies for the remainder of the ecosystem, and these may be structural (e.g. species composition and densities) or functional aspects (e.g. decomposition rates, metabolic rates). Successful biological indicators of aquatic ecosystems should (Marchant et al. 2006):

1. provide early warning of a range of environmental stressors
2. demonstrate a change and provide a diagnostic for such a change
3. be cost-efficient
4. yield interpretable outputs.

Given the large array of physical and chemical drivers of these biological systems, how does one determine if a given management objective for conservation of aquatic and riparian biodiversity has been met? Moreover, these are naturally dynamic systems, so choosing the appropriate spatial and temporal scales at which to answer the above question is a serious challenge.

Monitoring

Monitoring populations, communities, or even ecosystems, needs to take into account the unique features of each site. The specifics of a particular stream are a complex function of their physico-chemical attributes, as well as details of the community. What one would find in a particular stream may not be easily predicted solely from nearby "similar" streams. One of the primary statistical designs intended to accommodate these subtle idiosyncrasies is the well-known before–after, control–impact (BACI) design, which is intended to control for the stream itself before versus after some planned activity, using other reference sites where no specific change is expected. Using this relatively powerful statistical design in resource management still does not specify when the change or changes have been excessive or unrecoverable in an appropriate time frame (Richardson 2004). Moreover, this is only available as a tool when carefully planned designs are in place well in advance of any anthropogenic changes, which is a situation that is perhaps less common that one might hope.

Measuring changes from some reference state (which may be variously defined) for a specific land-use practice depends on statistical design and systems considerations. From a statistical point of view, the ability to detect change depends in part on the statistical power of the selected tests. Frequently, field studies are constrained by the ability to provide sufficient replication to statistically detect significant changes against the sometimes noisy background of natural systems. A low statistical power may imply that it is not possible to reject the null hypothesis that nothing has changed, when in fact it has (type II error). If it were possible to specify the acceptable magnitude of change in particular measures, it might be easier to design compliance monitoring to actually assess these changes with sufficient statistical power to evaluate the outcomes. This is rarely done. Important natural variations through time and across sites make this difficult, but not impossible.

Setting measurable targets

There are likely to be many instances in which setting targets based on rigorous scientific study and past experience is not possible. The complications of natural systems and the dearth of experimental trials at appropriate scales leads to the frequent application of expert opinion and risk management to the setting of targets. Target setting in such a context should be accompanied by a well-designed, adaptive management trial to assess the outcomes, but such trials are rarely applied at the catchment and landscape scales.

We feel that it is critical to remind readers that the world is not a stationary system, and the global context in which targets are set needs to be cognizant of background changes. For instance, factors such as climate change, harvesting of old-growth forest, and other processes will interact with management practices in a way that is not easily predicted solely from past experience.

Is it possible to set targets at the appropriate temporal and spatial scales, without being trapped into long-term and large spatial scale averages? Biological criteria as targets seem appallingly difficult to implement based on the limitations described above. Hydrological targets may be similarly difficult to appropriately address, especially given the amount of instrumentation and calibration necessary. Water quality parameters may be useful, but may also be so transient that they become irrelevant. But then, one would expect to be able to see particular and measurable changes in the biological system that could be used as targets. Compensation within ecosystems (functions of a species declining in abundance may be fulfilled by a similar species) may make the presence of a particular species less useful as a conservation target if we are primarily interested in protection of ecosystem function. This is certainly problematic if one's focus remains on selected species of cool-water fish. What is needed are structural and functional targets that are not susceptible to compensation and other changes associated with natural dynamics.

A set of measurable targets for evaluating success at conservation of water resources in managed forest landscapes would be met with great enthusiasm. The use of conceptual models to envision the relationships between management and targets, and the development of those models into more sophisticated analytical tools (see Box 12.2) provides an exciting avenue for this to occur. However, there is a critical need for research to understand the sensitivity of different types of targets to particular management activities. This is particularly true in forested systems, where our understanding of the effects of forestry activities, for instance, on even commonly applied indices is relatively poor. Once these data have been gathered however, there is powerful potential to use Bayesian techniques to generate decision support tools which can predict the effects of multiple stressors

Box 12.2 Quantitatively analysing ecological data

Statistical analysis of trends in indices of aquatic health and the achievement of conservation targets is a highly sophisticated area, which has developed rapidly in recent years.

Classical statistical methods are likely to be most familiar, and include analysis of variance and *t*-tests. These methods test whether means in data differ significantly from a null hypothesis of no significant differences. The underlying assumptions for classical statistics require that data be normally distributed and that variability be similar between treatments. Finding a significant effect will depend on the magnitude of tested effects, on the sample size, and on the background environmental variability. Because ecosystems tend to be highly variable, a high level of replication (i.e. large sample size) is generally required.

Likelihood and information-theoretic methods help identify statistical models that best fit the observed data for a given model (or group of models) and error distribution. These techniques are highly flexible and have less stringent assumptions than classical statistics, including an ability to fit linear or non-linear models to data that are strongly skewed and do not require that the assumption of normality be respected. Information-theoretic methods compare the fit of a range of models to the data and identify the "best" model. However these methods can be complicated and computationally intensive. In addition, there are no commonly reported, universally accepted statistics of model fit, meaning that a best model may still have poor explanatory power (Mueller 1996).

Bayesian statistics estimate the probability that a hypothesis is true, given prior knowledge and current data. Bayesian methods are designed to incorporate information from multiple sources explicitly using results of past studies as well as current experiments. These approaches are particularly amenable to restoration and conservation studies, because the hypothesis that a target is being met can be explicitly tested, and the methods are robust to low sample sizes. An overview of Bayesian statistics can be found in Berger *et al.* (2007).

on conservation objectives. The establishment of specific targets for these objectives is important, but must take into account background variability and must be carried out in a pragmatic way. We consider it essential that management objectives for managed forests, for instance, reflect the best possible compromise between conservation and production, rather than unrealistically comparing production landscape streams to those not subject to any form of anthropogenic disturbance. This objective setting can be aided by decision support tools which take into account variability and uncertainty about the interaction of multiple stressors. The establishment of those objectives could lead to quantitative targets within the next decade.

CONCLUSIONS

To establish and monitor conservation targets for forested catchments, researchers and managers should pay attention to the following issues.

- Clear quantitative targets (as achieved for the various biotic indices of health) are informative and provide key information for managers in appraising the current state of the environment and long-term trends.
- Conservation targets must be appraised for likely sensitivity to changes in forest management. In many cases, top predators such as fish may be slow to respond to such changes.
- Data taken prior to applying management or restoration activities and data from control sites are absolutely essential and rarely collected, particularly during restoration activities. The absence of such data, or failure to analyse them properly, makes it impossible to establish clear quantitative targets or evaluate success.
- Long time series of data are crucial given the high degree of interannual variability in most ecosystems. Persistence with a particular index over a longer period is likely to be more fruitful than changing indices, even if the new index is considered more sensitive.
- Conservation targets should take into account the dynamics of aquatic systems in terms of stochastic events (e.g. floods) and longer term trends (e.g. climate change). Sampling across a range of sites undergoing differing management regimes is the only way to clearly establish conservation target responses to changes in management.
- Assessing improvement quantitatively is difficult using classical statistical techniques and is likely to be best approached using Bayesian methods.

ACKNOWLEDGEMENTS

We thank Marc-André Villard, André St-Hilaire, and Roland Cormier for helpful comments on an earlier version of this chapter.

References

ANZECC. 2000. Australian Guidelines for Fresh and Marine Water Quality. Australian and New Zealand Environment and Conservation Council. Available online at www.ea.gov.au/water/quality/nwqms/#quality.

Armitage, P. D. 1989. The application of a classification and prediction technique based on macroinvertebrates to assess the effects of river regulation. Pp. 267–93 in J. A. Gore and G. E. Petts (eds.) *Alternatives in Regulated River Management*. Boca Raton, FL: CRC Press Inc.

Bailey R. C., R. H. Norris and T. B. Reynoldson. 2004. *Bioassessment of Freshwater Ecosystems – Using the Reference Condition Approach*. Boston, MA: Kluwer Academic Publishers.

Baxter, C. V., K. D. Fausch and W. C. Saunders. 2005. Tangled webs: reciprocal flows of invertebrate prey link streams and riparian zones. *Freshwater Biology* 50:201–20.

Benfield, E. F., J. R. Webster, J. L. Tank and J. J. Hutchens. 2001. Long-term patterns in leaf breakdown in streams in response to watershed logging. *Internationale Revue der Gesamten Hydrobiologie* 86:467–74.

Benke, A. C. and J. B. Wallace. 1997. Trophic basis of production among riverine caddisflies: implications for food web analysis. *Ecology* 78:1132–45.

Berger, J. O., A. P. Dawid and D. Heckerman (authors), J. M. Bernardo and M. J. Bayarri (eds.) 2007. *Bayesian Statistics 8*. London: Oxford University Press.

Bernhardt, E. S., M. A. Palmer, J. D. Allan *et al.* 2005. Synthesizing U.S. river restoration efforts. *Science* 308:636–7.

Beschta, R. L. 1978. Long-term patterns of sediment production following road construction and logging in the Oregon Coast Range. *Water Resources Research* 14:1011–16.

Bilby, R. E. and J. W. Ward. 1991. Characteristics and function of large woody debris in streams draining old-growth, clear-cut, and 2nd-growth forests in southwestern Washington. *Canadian Journal of Fisheries and Aquatic Sciences* 48:2499–508.

Boothroyd, I. K. G., J. M. Quinn, E. R. Langer, K. J. Costley and G. Steward. 2004. Riparian buffers mitigate effects of pine plantation logging on New Zealand streams – 1. Riparian vegetation structure, stream geomorphology and periphyton. *Forest Ecology and Management* 194:199–213.

Bormann, F. H., G. E. Likens, T. G. Siccama, R. S. Pierce and J. S. Eaton. 1974. Export of nutrients and recovery of stable conditions following deforestation at Hubbard Brook. *Ecological Monographs* 44:255–77.

Bovee, K., B. Lamb, J. M. Bartholow *et al.* 1998. *Stream Habitat Analysis using the Instream Flow Incremental Methodology*. USGS Information technology report 1998–2004.

Brinson, M. M. and R. Rheinhardt. 1996. The role of reference wetlands in functional assessment and mitigation. *Ecological Applications* 6:69–76.

Broadmeadow, S. and T. R. Nisbet. 2004. The effects of riparian forest management on the freshwater environment: a literature review of best management practice. *Hydrology and Earth System Sciences* 8:286–305.

Brooks, S. S., M. A. Palmer, B. J. Cardinale, C. M. Swan and S. Ribblett. 2002. Assessing stream ecosystem rehabilitation: limitations of community structure data. *Restoration Ecology* 10:156–68.

Bunn, S. E. 1995. Biological monitoring of water quality in Australia: workshop summary and future directions. *Australian Journal of Ecology* 20:220–7.

Bunn, S. E. and A. H. Arthington. 2002. Basic principles and ecological consequences of altered flow regimes for aquatic biodiversity. *Environmental Management* 30:492–507.

Bunn, S. E., P. M. Davies and T. D. Mosisch. 1999. Ecosystem measures of river health and their response to riparian and catchment degradation. *Freshwater Biology* 41:333–45.

Davies-Colley, R. J. 1997. Stream channels are narrower in pasture than in forest. *New Zealand Journal of Marine and Freshwater Research* 31:599–608.

Dudgeon, D. 2006. The impacts of human disturbance on stream benthic invertebrates and their drift in North Sulawesi, Indonesia. *Freshwater Biology* 51:1710–29.

Dudgeon, D. and R. E. W. Smith. 2006. Exotic species, fisheries and conservation of freshwater biodiversity in tropical Asia: the case of the Sepik River, Papua New Guinea. *Aquatic Conservation-Marine and Freshwater Ecosystems* 16:203–15.

FAO. 2005. *State of the World's Forests.* Rome, Italy: Food and Agriculture Organisation of the United Nations.

Flecker, A. S., B. W. Taylor, E. S. Bernhardt *et al.* 2002. Interactions between herbivorous fishes and limiting nutrients in a tropical stream ecosystem. *Ecology* 83:1831–44.

Forsberg, B. R., C. Araujolima, L. A. Martinelli, R. L. Victoria and J. A. Bonassi. 1993. Autotrophic carbon-sources for fish of the Central Amazon. *Ecology* 74:643–52.

Gessner, M. O. and E. Chauvet. 2002. A case for using litter breakdown to assess functional stream integrity. *Ecological Applications* 12:498–510.

Gomi, T., R. C. Sidle and J. S. Richardson. 2002. Headwater and channel network – understanding processes and downstream linkages of headwater systems. *BioScience* 52:905–16.

Gregory, S. V., F. J. Swanson, W. A. McKee and K. W. Cummins. 1991. An ecosystem perspective of riparian zones. *BioScience* 41:540–51.

Griffith, M. B. and S. A. Perry. 1991. Leaf pack processing in two Appalachian mountain streams draining catchments with different management histories. *Hydrobiologia* 220:247–54.

Hutchens, J. J. Jr. and E. F. Benfield. 2000. Effects of forest defoliation by the gypsy moth on detritus processing in southern Appalachian streams. *American Midland Naturalist* 143:397–404.

Harper, D. J. and J. T. Quigley. 2005. No net loss of fish habitat: a review and analysis of habitat compensation in Canada. *Environmental Management* 36:343–55.

Hynes, H. B. N. 1960. *The Biology of Polluted Waters.* Liverpool, UK: Liverpool University Press.

Karr, J. R. 1981. Assessment of biotic integrity using fish communities. *Fisheries* 6:21–7.

Kiffney, P. M., J. S. Richardson and J. P. Bull. 2003. Responses of periphyton and insects to experimental manipulation of riparian buffer width along forest streams. *Journal of Applied Ecology* 40:1060–76.

Lecerf, A., P. Usseglio-Polatera, J. Y. Charcosset *et al.* 2006. Assessment of functional integrity of eutrophic streams using litter breakdown and benthic macroinvertebrates. *Archiv für Hydrobiologie* 165:105–26.

Lee, P., C. Smyth and S. Boutin. 2004. Quantitative review of riparian buffer width guidelines from Canada and the United States. *Journal of Environmental Management* 70:165–80.

Likens, G. E., F. H. Bormann and N. M. Johnson. 1969. Nitrification – importance to nutrient losses from a cutover forested ecosystem. *Science* 163:1205–6.

Marchant, R., R. H. Norris and A. Milligan. 2006. Evaluation and application of methods for biological assessment of streams: summary of papers. *Hydrobiologia* 572:1–7.

Marczak, L. B., R. M. Thompson and J. S. Richardson. 2007. A meta-analysis of the role of trophic position, habitat type and habitat productivity in determining the food web effects of resource subsidies. *Ecology* 88:140–8.

McEachern, P., E. E. Prepas and D. S. Chanasyk. 2006. Landscape control of water chemistry in northern boreal streams of Alberta. *Journal of Hydrology* 323:303–24.

Minns, C. K. and J. E. Moore. 2003. Assessment of net change of productive capacity of fish habitats: the role of uncertainty and complexity in decision making. *Canadian Journal of Fisheries and Aquatic Sciences* 60:100–16.

Moore, R. D. and S. M. Wondzell. 2005. Physical hydrology and the effects of forest harvesting in the Pacific Northwest: a review. *Journal of the American Water Resources Association* 41:753–84.

Moore, R. D., D. L. Spittlehouse and A. Story. 2005. Riparian microclimate and stream temperature response to forest harvesting – a review. *Journal of the American Water Resources Association* 41:813–34.

Mueller, R. O. 1996. *Basic Principles of Structural Equation Modelling*. New York, NY: Springer-Verlag.

Neal C., S. J. Ormerod, S. J. Langan, T. R. Nisbet and J. Roberts. 2004. Sustainability of UK forestry: contemporary issues for the protection of freshwaters, a conclusion. *Hydrology and Earth System Sciences* 8:589–95.

Neill, C., L. A. Deegan and S. M. Thomas. 2001. Deforestation for pasture alters nitrogen and phosphorus in small Amazonian streams. *Ecological Applications* 11:1817–28.

Ormerod, S. J., A. P. Donald and S. J. Brown. 1989. The influence of plantation forestry on the pH and aluminum concentration of upland Welsh streams – a reexamination. *Environmental Pollution* 62:47–62.

Ormerod, S. J., B. R. Lewis, R. A. Kowalik, J. F. Murphy and J. Davy-Bowker. 2006. Field testing the AWIC index for detecting acidification in British streams. *Archiv Für Hydrobiologie* 166:99–115.

Palmer, M. A., E. S. Bernhardt, J. D. Allan *et al.* 2005. Standards for ecologically successful river restoration. *Journal of Applied Ecology* 42:208–17.

Prepas, E. E., J. M. Burke, I. R. Whitson, G. Putz and D. W. Smith. 2006. Associations between watershed characteristics, runoff, and stream water quality: hypothesis development for watershed disturbance experiments and modelling in the Forest Watershed and Riparian Disturbance (FORWARD) project. *Journal of Environmental Engineering and Science* 5:S27–S37.

Quigley, J. T. and D. J. Harper. 2006a. Compliance with Canada's Fisheries Act: a field audit of habitat compensation projects. *Environmental Management* 37:336–50.

Quigley, J. T. and D. J. Harper. 2006b. Effectiveness of fish habitat compensation in Canada in achieving no net loss. *Environmental Management* 37:351–66.

Revenga, C., I. Campbell, R. Abell, P. de Villers and M. Bryer. 2005. Prospects for monitoring freshwater ecosystems towards the 2010 targets. *Philosophical Transactions of the Royal Society* B 360:397–413.

Reynoldson, T. B., R. C. Bailey, K. E. Day and R. H. Norris. 1995. Biological guidelines for freshwater sediment based on BEnthic Assessment of SedimenT (the BEAST) using a multivariate approach for predicting biological state. *Australian Journal of Ecology* 20:198–219.

Richardson, J. S. 2004. Meeting the conflicting objectives of stream conservation and land use through riparian management: another balancing act. Pp. 1–6 in G. J. Scrimgeour, G. Eisler, B. McCulloch, U. Silins and M. Monita (eds.) *Forest-Land-Fish Conference II – Ecosystem Stewardship Through Collaboration*. Proceedings of the Forest-Land-Fish Conference II, April 26–28, 2004, Edmonton, Alberta.

Richardson, J. S. 2008. Aquatic arthropods and forestry: effects of large-scale land use on aquatic systems in Nearctic temperate regions. *Canadian Entomologist* **140**:495–509.

Richardson, J. S. and R. J. Danehy. 2007. A synthesis of the ecology of headwater streams and their riparian zones in temperate forests. *Forest Science* **53**:131–47.

Richardson, J. S., R. E. Bilby and C. A. Bondar. 2005a. Organic matter dynamics in small streams of the Pacific Northwest. *Journal of the American Water Resources Association* **41**:921–34.

Richardson, J. S., R. J. Naiman, F. J. Swanson and D. E. Hibbs. 2005b. Riparian communities associated with Pacific Northwest headwater streams: assemblages, processes, and uniqueness. *Journal of the American Water Resources Association* **41**:935–47.

Richmond, A. D. and K. D. Fausch. 1995. Characteristics and function of large woody debris in sub-alpine Rocky-Mountain streams in northern Colorado. *Canadian Journal of Fisheries and Aquatic Sciences* **52**:1789–802.

Roni, P., T. J. Beechie, R. E. Bilby *et al.* 2002. A review of stream restoration techniques and a hierarchical strategy for prioritizing restoration in Pacific Northwest watersheds. *North American Journal of Fisheries Management* **22**:1–20.

Sabo, J. L., R. Sponseller, M. Dixon *et al.* 2005. Riparian zones increase regional species richness by harboring different, not more, species. *Ecology* **86**:56–62.

Shaw, E. A. and J. S. Richardson. 2001. Effects of fine inorganic sediment on stream invertebrate assemblages and rainbow trout (*Oncorhynchus mykiss*) growth and survival: implications of exposure duration. *Canadian Journal of Fisheries and Aquatic Sciences* **58**:2213–21.

Stoddard, M. A. and J. P. Hayes. 2005. The influence of forest management on headwater stream amphibians at multiple spatial scales. *Ecological Applications* **15**:811–23.

Stone, M. K. and J. B. Wallace. 1998. Long-term recovery of a mountain stream from clearcut logging: the effects of forest succession on benthic invertebrate community structure. *Freshwater Biology* **39**:151–69.

Stott, T. and N. Mount. 2004. Plantation forestry impacts on sediment yields and downstream channel dynamics in the UK: a review. *Progress in Physical Geography* **28**:197–240.

Swank, W. T., J. M. Vose and K. J. Elliott. 2001. Long-term hydrologic and water quality responses following commercial clearcutting of mixed hardwoods on a southern Appalachian catchment. *Forest Ecology and Management* **143**:163–78.

Tank, J. L. and W. K. Dodds. 2003. Nutrient limitation of epilithic and epixylic biofilms in ten North American streams. *Freshwater Biology* **48**:1031–49.

Thompson, R. M. and C. R. Townsend. 2004. Landuse influences on New Zealand stream communities: effects on species composition, functional organisation, and food-web structure. *New Zealand Journal of Marine and Freshwater Research* **38**:595–608.

Thompson, R. M., N. R. Phillips and C. R. Townsend. 2008. Biological consequences of clear-cut logging around streams – moderating effects of management. *Forest Ecology and Management*. (In press.)

Townsend, C. R., C. J. Arbuckle, T. A. Crowl and M. R. Scarsbrook. 1997. The relationship between land use and physicochemistry, food resources and macroinvertebrate communities in tributaries of the Taieri River, New Zealand: a hierarchically scaled approach. *Freshwater Biology* **37**:177–91.

Turak, E., L. K. Flack, R. H. Norris, J. Simpson and N. Waddell. 1999. Assessment of river condition at a large spatial scale using predictive models. *Freshwater Biology* **41**:283–98.

Weatherley, N. S., E. C. Lloyd, S. D. Rundle and S. J. Ormerod. 1993. Management of conifer plantations for the conservation of stream macroinvertebrates. *Biological Conservation* **63**:171–6.

Webster, J. R. and J. B. Waide. 1982. Effects of forest clearcutting on leaf breakdown in a southern Appalachian stream. *Freshwater Biology* **12**:331–44.

Wipfli, M. S., J. S. Richardson and R. J. Naiman. 2007. Ecological linkages between headwaters and downstream ecosystems: transport of organic matter, invertebrates, and wood down headwater channels. *Journal of the American Water Resources Association* **43**:72–85.

Woodward, G., J. I. Jones and A. G. Hildrew. 2002. Community persistence in Broadstone Stream (UK) over three decades. *Freshwater Biology* **47**:1419–35.

Setting quantitative targets for recovery of threatened species

DOUG P. ARMSTRONG AND HEIKO U. WITTMER

INTRODUCTION

When considering targets in conservation biology, we are likely to first think of the recent literature on setting of ecosystem-level targets. The development of "systematic conservation planning" (Margules and Pressey 2000) has greatly facilitated the ability of conservation bodies to make objective decisions in development of reserve networks. At an even broader scale, research has been conducted to assess the proportion of the Earth's land surface that needs to be protected to maintain biodiversity and ecosystem function (e.g. Svancara *et al.* 2005), potentially allowing decision-makers to move beyond the traditional rule-of-thumb of converting 10% of the Earth's land surface into protected areas (IUCN 1993). However, population-level conservation targets have a much longer history, given that traditional management of wildlife, fisheries, and forests has involved regulating harvests from populations in order to achieve maximum sustainable yields (Holt and Talbot 1978). Although species recovery is a more recently developed field, the process of setting and meeting targets is not fundamentally different from that of traditional wildlife management. The primary goal in both cases is to manage human activity to allow species and populations to persist, regardless of whether those species are valued for utilitarian or other reasons.

There is often tension between goals of ecosystem and species-level conservation, with people sometimes having diametrically opposing views on how research effort and resources should be allocated. Advocates of

Setting Conservation Targets for Managed Forest Landscapes, ed. M.-A. Villard and B. G. Jonsson. Published by Cambridge University Press.
© Cambridge University Press 2009.

ecosystem management rightly point out that it is impossible to manage all species one-by-one, and that it is important to consider species interactions and ecosystem-level processes as well as species composition (Walker 1989; Grumbine 1994). On the other hand, species management is much more tractable than ecosystem management and usually has clearer goals (Simberloff 1998; Goldstein 1999). We see both approaches as essential, and advocate the setting of species recovery targets within a broader framework of ecosystem management.

In this chapter we focus specifically on targets for species recovery, but illustrate how research and management focusing on such targets may lead to insights into ecosystem-level processes that would not otherwise have been considered. We first propose a general framework for setting and meeting quantitative recovery targets, then illustrate the proposed framework through two case studies. These cases are not necessarily ideal examples of how targets should be set, but illustrate the framework in the context of real-world situations.

A FRAMEWORK FOR SETTING AND MEETING SPECIES RECOVERY TARGETS

Aspects of target setting can be conceptualized in many different ways, as illustrated in this volume. Here we outline a framework for both setting and meeting quantitative targets for species recovery, and suggest that there is an essential feedback loop between these two processes (Fig. 13.1). The framework has four essential elements, as outlined below.

A hierarchy of goals and targets

It is useful to make a distinction between qualitative *recovery goals* and quantitative *recovery targets* when developing conservation strategies for endangered species (Tear et al. 2005). Recovery goals are general goals or policy statements that reflect societal value and political or institutional intent, but lack the detail required for implementation. Setting these general goals forces us to acknowledge that conservation is ultimately derived by human values. The goal-setting process also facilitates involvement by a range of stakeholders, many of whom will have little scientific or quantitative background. The three guidelines of representation (establishing populations across the full array of potential habitat), resiliency (protecting populations large enough to remain viable), and redundancy (saving enough different populations that some can be lost without a loss of the species) can be invoked in setting recovery goals (Shaffer and Stein 2000).

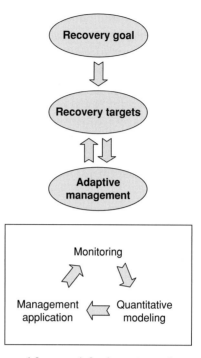

Figure 13.1. Conceptual framework for the setting and meeting of quantitative recovery targets for threatened species. The framework emphasizes that recovery targets should be subject to ongoing re-evaluation based on information gained through adaptive management. The box illustrates the components of the adaptive management process.

To make conservation policy accountable, it is essential to translate recovery goals into research-based quantitative recovery targets (see Chapter 1, this volume). It should be noted that recovery targets differ from other types of conservation target because, in the vast majority of cases, researchers have access to very little empirical data on the system at hand owing to the very rarity of the focal species. Most importantly, there is initially little information on what management is needed to achieve population growth, let alone meet other targets; hence it is impossible to assess the costs and feasibilities of different targets. Initial recovery targets will therefore often be highly tentative, meaning that target setting should be viewed as an ongoing process subject to updating as improved information becomes available.

By definition, the main goal of species recovery is an increase in abundance, through recovery of remnant populations and/or establishment of new populations. Consequently, the most fundamental target in species recovery is to achieve population growth, meaning that the finite rate of increase (λ) must be > 1. Additional targets can include the desired sizes or densities of populations, the number of populations to be maintained, and a desired degree of connectivity among populations. Such targets can initially be based on historical information on distribution and abundance (Marsh *et al.* 2005), genetic considerations (Franklin 1980; Mills and Allendorf 1996), or expert opinion (Fazey *et al.* 2006). Where more information is available, more quantitative approaches such as minimum viable population size (Nunney and Campbell 1993), ecological carrying capacity (Marsh *et al.* 2005), or detailed ecosystem modeling (Lessard *et al.* 2005) can be applied.

To determine what management is needed to meet recovery targets, it is useful to nominate *management action targets*. A management action target reflects the intensity, or type, of management initially thought necessary to achieve a recovery target. For example, many species recovery programs in New Zealand involve control of exotic mammals, and the effectiveness of control programs is assessed regularly through indices based on tracking (proportion of footprint tunnels tracked) or residual trap catch (proportion of kill traps catching an animal). The initial target for tracking or trapping indices is typically 5%, but such values can be updated for any species and system by modeling the relationship between tracking or trapping indices and species recovery targets (Armstrong *et al.* 2006). Once the intensity of management needed to meet a recovery target is estimated, and the associated costs known, the recovery target can potentially be revised.

Adaptive management

The obvious process for understanding the relationship between management action and species recovery is adaptive management (Holling 1978; Walters 1986). The most essential component of adaptive management is that management actions are treated as experiments, or as Walters (1986) put it, managers "probe the system" to gain information needed for further management. This sounds easy in principle. However, managers involved in species recovery programs want to do what they think is best for the species, and are understandably reluctant to change what they are doing or relax their efforts. The potential cost is that resources may be invested in ineffective or unnecessary management, and that better alternatives may never be discovered. The key is to acknowledge that we do not completely understand the systems we are working with, and that whatever understanding we have should be treated as a model that needs to be tested and updated.

There are two ways in which we can use adaptive management to improve our ability to meet and revise species recovery targets. First, we can test hypotheses about the factors limiting populations. These are usually the same factors thought to have caused the original decline or extirpation, although this is not necessarily the case. Caughley and Gunn (1996) used the term "diagnosis" to describe hypotheses for causes of decline, and stressed that all potential sources of information should be considered during the diagnosis phase. They then described how management experiments can be used to test these diagnoses. While traditional experiments would involve multiple replicates and controls, such experiments are unlikely to be possible or desirable with species recovery programs (Armstrong et al. 1994). A more feasible approach is a flexible series of management treatments, with ongoing selection of treatments based on previous results and further information needs. Once we have clear evidence that a particular factor is important, the second application of adaptive management is to vary the intensity of management to assess what is necessary to meet and revise recovery targets. The New Zealand pest management programs discussed above are good examples of this second application, as we have clear evidence that exotic mammals are impacting a range of native species, but need more data on intensities of mammal control needed to allow recovery.

Quantitative modeling

An essential component of any adaptive management exercise is quantitative modeling. Although quantitative models have been used for many decades to assess whether targets are likely to be met, such modeling was not commonly applied to endangered species until the advent of population viability analysis (PVA) in the 1980s (Beissinger and McCullough 2002). The initial focus of PVA was to estimate the long-term probability of extinction in small populations, taking into account genetic, demographic, and environmental stochasticity (Shaffer 1981). These PVAs played a useful role in highlighting the challenge likely to be faced in maintaining populations of area-demanding species such as grizzly bears (*Ursus arctos*). However, it is now well known that long-term extinction probabilities are impossible to estimate precisely without huge amounts of data unless the probability is close to zero or 100% (Fieberg and Ellner 2000; Ellner et al. 2002).

Three key steps have been taken to improve the practical value as well as the defensibility of modeling exercises for threatened species (Possingham *et al.* 1993; Beissinger and Westphal 1998). First, PVA has increasingly been treated as a component of adaptive management in species recovery. That is, modeling is conducted on an ongoing basis to evaluate management strategies and guide future management rather than used to make one-off predictions. Second, the focus of PVA has shifted away from long-term probability of extinction to more tractable recovery targets. We suggest that at least some targets focus on relatively simple parameters such as λ and that projections be restricted to time frames of no more than 5–10 years. Third, methods have been developed to quantify uncertainty in projections (see next section).

Incorporating uncertainty

Incorporation of uncertainty is the most complex part of making modeling projections, requiring far more time than determining the most likely outcome under any management scenario. However, the uncertainty around predictions can be critical for decisions about management targets, as illustrated in the examples below. There are two sources of uncertainty to be considered: uncertainty in outcomes due to demographic and environmental stochasticity, and uncertainty in parameters such as survival and reproduction rates. Although stochasticity has been a mainstay of PVA modeling since its inception (Shaffer 1981) and incorporated into all commonly used PVA packages (e.g. Lacy 2000), the other sources of uncertainty have tended to be ignored until recently (White 2000; Taylor *et al.* 2002; Wade 2002). However, in our experience, uncertainty in parameter estimation can overwhelm the effects of stochasticity, even after several years of intensive data collection in easily monitored populations. Uncertainty in parameter estimation depends not only on sample sizes, but also on the structure of models used. Models that fail to account for key factors will have biased parameter estimates when fitted to data, whereas complex models will have poor precision (Burnham and Anderson 2002). We usually select models based on Akaike's Information Criterion (AIC), which allows alternative models to be weighted based on the optimal compromise between bias and precision. Model averaging can then be used to obtain an overall model that incorporates uncertainty in model structure when estimating precision in parameter estimates.

We will now consider how the proposed framework applies to the recovery of the hihi (stitchbird, *Notiomystis cincta*), an endemic New Zealand forest bird, and the recovery of woodland caribou (*Rangifer tarandus caribou*) in British Columbia, Canada. Although these case studies contrast in taxa, geographical region, and scale, they converge on similar issues and both illustrate how long-term persistence of species may depend on forest management at the ecosystem level.

RECOVERY OF HIHI IN NEW ZEALAND

Background

The hihi is a forest bird endemic to the North Island of New Zealand and its surrounding islands. Hihi feed extensively on nectar and fruit as well as invertebrates, and were traditionally classified in the honeyeater (Meliphagidae) family. However, recent genetic evidence has shown that they are clearly not a honeyeater (Ewen *et al.* 2006). Hihi had disappeared from most of their range by the late nineteenth century, surviving only on Hauturu, a 3,083 ha offshore island. Their decline is thought to be due to exotic mammalian predators, as well as forest clearance and possibly disease (Taylor *et al.* 2005). Consequently, recovery efforts have focused on translocation of hihi to islands free of mammalian predators. Attempts to establish hihi on three islands (Hen, Cuvier, and Kapiti) in the 1980s were unsuccessful, with two populations declining to extinction and the population on Kapiti Island persisting only through periodic re-stocking from Hauturu (Taylor *et al.* 2005). In the mid-1990s, hihi were translocated to two further islands, Mokoia and Tiritiri Matangi.

Recovery goal and targets

The overall goal of the first recovery plan for hihi (Rasch *et al.* 1996) was "to increase the number of self-sustaining populations in locations other than Hauturu", with self-sustaining meaning that no re-stocking or other management was required to sustain populations. The recovery target was "to increase the number of self-sustaining hihi populations to five". This initial target was chosen subjectively, but was based on two types of rationale. First, that it was risky to have a species confined to one, or even two, small islands. Second, that it was unrealistic to restore the species to most of its natural range, owing to the prevalence of exotic predators, and unrealistic to aim for more than a handful of island populations given the previous failures in establishing such populations. However, it was impossible to assess the feasibility of the target directly until research had been done to assess why reintroduced populations were failing to grow.

Adaptive management and modeling

The New Zealand Department of Conservation approached Massey University for research support aimed at determining conditions needed for growth of hihi populations. Castro *et al.* (1994) studied the ecology of hihi reintroduced to Kapiti, and hypothesized that hihi were limited by availability of nectar and fruit at the reintroduction sites, where the forest was at an earlier successional stage than the mature forest found on Hauturu, and also that nest cavities might be limiting. Consequently, when hihi were reintroduced to Mokoia, an adaptive management program was established to assess the effect of food supplementation on that population (Armstrong *et al.* 2007) and artificial nest boxes were provided. The program involved providing food at some times but not others, providing individual feeders to some nesting females, and providing either sugar water or a complete food supplement including protein and minerals. It also involved control of nest mites after it was discovered that nest mites (*Ornithonyssus bursa*) could kill hihi broods, and data were collected on which broods were likely to have survived or been killed without intervention. Management treatments were decided annually based on previous results and further information needs. A population model was created early in the program, and updated annually. This modeling followed the approach described above, i.e. a limited number of plausible models for survival and reproduction were compared based on AIC. The results were then combined into a population model that was used to predict λ and population size under different management options, and uncertainty associated with demographic stochasticity, model selection, and parameter estimation was incorporated into projections.

The results showed that the Mokoia population would quickly decline to extinction ($\lambda < 0.6$) without supplementary feeding, but that λ could be substantially increased through provision of sugar-water feeders and control of nest mites (Fig. 13.2) (Armstrong *et al.* 2007). Provision of a complete food supplement did not have a clear benefit in comparison to provision of sugar water, and provision of individual feeders did not have a clear benefit in comparison to a lower number of communal feeders. Although λ was estimated to be > 1 under management, there was great uncertainty about whether the population would increase under any management regime, even after eight years of research. The population was limited by a high adult mortality, and dead hihi recovered were found to have mostly died from extensive infection by the fungus *Aspergillus fumigatus* (Alley *et al.* 1999). Perrott (2001) subsequently found that soil densities of *A. fumigatus* are much higher on Mokoia than on Hauturu and Tiritiri Matangi, where hihi have had lower mortality, suggesting that hihi on Mokoia were ultimately limited by a problem that could not be corrected by management.

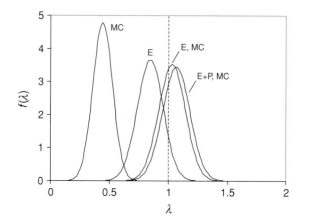

Figure 13.2. Probability density functions for the finite rate of increase (λ) of the hihi population on Mokoia Island under alternative management regimes: E+P, supplementary energy and protein; E, supplementary energy; MC, nests managed to ensure broods not killed by mites. Data were obtained during an adaptive management program conducted from 1995–2002 (from Armstrong *et al.* 2007).

Application of research results

Results from Mokoia were quickly applied to other reintroduced populations, leading to rapid growth of the Tiritiri Matangi and Kapiti populations by the late 1990s through sugar-water supplementation and nest mite control. In 2005 a further population was established at Karori, a predator-fenced mainland reserve, and this population has also grown rapidly. In 2002, the remaining hihi on Mokoia were relocated to Kapiti (Taylor *et al.* 2005).

Management action targets

The management protocol developed on Mokoia (communal sugar-water feeders and nest mite control) was incorporated into a set of standard operating procedures for hihi (Taylor and Castro 2000). The revised recovery plan for hihi (Taylor *et al.* 2005) included the implementation of this protocol for all reintroduced hihi populations. Surprisingly, however, there was no target given for the number of populations, or total number of hihi, to be maintained under this supportive management. The stated recovery goal and target remained focused on self-sustaining populations (i.e. those with no supportive management), the slightly revised target being to increase "the number of self-sustaining hihi populations to *at least* five".

RECOVERY OF WOODLAND CARIBOU IN BRITISH COLUMBIA

Background

The woodland caribou is a taxon of concern in British Columbia, particularly the threatened "mountain caribou" ecotype (COSEWIC 2002). Mountain caribou differ from other woodland caribou in that they feed almost exclusively on arboreal lichen (*Bryoria* spp. and *Alectoria sarmentosa*) in late-successional forest stands, particularly in late winter when deep snow (generally > 2 m) covers all terrestrial food (Terry *et al.* 2000). Landscapes with high proportions of old forests also provide refuge from alternative ungulate prey species and their predators (Wittmer *et al.* 2005a). However, these old forests are highly valuable to the forest industry, resulting in a conflict between forest management for fiber extraction and caribou life-history requirements.

Recovery goal and targets

A recovery plan for mountain caribou in British Columbia was completed in 2002 (Hatter *et al.* 2002). The goal of the recovery strategy was "the maintenance of caribou and their habitat in perpetuity throughout British Columbia's mountain caribou range", thus indicating political and institutional commitment to caribou conservation. At the time the recovery plan was finalized, the distribution and abundance of mountain caribou had declined from historical numbers and totaled fewer than 1,900 individuals fragmented into 18 isolated populations (Wittmer *et al.* 2005a,b). Data on historic abundances and estimates of current carrying capacity (based on availability of suitable foraging habitat) were both used to set an initial recovery target of "a metapopulation of 2500–3000 mountain caribou distributed throughout their current range" (Hatter *et al.* 2002). However, although the recovery plan recognized forestry as the greatest concern to caribou viability, neither the underlying mechanism of decline nor the type and intensity of management required to meet the recovery target had been determined.

Adaptive management and modeling

Using experimental methods to distinguish between potential causes of decline is challenging in wide-ranging species such as caribou. However, natural experiments that provide variation in external factors influencing population dynamics can also be used to differentiate between competing hypotheses (Sinclair 1991). Because of the significant conflict between

Figure 13.3. An example of changes to the composition of mountain caribou habitat (photos B. McLellan). Large-scale increases in early-seral forests result in more abundant alternative prey and their predators. Mountain caribou populations only remain viable in landscapes where early-seral forests are rare (see Fig. 13.4).

caribou habitat requirements and logging, mountain caribou population dynamics have been monitored over their entire range for over 20 years, resulting in data from more than 350 radio-collared individuals. Using these data and comparing dynamics among identified populations, Wittmer *et al.* (2005a) assessed whether population declines of mountain caribou were attributable to food limitation (i.e. reductions in availability of arboreal lichen from logging), predation-sensitive foraging, or predation. They concluded that unsustainable predation in the form of apparent competition (*sensu* Holt and Lawton 1994) was the major cause of decline. That is, increases in the abundance of other ungulates, such as moose (*Alces alces*) and deer (*Odocoileus* spp.) following conversion to early-seral forests, allowed predator numbers to increase, resulting in the decline and extirpation of caribou populations (Fig. 13.3).

A PVA using estimates of survival and recruitment was conducted (Wittmer 2004). Results suggested that mountain caribou were at an imminent risk of extinction over large parts of their distribution, and that mountain caribou only persisted in those parts of their historic range with the highest proportions of old-growth forest (Apps and McLellan 2006). Developing suitable management targets therefore required quantifying the relationship between forest composition and adult female survival, the vital rate that most strongly influenced population declines (Wittmer *et al.* 2005b). The relationship between forest composition and survival was analysed from a set of capture–recapture models. Survival probability was negatively correlated with the proportion of young (<40 years) forest, and also positively correlated with population density (Wittmer *et al.* 2007). In the best model, survival of adult females is predicted to start declining when the proportion of young forest within a population's range exceeds 0.09 (Fig. 13.4).

Application of research results

The designation of mountain caribou as threatened in Canada requires British Columbia to protect their habitats (under the *Accord for the Protection of Species at Risk* and the federal *Species at Risk Act*) (FPB 2004). Current forest management practices, however, were developed in the 1980s and 1990s, when researchers thought that the decline of mountain caribou was primarily a consequence of reductions in the availability of arboreal lichen (Stevenson *et al.* 2001). These management practices are insufficient to reverse the observed population declines, as highlighted by the extirpation of two of the remaining 18 populations since 2004. This failure has been recognized and site-specific management recommendations that

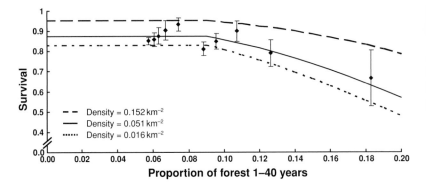

Figure 13.4. Correlation between proportion of young (<40 years) forest and survival rates of adult female mountain caribou in British Columbia, Canada. The lines show trends predicted by the most parsimonious model, where survival was reduced as a function of forest age only in populations where the proportion of young forest exceeds 0.09. Survival was also positively correlated with population density, and the three relationships are for the minimum, mean, and maximum densities that have been observed. Data points show population-specific survival estimates (±SE) (from Wittmer *et al.* 2007).

outline limited and no timber harvest zones at a larger scale have since been developed. However, these management recommendations are not binding under current legislation, and thus their implementation depends on the commitment of policy-makers (FPB 2004).

Management action targets

The modeled relationship between landscape composition and vital rates now allows implementation and assessment of management action targets that may result in population recovery, although uncertainty in λ remains to be quantified. It is unlikely that the alteration of the predator–prey system following changes to the forest-age structure can be rectified in time to maintain mountain caribou. Thus, the required management includes a temporary reduction of predators combined with continuous reduction in their primary prey until young forest cover decreases and, thus, the landscape becomes less favorable to the primary prey. Predator control may initially be achieved by simply increasing the number of hunting permits. The optimal intensity of predator–prey management required, however, cannot be easily quantified in complex multiprey, multipredator systems. Thus, an adaptive management approach is urgently required. Under such an adaptive management approach, the intensity of both predator and alternate prey management need to be varied significantly to determine management targets. In the case of mountain caribou, this variation is best achieved by varying treatments across the spatial distribution of caribou in British Columbia.

CONCLUDING REMARKS

In this chapter, we have argued that setting quantitative targets should be seen as an ongoing process whereby initial targets are continuously revised. We used two case studies to outline the central role of hypothesis testing and quantitative modeling in meeting and updating targets. This is especially true in the context of species recovery, where initial targets must often be adopted in the absence of some important pieces of information. The hihi and mountain caribou had both substantially declined from their original ranges through a combination of predation and forest modification, so the broad recovery goal of each program involved an increase in numbers. Initial recovery targets were nominated for number of populations (hihi) or total population (caribou) to be maintained. However, at the time the targets were nominated, there was little understanding of management needed to reverse the declines, hence no information that could be used either to set the targets or to quantitatively assess their feasibility. Subsequent research has provided information on management needs, and in doing so has provided insights into ecosystem-level processes associated with forest modification. The hihi research not only supported the hypothesis that secondary forest had insufficient fruit and nectar production to support hihi, but also led to novel research on changes to soil fungi in modified forests. The caribou research did not support the original hypothesis that caribou were limited by lack of arboreal lichen in secondary forest, but instead suggested complex predator–prey dynamics involving multiple species. These results illustrate not only that the fates of species may be determined by complex ecosystem dynamics, as noted by Sinclair and Byrom (2006), but that single-species recovery programs can provide an impetus for uncovering those processes.

With hihi, the small scale of the islands and ease of manipulation meant that adaptive management was possible. It has been demonstrated that population growth could be substantially increased with food supplementation and mite control, and that rapid growth could be achieved in some reintroduced populations under these protocols. The costs of these protocols are known; hence it is now possible to weigh these costs against the perceived benefits of maintaining populations, and to derive an informed target for the number of populations to be maintained through supportive management. There is scope for further adaptive management whereby intensity of management is varied (e.g. number of feeders available and proportion of time available) to model the relationship between management cost and projected population size, and also to model the effect of population size on loss of genetic variation, potentially leading to further refinement of the recovery target. However, because the existing protocol has been shown to be effective and has been written into standard operating procedures (Taylor and Castro 2000), the recovery group is currently reluctant to try any relaxation of the protocol.

With mountain caribou, the program is at an earlier stage in that there is no clear evidence that population decline can be reversed under any particular management regime. While >60% of caribou habitat is already being managed under guidelines that aim to increase the availability of arboreal lichen, modeling results suggest that these policies will be insufficient to reverse the observed population declines. It is likely that management recommendations based on supplying sufficient amounts of arboreal lichen are substantially different from thresholds of old forests required to prevent changes in the predator–prey system (i.e. increases in alternate ungulate populations to the point where they support predator numbers that are too high for caribou). To address these uncertainties, it is therefore required to assess levels of alternate prey and predators that will allow caribou to persist. This requires a carefully designed adaptive management approach where levels of predators and prey are varied to determine requirements for caribou persistence. Finally, given the high social and economic costs associated with implementing these recommendations over an even larger scale, there will be ongoing political pressure to revise management action targets for the proportion of young forests, especially if positive growth cannot be demonstrated in caribou populations.

Initial recovery targets of endangered species are necessarily based on incomplete information. However, the ultimate success of every recovery strategy depends on an understanding of both the causes of decline and the relationship between management actions and population recovery. Our proposed framework outlines a rigorous scientific approach embedded within the adaptive management paradigm that allows resource managers to move from initial recovery targets based on insufficient data to research-based quantitative targets. However, achieving such understanding is likely to be a long and challenging process, especially with endangered species.

References

Alley, M. R., I. Castro and J. E. B. Hunter. 1999. Aspergillosis in hihi (*Notiomystis cincta*) on Mokoia Island. *New Zealand Veterinary Journal* 47:88–91.

Apps, C. D. and B. N. McLellan. 2006. Factors influencing the dispersion and fragmentation of endangered mountain caribou populations. *Biological Conservation* 130:84–97.

Armstrong, D. P., T. Soderquist and R. Southgate. 1994. Designing experimental reintroductions as experiments. Pp. 27–9 in M. Serena (ed.) *Reintroduction Biology of Australian and New Zealand Fauna*. Chipping Norton, Australia: Surrey Beatty & Sons.

Armstrong, D. P., E. H. Raeburn, R. M. Lewis and D. Ravine. 2006. Estimating the viability of a reintroduced New Zealand robin population as a function of predator control. *Journal of Wildlife Management* 70:1020–7.

Armstrong, D. P., I. Castro and R. G. Griffiths. 2007. Using adaptive management to determine requirements of reintroduced populations: the case of the New Zealand hihi. *Journal of Applied Ecology* 44:953–62.

Beissinger, S. R. and M. I. Westphal. 1998. On the use of demographic models of population viability in endangered species management. *Journal of Wildlife Management* 62:821–41.

Beissinger, S. R. and D. R. McCullough. 2002. *Population Viability Analysis*. Chicago, IL: University of Chicago Press.

Burnham, K. P. and D. R. Anderson. 2002. *Model Selection and Multimodal Inference: A Practical Information-Theoretic Approach* (2nd edn). New York, NY: Springer-Verlag.

Castro, I., E. O. Minot and J. C. Alley. 1994. Feeding and breeding behaviour of hihi or stitchbirds (*Notiomystis cincta*) recently transferred to Kapiti Island, New Zealand, and possible management alternatives. Pp. 121–8 in M. Serena (ed.) *Reintroduction Biology of Australian and New Zealand Fauna*. Chipping Norton, Australia: Surrey Beatty & Sons.

Caughley, G. and A. Gunn. 1996. *Conservation Biology in Theory and Practice*. Melbourne, Australia: Blackwell Science.

COSEWIC. 2002. *COSEWIC Assessment and Update Status Report on the Woodland Caribou Rangifer tarandus caribou in Canada*. Ottawa, ON, Canada: Committee on the Status of Endangered Wildlife in Canada.

Ellner, S. P., J. Fieberg, D. Ludwig and C. Wilcox, C. 2002. Precision of population viability analysis. *Conservation Biology* 16:258–61.

Ewen, J. G., I. Flux and P. G. P. Ericson. 2006. Systematic affinities of two enigmatic New Zealand passerines of high conservation priority, the hihi or stitchbird *Notiomystis cincta* and the kokako *Callaeas cinerea*. *Molecular Phylogenetics and Evolution* 40:281–4.

Fazey, I., J. Fazey, J. G. Salisbury, D. B. Lindenmayer and S. Dovers. 2006. The nature and role of experiental knowledge for environmental conservation. *Environmental Conservation* 33:1–10.

Fieberg, J. and S. P. Ellner. 2000. When is it meaningful to estimate an extinction probability? *Ecology* 81:2040–7.

FPB. 2004. *BC's Mountain Caribou: Last Chance for Conservation*. Special report. Vancouver, British Columbia, Canada: Forest Practices Board.

Franklin, I. R. 1980. Evolutionary change in small populations. Pp. 135–49 in M. E. Soulé and B. A. Wilcox (eds.) *Conservation Biology: An Evolutionary-Ecological Perspective*. Sunderland, MA: Sinauer Associates.

Goldstein, P. A. 1999. Functional ecosystems and biodiversity buzzwords. *Conservation Biology* **13**:247–55.

Grumbine, R. E. 1994. What is ecosystem management? *Conservation Biology* **8**:27–38.

Hatter, I., D. Butler, A. Fontana *et al.* 2002. *A Strategy for the Recovery of Mountain Caribou in British Columbia*. Victoria, British Columbia, Canada: Ministry of Water, Land and Air Protection.

Holling, C. S. 1978. *Adaptive Environmental Assessment and Management*. Chichester, UK: John Wiley & Sons.

Holt, R. D. and J. H. Lawton. 1994. The ecological consequences of shared natural enemies. *Annual Reviews in Ecology and Systematics* **25**:495–520.

Holt, S. J. and L. M. Talbot. 1978. New principles for the conservation of natural living resources. *Wildlife Monographs* **59**:1–33.

IUCN. 1993. *Parks for Life: Report of the IVth World Congress on National Parks and Protected Areas*. Gland, Switzerland: IUCN.

Lacy, R. C. 2000. Structure of the VORTEX simulation model for population viability analysis. *Ecological Bulletins* **48**:191–293.

Lessard, R. B., S. J. D. Martell, C. J. Walters, T. E. Essingtons and J. F. Kitchell. 2005. Should ecosystem management involve active control of species abundances? *Ecology and Society* **10**:1–21.

Margules, C. R. and R. L. Pressey. 2000. Systematic conservation planning. *Nature* **405**:243–53.

Marsh, H., G. De'Ath, N. Gribble and B. Lane. 2005. Historical marine population estimates: triggers or targets for conservation? The dugong case study. *Ecological Applications* **15**:481–92.

Mills, L. S. and F. W. Allendorf. 1996. The one-migrant-per-generation rule in conservation and management. *Conservation Biology* **10**:1509–18.

Nunney, L. and K. A. Campbell. 1993. Assessing minimum viable population size: demography meets population genetics. *Trends in Ecology and Evolution* **8**:234–9.

Perrott, J. K. 2001. The ecology of *Aspergillus fumigatus*, and implications for wildlife conservation in modified environments. Ph.D. thesis, Massey University, New Zealand.

Possingham, H. P., D. B. Lindenmayer and T. W. Norton. 1993. A framework for the improved management of threatened species based on Population Viability Analysis (PVA). *Pacific Conservation Biology* **1**:39–45.

Rasch, G., S. Boyd and S. Clegg. 1996. Stitchbird (hihi), *Notiomystis cincta* recovery plan. Wellington, New Zealand: Department of Conservation.

Shaffer, M. L. 1981. Minimum population sizes for species conservation. *BioScience* **31**:131–4.

Shaffer, M. L. and B. A. Stein. 2000. Safeguarding our precious heritage. Pp. 301–21 in B. A. Stein, L. S. Kutner and J. S. Adams (eds.) *Precious Heritage: The Status of Biodiversity in the United States*. New York, NY: Oxford University Press.

Simberloff, D. 1998. Flagships, umbrellas and keystones: is single-species management passé in the landscape era? *Biological Conservation* **83**: 247–57.

Sinclair, A. R. E. 1991. Science and the practice of wildlife management. *Journal of Wildlife Management* **55**:767–73.

Sinclair, A. R. E. and A. E. Byrom. 2006. Understanding ecosystem dynamics for conservation of biota. *Journal of Animal Ecology* **75**:64–79.

Stevenson, S. K., H. M. Armleder, M. J. Jull *et al.* 2001. *Mountain Caribou in Managed Forests: Recommendations for Managers*. Wildlife report No. R-26. Victoria, British Columbia, Canada: Ministry of Environment, Lands and Parks.

Svancara, L. K., R. Brannon, J. M. Scott *et al.* 2005. Policy-driven versus evidence-based conservation: a review of political targets and biological needs. *BioScience* **55**:989–95.

Taylor, B. L., P. R. Wade, U. Ramakrishnan, M. Gilpin and H. R. Akcakaya. 2002. Incorporating uncertainty in population viability analyses for the purpose of classifying species at risk. Pp. 239–83 in S. R. Beissinger and G. M. McCullough (eds). *Population Viability Analysis*. Chicago, IL: University of Chicago Press.

Taylor, S. and I. Castro 2000. *Hihi Standard Operating Procedures*. Auckland, New Zealand: Department of Conservation.

Taylor, S., I. Castro and R. Griffiths. 2005. *Hihi/stitchbird* (Notiomystis cincta) *Recovery Plan 2004–09*. Wellington, New Zealand: Department of Conservation.

Tear, T. H., P. Kareiva, P. L. Angermeier *et al.* 2005. How much is enough? The recurrent problem of setting measurable objectives in conservation. *BioScience* **55**:835–49.

Terry, E. L., B. N. McLellan and G. S. Watts. 2000. Winter habitat ecology of mountain caribou in relation to forest management. *Journal of Applied Ecology* **37**:589–602.

Wade, P. R. 2002. Bayesian population viability analysis. Pp. 213–38 in S. R. Beissinger and D. R. McCullough (eds). *Population Viability Analysis*. Chicago, IL: University of Chicago Press.

Walker, B. 1989. Diversity and stability in ecosystem conservation. Pp. 121–30 in D. Western and M. C. Pearl (eds). *Conservation for the Twenty-First Century*. Oxford, UK: Oxford University Press.

Walters, C. J. 1986. *Adaptive Management of Renewable Resources*. New York, NY: Macmillan.

White, G. C. 2000. Population viability analysis: data requirements and essential analyses. Pp. 287–331 in L. Boitani and T. K. Fuller (eds.) *Research Techniques in Animal Ecology: Controversies and Consequences*. New York, NY: Columbia University Press.

Wittmer, H. U. 2004. Mechanisms underlying the decline of mountain caribou (*Rangifer tarandus caribou*) in British Columbia. Ph.D. thesis, University of British Columbia, Canada.

Wittmer, H. U., A. R. E. Sinclair and B. N. McLellan. 2005a. The role of predation in the decline and extirpation of woodland caribou. *Oecologia* **144**:257–67.

Wittmer, H. U., B. N. McLellan, D. R. Seip *et al.* 2005b. Population dynamics of the endangered mountain ecotype of woodland caribou (*Rangifer tarandus caribou*) in British Columbia, Canada. *Canadian Journal of Zoology* **83**:407–18.

Wittmer, H. U., B. N. McLellan, R. Serrouya and C. D. Apps. 2007. Changes in landscape composition influence the decline of a threatened woodland caribou population. *Journal of Animal Ecology* **76**:568–79.

(14)

Allocation of conservation efforts over the landscape: the TRIAD approach

DAVID A. MACLEAN, ROBERT S. SEYMOUR,
MICHAEL K. MONTIGNY, AND CHRISTIAN MESSIER

INTRODUCTION

The TRIAD forest management concept involves designating forest reserves and intensively managed areas within a landscape matrix managed by silvicultural systems derived from principles of ecological forestry (Seymour and Hunter 1999). By increasing timber yields per hectare in a strategically chosen zone, many fewer hectares are needed to produce the same forest-wide harvest, thus enhancing managers' ability to address other values such as biodiversity on the remaining areas (Sedjo and Botkin 1997). Introduced by Seymour and Hunter (1992), the concept can be traced to earlier work of Clawson (1974, 1977), Seymour and McCormack (1989), and Gladstone and Ledig (1990). Contemporary examples include grassland and aquatic ecosystems (Hunter and Calhoun 1996), an organizing framework for silvicultural research and management in the Great Lakes region (Palik et al. 2004), an illustration of "biodiversity exchanges" (Brown et al. 2006), and an analysis of public forest land in west Australia (Stoneman 2007). Indeed, many authors (e.g. Binkley 1997; Sahajananthan et al. 1998; Messier and Kneeshaw 1999; Taylor 1999) have explored the single-use zoning concept under various naming conventions.

The early 1990s was a tumultuous time in North American forestry, as influential ecologists began to question publicly the agricultural and "manage-everywhere" paradigms of traditional sustained yield forestry and outlined an alternative "New Forestry" (Franklin 1989; Gillis 1990), a

Setting Conservation Targets for Managed Forest Landscapes, ed. M.-A. Villard and
B. G. Jonsson. Published by Cambridge University Press.
© Cambridge University Press 2009.

concept that quickly morphed into ecosystem management as it was embraced by the USDA Forest Service (Salwasser 1994). Unlike Canada, where forests are largely owned by the provincial governments and managed by licensees under long-term agreements, during this era Maine was dominated by large contiguous industrial ownerships affiliated with large paper and sawmills facing wood shortages (Seymour and Lemin 1989). This was the context when Seymour and Hunter (1992) proposed the TRIAD to resolve a seemingly irreconcilable conflict in Maine between industrial interests concerned over predicted timber shortages (Seymour 1985) and conservation biologists who advocated creating a substantial network of unmanaged ecological reserves (McMahon 1993). In essence, the TRIAD envisions a landscape or regional *quid pro quo* – foresters historically accustomed to managing everywhere would accept some "set-asides", and ecologists would accept agronomic high-yield silvicultural practices if limited in area. In forest management jargon, the allowable cut effect[1] resulting from expanded production forestry is taken in the form of unmanaged ecological reserves and lower harvests in the matrix, not increased timber harvest levels. In many jurisdictions in Canada and elsewhere, "annual allowable cut" (AAC), also termed long-term sustainable harvest level, is determined by a long-term sustainability calculation that has ample constraints for biodiversity, for example "no type conversion of northern hardwoods" or "maintain a specified area of old-growth forest". Rather than attempting to manage every hectare for multiple values, which economic theory suggests is inefficient (Sahajananthan *et al.* 1998), TRIAD zoning demands management specialization. A specific, unique set of values is managed for in each zone, with the purpose of providing a forest-level full set of values through the collective outcomes across all zones. The concept thus acknowledges that no single type of forestry will meet all objectives well, and that competing interests of various stakeholders must, in practice, be addressed by a "balanced forestry" (Seymour and Hunter 1999, after Kimmins 1992) on any given forest landscape.

In early public discussions of the TRIAD, it quickly became apparent that nearly everyone embraced two-thirds of the TRIAD – just not the *same* two-thirds. Environmentalists fully supported reserves and a more ecologically

---

[1] *Allowable cut effect* is the immediate increase in annual harvest level resulting from expanded planting, thinning, or other yield-enhancing investments, even though the areas treated will not yield merchantable timber for perhaps decades. This works because the older, currently merchantable forest does not need to "last" as long in order to sustain a particular harvest level owing to the accelerated yields of the young stands.

based approach to forest management, but questioned the need for any high-yield silviculture. Meanwhile, large private landowners appreciated the logic that lands be managed under various levels of intensity (e.g. giving ecological values priority over commodity extraction in riparian zones), but were quite sceptical of "taking lands out of production."

Forest management planning is all about determining what allocation of treatments in time and space will result in forest conditions best able to provide the values sought for the forest in question. Forests provide a wide variety of timber and non-timber values, and selecting the appropriate mix of zones and area allocation is a function of desired values (Erdle 1999). This becomes more challenging when one value occurs at the expense of others, as occurred when comparing scenarios with increased intensively managed and reserve areas (Montigny and MacLean 2006). Forest management planning thus requires measuring management strategy outcomes in terms that reflect the breadth of economic, environmental, and social dimensions that characterize contemporary values sets. To this, the TRIAD concept introduces two additional questions: (1) how much area should be allocated to each of the three types of zones, and (2) how should the different types of zoning be intermixed to produce the best overall provision of values from the forest as a whole. In this context, "best" is clearly dependent upon the values desired by the landowner, or society in the case of publicly owned lands or the perceptions of the public. In some cases, it might not be socially, environmentally, or economically desirable to have the intensive zone divided into large blocks of thousands of hectares. Instead, it might be better to have it divided into small 1–10 ha blocks intermixed within the extensive zone.

Each TRIAD zone has specific objectives and a defined set of management treatments that can be implemented to meet those objectives. Intensive management zones are managed primarily for the production of timber products, and although other values may be obtained, they are secondary (Seymour and Hunter 1992). Careful stocking and density control, genetically improved stock, and short rotations or frequent harvest entries may all be employed to produce high yields. Extensive management zones are managed less intensively for timber production and in some cases with priority also given to non-timber values such as habitat or water quality. Natural disturbance-based silviculture may be implemented to protect these other values (Bergeron et al. 1999; Seymour and Hunter 1999), frequently involving longer harvest rotations or cutting cycles, and stand structure retention consistent with the natural disturbance dynamics of the stand types in question. Such practices result in lower timber production than that resulting from intensive management. Reserves are managed to provide ecological benchmarks and to represent forest conditions unaffected by timber management practices. As such, no timber is extracted from reserves and, ideally, natural ecological processes are allowed to occur (although major natural disturbances may be controlled depending upon the specific forest management plan).

In this chapter, we present three specific case studies of approaches to TRIAD zoning, in Maine, New Brunswick, and Québec, and then draw some general conclusions regarding the future of the approach.

CASE STUDY 1: THE TRIAD IN MAINE

Early reactions and acceptance

In an attempt to allay philosophical concerns among private landowners over expanding ecological reserves, Seymour and Hunter, the original proponents of the TRIAD, were careful to distinguish between the need for a scientifically designed, representative system of unmanaged ecological communities (as embodied in the TRIAD) versus the largely political agendas of those advocating large-scale wilderness areas strictly for spiritual and cultural reasons. They further argued that many foresters' assertion about managing successfully for biodiversity on every hectare is largely unsupported and can only be tested by benchmarking enlightened management against naturally functioning, unmanaged ecosystems. Although the concept remained controversial, Champion International Corporation, a large multinational industrial landowner that owned over 400,000 ha in northern New England, began to promote and apply the TRIAD concept after an extensive public involvement initiative in 1994. Champion's approach included high-yield and reserve areas, neither of which were extensive, and subdivided the matrix into "general management" and "special value" zones (Redelsheimer 1996).

An important development was the formation in 1994 of the Maine Forest Biodiversity Project, a group of large landowners, environmentalists, foresters, and scientists. After meeting for several years to discuss how biodiversity could be better incorporated into forest management, this group produced a feasibility study (McMahon 1998) of establishing an ecological reserve system in Maine's public forests managed by the Bureau of Parks and Lands (BPL), most of which has been under conservative multiple-use management since the early 1970s. In 1999 the Maine Legislature passed Public Law 1997 establishing an ecological reserve system on its public lands. The law stipulates that the total area of reserves cannot exceed

15% of total land under BPL jurisdiction, 6% of operable timberland, or 40,000 ha, whichever is least (Maine Statutes 2006). One can see a clear example of TRIAD logic embodied in the statute's final provision: "The designation of land as an ecological reserve may not result in a decline in the volume of timber harvested on land under the jurisdiction of the bureau." Capping the area in reserves and mandating no reduction in harvests gained the crucial support of the Maine Forest Products Council, the State's leading advocacy group for commercial forestry interests. By 2001, the BPL reserve system, encompassing about 30,000 ha was in place, incorporating most of the recommendations in McMahon's (1998) report.

Reflections

It is perhaps ironic that the most divisive feature of the TRIAD in 1992 – designating large ecological reserves on which all commodity extraction is prohibited – only seven years later became the first demonstrable contribution of the TRIAD in Maine. Indeed, after some small gains in the mid-1990s, the high-yield-forestry leg of the TRIAD has actually declined significantly since the late 1990s, as all but one large industrial ownership have been dissociated from manufacturing plants and converted to instruments of short-term investment (typically ten years). Most large private ownerships in Maine are now managed by timber investment and management companies (TIMOs) and real estate investment trusts (REITs) who have largely halted planting and precommercial thinning programs, or are held in large family estates. The progressive initiatives of Champion International in the mid-1990s are now a distant memory; the corporation was acquired by International Paper in 2000, which has since sold all their lands to a TIMO and halted all investments in silviculture. The notable exception to this pattern is J. D. Irving, Ltd., a large Canadian enterprise that is both a privately held company and a large manufacturer of softwood lumber, and also the subject of a prominent TRIAD test case in New Brunswick, discussed below.

Maine's forest is certainly very different from 1992 when the TRIAD was introduced, mainly owing to the wholesale change in land ownership. Environmental NGOs such as The Nature Conservancy, Appalachian Mountain Club, the Forest Society of Maine, and several other land trusts have recently acquired substantial ownerships of high conservation value from which they expect to derive important income from forest management. Management plans for these properties emphasize ecological forestry in the matrix and typically reserve 20%–40% of the productive area from harvesting. Although the NGOs' actions augment the very modest reserve system on the public forest lands, the total area in reserves is much less than 3% of all forest land in the State and thus quite inadequate in the view of conservation biologists. Demonstrated commitments to ecological forestry can be found on a few large public and family ownerships certified by the Forest Stewardship Council (FSC), collectively amounting to perhaps 10% of Maine's forest, but not elsewhere. Another 5% at most has been treated by intensive silviculture, largely a legacy of previous industrial owners that is not being sustained. So, although one can readily find examples of all the TRIAD's parts in Maine, it is difficult to argue, given recent trends, that the modest expansions for biodiversity (ecological matrix and reserves) have been "paid for" by expanded long-term investments in high-yield silviculture.

CASE STUDY 2: TRIAD ZONING SCENARIO ANALYSIS IN NEW BRUNSWICK

Some elements of a TRIAD zoning approach developed in New Brunswick before there was any consideration of the name. J. D. Irving, Ltd. actively pursued an intensive approach to forest management, especially on their privately owned land, beginning in the late 1950s. By the end of the twenti-eth century, the Irving Black Brook District in northern New Brunswick encompassed more than 60,000 ha of spruce plantations. Also, set-aside/protected areas received increased interest, culminating in the estab-lishment of a network of ten large protected areas on Crown land in New Brunswick in the 1990s. Over this period, J. D. Irving, Ltd. also set aside some benchmark scientific reserves on their privately owned land, so to an extent, elements of a TRIAD approach were in place. Impetus for fur-ther study of the possibilities of such an approach came with the develop-ment within the Canada Sustainable Forest Management Network Center of Excellence (SFMN) of an "innovative zoning" research program. The J. D. Irving, Ltd. Forest Research Advisory Committee, a group of company staff and researchers from academia and government, jointly decided that a scenario planning approach to exploring TRIAD zoning would be of interest to the company, and this resulted in the following specific case study.

Montigny and MacLean (2006) conducted a study of TRIAD forest man-agement scenarios on the 190,000 ha Black Brook District, owned by J. D. Irving, Ltd., in north-western New Brunswick, Canada (Fig. 14.1B). This landbase is characterized as one of the most intensively managed forests in Canada, with over 60,000 ha of primarily spruce (*Picea* sp.) plantations in the 5–40 year old age classes as a result of reforestation programs initiated

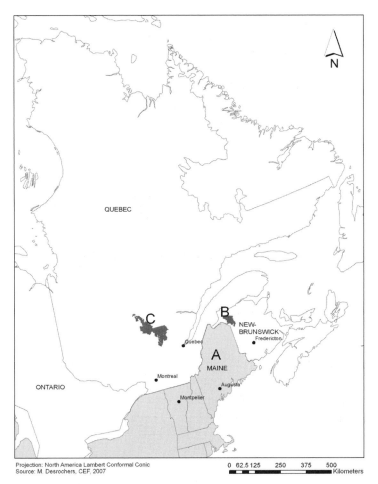

Figure 14.1. Locations of three TRIAD zoning case study areas: (A) State of Maine, (B) the 190,000 ha Black Brook District in northern New Brunswick, and (C) the 1 million ha management unit about 300 km north-east of Montréal, Quebec.

in the mid-1950s. Currently, the landowner has allocated over 7,000 ha of benchmark scientific reserves (Fig. 14.2a), which were selected with input from the World Wildlife Fund, with emphasis on large, unharvested, and unroaded areas on the landbase. These reserves include 2,600 ha designated as adaptive management areas, which are being used to develop and test natural disturbance (primarily spruce budworm, *Choristoneura fumiferana*, outbreak)-based silviculture, and to act as a control, 4,750 ha of core reserve areas (Fig. 14.2a). Currently, the allocation of TRIAD zones consists

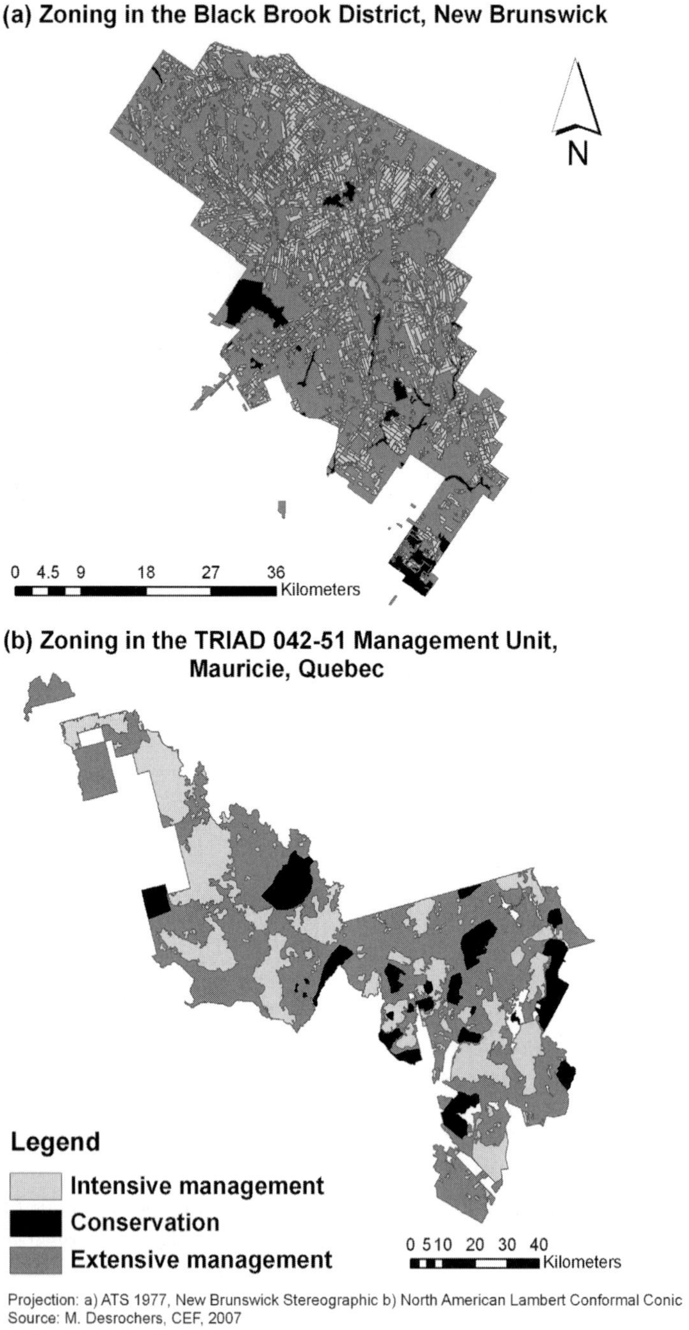

(a) Zoning in the Black Brook District, New Brunswick

0 4.5 9   18   27   36
                                Kilometers

(b) Zoning in the TRIAD 042-51 Management Unit, Mauricie, Quebec

Legend

Intensive management

Conservation

Extensive management

0 5 10 20 30 40
                    Kilometers

Projection: a) ATS 1977, New Brunswick Stereographic b) North American Lambert Conformal Conic
Source: M. Desrochers, CEF, 2007

Figure 14.2. Zonings for the management units, in terms of intensively managed, extensively managed, and conservation (protected areas): (a) Black Brook District, New Brunswick case study in 2002; and (b) the Quebec TRIAD case study area near Mauricie, Québec (the intensive management zone is further divided into three sub zones).

of 5% reserves, 39% intensively managed, and 56% extensively managed areas.

Scenario planning (Schoemaker 1995) was used to simulate effects of 64 allocation scenarios (0%–15% reserve area, 39%–64% intensively managed softwood, and 21%–61% extensively managed) on tree species composition, age class distribution, timber growing stock, harvest levels, and old forest habitat of the entire forest landbase over an 80-year planning horizon. Candidate reserve areas were identified with a selection algorithm (Montigny and MacLean 2005) prior to scenario analysis. Areas were sequentially added to the reserve network, as required, to fulfill the 0%–15% percent area target defined in each scenario and a no-harvest constraint was applied to each reserve. A method was needed to control either the amount of intensively or extensively managed areas (the other would be controlled by default as the remaining area). In the Montigny and MacLean (2006) analysis, intensively managed areas were not assigned within a spatially delineated zone, but rather areas for specific intensive management treatments were selected by using linear optimization in the wood supply model. Choices were constrained by treatment types, stand eligibility for treatment, and timing of treatments. In this sense, the TRIAD intensively managed zone is assigned to a target proportion of the area, which can be optimally spatially distributed, rather than predefining zoned locations for intensive management.

After 35 years of simulated management, the area of intensive management directly determined the softwood annual allowable cut level, which ranged from 3.8 million to 4.2 million m³ per 5-year period (Montigny and MacLean 2006). Projected hardwood harvest levels were insensitive to increased intensively managed area but an increased area of reserves reduced hardwood harvest (e.g., 0.7 million m³ per 5-year period with 15% reserves versus 0.9 million m³ per 5-year period with no reserves).

Results from the Montigny and MacLean (2006) TRIAD zoning analysis highlighted three key messages. First, increasing the area zoned for intensive softwood management from 39% to 64% increased softwood harvest by 1.4 million m³ per period after period 5. This is not a surprise, but the study provides a useful quantitative example. Second, softwood harvest level was relatively insensitive to the area of reserves, and increases from the current 5% reserves to 10% and 15% significantly increased old softwood and mixedwood habitat and the proportion of older stands. Third, intensive softwood and high-quality hardwood management resulted in increases in both annual allowable cut and the proportion of high-value products: the proportion of hardwood sawlogs doubled, while softwood studwood and logs increased by 88% and 57%, respectively, over the 80-year forecast period.

There is no single, or simple, answer to the question of how much area to zone to intensively managed, extensively managed, or reserve area on a landbase. Each zone provided benefits to the land manager; the amount of area dedicated to each zone will depend on the overall goals of management. There are advantages and disadvantages, depending on the value of interest, associated with increased reserves and intensively managed areas. However, management of the J. D. Irving, Ltd. test landbase is focused on timber production, and intensive management clearly provided major increases in timber yield. It also could permit setting aside additional reserve area; old mixedwood habitat in particular was in short supply (Montigny and MacLean 2006). Although the range of desired values may differ on other landbases, scenario analyses of alternative zoning are an effective means to select a management strategy.

The Montigny and MacLean (2006) TRIAD analysis used a spatial optimization function to assign stands to intensive or extensive management treatments, and thereby, to TRIAD zones. Another approach to area control could involve spatially identifying areas for intensive management in a similar way to that in which reserve areas are assigned. By spatially identifying areas, a land manager would be certain that sites most suited for intensive management (e.g. high site productivity, proximity to processing facility) would be selected. Norfolk and Erdle (2005) provided such a framework to select potential intensive management zone areas. By providing operationally feasible options prior to forest management planning, a land manager can make better use of the results from scenario analysis.

CASE STUDY 3: FUNCTIONAL TRIAD ZONING IN QUÉBEC

The idea of managing Québec's public forest following some kind of functional zoning concept has been discussed for many years, but recently a group of forest companies led by Abitibi-Consolidated, municipalities, various recreational organizations, the provincial government, and many researchers have agreed to work together to implement the concept on a 1 million ha unit in central Québec (Figure 14.1B). This management unit covers mainly two large ecological units: the boreal mixedwood forest, composed mainly of *Abies balsamea, Pinus banksiana, Betula papyrifera, Betula alleghaniensis, Populus tremuloides, Picea glauca,* and *Pinus strobus*; and the northern temperate deciduous forest, composed mainly of *Acer saccharum,*

Betula alleghaniensis, Betula papyrifera, Acer rubrum, Picea rubens, and *Pinus strobus.*

Reasons for the various stakeholders to be interested in this new concept varied, but the main reason was a general fear of declining amounts of harvesting due to the strong public pressure for increasing the proportion of protected areas and implementing new ecosystem-based management practices. As little as 4% of the public forest is fully protected from any kind of industrial forestry in Québec, and the short-term aim is to reach 8%. However, many environmentalists and ecologists are requesting this proportion to be much higher. At the same time, a report published by the Coulombe Commission in 2003 (Commission d'étude sur la gestion de la forêt publique Québécoise 2004) indicated that the public forest of Québec has been overcut in the past, and suggested decreasing the allowable cut for the coniferous portion of the public forest by as much as 20%. It also suggested that the government implement the principle of ecosystem-based management for a large portion of the forest, in order to maintain ecological integrity. Thus three factors combined – (1) the need to increase protected areas, (2) the need to implement some form of ecosystem management of the forest, and (3) the declining yield of the public forest – brought the idea of the TRIAD to the forefront in Québec. Messier *et al.* (2003) suggested dividing the public forest of Québec into four zones (QUAD) instead of the traditional three, recognizing that traditional intensive plantation using native species, vegetation management, thinning, fertilization, and genetic improvement was totally different from short-rotation management using hybrid larch and poplar and agriculture-like approaches to stand tending.

Adopting a modified version of the TRIAD with five zones

As part of a large-scale Québec TRIAD project, five different functional zones are being used in preliminary analyses: (1) a totally protected area, (2) an area where only ecosystem-based management is implemented, (3) an area where a mixture of ecosystem-based and traditional forestry is implemented, (4) an area where only traditional intensive forestry is implemented (Figure 14.3B), and (5) an area where short-rotation plantations are prioritized (Figure 14.3C). From the beginning, it became clear that first the zoning for the protected and short-rotation plantation areas needed to be determined. For both zones, some simple and easy-to-implement indicators were used to locate the best sites. For the protected area, since old-growth and large tracts of intact forests without roads are rare in the region, these two indicators were initially used to identify some potential protected areas.

After that, further areas were selected according to criteria of minimum size and ensuring that all ecologically recognizable units in the landscape, especially rare units, were represented in protected areas. Following these criteria, it was relatively easy to come out with around 10% protected areas for the management unit. Because younger succession stages after natural disturbance are relatively abundant, protected areas focus on the rarer old-growth and unroaded areas. Second, since short-rotation plantations require relatively rich soils and flat terrain, these two indicators were used to determine potential sites for implementing high-yielding plantations. Once these protected and intensive, short-rotation plantation zones were selected, it was relatively easy to determine where the traditional intensive and ecosystem-based management zone would be situated. The traditional intensive zone is situated as close as possible to the mills and permanent roads on gentle terrain, to facilitate its management. The fourth zone, the so-called status-quo zone where the current management will be implemented, was situated in areas where there are presently very few activities other than forestry. This is a low-intensity zone where mainly natural regeneration is used and traditional forestry is implemented. Finally, all other areas were put *de facto* into the ecosystem-based management zone. Figure 14.2b illustrates the final result of the first zoning assessment done for the area.

Out of the five zones, the status quo and traditional intensive management are probably the easiest zoning to implement, since most foresters feel comfortable with this traditional way of doing forestry that has been taught in forestry schools until very recently. Furthermore, current legislation does not need to be changed since it was often developed with this type of practice in mind. However, because monospecific plantations are often not socially and/or ecologically acceptable, we are investigating the use of mixtures of two to five species (e.g. Fig. 14.3A) instead of the traditional monoculture. There are many ecological and social advantages to doing this. First, socially, mixed plantations are perceived by the public as more "natural". Second, ecologically, it is well known that mixtures are less sensitive to insect outbreaks and diseases than monocultures. Third, by using the right combination of species we could, theoretically at least, increase the overall yield of mixed stands. In particular, there is interest in mixtures of shade-tolerant species such as red spruce, white spruce, and Norway spruce with more shade-intolerant species such as white pine, yellow birch, white birch, hybrid poplar, and hybrid larch.

The main principle for the ecosystem-based management zone was the need to recreate, as much as possible, the structure and composition

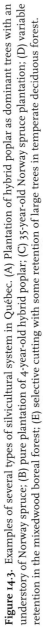

Figure 14.3. Examples of several types of silvicultural system in Québec. (A) Plantation of hybrid poplar as dominant trees with an understory of Norway spruce; (B) pure plantation of 4-year-old hybrid poplar; (C) 35-year-old Norway spruce plantation; (D) variable retention of large trees in temperate deciduous forest.

found in the pre-industrial forest of the region. To do so, existing information regarding past fires and insect epidemics was used to determine the target forest composition and stand structures. A preliminary examination showed that (1) old-growth forests of irregular structure have declined greatly in the past 100 years, (2) jack pine stands are less abundant now than when the natural fire regime dominated, (3) there are fewer conifer-dominated forests, and (4) the proportions of spruce (in the north of the area) and white pine (in the south) have declined greatly in the past 100 years. Following an evaluation of operational constraints for this particular area, the following management strategies were proposed as a first attempt to implement ecosystem-based management: (1) increase the proportion of stands that will be harvested following some kind of selective cutting (up to 40% from less than 5% now) to increase the proportion of forest with irregular structure; (2) implement the principle of variable retention on all cut blocks (Fig. 14.3D), with retention varying between 5% and 30%; (3) develop landscape-level cutting patterns that will maintain forest fragments as large as possible; and (4) develop a strategy to reintroduce white pine and red spruce into the forest. A preliminary analysis using spatially explicit landscape modeling showed that the zoning adopted increased the average size of forest fragments four-fold, from around 200 to 800 ha, compared with the status quo approach (Côté 2006).

The need for more flexible regulations

Very early on, it became clear that many elements of legislation that regulate how the forest should be harvested and managed would need to be changed or not implemented if one wanted to successfully adopt the functional zoning approach. The Québec provincial government decided to make the TRIAD study area a "special project" where many of the current regulations could be relaxed. Regulations that needed to be "relaxed" in order to allow for the successful implementation of a functional zoning approach included: (1) revision of the concept of wasted timber in light of the need for ecosystem-based management to leave many more dead and live trees (under current regulations, managers cannot leave more than 3.5 m³ of harvestable wood, whereas up to 50 m³ of harvestable wood will be left in some cutovers as part of the variable retention approach); and (2) elimination of the concept of the "best" treatment for a particular forest. Natural forests are naturally complex and varied and therefore forestry interventions that are part of ecosystem-based management need to be much more varied and complex than currently done.

Research as part of an adaptive management approach

Many of the ideas behind the TRIAD zoning approach are new, especially those relating to emulating natural disturbance and natural landscape patterns, developing short-rotation very intensive forestry, accepting that forest management should foster complexity at the stand and landscape levels, etc. Therefore, research teams were established to work closely with the practitioners to develop zoning approaches. Since research is slow at getting results, the teams quickly embraced the adaptive management approach. Within this approach, researchers were asked to come up with new practices *before* the results from their research were available. Preliminary analyses done with some new modeling tools (SELES: Fall *et al.* 2004; Côté 2006; SORTIE: Coates *et al.* 2003) were used to evaluate a series of alternative possibilities that could be implemented, and from those, a series of practices are being piloted in the field. Although we know that these new practices are not perfect, they are based on the best science available and some preliminary computer simulations that have allowed us to select the most promising approach. However, they are part of the ongoing research effort and these first new treatments will be monitored closely, so that improved practices will be implemented in the future.

In the Québec study, some preliminary long-term simulations have been done using different zoning scenarios (Côté 2006). Basically, the status quo (with 2% protected areas and around 10% ecosystem-based management) provided approximately the same level of allowable cut as the TRIAD scenario but modified strongly the composition and structure of the forest compared with the pre-industrial one. It also created the smallest average forest fragment of all scenarios evaluated. All other zoning scenarios (with 10%–20% protected area and between 45% and 70% ecosystem-based management) increased the average size of forest fragments by about four times, which decreases fragmentation of the forest. This was due to the elimination of the "mosaic cut" currently used in Québec, which tends to fragment the landscape, and the increased proportion of partial cuts implemented as part of an ecosystem-based management system.

Economically, the Québec team is also looking at new ways to consider the cost-benefit ratio of different zoning options. For example, most economic analyses of traditional intensive or short-rotation plantations do not consider the indirect benefit that such management has in increasing protected areas and allowing a larger proportion of the landscape to be managed under the ecosystem-based system. Such new analyses are likely to find intensive and short-rotation plantations much more economically attractive than first thought! Furthermore, these direct and indirect values are being included in new analyses using the theory of real options in economics. In a few words, real options take into consideration the cost of making decisions right now that reduce our ability to benefit from alternative future conditions. These new analyses may result in the current decision being not economically optimal today, in order to leave more options open in the future.

CONCLUSIONS

Although controversial when introduced, the TRIAD has proven to be an effective way to consider simultaneously both the economic and environmental interests of society in their forests, using concrete criteria on specific pieces of forest landscape. By explicitly recognizing the validity of all stakeholders' interests, the TRIAD moves beyond the highly polarized discussions of the 1980s when debates were too often about "all-or-nothing" choices between intensive management and preservation. To some extent, zoning has always been done but without "official" recognition. In the past, some jurisdictions, like Québec, had forest reserves that were set aside not for conservation, but for possible future timber needs; although now long gone, these "reserves" were a form of zoning. In Europe, much of the landscape is divided among exotic fast-growing plantations (hybrid poplar and Douglas fir), intensive native conifer, and the less intensive hardwood native species.

Evaluation of potential TRIAD approaches clearly requires consideration of effects on biodiversity "proxies". These typically include the distribution of species composition, age classes, and sizes of stands in the region, relative to knowledge of these variables under natural disturbance regimes. Area of old forest habitats is a particularly key variable in that it often has been dramatically reduced by management. In addition to these "coarse-filter" biodiversity measures, attention also needs to be paid to "fine-filter" biodiversity measures, such as particular stand structures (e.g. downed woody debris, snags, large trees), but these are usually implemented by best management practices or biodiversity guidelines, rather than forest-level planning.

From our experience working and interacting with various stakeholders and the general public over the past few years, it seems that the general principle of the TRIAD approach, which is to use more intensive forestry on a small portion (less than 25%) of the landscape to allow for more protected areas and "ecological" forestry practices on the majority of the landscape, is generally very well received. As an example, in Québec, Christian Messier was recently invited by the environmental group L'Action boréale, led by singer Richard Desjardins, to present the TRIAD concept at one of their meetings, and the response was enthusiastic. Even the mention that herbicides should be used in some very intensive forest to reduce cost and increase yield, so that the added production could be used to increase protected areas and ecosystem-based management, received some acceptance. Furthermore, many of the initial negative reactions encountered towards traditional intensive or short-rotation plantations come from the "monoculture" and simplified look of these plantations. Therefore, any attempt at developing more intensive plantations using two or more species together is likely to greatly reduce this negative reaction toward plantation forestry. Also, research in Québec will evaluate the pros and cons, socially, economically, and ecologically, of interspersing 1–5 ha intensive and super-intensive plantations within the larger areas of ecosystem-based management forestry instead of aggregating all plantations into specific larger zones. It may well not be socially acceptable to have many hundreds or thousands of hectares of intensive monoculture plantations in large blocks. Spatial considerations also definitely need attention in designing protected areas, including such issues as dispersal ranges of target species and isolation. Montigny and MacLean (2005) used three spatial criteria in selecting additional reserve areas (listed from lowest to highest priority): (1) select areas predicted to contain rare plants, based upon the assumption that they would contribute both at a coarse- and a fine-filter level; (2) aggregate proposed reserves to make them as large and round as possible, to increase core area and reduce amount of edge; and (3) distribute the total maximum reserve area to try to include all ecosites.

In the following, we summarize ten considerations (advantages or things to consider) for TRIAD management.

1. *"Having our forest and harvesting too."* Potentially TRIAD offers more protected areas, more aggregate forest-level production, and better, ecosystem-based management in the matrix. It allows more objectives to be reached optimally than trying to achieve all objectives everywhere.
2. *Public acceptability.* We believe that a total package, which includes limited increased intensive management that goes hand-in-hand with more protected areas and more ecological management of the matrix, could be broadly socially acceptable.
3. *Green accounting value.* Although traditional, discounted accounting analyses are often not in favor of intensive forestry practices because of the long-term (rotation-length) investments required, "green",

total-system accounting procedures coming into use that value increased protected areas and improved ecosystem management may well show different results.

4. *Spatial advantages.* Concentrating on growing trees for timber production on a portion of the area would permit optimal site selection, better protection against insects, disease, and fire, and reduced transportation costs.

5. *Adaptive approach to zone allocation?* Potentially, with a rigorous science and monitoring program, it might be possible over time to reduce the requirement for some protected areas, depending upon how "intense" is the ecosystem-based approach. For example, it may be possible to have smaller and less strictly protected areas, if they are well surrounded by a matrix of ecosystem management stands that provide large dead snags, woody debris, irregular structures, etc.

6. *How much of each?* The question of how much of each zone/treatment is clearly dependent upon the desired values, which differ among constituencies.

7. *Complex implementation.* TRIAD planning and implementation may well be more complex than current management regimes in most jurisdictions, and will require good spatial management and monitoring.

8. *Time to results.* Even if TRIAD is adopted today, its effects on the landscape will be slow to show, and it will require a long-term commitment from governments and industry to stick to the plan.

9. *Not a panacea.* TRIAD may not be a helpful solution in areas where much of the landscape is already under intensive management (which is the case for large parts of European forests), because allowable-cut effects have already been taken in the form of increased harvests. However, it may well be a basis for planned transition of such areas to more ecosystem-based management.

10. *Effective communication.* TRIAD zoning would require effective communication of the intent, limits, approaches, etc. to a wide range of constituencies, to demonstrate what each zone is providing. This is no different from any effective management regime, but it is a shortcoming almost everywhere at present.

One note of caution is that although the TRIAD concept embodies the idea that high-yield production forestry can allow expansion of no-management ecological reserve zones, this feature alone is not sufficient if the remaining matrix lands are not also managed under an ecologically sustainable framework. If matrix lands remain under "extensive management" – a term that too often serves as a euphemism for high-grading and other non-sustainable, exploitative practices – or ignore biodiversity, public pressure will mount to halt commodity extraction from the matrix lands. If matrix lands are privately owned, as in much of the eastern United States, there will be strong pressure to bring them under public or conservation ownership and permanently remove them from harvesting, thus making them part of the overall reserved portion of the landscape. Under these scenarios, the TRIAD thus degenerates into a BIAD, following the developments in New Zealand and much of mainland Australia (Hickey and Brown 2003; Norton 2003).

In conclusion, and to link back to the main topic of this book, we believe that TRIAD or other zoning approaches (with perhaps more than three specific types of zone), offer at least two major advantages to conservation of managed forest landscapes: (1) greater extent of protected areas without reduced production; and (2) better ecosystem-based management of what will undoubtedly be the largest forest zone, the "matrix" forest within which protected areas and intensively managed areas are located. As noted earlier, nearly everyone agrees with two-thirds of the TRIAD, but not the same two-thirds. Linking intensively managed and protected forest areas together, toward meeting agreed-upon forest production and conservation goals, seems to be a viable way forward.

References

Bergeron, Y., B. Harvey, A. Leduc and S. Gauthier. 1999. Forest management guidelines based on natural disturbance dynamics: stand- and forest-level considerations. *Forestry Chronicle* 75:49–54.

Binkley, C. S. 1997. Preserving nature through intensive plantation forestry: the case for forestland allocation with illustrations from British Columbia. *Forestry Chronicle* 73:553–9.

Brown, S., E. Palola and M. Lorenzo. 2006. *The Possibility of Plantations: Integrating Ecological Forestry into Plantation Systems*. Reston, VA: National Wildlife Federation.

Clawson, M. 1974. Conflicts, strategies, and possibilities for consensus in forest land use and management. Pp. 101–91 in M. Clawson (ed.) *Forest Policy for the Future: Papers and Discussions from a Forum on Forest Policy for the Future*. Washington, D.C.: Resources for the Future, Inc.

Clawson, M. 1977. American forests in a dynamic world. Pp. 37–82 in M. Clawson (ed.) *Research in Forest Economics and Forest Policy*. Washington, D.C.: Resources for the Future, Inc.

Coates, K. D., C. Messier, M. Beaudet and C. D. Canham. 2003. SORTIE: a resource mediated, spatially-explicit and individual-tree model that simulates stand dynamics in forest ecosystems. *Forest Ecology and Management* 186:297–310.

Commission d'étude sur la gestion de la forêt publique Québécoise. 2004. *Rapport*. Québec.

Côté, P. 2006. *Évaluation de différentes stratégies de zonages forestiers dans le cadre du projet TRIADE de la haute Mauricie*. Mémoire de Maîtrise. Montréal, Québec: Université Québec à Montréal.

Erdle, T. A. 1999. The conflict in managing New Brunswick's forests for timber and other values. *Forestry Chronicle* 75:945–54.

Fall, A., Fortin, M. J., Kneeshaw, D. D. *et al.* 2004. Consequences of various landscape-scale ecosystem management strategies and fire cycles on age-class structure and harvest in boreal forests. *Canadian Journal of Forest Research* 34:310–22.

Franklin, J. F. 1989. Towards a new forestry. *American Forests* (Nov.–Dec.):37–44.

Gillis, A. M. 1990. The new forestry: an ecosystem approach to land management. *BioScience* 40:558–62.

Gladstone, W. T. and F. T. Ledig. 1990. Reducing pressure on natural forests through high-yield forestry. *Forest Ecology and Management* 35:69–78.

Hickey, J. E. and M. J. Brown. 2003. Towards ecological forestry in Tasmania. Pp. 31–46 in J. F. Franklin and D. B. Lindenmayer (eds.) *Towards Forest Sustainability*. Washington, D.C.: Island Press.

Hunter, M. L., Jr. and A. Calhoun. 1996. A triad approach to land-use allocation. Pp. 477–91 in R. C. Szaro and D. W. Johnston (eds.). *Biodiversity in Managed Landscapes*. New York, NY: Oxford University Press.

Kimmins, H. 1992. *Balancing Act: Environmental Issues in Forestry*. Vancouver, BC: University of British Columbia Press.

Maine Statutes. 2006. *Designation of Ecological Reserve*. Title 12, Chapter 220, Section 1805. Available online at http://janus.state.me.us/legis/statutes/12/title12sec1805.html.

McMahon, J. 1993. *An Ecological Reserve System for Maine: Benchmarks in a Changing Landscape*. Augusta, ME: Maine State Planning Office.

McMahon, J. 1998. *An Ecological Reserves System Inventory: Potential Ecological Reserves on Maine's Existing Public and Private Conservation Lands*. Augusta, ME: Maine State Planning Office.

Messier, C. and D. D. Kneeshaw. 1999. Thinking and acting differently for sustainable management of the boreal forest. *Forestry Chronicle* 75: 929–38.

Messier, C., C. Bigué and L. Bernier. 2003. Using fast-growing plantations to promote forest ecosystem protection in Canada. *Unasylva* 54:59–63.

Montigny, M. K. and D. A. MacLean. 2005. Using heterogeneity and representation of ecosite criteria to select forest reserves in an intensively managed industrial forest. *Biological Conservation* 125:237–48.

Montigny, M. K. and D. A. MacLean. 2006. Triad forest management: scenario analysis of effects of forest zoning on timber and non-timber values in northwestern New Brunswick, Canada. *Forestry Chronicle* 82:496–511.

Norfolk, C. J. and T. A. Erdle. 2005. Selecting intensive timber management zones as part of a forest land allocation strategy. *Forestry Chronicle* 81:245–55.

Norton, D. 2003. Sustainable forest management in New Zealand. Pp. 167–88 in J. F. Franklin and D. B. Lindenmayer (eds.) *Towards Forest Sustainability*. Washington, D.C.: Island Press.

Palik, B., L. Levy and T. Crow. 2004. The Great Lakes silviculture summit: an introduction and organizing framework. Pp. 1–4 in B. Palik and L. Levy (eds). *Proceedings of the Great Lakes Silviculture Summit.* Houghton, MI, April 22, 2003. USDA Forest Service GTR-NC-254.

Redelsheimer, C. L. 1996. Enhancing forest management through public involvement: an industrial landowner's experience. *Journal of Forestry* **94**(5):24–7.

Sahajananthan, S. D., D. Haley and J. Nelson. 1998. Planning for sustainable forests in British Columbia through land use zoning. *Canadian Public Policy* **24**:S73–S81.

Salwasser, H. 1994. Ecosystem management: can it sustain diversity and productivity? *Journal of Forestry* **92**(8):6–10.

Schoemaker, P. J. H. 1995. Scenario planning: a tool for strategic thinking. *Sloan Management Review* (Winter): 25–40.

Sedjo, R. A. and D. Botkin. 1997. Using forest plantations to spare natural forests. *Environment* **39**:15–20.

Seymour, R. S. 1985. Forecasting growth and yield of budworm-infested forests. Part I: Eastern North America. Pp. 200–13 in *Recent Advances in Spruce Budworm Research: Proceedings of CANUSA Spruce Budworms Research Symposium.* Bangor, ME, Sept. 16–20, 1984. Ottawa, ON: Canadian Forest Service.

Seymour, R. S. and M. L. Hunter, Jr. 1992. *New Forestry in Eastern Spruce-Fir Forests: Principles and Applications to Maine.* Maine Agricultural Experiment Station, University of Maine, Miscellaneous Publication 716.

Seymour, R. S. and M. L. Hunter, Jr. 1999. Principles of ecological forestry. Pp. 22–61 in M. Hunter (ed.). *Maintaining Biodiversity in Forested Ecosystems.* Cambridge, UK: Cambridge University Press.

Seymour, R. S. and R. C. Lemin, Jr. 1989. *Timber Supply Projections for Maine,* 1980–2080. Cooperative Forest Research Unit Bulletin 7. (Maine Agricultural Experiment Station Miscellaneous Report 337.)

Seymour, R. S. and M. L. McCormack, Jr. 1989. Having our forests and harvesting too: the role of intensive silviculture in resolving land use conflicts. Pp. 207–13 in R. D. Briggs, W. B. Krohn, J. G. Trial, W. D. Ostrofsky and D. B. Field (eds.) *Forest Wildlife Management in New England – What Can We Afford?* (Maine Agric. Exp. Sta. Misc. Rep. 336.) Orono, ME: University of Maine.

Stoneman, G. L. 2007. Ecological forestry and eucalypt forests of south-western Australia. *Biological Conservation* **137**:558–66.

Taylor, N. W. (chair). 1999. *Competing Realities: The Boreal Forest at Risk.* Report of the Sub-Committee on Boreal Forest of the Standing Senate Committee on Agriculture and Forestry.

Forest landscape modeling as a tool to develop conservation targets

EMIN ZEKI BASKENT

INTRODUCTION

International agreements emerging from the United Nations Conference on Environment and Development in 1992 challenge the forestry sector to harmonize the ecological, economic, and socio-cultural values of forests. Criteria and Indicators (C&I) for the sustainable forest management initiative have been developed and implemented as part of the forest certification process. Within the past two decades, it has become clear that forest management regulations directly affect biodiversity conservation and thus have a critical role in moderating conservation values (Hunter 1999; Angelstam *et al.* 2004). The emerging idea of forest conservation in tandem with production has inspired researchers and forest managers to revisit the conventional philosophy of forest management. Various approaches, including timber management, integrated forest resource management, ecosystem management, landscape management, and spatial forest management have emerged to enhance sustainability.

A management planning process must follow a series of related activities. These typically begin with ecosystem surveys focusing on forest values such as wood, water, carbon, and biodiversity, followed by land stratification and the establishment of conservation targets and management objectives. Later, planning alternatives are developed to accommodate the principles, activities, or actions, and any constraints necessary for the sustainable management of forest ecosystems. Nearly all current forest management practices apply planning methods that are believed to have a positive impact

Setting Conservation Targets for Managed Forest Landscapes, ed. M.-A. Villard and B. G. Jonsson. Published by Cambridge University Press.

Figure 15.1. Biological remnants in Camili Bio-reserve Area, Artvin, Turkey.

on forest ecosystems and ecological sustainability. Forest management typically integrates conservation of forests with the production of goods and services such as recreation, wood production, water quality, soil protection, and biodiversity. The basic philosophy in managing forest landscapes is to maximize economic opportunity while minimizing the risk associated with managing the landscape. Specifically, management of forest landscapes must integrate the production of multiple values on a sustainable basis without jeopardizing long-term ecosystem health and integrity. In this regard, design as well as planning is indispensable.

Until the late twentieth century, forest management concentrated on the production of wood from forest landscapes. As such, forest management planning was designed to maximize wood production at the least cost. The design of forest management planning was relatively simple as the amount of wood could easily be quantified and forecast of timber production could simply be made over time. Nowadays, however, with the growing public and scientific concerns about the multifunctional role of forest landscapes, design and management of forest ecosystems as a whole have become a great challenge to foresters. While management interventions should comply with relevant regulations, they should also consider the ecological and socio-cultural dimensions of forestry (Fig. 15.1). Thus, based on the robust integration of economic, ecological, and socio-cultural compo-nents of forest ecosystems, the contemporary forest management concept has emerged. Given the multifaceted components, it is quite difficult and challenging to quantify various other forest values to set up operational conservation targets and management objectives.

Whatever management approach is taken, two components are crucial in this process: setting the conservation target and management objectives, and designing a management tool to achieve the objectives. When ecologi-cal, socio-cultural, and economic values are considered in forest landscape management, a holistic approach to landscape modeling becomes neces-sary. Therefore, this chapter focuses on introducing the emerging new concept of forest landscape management under conservation and sustain-able management initiatives. The chapter is organized into three major sections: the concept and the framework of forest landscape modeling with biodiversity conservation in focus, forest landscape modeling as a tool to achieve the target, and a summary with a few concluding remarks.

THE FRAMEWORK OF FOREST LANDSCAPE MODELING

A forest landscape is a spatial mosaic that contains distinct areas that func-tionally interact (Turner 1989). It consists of different forest types and stages of development distributed geographically. The landscape can be concep-tualized and quantified as the *composition* and *configuration* of *patches* that forest management attempts to control. A patch refers to a spatially dis-tinct unit of area that differs noticeably from surrounding areas in terms of its composition that is defined based on specific management objectives or conservation target. Composition refers to the non-spatial aspect of a landscape and is usually characterized by the species mix and their verti-cal structure within a patch. Configuration refers to the spatial aspect of a landscape such as the shape, size, and juxtaposition or the relative spatial arrangement of patches and their interconnections. The composition and configuration of patches across a landscape constitute landscape structure, and supports a number of functions and processes (Baskent and Jordan 1995).

Management of landscapes for composition and configuration has evolved towards a more holistic approach, generally called landscape man-agement or ecosystem management (Grumbine 1994; Salwasser 1994; Baskent *et al.* 2000). The approach attempts to manage for both commod-ity production and ecological values by controlling spatial structure of the landscape and its long-term dynamics. Control is achieved through the

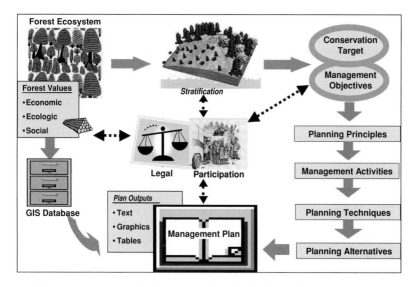

Figure 15.2. Framework of ecosystem-based multiple use forest management planning process (Baskent *et al.* 2008).

design of intervention (including harvesting) schedules. Interventions alter the spatial structure, and therefore forest values, through effects on stand development and the resultant spatial mosaic of forest conditions. Spatial requirements relate to the size, shape, juxtaposition, and distribution of management units (i.e. stands, harvest blocks, wildlife habitats, and age class), minimum and maximum harvest block size limits, adjacency restrictions (e.g. green-up delay), connectivity and proximity, and core area. The success of forest landscape control is measured with performance indicators based upon spatiotemporal changes. Designing a schedule of interventions that will achieve and maintain a desired future landscape structure – *the landscape target* – and thus forest values, is the focus of forest landscape management.

The Multiple Use Forest Management (MUFM) concept, as the working version of landscape management, relates to the design and implementation of management strategies with multiple values to achieve public demands on a participatory and sustainable basis. It focuses on the maintenance of biodiversity, productivity, regeneration capacity, and the potential to satisfy ecological, economic, and socio-cultural values without jeopardizing the long-term stability of forest ecosystems. The framework incorporates a number of components (Fig. 15.2). First, MUFM utilizes new inventory processes that consider biodiversity and other forest values. Second, MUFM incorporates participation of NGOs and local people along with institutions crucial in preparing an on-the-ground forest management plan. Third, it utilizes up-to-date information technologies such as Geographic Information Systems (GIS), remote sensing, global positioning systems, and database management systems to establish the necessary forest information system. Fourth, management objectives and actions are determined by consensus reached in meetings with the stakeholders as demonstrated by model forest programs (www.modelforest.net/cmfn/en/). Fifth, management objectives and conservation targets are formulated based on both public demand and potential forest values. Finally, silvicultural prescriptions are created with the conservation of biodiversity in mind.

Forest ecosystem inventory

The first step in multiple use forest management planning is to develop a survey of the forest ecosystem. Besides traditional characterization of stand types, their areas, and growth and yield, a sound approach is needed to survey other forest values such as water, recreation, soil erosion, and biodiversity. To characterize biodiversity, for example, species, ecosystem, and genetic diversity are considered in the inventory. Managers cannot measure everything of potential interest, so the choice of what to measure is critical (see Chapter 5, this volume).

The forest landscape is characterized in a hierarchical structure, from individual species, to patches, to the landscape (Noss 1989). At the species level (fine-scale approach), the species are listed along with their conservation status according to national and international criteria. This list is then used to find the *focal species* that are ecologically, economically, or socially critical for the maintenance of forest ecosystems. Among the kinds of species that might make good targets for planning and monitoring are area-limited species, dispersal-limited species, resource-limited species, process-limited species, keystone species, and narrow endemic species (Noss 1989). The objective is to identify a suite of focal species, each of which is used to define different attributes that must be present in a landscape if it is to retain its biota. At the patch level, critical or sensitive areas necessary for each target species are identified. Specifically, habitat areas are defined based on composition and spatial configuration. Major threats to habitat patches are assessed. At the landscape level, forests are defined as contiguous blocks of patches large and intact enough to sustain various values that the forests provide. The spatial configuration of patches across a landscape is needed to describe measurements of landscape pattern, for example, habitat fragmentation.

Characterizing forest values

Spatial structure consists of a mosaic of patches varying in content and scale and altered by natural events and by human interventions. The dynamics of spatial structure will determine the availability of desired values from the forest over time. For example, the sizes of harvest openings made today will determine the patches of economically available timber for harvesting in the distant future. Spatial structure affects not only wood value but also ecological processes (Harris 1984; Forman and Godron 1986; Turner 1989; Bissonette and Storch 2003). Ecological processes will determine the requisite forest conditions and the appropriate spatial arrangement necessary to sustain many forest values. For example, a number of bird species have been found to be sensitive to forest core area (Temple 1986; Loehle *et al.* 2006). Imposing management interventions can drastically alter the structural characteristics. Thus, it is crucial to characterize, understand, and control the spatial structure.

Fragmentation is often used as a general indicator of landscape structure. It has consequences for timber and non-timber values alike as fragmentation has a deleterious effect on many sensitive species (Harris 1984; Wilcove *et al.* 1986; Noss 1989). Reducing habitat loss should be a top priority since it is the main cause of species extinction (Simberloff 1993). Fragmentation can be described by an array of structural measurements to quantify the spatial pattern of forest ecosystems (Baskent and Jordan 1995; McGarigal and McComb 1995). However, it should be kept in mind that the indicators are just proxies; they are not one-to-one representations of landscape pattern for biodiversity conservation.

Setting conservation targets and management objectives

Management goals are a reflection of public demands on forest values. If the public demands clean water production, then the management goal creates as much clean water as possible besides other values. Depending on the intersection of forest values and demands, the general management policy can be set to maintain the long-term sustainability of forest ecosystems. Following this policy level target, major forest management objectives would include:

- maximizing the sustainable supply of timber while meeting identified non-timber objectives
- maintaining populations of focal species and the associated critical habitat
- minimizing the loss of soil

- increasing carbon storage
- protecting water quality and maintain aquatic habitat for fish and wildlife species
- helping to generate income and contribute to the local and national economy.

Embedded into these objectives are the ecological, economic, and socio-cultural aspects of sustainable forest management. Almost always the ecological sustainability of forests leads other objectives, as the sustainable flow of forest resources is assured with ecological stability and integrity. Only then would economic and social values be sustained. Ecological instability will jeopardize ecosystem capacity and its capability to satisfy tangible management objectives. Thus, harmonization as well as prioritization of forest objectives is necessary to prepare a forest management plan for multiple uses.

Any forest management objective will eventually affect the forest structure (composition and configuration of stands) and thus harvest levels. Given ecological integrity as a priority, a realistic allowable cut is set to minimize volume loss, including loss due to fire, insect, and wind damage. Similarly, conservation targets are set at the beginning. A conservation target generally refers to critical and unique faunal and floral species, and their requisite ecosystems and sites (DeGraaf and Miller 1996). For conservation targets, it is necessary to determine the area to be protected to create an effective protected-area network (Bunnell and Huggard 1999; Bücking 2003; Parviainen and Frank 2003). Historical dynamics in landscape pattern may also be used by managers to assess current landscape conditions and develop target configuration for management activities (Keane et al. 2002). Such a process will provide the basis for establishing the appropriate conservation targets. The important point in setting a conservation target is the consensus among stakeholders to delineate appropriately the boundaries for conservation areas and establish an effective mechanism to integrate conservation into management plans.

Commonly, two basic approaches are followed to develop conservation targets (Fig. 15.3) (Betts and Forbes 2005). The fine-filter approach is to identify focal species, determine their habitat requirements, and incorporate them into forest planning. The practice of using focal species was generally recognized because the value of biodiversity and the vast number of species may not be accounted for in traditional forest-wildlife planning. The premise of such an approach is that planning for the viability of an indicator species allows for the maintenance of many species, and saves on the cost and

Figure 15.3. An illustration of fine-filter or indicator species level approach (above) and coarse-filter or disturbance level approach (below).

logistics of planning for all species (Lindenmayer *et al.* 2000; Chapter 6, this volume). If the ecological requirements of these species are met, it is logical to assume that less sensitive species will also persist. The advantage of the indicator approach is that it allows managers to focus on a few species, and limit complexity in planning. The risk associated with the indicator approach, however, is that poorly selected indicators may not effectively represent other taxa (Chapter 5, this volume).

At the landscape or coarse level, management must consider the amount, type, size, and pattern of forest stands, as they are critical to the persistence of all wildlife species. The coarse-filter approach is based on the premise that the more forest management parallels natural patterns and processes, the greater the likelihood that biodiversity will be maintained (Betts and Forbes 2005). This is because biodiversity is the product of local conditions, disturbance, and available species. The natural disturbance paradigm was developed in response to the weaknesses of the single-species approach. The hypothesis is that species are adapted to disturbance regimes, and if we emulate local disturbance patterns, we may assume that the full complement of species will be maintained. The advantage of the natural template approach is that there is a greater likelihood that native species will persist if natural disturbance regimes are approximated by harvest, compared with harvest based on economic gain. Also, this approach does not require detailed knowledge of the habitat requirements of all species.

In setting the conservation target, the hybrid approach (mesofilter) is taken into consideration. Relying solely on a few indicator species may ignore the complexity associated with managing for biodiversity. However, the indicator approach provides the minimum level required by a species, and can, therefore, provide a lower level of a range of acceptable variability. Based on the premise that the thousands of species about which we know little are associated with enduring features and disturbance, objectives set based on natural conditions will provide confidence that habitat requirements of even lesser-known species are met (Betts and Forbes 2005).

Establishing the relationship between values and structure

In forest management modeling, it is highly crucial to set the functional relationship between forest structure and values to assess the marginal contribution of each forest patch to management objectives, as in landscape ecology (Gutzwiller 2002; Liu and Taylor 2002; Bissonette and Storch 2003). The ability to forecast the future forest condition necessitates the existence of the quantitative relationship. For example, wood productivity per unit area can be determined based on tree species composition in a site. Likewise, per area amount of soil loss and water production as a function of basal area can be determined by regression models (Karahalil 2003; Keleş 2003) (Fig. 15.4). The top left curve indicates that as the basal area increases the soil loss decreases, whereas the top right curve shows the gradual decrease of water production as the basal area increases. In addition, per area contribution to the value of wildlife conservation can be estimated by relating habitat requirements of focal species to stand structure. The relationship between stand structure and the focal species is reflected on the right and

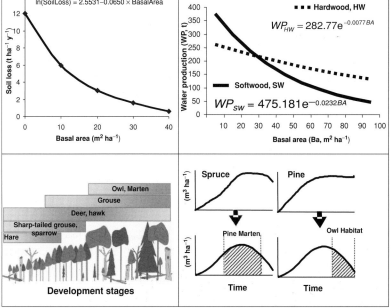

Figure 15.4. The relationships between various forest values (soil, water, timber, biodiversity) and stand development patterns.

left bottom curves in the same figure (Probst and Crow 1991). A MUFM plan should first establish basic relationships, then examine alternative management options to meet multiple objectives. For example, when management objectives are set to maximize timber production and conserve owl habitat, then certain stands exceeding the rotation age should be left as old-growth stands to contribute to owl habitat. Such an approach will obviously reduce the opportunity for timber production. So the relationship will provide an excellent basis for optimizing the objectives and reaching the target.

Developing management strategies

Forest management strategies are the means to achieve landscape objectives. A management strategy covers management policies, regulations, and prescriptions that include time, level, and location of a series of management actions to apply in a designated analysis area. Aside from policy and regulations, management prescriptions contain a set of rules for arranging stands for interventions, and a set of rates at which these activities would be carried out. Intervention rules such as harvesting from old stands are used to queue stands for certain treatments based on stand conditions and

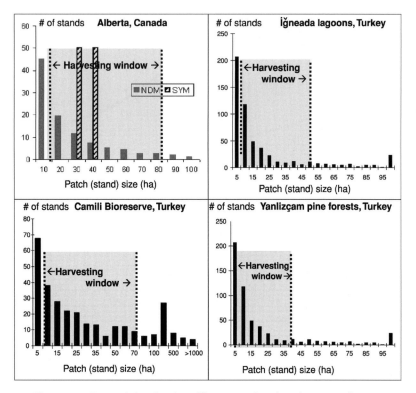

Figure 15.5. Determining the size of forest openings based on natural development of patch/stand sizes.

location. Spatial harvesting pattern dictates how a planned set of harvesting actions will be applied on the landscape. Then, the size of openings (Fig. 15.5), their spatial distribution, and progression of harvesting all become central issues in designing management strategies. For example, the natural distribution of patch sizes is an excellent indicator in determining harvest openings or cut block sizes. Four sample forest areas were evaluated with GIS to examine the natural distribution of patch sizes (Fig. 15.5). The analysis indicated that almost 90% of all patches are nearly within 15–85 ha size classes in Alberta, 10–70 ha in Camili Bioreserve area, 10–40 ha in Yanlızçam forests, and 5–35 ha in İğneada lagoon. Such information provides the basis to design the treatment sizes at a coarse level to create a more natural landscape. A uniform level of harvesting size of 40 ha, for example, would create a landscape structure different from a natural structure, which might impair the ecosystems in the future.

Figure 15.6. An illustration of 8% retention harvest.

In contrast, small openings create a more fragmented landscape whereas large openings create more clumped ones. When biodiversity conservation is a key objective, harvesting can then be an appropriate action to create a target landscape structure. For example, harvesting stands just entering their harvestable stage, before economic maturity, may be appropriate where too little open habitat exists. Alternatively, a number of spatially contiguous stands may be harvested in a progressive manner to reduce edge effects or to increase forest core area (Baskent and Jordan 1995; Ohman and Eriksson 1998). Few big openings and more small ones may be allowed, to mimic the pattern of natural disturbances such as wildfire. Furthermore, traditional clearcut harvesting may be modified to mimic natural disturbance by exercising retention harvest (Fig. 15.6). Beyond this, creating wider and more natural age class distributions (inverse J distribution) (Bergeron *et al.* 1999), extending rotation ages, leaving old-growth forests beyond economic rotation, setting aside unique ecosystems for protection, developing natural disturbance patterns, and adjusting cut block sizes so they are similar to the distribution of natural stand sizes (Fig. 15.5) are important principles for integrating multiple values into management planning.

FOREST LANDSCAPE MODELING AS A TOOL TO ACHIEVE A TARGET

Given the general framework, a key challenge for landscape management is to develop a comprehensive set of alternative management strategies to find the desirable combination of ecological, economic, and socio-cultural values. A very large number of alternative strategies create a difficult and complex decision-making environment. Therefore a model is necessary in controlling the composition and configuration of forest ecosystems to achieve the target among myriad choices in a complex setting.

Modeling, in fact, is a significant tool in decision-making today as the spatial and temporal arrangement of wildlife habitat and forest management activities is becoming increasingly important. Some forest regulations, for instance, place limits on the size and spatial relationships of harvest units. In addition, many forest management goals are now being specified by decision-makers in the form of desired landscape conditions: for example, a 60 ha opening size limit, 2-period adjacency delay, conservation of 10% of old-growth forest area, creation of core area, reduction of edges, and connection of habitats. Furthermore, the spotted owl, listed as a threatened species, requires retention of a 28.3 ha core area around owl nests during the nesting season (Bettinger *et al.* 2003). Most of the conservationists call for more than 10% of forests as reserves. Depending on ecosystems, reserves should be more than 50 ha and smaller reserves should be protected by buffer zones (Bücking 2003). Riparian buffers of at least one to two tree heights should be identified for reserve or light silviculture. Instead of uniform area distribution, inverse J distribution is advocated for natural management of forest (Bergeron *et al.* 1999; Davis *et al.* 2000). The number of snags from 8 m³ ha⁻¹ to 22 m³ ha⁻¹ is required to be maintained for biodiversity conservation in some Scandinavian countries. Forest landscape planning within this environment is therefore complex owing to compositional and configurational requirements in the form of the spatial and temporal constraints.

As an initial stage of modeling, a landscape is stratified for various uses before modeling it. For such *a priori* land stratification, forest landscapes are best viewed in advance with scientists and stakeholders, taking into account legislative mandates. In modeling forest landscape planning, the hybrid of both fine- and coarse-filter approaches is sequentially applied. First of all, the requirements of a fine-filter approach are determined by identifying the focal species and their required habitat in the form of composition and configuration. Important sites, unique patches, number of snags, and nesting and roosting areas are all identified for a determined number of focal species. Then, a landscape-level adjustment is made. Coarse-level arrangements such as minimum 35% of mature forest area, 10% of old-growth or overmature reserve, or minimum 75 ha of core area of mature forests, are applied to create the landscape level stratification.

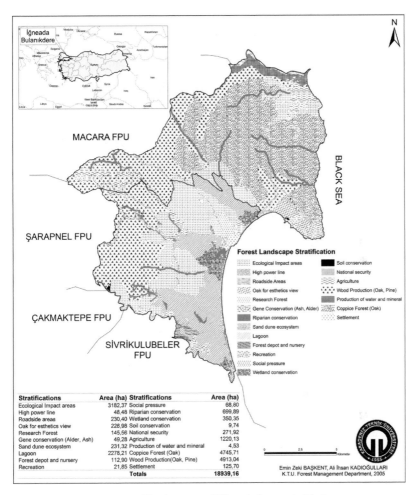

Figure 15.7. Forest stratification map of Iğneada lagoon in Turkey.

Two case study results may be given as examples here to illustrate the pre-stratification concept in landscape modeling. As part of a World Bank-supported GEF project, the Iğneada lagoon areas in Turkey were stratified into 12 land-use categories (Fig. 15.7) and the Camili Bioreserve areas into 17 land-use categories (Fig. 15.8) and mapped with GIS (Baskent *et al.* 2008). Necessary indicators were developed by scientists, managers, and the stakeholders and used by the planners (Table 15.1). In both landscapes, little area was left for wood production, as opposed to traditional planning where the majority of areas used to be managed for wood production. These examples indicated that, before modeling, a landscape has to be

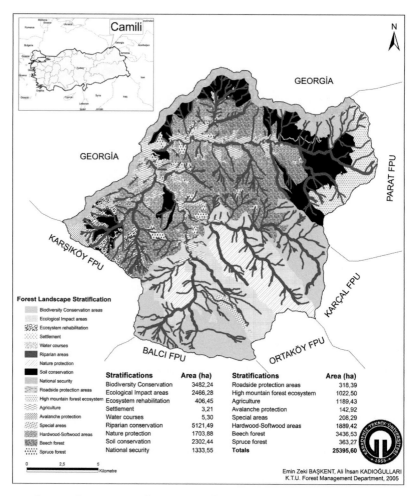

The following table appears within the figure:

Stratifications	Area (ha)	Stratifications	Area (ha)
Biodiversity Conservation	3482,24	Roadside protection areas	318,39
Ecological Impact areas	2466,28	High mountain forest ecosystem	1022,50
Ecosystem rehabilitation	406,45	Agriculture	1189,43
Settlement	3,21	Avalanche protection	142,92
Water courses	5,30	Special areas	208,29
Riparian conservation	5121,49	Hardwood-Softwood areas	1889,42
Nature protection	1703,88	Beech forest	3436,53
Soil conservation	2302,44	Spruce forest	363,27
National security	1333,55	**Totals**	**25395,60**

Emin Zeki BAŞKENT, Ali İhsan KADIOĞULLARI
K.T.U. Forest Management Department, 2005

Figure 15.8. Forest stratification map of Camili Bioreserve area in Turkey.

evaluated for a consensus-based allocation of the landscape into various forest values.

After the pre-stratification, a landscape planning model is developed to forecast the future status of forest based on management strategies. A forest is described spatially in terms of composition and configuration. Management objectives, constraints, and performance indicators include spatial characteristics; management strategies specify the spatial rules of interventions. To realize such a model, simulation and mathematical optimization solution techniques have been used.

Table 15.1. *Indicators used to stratify forest landscape in Camili and İğneada forests in Turkey*

Forest unit	Indicators
National security	Border areas with adjacent countries that are strategically important (500 m buffer) with Bulgaria and Georgia
Aesthetic and recreation	The pleasing areas with recreational values: over 2 ha in size and less than 20% of slope, There is no apparent threat by any natural disturbances such as landslide, avalanche, 500 m radius around İğneada residence, 200 m around the other important residences, 60 m buffer around some roads
Lagoon forests	Forests under frequently flooded areas or under natural stagnant water within the depth of 6 m
Ecological impact areas	To support the lagoon ecosystem, a 1 km buffer around the lakes and the lagoon, used also as corridor
Sand dune areas	The identified areas as sand dunes along the coast of Black Sea
Riparian buffers	60 m around large rivers, and 30 m around all other streams
General reserve areas	Minimum disturbed natural areas representing various ecosystems: area >100 ha of contiguous areas
Research areas	Areas identified by scientist to be unique in forest structure and composition
Biodiversity conservation	Areas specifically important for brown bear, black grouse, and other focal species
Nature reserves	Legally defined areas for strict protection
Old beech forest	Beech stands over 60 cm average stem diameter, no indication of human disturbance, with dead, living, and fallen logs that have resprouted
Special areas	Nursery, rivers, agriculture, settlements, etc.
Wood production	The remainder of the area

The traditional simulation approach sequentially schedules management interventions based on predefined amounts, rules, and limits of outputs, usually to achieve a single management objective. Spatial constraints are imposed in models as hard constraints. The simulation is efficient in developing cause–effect relationships of management activities. The results are, however, not guaranteed for optimality. GISFORMAN (Baskent and Jordan 2002), HARVEST (Gustafson and Crow 1999), and ATLAS (Nelson and Finn 1991) are some recognized simulation models. However, landscape management requires a modeling technique that is able to make intertemporal compromises among multiple objectives for an optimal solution. Simulation techniques fail in this regard. Optimization

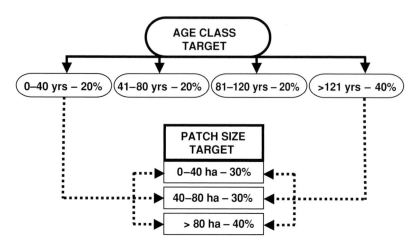

Figure 15.9. The distribution of age class and patch sizes as a landscape target (BC Ministry of Forests 1995).

techniques, e.g. linear/integer programming, can find optimal solutions where multiple objectives exist, provided the problem is amenable to linear formulation. A number of models based on linear programming, such as FORPLAN (Johnson *et al.* 1986), WOODSTOCK (Walters *et al.* 1999), and SPECTRUM (Anon. 2007) were developed and used in forest management planning.

These techniques, however, suffer limitations when spatial requirements are to be explicitly handled. As we introduce spatial constraints, such as adjacency delay, opening size, and landscape fragmentation, the problem becomes overwhelming. Forest planning models that optimize the spatial arrangement of activities can vary from the traditional optimization techniques, such as mixed integer programming (Hof *et al.* 1994; Boston and Bettinger 2001) to heuristics (Murray and Church 1995). Mixed integer programming techniques have been used to produce management plans that recognize green-up requirements, but have substantive limitations when applied to large combinatorial problems (Lockwood and Moore 1993). In addition, some non-linear objectives, such as maintenance of a desired patch size distribution, are inevitable. For example, British Columbia set age class and patch size distribution as targets in forest management planning (Fig. 15.9). Patch size distribution of each age class is targeted to create a desirable future forest landscape structure. For some structural objectives, finding a meaningful mathematical expression is exceedingly complex, even with overly simplified assumptions (Nurullah *et al.* 2000).

Landscape management therefore requires a spatial forest modeling approach. Management interventions and their timings are identified for each stand so that spatiotemporal characteristics of the forests can be predicted with respect to objectives. As each stand is subjected to multiple treatment regimes, landscape management becomes a combinatorial problem (Murray 1999; Nurullah *et al.* 2000). Particular classes of algorithm such as simulated annealing, taboo search, genetic algorithm, and cellular automata have been able to provide good enough solutions in solving spatial forest management problems in a reasonable time (Lockwood and Moore 1993; Bettinger *et al.* 1998; Baskent and Jordan 2002). In metaheuristic parlance, for example, a landscape management design problem would be represented as either minimizing or maximizing an objective function subject to some constraints such as:

$$\text{Minimize } E_o = \sum_{i=1}^{n} w_i F_i$$

where

E_o = the objective function value for the current treatment schedule

w_i = the weighting coefficient determining the relative importance of objective i

F_i = penalty cost functions for ith management objective such as control of timber flow and patch size distribution as *target*.

A few metaheuristic models such as STANLEY (Walters *et al.* 1999), HERO (Jumppanen *et al.* 2003), and ECHO (McGregor Model Forest Association 2001) have been developed to present landscape management. As reviewed by Baskent and Keleş (2005), different types of forest model have been developed and used as a tool to incorporate various forest values from water production to biodiversity conservation in developing effective management plans with conservation targets. Bettinger *et al.* (1998) used a taboo search technique to ensure the compatibility of aquatic habitat and commodity production goals in eastern Oregon. Radeloff *et al.* (2006) used LANDIS to test the effects of (a) cut unit size, (b) minimum harvest age, and (c) target species for management. The results showed that these choices have strong effects on forest composition and configuration. Cut unit size is the most important factor influencing configuration, target species for management the second most important, and minimum harvest age least important. Changes were most pronounced when clearcut size increased from 4 to

16 and then to 65 ha, but leveled off thereafter. Nelson and Finn (1991) presented that harvests constrained by 20–30-year exclusion periods were, respectively, an average of 15% and 30% below the progressive clearcutting solution. A combination of small openings and long exclusion periods led to significant reductions in harvests (43%) and caused a high percentage of the road network to be constructed in the early decades.

Similarly, Bettinger *et al.* (2005) evaluated the implications of policies that suggest clearcut size restrictions, minimum harvest ages, or the development of interior habitat areas. Simulations indicated that the minimum harvest age constraint has a stronger influence on even-flow harvest levels than do maximum clearcut size or interior habitat area constraints. Recently, Loehle *et al.* (2006) used a harvest scheduler to plan forest management over a 40-year horizon at a landscape scale under five scenarios: unmanaged, an unlimited block-size option both with and without riparian buffers, three cases with different harvest block-size restrictions, and a set-aside scenario in which older stands were withheld from cutting. Of nine bird species and guilds (canopy nesters, cavity nesters, neotropical migrants, and scrub-successional associates), none appeared to benefit from 50 m riparian buffers, response to an unmanaged scenario was mixed and expensive, and block-size restrictions provided no apparent benefit and in some cases were possibly detrimental to bird richness. A set-aside regime, however, appeared to provide significant benefits to all species and groups, probably through increased landscape heterogeneity and increased availability of older forest.

These are just a few examples to demonstrate the usefulness of forest landscape planning models in achieving the target. The models allowed managers to understand the causative basis of various management strategies and constraints. The implementation of an ecosystem-based multiple-use forest management planning concept, as explained in this chapter, in the form of a sound model becomes essential.

CONCLUSION

Based on the traditional forest management planning concept, a new ecosystem-based multiple use forest management planning approach has been introduced and its major components explained. Forest management will be more comprehensive as various forest values are integrated into the plans under stakeholders' participation. The forest management design focuses on spatially re-engineering a forest landscape for the production of ecological, economic, and socio-cultural values. This represents a fundamental shift in focus from resource-based to holistic management planning where the importance of spatial structure (composition and configuration) in determining multiple values can be taken into account. The requirements for a successful management calls for: (i) active stakeholder involvement in policy-making; (ii) an ability to quantitatively characterize spatial structure; (iii) creation of management objectives and conservation targets; (iv) access to spatial management strategies; and (v) spatial measurements of forest response as output. Here, the process accounts for spatial structure driven by ecosystem functions, and takes advantage of new emerging technologies such as GIS, remote sensing, and operations research.

Among other forest values, biodiversity conservation has now become a major planning principle. Both fine- and coarse-filter approaches are needed in management planning to accommodate biodiversity. At the species level, population dynamics of focal species are studied and species-specific conservation programs developed. Here, the focal species and their habitat requirements provide information for forest planners in generating quantitative proxy measures of biodiversity. To network the protected areas, a minimum size and rate of protected areas must be determined for different forest ecosystems, as illustrated by Bücking (2003). At a coarse level, core area, adjacency, and opening size restrictions along with their shape and spatial distribution to control fragmentation are essential components. Last, the protected areas are supported by leaving buffer zones around core zones with low level management activities. For effective conservation, specific targets for each identified eco-region are necessary. Priorities are given to relatively intact natural lands, sensitive areas, and areas rich in endemic species. Strong institutional willingness and support are needed in establishing the appropriate target.

Models are indispensable tools to realize ecosystem-based forest management plans. They require sophisticated analytical and mathematical functions to find the optimal combinations of alternatives. Sustainable forest management issues are too complex to presume that an optimal solution can be identified, particularly when there are other stakeholders involved (Mendoza and Prabhu 2006). Given the situation, models should rather be viewed as structuring tools to understand the problem, before they can be used as problem-solving methods to assist in decision-making. Here wisdom, perception, or intuition should encapsulate the models when they are used to make important decisions based on more theoretical data.

Performance indicators are used to measure model capability. Five characteristics can be considered to evaluate the indicators for sustainable management of forest ecosystems: scientific merit, ecological breadth, practicality, utility, and relevance (Hagan and Whitman 2006). The use of indicators seems to be an economically more efficient practice than to execute a large biodiversity survey for habitat protection (Juutinen and Mönkkönen 2004).

In order to implement the forest landscape management concept on the ground, a few initiatives should emerge. First of all, a common understanding should arise among the various users and stakeholders. Second, managers must have better decision-making tools and comprehensive spatial databases. Third, forest values must be quantified and managed on the basis of ecological sustainability. Fourth, alternative future management options should be evaluated. Finally, institutional capacity and the due management regulations for implementation of coordinated works are needed for the stability and continuity of personnel to implement the concept.

References
Angelstam, A., M. Dönz-Breuss and J. M. Roberge (eds.) 2004. Targets and tools for the maintenance of forest biodiversity. *Ecological Bulletins* 51.
Anonymous. 2007. *SPECTRUM, an Analytical Tool for Building Natural Resource Management Models*. Fort Collins, CO: USDA Forest Service, Inventory and Monitoring Institute.
Baskent, E. Z. and S. Keleş. 2005. Spatial forest planning: a review. *Ecological Modelling* 188:145–73.
Baskent, E. Z. and G. A. Jordan. 1995. Characterizing spatial structure of forest landscapes. *Canadian Journal of Forest Research* 25:1830–49.
Baskent, E. Z. and G. A. Jordan. 2002. Forest landscape management modeling using simulated annealing. *Forest Ecology and Management* 165:29–45.
Baskent, E. Z, G. A. Jordan and A. M. M. Nurullah. 2000. Designing forest landscape (ecosystems) management. *Forestry Chronicle* 76:739–42.
Baskent, E. Z., S. Terzioğlu and Ş. Başkaya. 2008. Developing and implementing multiple-use forest management planning in Turkey. *Environmental Management* 42:37–48.
BC Ministry of Forests. 1995. *Biodiversity Guidebook: Forest Practices Code of British Columbia*. Victoria, Canada.
Bergeron, Y., B. Harvey, A. Leduc and S. Gauthier. 1999. Forest management guidelines based on natural disturbance dynamics: stand and forest level considerations. *Forestry Chronicle* 75:49–54.
Bettinger, P., J. Sessions and K. N. Johnson. 1998. Ensuring the compatibility of aquatic habitat and commodity production goals in eastern Oregon with a taboo search procedure. *Forest Science* 44:96–112.
Bettinger, P., D. L. Johnson and K. N. Johnson. 2003. Spatial forest plan development with ecological and economic goals. *Ecological Modelling* 169:215–36.
Bettinger, P., B. K. Lennette, K. N. Johnson and T. A. Spies. 2005. A hierarchical spatial framework for forest landscape planning. *Ecological Modelling* 182:25–48.

Betts, M. and G. Forbes. 2005. *Forest Management Guidelines to Protect Native Biodiversity in the Greater Fundy Ecosystem*, 2nd edn. New Brunswick, NJ: Co-operative Fish and Wildlife Research Unit, University of New Brunswick.

Bissonette, J. A. and I. Storch (eds.) 2003. *Landscape Ecology and Resource Management: Linking Theory with Practice*. Washington, D.C.: Island Press.

Boston, K. and P. Bettinger. 2001. Development of spatially feasible forest plans: a comparison of two modeling approaches. *Silva Fennica* 35:425–35.

Bücking, W. 2003. Are there threshold numbers for protected forests? *Journal of Environmental Management* 67:37–45.

Bunnell, F. L. and D. J. Huggard. 1999. Biodiversity across spatial and temporal scales: problems and opportunities. *Forest Ecology and Management* 115: 113–26.

Davis, L., K. Johnson, P. Bettinger and T. E. Howard. 2000. *Forest Management*, 4th edn. New York, NY: McGraw-Hill.

DeGraaf, R. M. and R. I. Miller. 1996. *Conservation of Faunal Diversity in Forested Landscapes*. London: Chapman and Hall.

Forman, R. T. T. and M. Godron. 1986. *Landscape Ecology*. New York, NY: John Wiley and Sons.

Grumbine, R. E. 1994. What is ecosystem management? *Conservation Biology* 8:27–38.

Gustafson, E. J. and T. R. Crow. 1999. HARVEST: linking timber harvest strategies to landscape patterns. Pp. 309–32 in D. J. Mladenoff and W. L. Baker (eds.) *Spatial Modeling of Forest Landscapes: Approaches and Applications*. Cambridge, UK: Cambridge University Press.

Gutzwiller, K. J. 2002. Applying landscape ecology in biological conservation. New York, NY: Springer-Verlag.

Hagan, J. M. and A. A. Whitman. 2006. Biodiversity indicators for sustainable forestry: simplifying complexity. *Journal of Forestry* 104:203–10.

Harris, L. D. 1984. *The Fragmented Forest: Island Biogeography Theory and the Preservation of Biotic Diversity*. Chicago, IL: University of Chicago Press.

Hof, J., M. Bevers, L. Joyce and B. Kent. 1994. An integer programming approach for spatially and temporally optimizing wildlife populations. *Forest Science* 40:177–91.

Hunter, M. L. (ed.) 1999. *Maintaining Biodiversity in Forest Ecosystems*. Cambridge, UK: Cambridge University Press.

Johnson, K. N., T. Stuart and S. A. Crimm. 1986. *FORPLAN, Version 2: An overview*. Washington, D.C.: USDA Forest Service, Land Management Planning Systems Section.

Jumppanen, J., M. Kurttila, T. Pukkala and J. Uuttera. 2003. Spatial harvest scheduling approach for areas involving multiple ownership. *Forest Ecology and Management* 5:27–38.

Juutinen, A. and M. Mönkkönen. 2004. Testing alternative indicators for biodiversity conservation in old-growth boreal forests: ecology and economics. *Ecological Economics* 50:35–48.

Karahalil, U. 2003. Toprak Koruma ve Odun Üretimi Fonksiyonlarının Doğrusal Programlama İle Modellenmesi (Karanlıkdere Planlama Birimi Örneği). Yüksek Lisans Tezi. Karadeniz Teknik Üniversitesi, Fen Bilimleri Enstitüsü.

Keane, R. E., R. A. Parsons and P. F. Hessburg. 2002. Estimating historical range and variation of landscape patch dynamics: limitations of the simulation approach, *Ecological Modelling* 151:29–49.

Keleş, S. 2003. Ormanların Su ve Odun Üretimi Fonksiyonlarının Doğrusal Programlama Tekniği İle Optimizasyonu (Karanlıkdere Planlama Birimi Örneği). Yüksek Lisans Tezi. Karadeniz Teknik Üniversitesi, Fen Bilimleri Enstitüsü.

Kurttila, M. 2001. The spatial structure of forests in the optimization calculations of forest planning – a landscape ecological perspective. *Forest Ecology and Management* **142**:129–42.

Lindenmayer, D. B., C. R. Margules and D. B. Botkin. 2000. Indicators of biodiversity for ecologically sustainable forest management. *Conservation Biology* **14**:941–50.

Liu, G., J. D. Nelson and C. W. Wardman. 2000. A target-oriented approach to forest ecosystem design – changing the rules of forest planning. *Ecological Modelling* **127**:269–81.

Liu, J. and W. W. Taylor. 2002. *Integrating Landscape Ecology and Resource Management.* Cambridge, UK: Cambridge University Press.

Lockwood, C. and T. Moore. 1993. Harvest scheduling with spatial constraints: a simulated annealing approach. *Canadian Journal of Forest Research* **23**: 468–78.

Loehle, C., P. V. Deusen, B. T. Wigley *et al.* 2006. A test of sustainable forestry guidelines using bird habitat models and the Habplan harvest scheduler. *Forest Ecology and Management* **232**:56–67.

McGarigal, K. and B. J. Marks. 1994. *FRAGSTATS: Spatial Pattern Analysis Program for Quantifying Landscape Structure.* Unpublished Report. Corvallis, OR: Forest Science Department, Oregon State University.

McGarigal, K. and W. J. McComb. 1995. Relationship between landscape structure and breeding birds in the Oregan Coast Range. *Ecological Monographs* **65**:235–60.

McGregor Model Forest Association. 2001. *ECHO Planning System Overview Manual.* Available online at www.mcgregor.bc.ca.

Mendoza, G. A. and R. Prabhu. 2006. Participatory modeling and analysis for sustainable forest management: overview of soft system dynamics models and applications. *Forest Policy and Economics* **9**:179–96.

Murray, A. T. 1999. Spatial restrictions in harvest scheduling. *Forest Science* **45**:45–52.

Murray, A. T. and R. L. Church. 1995. Heuristic solution approaches to operational forest planning problems. *OR Spectrum* **17**:193–203.

Nelson, J. D. and S. T. Finn. 1991. The influence of cut-block size and adjacency rules on harvest levels and road networks. *Canadian Journal of Forest Research* **21**:595–600.

Noss, R. F. 1989. Indicators for monitoring biodiversity: a hierarchical approach. *Conservation Biology* **4**:355–64.

Nurullah, A. M. M., G. A. Jordan and E. Z. Baskent. 2000. Spatial stratification. *Forestry Chronicle* **76**:311–17.

Ohman, K. and L. O. Eriksson. 1998. The core area concept in forming contiguous areas for long-term forest planning. *Canadian Journal of Forest Research* **28**:1032–9.

Parviainen, J. and G. Frank. 2003. Protected forests in Europe approaches – harmonizing the definitions for international comparison. *Journal of Environmental Management* **67**:27–37.

Probst, J. R. and T. R. Crow. 1991. Integrating biodiversity and resource management. *Journal of Forestry* **89**:12–17.

Radeloff, V. C., D. J. Mladenoff, E. J. Gustafson *et al.* 2006. Modeling forest harvesting effects on landscape pattern in the Northwest Wisconsin Pine Barrens. *Forest Ecology and Management* **236**:113–26.

Salwasser, H. 1994. Ecosystem management: can it sustain diversity and productivity? *Journal of Forestry* **92**:6–10.

Simberloff, D. 1993. How forest fragmentation hurts species and what to do about it. Pp. 85–90 in *Proceedings of Sustainable Ecological Systems: Implementing an Ecological Approach to Land Management*. July 12–15, 1993. Flagstaff, AZ: USDA Forest Service, General Technical Report RM-247.

Temple, A. S. 1986. Predicting impacts of habitat fragmentation on forest birds: a comparison of two models. Pp. 301–4 in J. Verner, M. L. Morrison and C. J. Ralph (eds.) *Wildlife 2000: Modeling Habitat Relationships of Terrestrial Vertebrates*. Madison, WI: University of Wisconsin Press.

Thomas, J. W., E. D. Forsman, J. B. Lint *et al.* 1990. A conservation strategy for the northern spotted owl: a report of the Interagency Scientific Committee to address the conservation of the northern spotted owl. USDA Forest Service, USDI BLM, Fish and Wildlife Service, National Park Service.

Turner, M. G. 1989. Landscape ecology: the effect of pattern on process. *Annual Review of Ecology and Systematics* **20**:171–97.

Walters, K. R., U. Feunekes, A. Cogswell and E. Cox. 1999. A forest planning system for solving spatial harvest scheduling problems. Canadian Operations Research Society National Conference, June 7–9, 1999. Windsor, Ontario, Canada.

Wilcove, D., C. H. McLellan and A. P. Dobson. 1986. Habitat fragmentation in the temperate zone. Pp. 237–356 in M. E. Soulé (ed.) *Conservation Biology: The Science of Scarcity and Diversity*. Sunderland, MA: Sinauer Associates.

Setting targets: tradeoffs between ecology and economics

MIKKO MÖNKKÖNEN, ARTTI JUUTINEN, AND EIJA HURME

INTRODUCTION

Habitat loss is the main threat to biodiversity. Conversion of land to urban sprawl and agricultural land is widespread, particularly in southern temperate regions. In the boreal forest zone, landscapes have remained primarily forested while undergoing spatial and temporal changes in composition and age structure. Within the seemingly intact forest cover, habitat degradation has resulted in habitat loss for many species. Common to these types of landscape changes is that human activities have resulted in a shortage of area for species and their habitats. Preventing further habitat loss, that is conservation, causes restrictions to other land-use types and often incurs considerable economic costs in terms of foregone opportunities. Therefore, there is an immanent tradeoff between alternative land-use practices. How much trading in ecological values we are willing to accept for increasing economic welfare is an important ethical question, and relates to the discussion of weak versus strong sustainability (Costanza 1996). From a scientific point of view, the tradeoff between ecological and economic targets calls for the development of procedures and methods to cope with it in a balanced way.

The tradeoff between ecological and economic targets reflects land-use demands. Market value of land varies widely across sites according to, for example, location, potential other uses, and primary productivity. Pressures to develop a parcel of land increase in proximity to dense human populations, yet social benefits from undeveloped land (e.g. recreation and

Setting Conservation Targets for Managed Forest Landscapes, ed. M.-A. Villard and B. G. Jonsson. Published by Cambridge University Press.

conservation) also increase with proximity. Therefore, land value tends to decrease with distance from cities. Land value also tends to increase with its productivity. Productivity is also a primary determinant of species richness (Currie 1991; Hawkins *et al.* 2003; Mönkkönen *et al.* 2006). These create potential conflict between conservation and commercial use of forests. The global network of protected areas is biased toward landscapes with low productivity that are not economically valuable for agricultural production or forestry (Pressey 1994). Also, in Fennoscandia, protected areas are located in remote areas and on less productive sites, particularly at high altitude or latitude (Nilsson and Götmark 1992; Virkkala 1996; Stokland 1997). Protected area networks on more productive soils and regions have often proved to be inadequate (Heikkinen *et al.* 2000; Angelstam and Andersson 2001). Moreover, the most productive sites, e.g. luxurious groves, have already largely been developed for agriculture, and such habitat types are the most endangered in many regions.

Conservation emphasis has largely focused on old-growth forests. This is because many habitat features that are important for biodiversity, such as snags and very large living trees, develop over long periods of time. Commercial forestry aims at high economic outcome via shorter forest rotations compared with natural forests. Forests that exceed the optimum rotation age cause economic losses. Nature conservation objectives, on the other hand, require extended harvest rotations, and are thus in conflict with economically efficient use of timber resources.

The tradeoffs are not confined to those between ecology and economics. A basic ecological principle is that each species has a unique ecological niche, i.e. no two species are identical in their ecological requirements. If a habitat or a landscape is managed for one species, this may not benefit others and may even be harmful for some. Alternative socio-economic objectives do not necessarily closely align either (e.g. timber harvesting versus recreation).

From a practical perspective we need methods to incorporate multiple objectives into a planning system to reveal tradeoffs and to find opportunities for simultaneously meeting the economic and ecological targets. Managing land for maintaining biodiversity and enhancing sustainability of resources is inherently a complicated problem involving ecological and socio-economic aspects. Therefore, target setting must also include multiple objectives. Conservation biologists often aim to identify particular parcels of land where conservation efforts should be directed, whether through protected areas or specific restoration activities. Conversely, for natural resource managers it is equally important to locate potential areas for development and resource extraction (e.g. timber harvest).

Thus, addressing economic–ecological tradeoffs can often be reduced to the problem of allocating parcels of land into protection versus production/ development. This refers to systematic conservation planning (*sensu* Margules and Pressey 2000), which has received much attention from conservation biologists (Pressey *et al.* 1993; Rodrigues *et al.* 2000; Cabeza and Moilanen 2001) and lately also among economists (Ando *et al.* 1998; Polasky *et al.* 2001; Haight *et al.* 2002). The site selection approach, where a land manager has to decide whether to harvest or to protect a stand, is particularly useful when considering the protection of old-growth forests, since clearcutting combined with regeneration is the dominant silvicultural method. However, forest biodiversity conservation can be achieved in a variety of ways, aside from strict protection, e.g. green tree retention, prescribed burning, and active management for some specific structural or floristic features (Chapters 5 and 6, this volume). Ecological knowledge suggests that aggregating such measures in space is more efficient than even or random distribution of conservation efforts (Hanski 2000). Therefore, even these alternative measures can be considered within the framework of systematic conservation planning. The core question is: what is the most efficient way to achieve the conservation target?

In this chapter, we first outline a general framework to address the tradeoff between ecology and economics. This framework is based on a simple species–area relationship and a subsequent cost–benefit approach. We then provide examples to illustrate practical cases where these concepts have been applied. Here, we particularly focus on site selection issues in forestry, i.e. land allocation to protection versus timber production. To demonstrate the features of species–area relationships, we refer to a site selection problem where the aim is to maximize the number of species in the selected protected area network, subject to a given resource constraint (maximum coverage problem). We also provide an example where multiple ecological objectives are incorporated in a site selection problem. Finally, we consider a case where long-term population persistence is the objective, along with economically sustainable forestry.

CONCEPTUAL BACKGROUND

Species–area relationship and costs versus benefits of conservation

One of the few general laws in ecology is that species richness increases with the area surveyed. This species–area relationship is commonly used to make predictions about species loss with habitat loss and fragmentation (Pimm and Askins 1995; Manne *et al.* 1999; Hanski 2005). A rule of thumb derived from this relationship is that 90% habitat loss results in 50% species loss

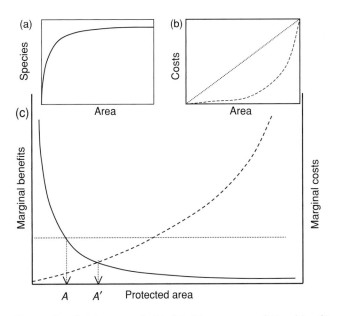

Figure 16.1. Species–area relationship (a), cost–area relationships (b), and derived marginal benefit curve (continuous line) as a function of protected area (c). Costs (b) and marginal costs (c) are drawn assuming constant (or ignored) costs per unit area (dotted line) and variable costs per unit area (dashed line).

(Wilson 1992). In a similar vein, species–area relationships can be used to predict species gain if habitat area is increased. We can, for example, predict the increment in the number of species obtained from the area added to an existing protected area network, and the effects of habitat restoration on species richness by the area of restored habitat.

Although there are several alternative equations to describe the species–area relationship (SAR) the most commonly used and generally accurate description is $S = cA^z$, where S is species richness, A is area and c and z are constants. Parameter z is dimensionless and typically varies between 0.1 and 0.4; c is scale-sensitive and depends on the units used to express the area (Rosenzweig 1995).

When the conservation goal is to protect the maximum number of species (maximum coverage problem) SAR can be used to estimate the benefits of increasing the total protected area. First, if only very little protected area exists, benefits are large, as each unit increment in area results in a considerable increase in species richness. At a higher level of protection, benefits level off following the SAR (Fig. 16.1a). In other words, marginal benefits, which can be estimated with the first derivative of the SAR, i.e.

$S' = czA^{z-1}$, is a decreasing convex function of increasing area of protection (Fig. 16.1c).

If each parcel of land has an equal market value per unit area, then costs of protecting areas increase linearly (Fig. 16.1b) and marginal cost is a flat function of area (Fig. 16.1c). From the point of view of society, the optimal solution is at the point where marginal costs equal marginal benefits. In practice, however, land values vary considerably. When protection can be started from the sites with a low opportunity cost and high ecological value, the result is a convex non-linear cost curve (Fig. 16.1b) and hence increasing marginal costs with area (Fig. 16.1c). If costs (foregone opportunities) and benefits (increment in the number of species protected) could be measured by using a commensurate scale, an exact conservation target could be defined. This, however, is seldom possible because translating biodiversity into exact monetary value is an elusive goal (Costanza *et al.* 1997; Montgomery *et al.* 1999). Nevertheless, one implication is still evident. If land value per unit area is assumed to be constant (implying constant marginal cost for protected areas), less area can be protected for a given budget level than when opportunity costs are considered (compare A and A' in Fig. 16.1). The resources saved by selecting sites with low cost in the beginning allow a larger total area to be protected. This clearly emphasizes the benefits from integrated planning where ecological and economic objectives are simultaneously considered.

Consider a forest manager whose task is to create a protected area network aiming to maximize species coverage – given a conservation budget – in a region where very little or no forest has been protected before. The manager has fairly little knowledge of the ecological characteristics of alternative sites, except for some surrogate information based on structural characteristics (e.g. naturalness; see, for example, Mrosek 2001) from which to conduct a pre-selection of potential sites. Because of the non-linearity of SAR, the planner has a high certainty that, in this case, maximizing the area under protection will result in a rapid increase in the coverage of species. Therefore, the most efficient procedure would be first to select, among the pre-selected sites, the ones with low opportunity costs to maximize total area within the network.

With increasing budget and protected area, the certainty declines that maximizing area alone would result in a maximum increment in species richness, because the rate of increase predicted by SAR rapidly levels off. What becomes important is the species composition in alternative potential sites. This means that an existing network will best be completed if additional sites are selected so that they maximize the increment of species representation, i.e. if new sites are selected based on the complementarity of their species assemblages rather than as a function of their species richness *per se* (Church *et al.* 1996; Csuti *et al.* 1997).

The conservation ecology literature provides an abundance of methods and case studies where the maximum coverage problem and complementarity of sites have been addressed, but rather few studies have incorporated economic aspects into optimal site selection (Ando *et al.* 1998; Balmford *et al.* 2000; Polasky *et al.* 2001). The complementarity approach makes planning more complicated and expensive because it requires detailed ecological information. Efficient site selection can only be made if species composition or other ecological characteristics of alternative sites are adequately known. Then, one must determine whether it is reasonable to use limited conservation funds to acquire good quality ecological data on which conservation planning can be conducted on a firm basis, or whether it is more cost-efficient to complete the existing network in spite of limited information. The answer depends on the overall level of protection and on the relative cost of information gathering (Juutinen and Mönkkönen 2004). Reliable and cost-efficient indicators of biodiversity and complementarity are certainly welcome (Caro and O'Doherty 1999; Andelman and Fagan 2000; Roberge and Angelstam 2004).

Recent work on species abundance distributions has shown that there is a long and negatively skewed tail of uncommon species (Hubbell 2001). Each region has a high number of rare species with restricted ranges, low population densities, and/or specialized habitat requirements. Together with the species–area relationship, this implies that some species will be lost with habitat loss, even though most of an area remains intact. That is, to cover all species within a protected area network, very large areas and an excessively large conservation budget are needed. Solutions to this problem include more careful planning based on knowledge of the distribution and natural histories of the most demanding species. In practice, special objectives for rare or red-listed species further complicate site selection problems and provide yet another potential tradeoff (Arthur *et al.* 2004). Moreover, there is a tradeoff between species representation and viability to be considered (Haight *et al.* 2000).

EMPIRICAL EXAMPLES

The case studies we use in this section all originate from the northern and central boreal forests of Finland. We demonstrate how ecological and economic objectives have been simultaneously integrated into landscape management for sustainable forestry. We particularly focus on old-growth (or overmature) forests where the ecology vs. economy tradeoffs are particularly pronounced. The remaining unprotected patches of old-growth forests in the region are considered crucially important for biodiversity, yet are under pressure of forest harvesting owing to their importance for the local economy. All the examples address the site selection question from ecological and economic viewpoints. We consider benefits from incorporating multiple objectives in management planning, costs and benefits of precise information, and multiple objective setting in general and in dynamic boreal landscapes in particular.

Ecological site selection

Here we present the results of the analysis of a database that included 32 state-owned semi-natural old forest stands located in northern Finland. Four forest types (eight stands from each type) were surveyed among potential set-aside areas. These stands cover the entire gradient of forest site types in this region and represent a fertility gradient ranging from barren pine heaths to forests with a rich herbaceous understory. The database included information on 103 vascular plant, 30 bird, 64 wood-inhabiting fungus, and 435 beetle species, the total number of species being 632. These taxa cover a wide array of dispersal potential and life forms and, thus, a high potential for generality. Species surveys were conducted in 1997–98 (see Similä *et al.* 2006 for survey methods and a detailed description of the data set).

First, consider a case where the objective is to cover a maximum number of species within a network of protected sites. Sites are assumed to have equal economic value and the resource constraint is expressed in terms of a given upper bound for the number of selected stands (i.e. variation in area not considered). A set of sites is selected so that species richness within the whole set is maximized, but the most species-rich individual stands are not necessarily selected. This selection can be named "ecological selection", because it takes into account only the ecological features of sites (number of species), ignoring variation in economic values (Juutinen *et al.* 2004; Box 16.1). To emphasize the efficiency of this selection from a conservation viewpoint, we can compare this selection with a random selection (Juutinen *et al.* 2006). This comparison, applied to the 32 stands, is depicted in Figure 16.2.

Even if the sites are selected randomly, a typical concave species–area curve appears (Fig. 16.2). This is because sites are always strategic substitutes in terms of number of species (Koskela and Ollikainen 2001). The marginal benefit of protecting a given site will decrease, given that some

Box 16.1 Ecological and integrated site selection

Ecological selection maximizes the representation of natural features, such as species, in the selected protected area network given an upper limit for the number of selected sites.

We use the following notation:

$x_j = 1$ if site j is selected and 0 otherwise,

$n =$ the number of potential sites included in the site selection,

$y_i = 1$ if feature i is contained in at least one of the selected sites and otherwise 0,

$m =$ the number of ecological features included in the site selection,

$N_i =$ the subset of candidate reserve sites that contains feature i,

$k =$ the given upper limit for the number of sites in the protected area network.

The formal presentation of the ecological model is:

$$\underset{x,y}{Max} \sum_{i=1}^{m} y_i \tag{1}$$

subject to

$$\sum_{j \in Ni} x_j \geq y_i, i = 1, \ldots, m \tag{2}$$

$$\sum_{j=1}^{n} x_j \leq k, \tag{3}$$

$$y_i = (0, 1), i = 1, \ldots, m \tag{4}$$

$$x_j = (0, 1), j = 1, \ldots, n. \tag{5}$$

The objective function (1) sums up the number of features represented in the selected sites. Constraint set (2) ensures that feature i is counted as being represented when at least one of the sites where it occurs is selected. Constraint (3) sums up the number of selected sites and ensures that this sum will not exceed the given threshold value. The constraint sets (4) and (5) indicate that the choice variables must be binary, i.e. the sites are either protected or not, and the features are represented or not represented, in their entirety.

Given this model structure, the decision variable y_i will always have a value of unity, because the objective is to maximize the number of features, except in the case that the particular feature is not represented in the selected sites, when y_i is forced to have value zero owing to constraint sets (2) and (4). A feature found from more than one selected sites is counted only once as represented. A site will likely have many ecological features and some of them are also found from other sites. Therefore, it is optimal to select sites that complement each other with respect to the objective. Note that the sites are treated as having equal size and each ecological feature is equally important. Further, the sites are implicitly assumed to have equal economic value due to constraint (3). By varying the threshold value for the number of protected sites used in constraint (3) it is possible to reveal the tradeoff between the number of represented features and the number of protected sites.

Integrated selection maximizes the representation of natural features, such as species, in the selected protected area network given an upper limit for the total costs of conservation.

Ecological selection can be easily transformed to the integrated selection by replacing constraint (3) by the following constraint:

$$\sum_{j=1}^{n} b_j x_j \leq B \qquad (3)'$$

where b_j denotes the opportunity costs of protecting site j and B is the budget allowable for protection. Thus, equation (3) is the budget constraint requiring that the sum of opportunity costs of the selected sites do not exceed the funds allowable for a protected area network. Each site may have different opportunity costs. The opportunity costs represent the forgone benefits from other potential land uses than protection for production of biodiversity services, such as lost timber revenues. By varying the budget value used in constraint (3)' it is possible to reveal the tradeoff between the number of features represented and the budget allowable for conservation.

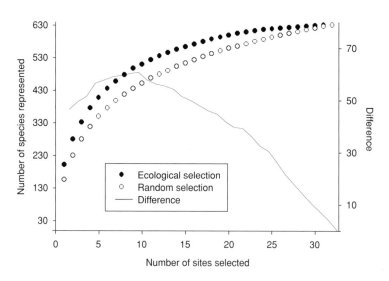

Figure 16.2. The number of species represented in the protected area network, plotted as a function of the number of sites selected (left ordinate). Ecological selection refers to procedure where stands were selected to maximize species richness within the network. Random selection depicts species richness within a set of randomly selected sites as an average over 1,000 simulations at each level of the number of sites protected. The solid line denotes absolute difference in species richness between random and ecological selection (right ordinate).

other site will also be protected because there is overlap in species composition among sites. However, some (rare) species only occur in a few
sites. If sites are selected so that this variation in species composition and
complementarity between sites are taken into account, more species can
be protected with a given number of sites than in the random selection.
Thus, the empirical SAR is more concave in the ecological selection than
in the random selection, indicating the greater efficiency of the former.
The difference between ecological and random selection is relatively small
in absolute measures in the beginning (<5 stands selected) but increases
when more stands have become selected. The difference is at the largest
when 9–10 stands have been selected.

Integrating economic information

Conservation efficiency can be improved by taking into account the variation
in the economic value of sites when selecting areas for species protection. In
line with this argument, Juutinen et al. (2004) compared three alternative
selections, namely ecological selection (see above), integrated selection,
and penny-pincher selection. Integrated selection takes into account both
ecological and commercial values of the stands, and defines a cost-efficient
solution to site selection problems (Box 16.1). The difference relative to
ecological selection is that integrated selection considers – in addition to
variation in species composition – the variation in opportunity costs among
stands. The economic aspect is presented in terms of lost timber revenues
when the stands are protected.

Penny-pincher selection represents an *ad hoc* conservation procedure
where the stands having the lowest commercial value, irrespective of their
ecological features, are selected. The difference to the integrated selection
is the assumption that all stands are equally valuable ecologically. Penny-
pincher selection may sound naive but, in reality, this type of procedure has
frequently been used across the world, judging from the fact that protected
areas tend to be located on infertile land that is not economically valuable
(Pressey 1994).

The results of this comparison are presented in Fig. 16.3. Ecological
selection usually has several optimal solutions (with several sets of stands
all containing the same number of species and the same number of stands).
This is exemplified with the minimum (a given number of species and areas
are selected to a minimum cost) and maximum (a given number of species
and areas are selected to a maximum cost) opportunity costs to show the
variation in the results. The cases are named minimum and maximum cost
solutions.

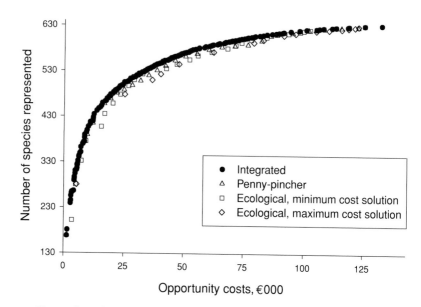

Figure 16.3. The number of species represented in the selected protected area network, plotted as a function of opportunity costs, resulting form alternative priority-setting methods. When the minimum and the maximum cost solutions of ecological selection are the same, for clarity, only the minimum cost solution is plotted. (Modified from Juutinen *et al.* 2004.)

The species–costs relationship (SCR) is slightly more concave in the integrated selection than in the ecological and penny-pincher selections (Fig. 16.3). Thus, the integrated selection is more efficient than the other two selection methods. Juutinen *et al.* (2004) estimated that penny-pincher selection causes, on average, 9% higher costs than integrated selection for a given number of species represented within the selected network. The respective figure for ecological selection varies between 15% and 19% depending on whether the minimum or the maximum cost solution is considered (see also Ando *et al.* 1998; Balmford *et al.* 2000; Polasky *et al.* 2001). Interestingly, the penny-pincher selection can yield species coverage equal to that of the ecological selection, but with lower average costs.

When inspecting the SCR in Fig. 16.3 more closely, it is obvious that when a low amount of funds is devoted to conservation, the optimal species coverage is a steeply increasing function of the area, i.e. number of stands included in the network. The €16,000 budget proved to be a critical threshold value (Juutinen *et al.* 2004). Below this threshold, it is optimal to select stands with the lowest opportunity costs (penny-pincher selection) and to establish as large a network as possible, since any increase in the number of stands rapidly increases the coverage of species. Above this threshold and given that the network includes eight stands, the complementarity of selected stands becomes more important than the size of the network as such. It is no longer optimal to select the nine cheapest stands, for example, because with this budget there is a combination of eight stands available covering a larger number of species. In other words, above the €16,000 threshold, the points in Fig. 16.3 for integrated selection are always above those of other selections, and thus marginal benefits for a given marginal cost are higher. This provides empirical support for the prediction we derived from SAR above, that at low level of protection, maximizing area within the network is a reasonable strategy, but increasing conservation efforts to obtain information on species composition among sites becomes a prerequisite.

At high budget levels when almost all species are covered, the objective function becomes flat (Fig. 16.3). The species not yet covered are likely to be restricted to one or very few stands. These stands inevitably have rather high timber values (opportunity costs) because the cheap ones were selected earlier. Therefore, saving the last few species is increasingly costly. In this specific case, covering all species requires that all stands are included in the protected area network and, therefore, there are no differences among alternative selection procedures in the end (see Figs. 16.2 and 16.3).

Costs and benefits of information

The previous section suggests that it may be important to know the species composition of sites in order to apply the complementarity approach. However, detailed species inventories tend to be time-consuming and expensive and, therefore, one has to consider the tradeoffs between the costs and quality of ecological information.

Juutinen and Mönkkönen (2004) assessed, for a given species coverage, whether it would be more efficient to use indicator species groups or to gather data on all species. For this purpose, beetles, birds, vascular plants, wood-inhabiting fungi, and a specified sub-group of presumed old-forest indicator species were tested. Inventory costs (field sampling, data preparation, and species identification) varied considerably among the alternative indicators. The site selection procedure used information on species composition, inventory costs, and the opportunity costs of conservation. Inventory costs were fixed for a given indicator group because all potential sites had to be surveyed irrespective of how many would eventually be protected. Opportunity costs increased with the number of protected stands.

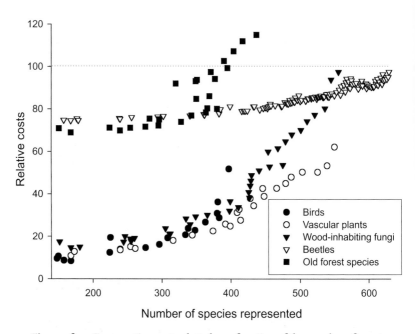

Figure 16.4. Conservation costs plotted as a function of the number of species represented in the protected area network selected by the indicator models. Costs are presented in relative terms such that the costs of integrated model, taking all species into account, is attributed a value of 100 at each level of number of species represented (dotted line). (Modified from Juutinen and Mönkkönen 2004.)

Integrated selection based on information from all species was used as a benchmark. Thus, the benchmark selection represents, by definition, the maximum level of biodiversity in the region at a given level of resources devoted to conservation. To compare with the benchmark, we selected sites by using information on the indicator group only, and calculated how many species in total (including also other than indicator taxa) were included into the selected set. We then calculated the sum of inventory and opportunity costs for all solutions. Comparison of costs from alternative indicator groups with the costs from benchmark selection reveals how efficiently species become covered by the selected network when using information on indicators only.

It seems that the use of indicators usually costs less than the benchmark, suggesting that extensive species inventories are not cost-efficient but the use of indicators is more beneficial (Fig. 16.4). To interpret this outcome, recall that the cost functions include two parts: the inventory costs and opportunity costs of conservation. Because the inventory costs are independent of the level of protection, at low levels of protection the share of inventory costs from total costs is high, and they may dominate the cost pattern. This is clearly the case when we consider the benchmark or the costs of using beetles or old-growth forest indicator species as an indicator group. These two indicator groups only reduce total costs by c. 10–15% compared with the benchmark.

In other groups, the inventory costs do not seem to have strong effects on cost functions. In particular, at a low level of protection the cost difference between the benchmark and vascular plants, wood-inhabiting fungi, and birds is rather large, and using indicators results in c. 80% reductions in total costs of protection (Juutinen and Mönkkönen 2004). Therefore, an experienced forest manager could do efficient conservation planning by using these three indicator groups. Devising a combination of these three groups may be particularly useful as they stand for different ecological features. Vascular plants have been shown to be a useful surrogate species group in complementarity site selection for many other taxa (Saetersdal et al. 2003). Species richness of wood-inhabiting fungi indicates long-term availability of dead wood (Siitonen 2001) and viable populations of selected bird species reflect appropriate amounts of habitat at the landscape scale (Angelstam 1992; Roberge and Angelstam 2006; Chapter 9, this volume).

Relative to the benchmark, the use of indicator groups become less efficient, i.e. relative costs become more similar, with increasing species coverage. This suggests that indicator species groups, or incomplete information in general, is particularly beneficial at a low level of species coverage. This is fortunate because information quality becomes more important at higher levels of protection, as indicated by the conceptual framework based on SAR and by the empirical results above.

Multiple objectives

So far, we have considered only a single ecological objective in conservation. In practice, however, decision-makers must meet several objectives simultaneously. For example, threatened or rare species deserve special attention in conservation action together with more general objectives to maintain ecological assemblages typical of a region. Moreover, the ultimate conservation goal is to maintain viable populations of species, not just to maximize species coverage in the current protected area network. There may be tradeoffs between the alternative ecological objectives.

Arthur et al. (2004) developed a methodology to reveal the tradeoffs between multiple objectives in a site selection framework. They demonstrated tradeoffs between the maximum species coverage objective and the objective to maximize the likelihood that a subset of endangered species is represented. In a similar vein, Juutinen (2005) examined the relative merits of alternative biodiversity conservation objectives for forestry. In what follows we will present three integrated models. The models differed in terms of their specific objectives, giving unequal weight to species according to three criteria: representation, conservation status, and abundance. Comparing these budget-constrained solutions, we analyse the pros and cons of achieving alternative goals.

Model 1 maximizes the number of species in the selected protected area network for a given budget. Thus, it is the basic integrated benchmark model described earlier. In model 2, the objective is also to maximize the number of species, but the threatened and vulnerable species are given a higher weight than other species. Respectively, red-listed species are preferred to species of least concern in site selection. Model 3 is similar to model 2, but it also takes into account species abundance together with their representation and conservation status. Sites with high abundance values are favored relative to sites with low abundance. This will likely improve species persistence in the long run.

To examine the tradeoffs between alternative ecological objectives it is informative to depict how the size of conservation budget (costs) affects the achievement of these goals (benefits). In Fig. 16.5, the achieved conservation is expressed as relative biodiversity (actual conservation level/conservation when all stands are protected). In other words, the different objectives are scaled to the same metrics to assist comparison. One should note that the size of conservation budget in Fig. 16.5 is just another way to state the level of opportunity costs used in previous figures.

Alternative conservation objectives yield cost–benefit curves of different shapes (Fig. 16.5). With the objective to maximize species richness or the number of red-listed species, the resulting function is strongly concave (Fig. 16.5). In other words, the majority of the objective can be achieved with a fraction of the costs needed to achieve the objective in full. Marginal costs dramatically increase and marginal benefits decrease when approaching the full objective (Fig. 16.1). It is hard to obtain general acceptance for environmental policy, which requires a high cost relative to the associated benefits and, therefore, all the potential areas may not be protected under these targets. By contrast, a large protected area network is more justified when the objective is to enhance species persistence because the cost–benefit function is less concave (Fig. 16.5) and, thus, considerable benefits per unit investment are obtained, even at high budget levels. In other

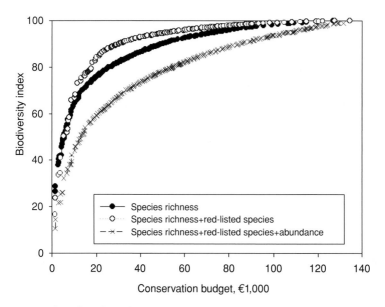

Figure 16.5. The relative biodiversity in the selected protected area network, plotted as a function of conservation budget, for alternative site selection procedures. The relative biodiversity is defined so that the maximum value for the biodiversity measure when all the stands are protected equals 100 in each model.

words, the objective of enhancing persistence is more appropriate than the one of maximizing species richness, and enhancing persistence may avoid choosing a policy that fails to achieve a meaningful goal. The size of the protected area network is an important factor for species persistence because larger total area can foster larger and hence more viable populations.

When inspecting the above results more closely, it becomes obvious that the conflict between protecting red-listed species and the other species is quite clear at low budget levels. Red-listed species are not totally covered in the protected area network if this aspect is not incorporated in the area selection process; conversely, if areas are selected by preferring the red-listed species, the other species become rather poorly represented. At high budget levels, favoring red-listed species relative to other species does not appreciably reduce the total number of species represented in the protected area network. The conflict between number of species and species abundance is minor. In particular, species abundance can be increased to some extent without sacrificing the representation of all species (see also Juutinen and Mönkkönen 2007).

Conservation targets in dynamic landscapes

So far, the examples we have considered have not dealt with the temporal dimension, i.e. the fact that forested landscapes are dynamic patchworks of stands where disturbances, both natural and human-induced, and subsequent succession processes, constantly modify the composition and configuration of habitats. From the perspective of population viability, these dynamics are essential as persistence, by definition, involves much more than just a snapshot of present distribution of individuals and species. For example, Nalle et al. (2004) developed a method that combines economic and ecological models in a dynamic and spatial analysis to evaluate land-use decisions and find cost-effective land-use alternatives. They compared the dynamic approach with a static reserve approach and found that the dynamic procedure was substantially more efficient than the static procedure.

Our final example considers a case where long-term population persistence is the objective, together with economically sustainable forestry. This case focuses on the Siberian flying squirrel (*Pteromys volans*), an arboreal mammal that is categorized as vulnerable in Finland (Rassi et al. 2001). The flying squirrel prefers old spruce-dominated forests with deciduous trees in the mixture within the northern boreal vegetation zone (e.g. Reunanen et al. 2000; Hurme et al. 2005). It can also be seen as a potential umbrella species for a wide range of forest-associated species inhabiting similar habitats (Hurme et al. 2008): ensuring persistence of the flying squirrel would increase the likelihood that species under the umbrella are also maintained in the system (Chapter 6, this volume). Moreover, flying squirrel distribution in the region is dependent on habitat connectivity, i.e. on effective dispersal routes among patches of suitable habitat (Mönkkönen et al. 1997; Reunanen et al. 2000; Hurme et al. 2007a). Dispersal is only possible along forested connections because the species is incapable of traversing totally open areas longer than a few hundred meters (Hanski et al. 2000; Selonen and Hanski 2003). There is a potential conflict between commercial forestry and flying squirrel persistence within the northern part of its range because the flying squirrel requires mature spruce-dominated, mixed forests, the most productive forest type in the region, and there is considerable pressure for harvesting the remaining mature spruce stands (Hurme et al. 2007a).

In this case study, the aim was to incorporate the known habitat and landscape requirements of the species into dynamic long-term forest planning simulations (Hurme et al. 2007b). The ecological objective was to increase the amount of suitable habitat for the flying squirrel in the landscape. A stand was assigned as flying squirrel habitat (FSH) if it had a predicted probability for the occurrence of the flying squirrel higher than 50%. The probability was based on a predictive model built with empirical data on flying squirrel occurrence (Hurme *et al.* 2005). The economic objective was to ensure a constant timber flow from the landscape.

Here, we consider four alternative scenarios that were created with different targets for flying squirrel habitat and timber production (Hurme *et al.* 2007b). The first scenario (termed "Forest Service") followed the landscape ecological guidelines used for state-owned forests in Finland (Karvonen 2000) that aim to maximize timber production (growing stock volume at the end of the planning period and cutting volume over the 60-year planning period) and to protect old forests and broad-leaved trees (maximizing the area of old forest (age ≥140 years) and volume of broad-leaved trees). In the second scenario ("Max FSH"), the objective was to maximize only the amount of flying squirrel habitat in the landscape, and timber harvesting was only allowed on stands not suitable for FSH. The third scenario ("Max NPV") aimed to maximize only the net present value of income from timber harvesting with a 3% interest rate subject to specified growing stock volume objectives at the end of the planning period. Integrated fourth scenario ("FSH & timber") aimed to maximize both the amount of flying squirrel habitat and timber production (growing stock and cutting volumes) over the planning period.

Initially, flying squirrel habitat covered some 8% of the landscape of 10,000 hectares (Hurme *et al.* 2007b). The results from a comparison among alternative scenarios showed that, in all scenarios, the amount of flying squirrel habitat considerably increased over the 60-year planning period and varied between 25% and 33% in the end, i.e. it at least tripled. Timber flow was also relatively equal except with the "Max FSH" scenario, which yielded *c.* 28% less timber than the other planning scenarios. Total net present value of harvests followed the same pattern, and "Max FSH" produced some 30% less income than other scenarios (Fig. 16.6). It is notable that the integrated scenario "FSH & timber" performed well in comparison with other scenarios: it resulted in the second highest amount of suitable habitat over the 60-year planning period and, when compared with the "Max NPV", only a 2% reduction in the maximum net present value of harvests (Hurme *et al.* 2007b).

The performance of alternative scenarios can be assessed by using a production possibility frontier (e.g. Mas-Colell *et al.* 1995; Calkin *et al.* 2002), a curve that in this study reflects the tradeoff between the net present value of forest harvest income and the amount of flying squirrel habitat. The production possibility frontier was calculated by maximizing the area of flying

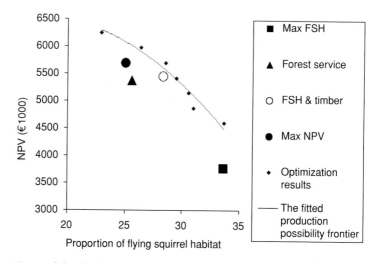

Figure 16.6. The location of four alternative forestry plans in relation to the production possibility frontier, which shows here the relative tradeoff between the proportion of suitable habitat for the flying squirrel and the net present value of cutting income. (Modified from Hurme *et al.* 2007b.)

squirrel habitat for a given NPV constraint (see fixed values on the *y*-axis in Fig. 16.6). The calculation of the values for the frontier differed from that of the scenarios, as scenarios did not have NPV constraints. Scenarios either had a growing stock constraint ("Max NPV") or had no constraints at all (other scenarios). In particular, "FSH & timber" is quite close to optimum with respect to flying squirrel habitat and NPV, as it is located very close to the frontier (Fig. 16.6). All other scenarios seem equally sub-optimal. This again indicates that combining multiple objectives into planning procedures yields solutions that are closer to optimum than planning with detached objectives.

CONCLUSION

A conservation budget is usually determined through a political process. The size of this budget determines the size of a protected area network. However, consideration of marginal costs and benefits ought to play a central role in determining the size of the budget in informed decision-making. Cost–benefit analysis based on species richness does not yield a very large conservation budget because marginal benefits rapidly decline with increasing area and may fall below marginal costs at a low level of protection

(Fig. 16.1c). This is a consequence of SAR: the rate of increase in species richness soon levels off as the protected area increases (Fig. 16.1a). Therefore, as part of the political process, the issue of choice of the conservation goal is important. Do we maximize species richness, or species persistence, or do we try to maintain ecological function (e.g. dispersal)? Maximizing species richness in a protected area network does not necessarily maximize species persistence and, in fact, minimum set coverage solutions in site selection (e.g. a minimum total area or minimum number of areas that represent at least one population of each species) very likely maximize species loss (Cabeza and Moilanen 2001).

The ultimate ecological goal of protected area networks is to maintain viable populations of species over time. Our analyses suggest that when devising to augment an existing large protected area network, enhancing population persistence within the network is a more appropriate goal than maximizing species richness also from a socio-economic perspective. This is because marginal benefits from enhancing population persistence can be considerable even in situations where marginal benefits from maximizing species richness are negligible (Fig. 16.5). Setting the right ecological objectives is therefore of crucial importance in choosing a policy that has an achievable and meaningful goal.

The results of the case studies indicate, in line with the conceptual framework derived from SAR, that if the budget is very low it may be reasonable first to make a pre-selection by using available ecological information to determine the potential objectives and then to select the cheapest areas into the protected area network within the budget. If the budget exceeds a case-specific threshold value, then it is important to take into account the complementarity between sites in the site selection. This provides empirical support for the prediction we derived from SAR (above) that at low levels of protection, maximizing area within the network is a reasonable strategy but with increasing conservation efforts, information on species composition among sites becomes a prerequisite for cost-efficient conservation. This is likely to require specific field inventories in practice. However, at this budget level, it may be reasonable to prefer red-listed species to common species, because they need protection most urgently. Also, it is justified to protect sites where species abundance is high to enhance species persistence. If the budget is large enough, then the complementarity may not be so important an aspect any more, and population persistence should be given the highest priority. In practice, this could mean, for example, that protected areas are selected to avoid fragmentation of forest landscapes through increasing connectivity, i.e. improving possibilities for species to move among habitat patches by designing movement corridors and stepping stones.

Indicators and umbrella species are useful tools in conservation planning, but only if data concerning their distribution are relatively easy and inexpensive to collect. All examples we discussed above clearly indicate that an integrated planning procedure where alternative and potentially conflicting objectives are simultaneously taken into account provides solutions that are closest to optimum. Moreover, a dynamic planning procedure – taking the development of habitats over time into consideration – will likely result in a more efficient outcome than a static approach.

ACKNOWLEDGEMENTS

We are grateful to the Ministry of Agriculture and Forestry and to the Ministry of Environment for financial support, as well as to B. G. Jonsson, T. Lämås, D. Ludwig, and M.-A. Villard for fruitful comments on an earlier version of this chapter.

References

Andelman, S. J. and W. F. Fagan. 2000. Umbrellas and flagships: efficient conservation surrogates or expensive mistakes? *Proceedings of the National Academy of Sciences of the United States of America* **97**:5954–9.

Ando, A., J. Camm, S. Polasky and A. Solow. 1998. Species distributions, land values, and efficient conservation. *Science* **279**:2126–8.

Angelstam, P. 1992. Conservation of communities – the importance of edges, surroundings and landscape mosaic structure. Pp. 9–70 in L. Hansson (ed.) *Ecological Principles of Nature Conservation: Applications in Temperate and Boreal Environments*. Boston, MA: Kluwer Academic Publishing.

Angelstam, P. and L. Andersson. 2001. Estimates of the needs for forest reserves in Sweden. *Scandinavian Journal of Forest Research*, Supplement No. **3**:38–51.

Arthur, J. L., J. D. Camm, R. G. Haight, C. A. Montgomery and S. Polasky. 2004. Weighing conservation objectives: maximum expected coverage versus endangered species protection. *Ecological Applications* **14**:1936–45.

Balmford, A., K. J. Gaston, A. S. L. Rodriques and A. James. 2000. Integrating costs of conservation into international priority setting. *Conservation Biology* **14**:597–605.

Cabeza, M. and A. Moilanen. 2001. Design of reserve networks and the persistence of biodiversity. *Trends in Ecology and Evolution* **16**:242–8.

Calkin, D. E., C. A. Montgomery, N. H. Schumaker *et al.* 2002. Developing a production possibility set of wildlife species persistence and timber harvest value. *Canadian Journal of Forest Research* **32**:1329–42.

Caro, T. M. and G. O'Doherty. 1999. On the use of surrogate species in conservation biology. *Conservation Biology* **13**:805–14.

Church, R. L., D. M. Stoms and F. W. Davis. 1996. Reserve selection as a maximal covering location problem. *Biological Conservation* 76:105–12.

Costanza, R. 1996. Ecological economics: reintegrating the study of humans and nature. *Ecological Applications* 6:978–90.

Costanza, R., R. d'Arge, R. de Groot *et al.* 1997. The value of the world's ecosystem services and natural capital. *Nature* 387:253–60.

Currie, D. J. 1991. Energy and large-scale patterns of animal-species and plant-species richness. *American Naturalist* 137:27–49.

Csuti, B., S. Polasky, P. Williams *et al.* 1997. A comparison of reserve selection algorithms using data on terrestrial vertebrates in Oregon. *Biological Conservation* 80:83–97.

Haight, R. G., C. Revelle and S. Snyder. 2000. An integer optimization approach to a probabilistic reserve site selection problem. *Operations Research* 48:697–708.

Haight, R. G., B. Cypher, P. A. Kelly *et al.* 2002. Optimizing habitat protection using demographic models of population viability. *Conservation Biology* 16:1–13.

Hanski, I. 2000. Extinction debt and species credit in boreal forests: modelling the consequences of different approaches to biodiversity conservation. *Annales Zoologici Fennici* 37:271–80.

Hanski, I. 2005. *The Shrinking World: Ecological Consequences of Habitat Loss.* Excellence in Ecology, Vol. 14. Oldendorf/Luhe, Germany: International Ecology Institute.

Hanski, I. K., P. Stevens, P. Ihalempiä and V. Selonen. 2000. Home range size, movements and nest site use in the Siberian flying squirrel *Pteromys volans. Journal of Mammalogy* 81:798–809.

Hawkins, B. A., R. Field, H. V. Cornell *et al.* 2003. Energy, water, and broad-scale geographic patterns of species richness. *Ecology* 84:3105–17.

Heikkinen, R., P. Punttila, R. Virkkala and A. Rajasärkkä. 2000. The significance of protected area network for forest-dwelling species: vascular plants of herb-rich forests, beetles dependent on dead wood, birds of coniferous and mixed forests. *The Finnish Environment* 440.

Hubbell, S. P. 2001. *The Unified Neutral Theory of Biodiversity and Biogeography.* Princeton, NJ: Princeton University Press.

Hurme, E., M. Mönkkönen, A. Nikula *et al.* 2005. Building and evaluating predictive occupancy models for the Siberian flying squirrel using forest planning data. *Forest Ecology and Management* 216:241–56.

Hurme, E., P. Reunanen, M. Mönkkönen *et al.* 2007a. Local habitat patch pattern of the Siberian flying squirrel in a managed boreal forest landscape. *Ecography* 30:277–87.

Hurme, E., M. Kurttila, M. Mönkkönen, T. Heinonen and T. Pukkala. 2007b. Maintenance of flying squirrel habitat and timber harvest: a site-specific spatial model in forest planning calculations *Landscape Ecology* 22:243–56.

Hurme, E., M. Mönkkönen, A.-L. Sippola, H. Ylinen and M. Pentinsaari. 2008. The role of the Siberian flying squirrel as an umbrella species for biodiversity in northern boreal forests. *Ecological Indicators* 8:246–55.

Juutinen, A. 2005. Biodiversity conservation in forestry: essays on the economics of site selection. *Acta Universitatis Ouluensis* G18.

Juutinen, A. and M. Mönkkönen. 2004. Testing alternative indicators for biodiversity conservation in old-growth boreal forests: ecology and economics. *Ecological Economics* 50:35–48.

Juutinen, A. and M. Mönkkönen. 2007. Alternative targets and economic efficiency of selecting protected areas for biodiversity conservation in boreal forest. *Environmental and Resource Economics* 37:713–32.

Juutinen, A., E. Mäntymaa, M. Mönkkönen, J. Salmi and L. Svento. 2004. Cost-effective preservation of boreal old forest. *Forest Science* 50:527–39.

Juutinen, A., M. Mönkkönen and A.-L. Sippola. 2006. Cost-efficiency of decaying wood as a surrogate for overall species richness in boreal forests. *Conservation Biology* 20:74–84.

Karvonen, L. 2000. *Guidelines for Landscape Ecological Planning*. Forestry Publications of Metsähallitus.

Koskela, E. and M. Ollikainen. 2001. Optimal private and public harvesting under spatial and temporal interdependence. *Forest Science* 47:484–96.

Manne, L. L., T. M. Brooks and S. L. Pimm. 1999. Relative risk of extinction of passerine birds on continents and islands. *Nature* 399:258–61.

Margules, C. R. and R. L. Pressey. 2000. Systematic conservation planning. *Nature* 405:243–53.

Mas-Colell, A., M. D. Whinston and J. R. Green. 1995. *Microeconomic Theory*. New York, NY: Oxford University Press.

Mönkkönen, M., P. Reunanen, A. Nikula, J. Forsman and J. Inkeröinen. 1997. Landscape characteristics associated with the occurrence of the flying squirrel *Pteromys volans* L. in old-growth forests of northern Finland. *Ecography* 20:634–42.

Mönkkönen, M., J. T. Forsman and F. Bokma. 2006. Energy availability, abundance, energy-use and species-richness in forest bird communities: a test of the species-energy theory. *Global Ecology and Biogeography* 15:290–302.

Montgomery, C., R. Pollak, K. Freemark and D. White. 1999. Pricing biodiversity. *Journal of Environmental and Economic Management* 38:1–19.

Mrosek, T. 2001. Developing and testing of a method for the analysis and assessment of multiple forest use from a forest conservation perspective. *Forest Ecology and Management* 140:65–74.

Nalle, D., C. Montgomery, J. Arthur, S. Polasky and N. Schumaker. 2004. Modelling joint production of wildlife and timber. *Journal of Environmental Economics and Management* 48:997–1017.

Nilsson, C. and F. Götmark. 1992. Protected areas in Sweden: is natural variety adequately represented. *Conservation Biology* 6:232–42.

Pimm, S. L. and R. A. Askins. 1995. Forest losses predict bird extinctions in eastern North America. *Proceedings of the National Academy of Sciences of the United States of America* 92:9343–7.

Polasky, S., J. Camm and B. Garber-Yonts. 2001. Selecting biological reserves cost-effectively: an application to terrestrial vertebrate conservation in Oregon. *Land Economics* 77:68–78.

Pressey, R. L. 1994. Ad hoc reservations: forward or backward steps in developing representative reserve systems? *Conservation Biology* 8:662–8.

Pressey, R. L., C. J. Humphries, C. R. Margules, R. I. Vane-Wright and P. H. Williams. 1993. Beyond opportunism: key principles for systematic reserve selection. *Trends in Ecology and Evolution* **8**:124–8.

Rassi, P., A. Alanen, T. Kanerva and I. Mannerkoski (eds.) 2001. *Suomen Lajien Uhanalaisuus 2000*. Helsinki: Ympäristöministeriö & Suomen ympäristökeskus. (In Finnish with an English summary.)

Reunanen, P., M. Mönkkönen and A. Nikula. 2000. Managing boreal forest landscape for flying squirrels. *Conservation Biology* **14**:218–26.

Roberge, J.-M. and P. Angelstam. 2004. Usefulness of umbrella species concept as a conservation tool. *Conservation Biology* **18**:76–85.

Roberge, J.-M. and P. Angelstam. 2006. Indicator species among resident forest birds – a cross-regional evaluation in northern Europe. *Biological Conservation* **130**:134–47.

Rodrigues, A. S., K. J. Gaston and R. D. Gregory. 2000. Using presence-absence data to establish reserve selection procedures that are robust to temporal species turnover. *Proceedings of the Royal Society of London* B**267**:897–902.

Rosenzweig, M. L. 1995. *Species Diversity in Space and Time*. Cambridge, UK: Cambridge University Press.

Saetersdal, M., I. Gjerde, H. H. Blom *et al.* 2003. Vascular plants as a surrogate species group in complementarity site selection for bryophytes, macrolichens, spiders, carabids, staphylinids, snails, and wood living polypore fungi in a northern forest. *Biological Conservation* **115**:21–31.

Selonen, V. and I. K. Hanski. 2003. Movements of the flying squirrel *Pteromys volans* in corridors and in matrix habitat. *Ecography* **26**:641–51.

Siitonen, J. 2001. Forest management, coarse woody debris, and saproxylic organisms: Fennoscandian boreal forests as an example. *Ecological Bulletins* **49**:11–41.

Similä, M., J. Kouki, M. Mönkkönen, A.-L. Sippola and E. Huhta. 2006. Covariation and indicators of species diversity: can richness of forest-dwelling species be predicted in northern boreal forests? *Ecological Indicators* **6**:686–700.

Stokland, J. N. 1997 Representativeness and efficiency of bird and insect conservation in Norwegian boreal forest reserves. *Conservation Biology* **11**:101–11.

Virkkala, R. 1996. Reserve network of forests in Finland and the need for developing the network – an ecological approach. *The Finnish Environment* **16**.

Wilson, E. O. 1992. *The Diversity of Life*. New York, NY: W.W. Norton.

Setting, implementing, and monitoring targets as a basis for adaptive management: a Canadian forestry case study

ELSTON DZUS, BRIGITTE GROVER, SIMON DYER,
DAVE CHEYNE, DON POPE, AND JIM SCHIECK

INTRODUCTION

Forest management has seen a gradual transition from focusing on few to focusing on multiple values. Early forestry operations focused on production of timber. As the need for sustainability of the timber resource became apparent, foresters began developing production and regrowth strategies that focused on perpetuating the fiber source. This approach of harvest and regeneration, with a focus on trees, became known as sustained yield forestry. Throughout the latter half of the twentieth century there emerged a growing societal demand that forests provide not only fiber, but also ecological and social values. So began the transition from sustained yield forestry (with a focus primarily on economics) to sustainable forest management (with a focus on economic, ecological, and social values). Embedded within this transition from sustained yield to sustainable forest management was the concept of adaptive management.

Adaptive management is a "formal process for continually improving management policies and practices by learning from their outcomes" (Taylor *et al.* 1997). Many companies and government agencies utilize some form of adaptive management in their decision-making process. Passive adaptive management or "trial and error" approaches are the most

Setting Conservation Targets for Managed Forest Landscapes, ed. M.-A. Villard and
B. G. Jonsson. Published by Cambridge University Press.
© Cambridge University Press 2009.

Box 17.1 Key attributes of adaptive management

1. Decision-makers, scientists, and others work together and seek to enhance the understanding of the system that they manage.
2. Identification of:

  - **Indicators** (i.e. quantitative measures of the state or dynamics of the system that are relevant in the analysis of tradeoffs among management alternatives; for example, diversity of forest birds; cubic meters of hardwood; hectares of forest in different age classes);
  - **Actions** (management activities or policies that will affect the system; for example, type, location, and amount of roads; size, distribution, and type of timber harvest areas); and
  - **Ecological processes** that link actions to changes in the indicators.

3. Explicit predictions of outcomes of potential management actions (e.g. different target levels) on a suite of indicators, using simulation models or other projection tools. Exploration of tradeoffs among alternative approaches.
4. Identification of key uncertainties and knowledge gaps. These are prioritized based on how reducing these uncertainties will help in the tradeoff analysis. For example: if we knew X, would it help us to choose between management alternatives A and B?
5. Management experiments implemented at an operational scale, designed to test hypotheses or qualitative relationships between management actions (e.g. different target levels) and changes in indicators.
6. Monitoring of indicators.
7. Evaluation of observed and predicted changes, diagnosis of reasons for differences, and assessment of whether newly acquired knowledge justifies modification of the management plan. The adaptive management process is a continuous improvement process with feedback mechanisms that enable testing of the newly implemented management actions.

---

commonly used forms of adaptive management. A more strategic and defensible approach exists in the form of "active adaptive management" (Walters and Holling 1990; Taylor *et al.* 1997).

The term *adaptive management* describes an interactive process designed to improve the rate of learning about the management of complex systems (see Box 17.1). The process incorporates an explicit acknowledgement of uncertainties and knowledge gaps about the response of a system to management actions. Reducing these uncertainties (i.e. learning) becomes one management objective exercised by evaluating alternatives (e.g. different management approaches or different target levels within a management approach).

In a more abbreviated definition, active adaptive management is a systematic process of modeling, experimentation, and monitoring to compare the outcomes of alternate management actions. Relative to "trial and error" approaches, active adaptive management is more efficient as it tests alternative practices simultaneously in management experiments as opposed to sequentially. The rigor involved in the modeling and experimentation of alternative actions also makes decisions based on active adaptive management more defensible. Active adaptive management is thus a risk management strategy involving continual evaluation of the consequences of our forest management practices and other land-use practices on biota and ecological processes. The outcome of adaptive management is either a confirmation of existing practices or recommendations for implementation of alternative practices.

A commitment to monitor the outcome of management practices is a requirement of active adaptive management. Revision of practices is undertaken as new information becomes available. Communication between managers, scientists, government representatives, and stakeholders is as important to the active adaptive management process as analysis. Flexibility within the process is critical, and flexibility within policy and planning is essential to allow rapid implementation of new practices. Adaptive management can occur regardless of the type of forest tenure.

A unique opportunity to implement sustainable forest management with a new operation arose in north-eastern Alberta, Canada, in 1991 with the granting of a Forest Management Agreement (FMA)[1] to Alberta-Pacific Forest Industries Inc. (Al-Pac; Hebert et al. 2003). The FMA granted Al-Pac an area-based tenure right to the deciduous timber within the Al-Pac FMA area (Fig. 17.1). Allocation of conifer trees is shared through volume-based quotas between Al-Pac and a variety of pre-existing conifer harvesting companies. Unless otherwise stated, the forest management approaches described in this chapter are those of Al-Pac. Although softwood (e.g. pine and spruce) timber harvesting had been occurring in Alberta for many decades, deciduous trees (primarily trembling aspen (*Populus tremuloides*)

---

[1] A forest management agreement in Alberta is a tenure agreement between the provincial Government of Alberta (who manages the publicly owned forests on behalf of the citizens of Alberta) and a private company in which the province grants the company specific rights (and obligations) to access timber.

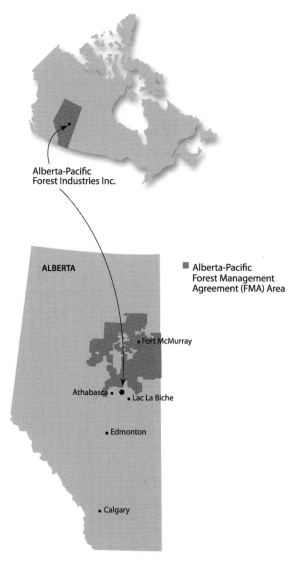

Figure 17.1. The 56,000 km² forest management area of Alberta-Pacific Forest Industries Inc. in north-eastern Alberta, Canada.

and balsam poplar (*P. balsamifera*) were previously viewed as undesirable "weeds" (see Box 17.2 for a description of the natural features of the Al-Pac area). Changes in paper markets and timber allocations allowed deciduous trees to be the primary fiber source for the Al-Pac pulp mill.

Box 17.2 Natural features of the Al-Pac area of north-eastern Alberta

The Al-Pac FMA area covers about 6,900,000 ha (approx. 5.6 million hectares net area) in north-eastern Alberta, Canada (see Fig. 17.1). Most (98%) of the Al-Pac FMA area lies within the Boreal Forest Natural Region. The FMA area is characterized by a continental boreal climate where winters are typically long and cold (mean winter temperature of −10.5 °C) and summers are short and cool (mean summer temperature of 13.8 °C). Approximately 36% of the FMA area is considered merchantable landbase (i.e. with trees suitable for harvest now or in the future). The remainder consists of non-merchantable lands, such as wetlands (including bogs, fens, swamps, and marshes), and protected areas.

Soil type, hydrology, and wildfire have played an important role in determining the vegetative cover within the sub-region. Mesic upland sites are typically vegetated by trembling aspen and balsam poplar stands interspersed and/or mixed with pockets of white spruce (*Picea glauca*). White spruce and balsam fir (*Abies balasmifera*) are the climax species; however, balsam fir is not well represented because fires restart the succession process at frequent intervals. Subxeric sites are often dominated by aspen stands. Xeric sites are represented by various densities of jack pine (*Pinus banksiana*), sometimes with a minor component of aspen. Extensive wet lowland areas are dominated by black spruce (*Picea mariana*) and larch (*Larix laricina*). Widespread fires in the early 1900s have resulted in large expanses of mature even-aged stands. Large fires continue to occur despite intensive fire suppression efforts in the past few decades (e.g. a 250,000 ha fire in 2002).

Corporate leaders were thus provided with an opportunity to implement sustainable forest management at multiple spatial and temporal scales in an area of the world relatively untouched by previous forest management activities (i.e. conifer quota holders operated <50 years).

At about the same time, the US Forest Service was exploring natural disturbance dynamics as a concept for forest management in the National Forests of the United States (Franklin 1989; Bourgeron and Jensen 1993). The primary agent of natural change in Canada's boreal forest is wildfire and subsequent forest succession. As most of Canada's forests have a relatively short history of large-scale commercial forestry (<50–100 years), under-standing natural patterns and processes in the forest provide a reasonable guide or template upon which to plan forest management activities. The need for a sound ecologically based forest management program allowed the integration of boreal forest fire dynamics with a program of "ecosystem-based management" (Kessler *et al.* 1992; Grumbine 1994). Indeed, it was believed the natural features and natural disturbance regime (primarily wildfire) of north-eastern Alberta were suitable for management according to a disturbance-approximation model. Central tenants of the natural disturbance model are the assumptions that if biodiversity has evolved with natural disturbance, and if management patterns can approximate those of nature, then biodiversity should be able to be maintained by using an ecosystem-based management approach (e.g. Perera *et al.* 2004). The primary contrasting forest management approach in Canada and the USA at the time was a sustained yield paradigm with constraints associated with a few selected wildlife species (e.g. charismatic megafauna such as moose, *Alces alces*) of social importance to local people. Thus a paradigm shift began with the first operational implementation of industrial forest ecosystem management in north-eastern Alberta in which the use of conservation targets and adaptive management are embedded in the management philosophy.

MANAGEMENT FRAMEWORKS

A number of concepts provide a framework for Al-Pac's management philosophy: *ecosystem-based management, TRIAD,* and *integrated landscape management.*

Ecosystem-based management (EBM) has been given a variety of definitions (see Quinn 2002). A working definition relevant to this book's theme of conservation targets is as follows: "management driven by objectives and made adaptable by monitoring and research based on our best understanding of the ecological interactions and processes necessary to sustain ecosystem composition, structure and function" (Christensen *et al.* 1996).

To implement forestry operations based on ecosystem management, we apply management practices at ecologically appropriate scales, hierarchically nested from stands to landscapes. An emphasis on research and monitoring, and, more importantly, the application of new knowledge in an effort to continuously improve, are required components of adaptive management.

A central tenet of EBM is sustainability (Quinn 2002). However, the dynamic nature of the boreal forest makes it rather challenging to define sustainability. Every aspect of wildfire and its concomitant effects on forest landscapes is variable, be it fire size, intensity, or frequency of recurrence (Johnson 1992). To apply EBM principles thus requires an understanding and application of the natural range of variation (NRV) in various ecological parameters (Forman and Godron 1986; Franklin 1993). We will outline below how NRV has been used in our planning and harvesting practices in terms of retention of live standing residual trees within harvest areas,

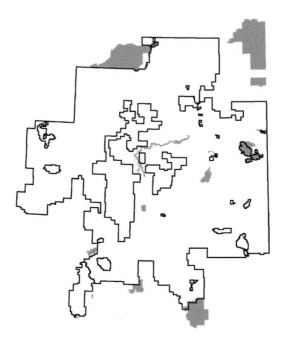

Figure 17.2. Protected areas (shown in dark gray) in and near the Al-Pac Forest Management Agreement area as of 2007.

establishing targets for sizes of harvest planning units, and determining the amount of old forest to be maintained at a landscape level.

Al-Pac has adopted a three-pronged approach to sustainable forest management known as the "**TRIAD**" (see Chapter 14, this volume). In this approach, there are three main categories: protected areas, multiple-use areas for sustainable forest management, and intensive management for timber production (e.g. Odum 1969; Hunter and Calhoun 1996; Seymour and Hunter 1992). Within the multiple-use area, the objective is to have a long-term economical supply of timber while maintaining biodiversity (landscape patterns and biota). The multiple-use area makes up the vast majority of Al-Pac's FMA area. In ecological benchmarks and other protected areas the primary goal is conservation or recreation, with ideally no industrial activity. Government-designated protected areas currently represent about 400,000 ha in and near the Al-Pac FMA area (Fig. 17.2). To offset the reduced commercial utilization of productive[2] forest land due to

---

[2] In Alberta from a *forestry* perspective the landbase is divided into "productive" and non-productive lands; areas capable of producing merchantable-sized trees are considered to be on "productive" land.

protected area commitments and multiple-use management, Al-Pac's current intensive arm of the TRIAD exists completely off the FMA area and relies on agro forestry to grow hybrid poplar on private lands owned or leased by the company. There is a wide range of management intensities possible under the TRIAD approach and there is no requirement that each management category be equally allocated across the management area.

Most of the natural resources in Canada are located on publicly owned land; access to these resources (timber, oil, natural gas, diamonds, gravel, etc.) is typically managed by the provincial government. The Alberta government distributes these resource rights to various companies and often there is overlapping tenure on a common landbase. Alberta is underlain with a multitude of deposits of oil and gas, including the world's largest deposits of oil sands (Schneider 2002). As a result, managing cumulative effects is another concept of direct relevance to forest management on the Al-Pac FMA area. Al-Pac has participated in an *Integrated Landscape Management* (ILM) program with other resource companies and the Government of Alberta to manage the amount, distribution, and duration of industrial "footprint" on the FMA area (Alberta Chamber of Resources 2005a,b).

In this chapter we discuss how Al-Pac has implemented ecosystem-based management following a natural disturbance model through the setting of conservation targets at both the stand and the landscape scale. Practices and management targets have been refined as research and monitoring provided further guidance for implementing the natural disturbance model in Canada's boreal forest. A section focuses on defining the multitude of resource activities that are ongoing in north-eastern Alberta and how management targets are being used in an ILM framework. Finally, we introduce a provincial biodiversity monitoring program that has been developed in Alberta to assist resource managers in an assessment of the effects of land-use change (both natural and anthropogenic) on biodiversity in meaningful space and time.

ECOSYSTEM-BASED MANAGEMENT: STAND-LEVEL TARGETS

Wildfire affects forest structure and biodiversity at the landscape scale as well as at the scale of forest stands. As a wildfire burns across a landscape it often does so in a non-continuous manner owing to changes such as flammability of different forest types, influences of water bodies, or changes in weather conditions. Fire skips will retain live individual trees, patches, or large unburned areas (referred to as residuals or as residual structure). Research has examined the amount of residual trees found within fires and the associated ecological benefits of the structure created by live and dead residual trees as well as snags and downed woody logs that they generate (e.g. Song 2002). Boreal ecosystems have evolved with wildfire and the associated live tree patch remnants remaining within the burnt landscape (Smyth et al. 2005). Similarly, retained residual patches in cutblocks[3] play a variety of temporal and spatial roles for biodiversity (Franklin et al. 1997). Residuals (patches of live trees, as well as scattered live and dead trees) in the cutblock may produce structural conditions that are more similar to those created by forest fires than to those resulting from traditional clearcut harvesting, especially as the forest regenerates. Residuals also positively affect microsite conditions to help establish the new vegetative community on cutovers. Residual patches may also act as stepping stones for dispersal or as "lifeboats" that permit fuller use of the disturbed area and more rapid recolonization of its interior by species characteristic of later successional stages.

Research exploring whether the structure provided by live residual trees creates older forest characteristics within young and mature regenerating stands indicated that biota associated with old forests benefit from residual structure (Hansen et al. 1991; Niemelä 1999; Merrill et al. 1998; Bradbury 2002a,b; Fisher and Wilkinson 2002; Schieck and Song 2002). Research focused on songbird communities indicated that partially harvested stands had bird communities more similar to old forest than did clearcut stands (Westworth and Telfer 1993; Norton and Hannon 1997; Steventon et al. 1998; Schieck et al. 2000a,b; Schieck and Song 2006). That association was also true for arthropods (Schowalter 1995), small mammals (Steventon et al. 1998), and some lichen groups (Peck and McCune 1997). Thus, residuals (post-wildfire and post-harvest) can serve as refuges for some biota, but just as importantly, they are hypothesized to introduce structural diversity into stands throughout succession, thus facilitating more rapid biotic convergence between harvested and fire-origin stands (Schieck and Hobson 2000).

In the past decade, an increasing number of studies have examined the amount and pattern of unburned residuals. Scientific guidance with regards to matching post-harvest structure to post-wildfire structure has focused on amount, composition, and distribution of residual trees and patches. The mean amount of residual material in boreal forest wildfires varies from 1.9% (Eberhart and Woodard 1987) to as much as 30% (Smyth et al. 2005). Bergeron et al. (2002) reviewed existing studies in the boreal

---

[3] The terms cutblock and harvest area will be used interchangeably in this chapter.

forest and found that undisturbed residual patches represented 3%–5% of the disturbed area. However, they found areas of lower tree mortality (lightly burned areas) composed up to 50% of the burn area and argued that the total amount of residual should be corrected to include these areas, resulting in a range of residuals from 15% to 20% of total burned area. In aspen-dominated forests, Smyth (1999) found that an average of 5.8% of fires were live residuals, with a range of 0.5%–16%. The considerable amount of variation may be attributed both to differences in study methods as well as differences in tree species and fire intensity across the boreal forest.

The three studies conducted in Alberta's boreal forest (Eberhart and Woodard 1987; Smyth 1999; Smyth et al. 2005) reported that the amount of residuals increased with the size of the wildfire. In general, wildfires <200 ha had less than 1% residuals whereas those larger than 2,000 ha had >5% unburned residuals. Smyth et al. (2005) examined 168 aspen stands from eight wildfires in the most intensive stand-level description of amount and pattern of live residual trees present post-fire to date.[4] They found the area of aspen stands affected not only the total amount of live residual material, but also the size of the residual patches. They reported that, with increased size of pre-fire aspen stands, the percent of area occupied by the residual patches as well as the proportion of larger residual patches increased.

Patch size distribution of wildfire residuals can range from single isolated trees to large patches several hectares in size. In general, the frequency distribution of residual size follows a negative exponential distribution (Eberhart 1986; Smyth 1999; Smyth et al. 2005). The most frequent residuals were smaller, ranging from 0.1 to 1 ha, but most of the area of residuals is found in larger patches ranging from 1 to 5 ha (Ontario Ministry of Natural Resources 2001; Smyth and Lee 2001). According to the data collected by Smyth et al. (2005) patch size of green residuals should increase as the pre-burn stand size increases.

In order to translate the patch distribution of fire residuals to harvest residuals, variability is key. Lee and Boutin (2008) suggest a two-pronged approach: stand-level retention and landscape-level retention to approximate the frequency distribution of patch sizes in fires while maintaining the total retention area appropriate to the size of fires. Residual patches of live trees within large wildfires (>50,000 ha) appear to plateau at 10.8%

[4] Al-Pac is collaborating on a study led by Dr David Andison to define residual patterns further following wildfire in northern Alberta (project completion in 2009).

of the total fire size (Eberhart and Woodard 1987; Smyth 1999). Lee and Boutin (2008) produced a curve estimating the translation of percent of retention from fires to harvest areas. They suggested that retention increase from 5.6% to 10.8% for harvest planning units[5] varying from 5,000 to more than 50,000 hectares. Lee and Boutin (2008) also recommend that, to translate fire residual pattern to harvest, patches under 5 ha in size be incorporated within cutblocks and patches over 5 ha in size be whole stands, planned at the landscape scale.

Size of patches and time since disturbance appear to be important in determining the response of biotic communities. The literature suggests that, in general, large, intact residual patches maintain more old-seral species than do smaller patches (Schieck et al. 2000a,b; Schieck and Song 2006). Large patches of residual trees were found to have bird communities that were more similar to communities in mature forest than were those in small residual patches (Schieck and Hobson 2000). Nelson and Halpern (2005) found that residual patches larger than 1 ha were required to prevent loss or declines in the presence of mosses and liverworts. Norton and Hannon (1997) reported that, immediately post-harvest, patches with residual values of 30%–40% retained significantly more old-seral species than did 8% residual. In another short-term post-harvest study, Steventon et al. (1998) suggested that bird communities were more similar to those of old-seral stages when 60% was retained, compared with 30%. It was unclear from these studies whether the degree of similarity to old growth was sufficient to be of long-term conservation value. In a retrospective study to evaluate long-term avian responses following fire vs. harvest, Schieck and Hobson (2000) found that bird communities continued to converge over time and that, by 60 years post-harvest, bird communities were very similar to those 60 years post-fire. Such convergence supports EBM approaches under the natural disturbance model.

Fire, or the absence of it, can dramatically affect forest composition, which includes the relative proportion of tree species or stand types and their respective age classes (see, for example, Carleton and MacLellan 1994; Cumming et al. 2000; Cumming 2001). As fires are recurring, overlapping disturbances retain residuals that will vary widely in composition and age.

---

[5] Planning unit is a forestry term describing a largely contiguous area of forest that will be planned for harvest within a defined (<15 year) period of time; in north-eastern Alberta there may be a considerable amount of non-merchantable forest interspersed with merchantable forest within a planning unit owing to the heterogeneous nature of the natural forest.

In contrast, harvest residuals are primarily derived from merchantable[6] -aged stands; as such, approximating the age structure following wildfire through harvest is problematic. Leaving patches of young forest (e.g. < 10 yr since fire) is redundant as it is too similar in structure to the recently logged stand to provide significant landscape heterogeneity or habitat to maintain biodiversity (Lee 2002). Some rotation ages may be extended to maintain older age classes on the landscape. Bergeron *et al.* (2002) suggested relying on structure within residuals to serve as surrogates for old-seral stages. Currently, it is unclear how much retention is required to compensate for the shortened rotation times (Lee *et al.* 1999; Song 2002).

While the processes of wildfire (thermo-chemical) and harvest (primarily mechanical) are different, the intent of a NDM approach to forest management is to approximate at the stand and landscape level the patterns left by fire. Decisions regarding the amount of live residual trees to retain within harvested areas are an ecological/economic tradeoff guided by amounts of live residual retained following wildfire. In addition to the amount of structure to be retained following a NDM approach, forest managers must make decisions regarding the age of trees to be retained as structure. Lee and Boutin (2008) suggest that in order to balance the economic constraints of timber harvest and the desire to retain heterogeneity on the landscape, within-block residual retention should reflect the age of the merchantable timber, and whole-stand retention should be separated by at least 25 years of age and left unharvested until the next rotation. Their rationale is that, immediately after harvest, all small retention patches within cutblocks would be mature or older seral stages since these are representative of harvest stands. Larger patches and whole-stand retention outside of cutblocks would be younger but develop old-seral characteristics earlier than the regenerating harvested areas.

IMPLEMENTATION AND MONITORING: APPROXIMATING NATURAL DISTURBANCE PATTERNS AT THE STAND LEVEL THROUGH RESIDUAL STRUCTURE RETENTION

Al-Pac implemented the concept of residual stand structure retention when operations commenced in 1992. Then, the protocol was to leave 1% of the merchantable volume or eight live trees per hectare scattered throughout the cutblock. As more research provided data on amount of live trees

---

[6] Merchantable (or merchantability) refers to the age (and size) of forested stands at which they are considered large enough for harvest.

after wildfire, the protocol was changed in 1995 to retain on average 5% live merchantable deciduous and 1% live merchantable conifer trees. The single-tree program remained unchanged at 1%, but an additional 4% merchantable structure was to be retained in clumps that should be the size of at least one swath of the fellerbuncher[7] (16 m in diameter). In 2006, the Forest Management Plan[8] included a new target, whereby the conifer structure on Al-Pac harvest areas was increased to 5% as well (Al-Pac 2006). Five percent retention within the harvest area boundary represents an ecological/economic tradeoff for retention at the stand level. Additional live (and dead) tree retention exists on the landscape in riparian buffers, steep slopes, and non-merchantable areas, so the total structural retention at the landscape level is significantly greater than 5%.

The intent was to leave 5% merchantable live trees (by volume) on average within harvest area boundaries but to be highly variable between blocks. To achieve this goal, the residual retention pattern was to be left to the fellerbuncher operators, who attend periodic training workshops to learn how to approximate the amount of 5% residual retention (Al-Pac 2000a). Although some operational logistics dictate where to leave structure, i.e. in-block and towards the cutblock boundary, not in decking areas,[9] there are still many variables to consider. The operators are encouraged to "think like fire" and approximate wildfire retention patterns, e.g. leave residuals in wet areas or draws, on north-facing or steep slopes, or totally randomly in the absence of block features. Wildlife areas, such as dens or mineral licks, are also to be protected with structure when identified prior to harvest. As with fire, the goal of operational structural retention is variability among and within harvested areas in the amount and distribution of live (and dead) residual trees.

Considerations also have to be given to the tree species and conformation to leave. Conifer trees, especially those existing below the forest canopy (referred to as understory trees), are to be left in clumps and/or windfirmed with deciduous trees to protect the shallow-rooted conifer trees from being blown down by strong winds. Trees with large or unusual crowns that are hard to handle by the mechanical delimbing process, and

---

[7] A fellerbuncher is a mechanized tree harvesting machine.

[8] In Alberta a Forest Management Plan is a document outlining forest management strategies and annual allowable cut (harvest) projections. It is typically developed by a forestry company (or companies) and approved by Alberta government officials responsible for forest management of forestry activities on publicly owned forest lands.

[9] A decking area is an area adjacent to a road in which harvested trees are piled following harvest; decking areas are typically within the cutblock and are temporary in nature, existing only until the logs are hauled to the mill.

trees containing large stick nests (e.g. those of raptors) are obvious choices for retention. Since a burn contains mostly dead trees, which are important to some species such as woodpeckers and other cavity-nesting birds, retaining existing dead trees (snags) in the cutblock will narrow the gap between cutblock and burn features. Operators are also encouraged to avoid disturbance of non-merchantable trees, such as immature understory or non-merchantable species.

A monitoring program has been implemented to capture the extent of merchantable residual structure remaining within the harvested areas. The area of merchantable residual clumps (>5 trees >15 m tall) is assessed by using 1:30,000 cutblock update photography (photographs are taken within two years of completion of harvest). The goal is to interpret aerial photography for at least 50% of Al-Pac's harvested areas annually. Up to 10 percent of the photo-assessed blocks will be ground surveyed to verify aerial photo evaluations. The single-tree program will be assessed in "ground survey" blocks only, as the remote assessment methodology was not suitable for single trees. Clumps of non-merchantable trees (5–15 m in height) will be quantified in half of the field survey blocks (which equals approximately 5% of total blocks).

Stand structure monitoring results will be reported annually by forest management unit (FMU[10]) since the annual allowable cut is calculated on an FMU basis. This will permit variation between cutblocks and even between planning units. For example, utilizing the 2003 and 2004 harvest area update photography, merchantable stand structure clumps (i.e. residuals) were measured in 56 harvest areas (1,802 ha) dispersed over seven FMUs. Retained stand structure ranged from 0.1% to 12.3% of the area, with an average of 3.8%. Single tree retention ranged from 0.4% to 2.3% of the volume with an area weighted average of 1.3%. Total stand structure thus met the intended target with an average of 5.1% merchantable residual being retained.

ECOSYSTEM-BASED MANAGEMENT: LANDSCAPE-LEVEL TARGETS

Currently, at large spatial scales, ecological factors do not figure prominently in forest management across Canada. Elkie and Rempel (2001) compared

---

[10] A forest management unit is the intermediate scale of landscape for forest management between the forest management agreement area and the planning unit. The Al-Pac Forest Management Agreement area is divided into 11 Forest Management Units that range in size from 120,000 to 1.5 million ha.

north-western Ontario (relatively little harvest or fire suppression) with north-eastern Ontario (long history of harvesting and fire suppression). When examining the scale of landscape patterns, they found the unharvested landscape with fire tended to create residual patches within a complex nested hierarchy of spatial scales, whereas the harvested landscape with fire suppression featured disturbances at a single spatial scale. Similarly, Johnson *et al.* (1998) argued the spatial scale of current cutblock management in the boreal forests of western Canada does not coincide with the mosaic of stand ages and sizes created by fire. The common practice of focusing on residual structure within cutblocks as part of a dispersed (multi-pass[11]) harvest pattern produces landscape structure that is rectilinear in shape and does not approximate wildfire-based landscape patterns.

Although dispersed multi-pass (often two-pass) harvest systems have some economic, social, and aesthetic benefits, they also have a number of ecological consequences (Spies *et al.* 1994; Wallin *et al.* 1994; Cissel *et al.* 1999). A traditional two-pass dispersed harvesting system removes 30%–70% of merchantable timber in the first entry, and the remaining fiber in the second entry. The consequence of harvesting in a two-pass pattern is a large road network that needs to be maintained over a long time period. Such roading has increased building and maintenance costs, as well as ecological risks associated with long-term access. Dispersed cutting produces an unnatural pattern of small openings with high amounts of edge and fragmentation that is very difficult to erase in the future unless radical changes are made to patch size or rotation time (Wallin *et al.* 1994). Patterning harvest on a wildfire template requires a greater degree of aggregation of harvest areas than does a two-pass dispersed harvest system. Although an aggregated pattern has a greater local effect, it is hypothesized to minimize the long-term risks to biodiversity relative to dispersed harvesting.

To implement further the natural disturbance model and ecosystem-based management, and maintain the heterogeneity on the landscape, a portion of the historical range of wildfire sizes could be used as a target to plan areas of aggregated harvest. Based on the Alberta Land and Forest Service (2000) fire database, the size distribution of fires follows a right-skewed distribution when based on frequency. There are many small wildfires and relatively few large wildfires. Fires up to 2 ha account for

---

[11] In a multi-pass harvest system there is a systematic pattern of harvest and non-harvested merchantable forest, typically following a rectilinear or "checkerboard" pattern. The unharvested areas of merchantable forest left on the first entry or "pass" are subsequently harvested at some time in the future (e.g. 10–40 years later).

Table 17.1. *Landscape level targets for planning unit size*

Planning unit size (ha)	Frequency (%)
1,000–5,000	56
5,001–10,000	19
10,001–25,000	16
25,001–50,000	7
50,001–75,000	2

74% of fires recorded in the provincial fire database from 1961 to 1998. Although larger fires are rare, they dominate the landscape in terms of area burned. Between 1961 and 1998, 98% of the total area burned was due to 5% of the largest fires in the distribution curve. Some of the largest fires exceeded 100,000 ha. Following the guidance of Lee and Boutin (2008), forestry operations within aggregated harvest areas would proceed over a period of approximately 10 years and essentially initiate or maintain dominance of a single seral stage. Stands initiated over this period are likely to exhibit relatively few structural and biotic differences (Song 2002). Lee and Boutin (2008) emphasize that, after this period of harvest, the aggregated planning unit would be closed for harvest until the next scheduled rotation.

The template of wildfire sizes suggests that a mixed distribution of planning units would have many small units with a few intermediate and fewer large units (see example in Table 17.1). However, most of the harvestable landbase will be found within the larger units. To translate landscape-scale fire patterns to harvest planning, Lee and Boutin (2008) suggest applying restrictions on the lower and upper size limits of planning units that deviate from a wildfire template. The lower limit would be planning units of 1,000 ha to ensure that harvest areas are large enough to be economically feasible, yet are small enough to fit into the range of wildfire sizes and be useful for naturally smaller planning units, such as mesic sites surrounded by non-productive landbase. To calculate the upper limit of landscape planning units, the currently regulated annual allowable cut would be spread over a 10–15 year harvest period. For example, if the annual allowable cut would translate to 2,000 ha per year (in terms of area) then the maximum planning unit size based on a 10 year harvest period would be 20,000 ha of merchantable forest. In the boreal forests of north-eastern Alberta where the majority (>60%) of the landbase is non-merchantable wetlands (bogs and fens), this would produce a total planning unit area of about 50,000 to 60,000 ha when including non-merchantable and non-productive forest (Lee and Boutin 2008). When harvesting from planning units smaller than the maximum, companies will have to schedule and balance their supply from two or more planning units. Social factors will also contribute to setting the upper limit of planning unit size based on a natural disturbance template. As such, timber harvesting (see Table 17.1) will occupy a middle portion of the fire size distribution, with natural wildfires contributing the very small (<1,000 ha) and very large (>75,000 ha) disturbances on the landscape.

Implementation and monitoring at a landscape level: approximating natural disturbance patterns through aggregated harvest

Al-Pac's approach to landscape-level implementation of the natural disturbance model was initiated in 2005 when the company initiated an active adaptive management experiment to compare a multi-pass dispersed harvest system to an aggregated harvest pattern (single pass). In this new approach, aggregated harvest areas are concentrated within a planning unit and the harvest occurs within a limited time period (up to 15 years, depending on the size of the planning unit). Harvest is followed by a long period of absence, ideally a whole rotation length. Under the aggregated harvest scenario, cutblock size is no longer bound by a 20 ha average rule but follows the original disturbance event up to a socially imposed constraint of 500 ha for single openings. By separating individual harvest openings with forested structure (e.g. stream side buffers, wildlife corridors) forest managers can aggregate harvest areas to fall within a variety of planning unit sizes. The 2006 Forest Management Plan describes how Al-Pac implements a gradient of planning unit size classes and frequencies (Al-Pac 2006; Table 17.1). The sizes and number of planning units per size class are part of an adaptive management approach and may change over time as social and ecological conditions change. From a risk management perspective based on NDM, aggregated harvest more closely approximates patterns following wildfire. As such, the majority of our planned harvest over the next 15 years will be planned by using an aggregated harvest approach, with the remaining units planned as two-pass harvest areas for comparison.

Residual patches several hectares in size are left within the aggregated harvest areas; these larger patches are selected by the planning team and identified in the field to be avoided by fellerbuncher operators. These planned patches are left in addition to the 5% operator stand structure (see previous section) and can increase overall residual structure within a cutblock up to 10%. As the goal is to retain on average 5% "in-block" residual structure on a FMU basis, operators are encouraged to leave less structure in small blocks.

Another important residual component other than within-cutblock (or -stand) structure is landscape structure consisting of whole polygons interspersed among the cutblocks. A large component of this landscape structure is forest consisting of non-productive timber such as black spruce, larch, and shrubs. However, there is also a considerable component of productive timber maintained on the landscape, found in riparian buffers, isolated stands, and non-operable areas, as well as juvenile stands. A rigorous monitoring program has been developed to account for stand (see previous section) and landscape structure. Landscape structure will be reported by merchantability and size classes, as maintenance of large polygons and core areas within a planning unit is critical.

A complicating factor for implementing aggregated single-pass harvesting in north-eastern Alberta is the overlapping tenure of deciduous and coniferous operators. Al-Pac harvests predominantly deciduous timber on the FMA area, whereas sawmill operations harvest most of the merchantable coniferous timber. A true single-pass, aggregated harvest can only be implemented with the cooperative effort of all forestry operators. With the cooperation of coniferous operators, single-pass harvesting was implemented in one aggregated planning unit as of 2007. In an integrated planning unit, the majority of merchantable timber is scheduled for harvesting regardless of species. Ideally, harvest operations among companies would coincide to enable completion of operations in a timely fashion. The cooperative effort also has certain economic advantages such as joint planning and cutblock layout[12] as well sharing of road construction, maintenance, and reclamation. Future harvest goals have Al-Pac and coniferous operators working towards a higher level of integration where operators are harvesting based on location rather than species and exchange the timber accordingly.

Managing for retention of old forest within the natural range of variation
Old, or overmature, forest stands are an integral part of boreal forest ecosystems and exhibit unique structural attributes and ecological processes (Stelfox 1995). The key structures of old stands develop over time due to

---

[12] "Layout" refers to the process by which a forested stand is marked in the field for identification by harvesting personnel. Different colors of flagging tape are tied to trees to identify the cutblock boundary, locations for roads, and areas of planned residual structure.

the mortality of individual trees, not age *per se*, and this mortality leads to gaps in the forest canopy (Stelfox 1995). Gaps contribute to the growth of herbaceous plants and "release" of immature trees that had been growing slowly in the understory, resulting in an "older" stand actually composed of a mixture of young and old trees (Stelfox 1995). Additionally, the older stands in boreal forests gradually accumulate an abundance of standing dead trees (snags) and downed woody material. Old-forest stands may exist as small isolated islands within a recently burned landscape or as large areas of forest that have escaped disturbance for extended periods of time. The result is a high level of structural diversity at the stand and landscape scale (Stelfox 1995). The complex structure of old stands[13] provides a large variety of habitat types for use by species with specialized habitat requirements.

Given the dynamics of natural disturbance in Alberta's boreal forests, the amount and distribution of old forest on a given landscape is constantly changing. Thus, a lack of change or a stationary balance of age classes within the forest as dictated in classic "sustained yield" forest management planning would not be consistent with ecosystem-based management and the natural disturbance model adopted by Al-Pac. Management for retention of old-forest stands within a landscape may similarly incorporate shifting locations and target amounts that fall within an NRV (see below) on large landscape units. Thus, variation inherent in natural patterns should form the basis for forest management strategies for older forest retention.

A shift in forest management allowed Al-Pac to direct planning to look at less traditional forest values. This shift was paralleled by public or social pressures, first dominated by "old-growth" generalizations and simplicity, which insisted that old-forest retention was a land-use issue, rather than a landscape biodiversity situation (Kimmins 2002). Accordingly, Al-Pac's first Detailed Forest Management Plan (Al-Pac 2000b) laid out an initial strategy for older forest stand retention throughout the landscape. Alberta's former forest inventory illustrated that the average older age class area (over 120 years old) for the past 100 years was approximately 8% of the productive forested landscape. This number was then the target average for old forest in the 200-year timber supply analysis. However, the distribution of these stands was not to be managed directly. Additionally, 8% represented all types of forest stands (conifers, mixedwoods, and hardwoods) with no

---

[13] Stand: a grouping of trees with similar characteristics (such as species, age, or condition) that can be distinguished from adjacent groups. A stand is usually treated as a single unit in a management plan.

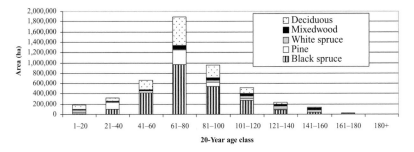

Figure 17.3. Forest age-class distribution of the Gross Forest Management Agreement Area (Al-Pac 2006).

weighting by actual hectare representation. The intent was to maintain the area of stands 120+ years old at the target percentage that has existed on the FMA over the past 100 years.

With the completion of a new forest inventory in 2001 (Al-Pac 2001) and an update in 2006 (Al-Pac 2006), Al-Pac received a clearer vision of the state of the boreal forest on the FMA area. Figure 17.3 summarizes the FMA area forest landbase by age classes from the 2006 forest inventory. The age-class distribution demonstrates that about 18% of the forest area is currently classified as old forest when summarized across forest types.

The 2006 forest inventory also highlighted that black spruce was the dominant tree species on the FMA area and that at any given time could represent most of the old-forest cohort. This situation would mean the old-forest strategy could in fact leave only black spruce stands and still achieve >120+ year target of 8% of the productive forest. It was also obvious that the entire forest landscape should contribute to ecological and social values, not just the productive forest, for the natural disturbance model deals with the entire forest community values, not just economic forest values.

Most forestry practices and timber supply models tend to sequence the harvest of older stands first. The result can be a gradual elimination of most old-forest stands in the productive forest landscape. Thus old-forest stands are at risk without special management strategies and a retention target with a defined old age. To better manage old forest, two main areas needed to be defined for the major forest cover groups in future forest forecasts: age definitions of old forest, and NRV. Explicit quantification of these attributes was essential for inclusion in goal-based timber supply models.

Typically, old-forest stands are defined as the overmature seral stage of the boreal forest. Different stand types develop old-forest characteristics at different ages. Additionally, aging is usually a slow and gradual process, but for Al-Pac's modeling analysis, exact old-forest commencement ages

Table 17.2. *Old-forest stand classification for the Al-Pac FMA area*

Main species cover type	Age (years)
Deciduous (aspen and balsam poplar)	100
White spruce	120
Mixedwood	100
Black spruce	120
Jack pine	100

were utilized for the five cover groups. Table 17.2 defines from a forest management perspective the age classification for "old-forest stands" in the FMA area (Andison 2003; Al-Pac 2006).

Natural range of variation

Al-Pac's old-forest management strategy also included the use of the NRV approach (see Box 17.3) of understanding and integrating natural disturbance patterns into long-term planning (Forman and Godron 1986; Franklin 1993). The NRV is defined by the maximum and minimum limits of a characteristic within a natural forest over a long period of time. In applying the NRV to old forest, the intent was to calculate the range of old-forest stand areas that existed prior to the effects of modern land use on the FMA area, and then design a management strategy to maintain the presence of old-forest stands (at or older than the defined old-forest age) on the FMA area within the NRV.

NRV predictions were not made on small landscapes such as FMUs, where natural disturbances can radically alter age-class diversity (Andison 2003). Within the FMA area, the location and size of forest fires are highly unpredictable and include very large fires (e.g. a 250,000 ha fire in 2002) that can significantly deplete old-forest stands at the meso-scale. However, the chance of depleting all old-forest stands is lessened when large landscapes are utilized. The total FMA area, excluding areas covered in water and areas lacking treed vegetation, was utilized for the modeling of old-forest stands. Based on these assumptions, the natural range of variation was predicted for each of the five major strata (white spruce, pine, black spruce, deciduous, and mixedwoods).

The NRV number should not be considered static for such a dynamic landscape, where a single percentage of old growth is irrelevant. Thus, to provide flexibility within the planning model, and be consistent with old-forest targets in Canada's boreal forests (set by the Forest Stewardship Council Canada Working Group 2004), Al-Pac decided to retain old-forest

Box 17.3 The FMA area NRV model was based on the following eight major assumptions[14]

1. Average fire cycle (the most critical factor) is 80 years in the FMA area boreal forest

   • Modeling work from neighboring landscapes in Saskatchewan has illustrated that the pre-industrial fire cycle is probably 40–60 years. However, fire cycle is one of the most debatable fire history parameters. The NRV model was run using both a 60-year and an 80-year fire cycle to provide a range of outcomes. The more conservative result from the 80-year run was used for the 2006 Forest Management Plan (Al-Pac 2006).

2. Fire size is random
   • Fire size is based on a combination of local historical data and fire size data from similar boreal forest areas. In the model, the probability of a large fire was far lower than a small one. The exact shape or size of fires is not very relevant to the non-spatial output.

3. Conifer burn probability is higher than deciduous

   • Andison's LANDMINE model spreads fires based on probabilities of burning based on stand fuel-type, which is determined by the age and species composition of the stand (Andison and Marshall 1998). The fuel-type categories adopted for the model are those used by the Canadian Fire Behaviour Prediction System (CFBPS), and the probabilities of burning are the rate-of-spread (ROS) estimates using the high fire threat (Forestry Canada Fire Danger Group 1992). Within that system, all else being equal, pine and spruce ROS levels are always higher than deciduous ROS levels.

4. Mixedwood is half as likely to burn as pine and spruce

   • This seems to be a reasonable assumption. Within the CFBPS system, all else being equal, mixedwood ROS levels are always higher than deciduous ROS levels.

5. The landscape is defined in five major strata: Deciduous, Mixedwood, White Spruce, Black Spruce, and Jack Pine. (Mixedwood is a combination of DC + CD: deciduous leading and conifer leading mixedwoods.)

   • These strata are the same categories used within the timber supply analysis. This allows the model's strategic output, as well as its assumptions, to be understood in the proper context.

6. The entire forested area of the FMA area was utilized, corresponding to 5.2 million hectares[15] within the gross FMA area (an area that can have an old-forest component.)

---

[14] From Andison (2003). Prepared in association with Al-Pac.
[15] 1.67 million hectares of land is (naturally) a mixture of water, bog, fen, brush, and grassland.

7. Topography is not a modeling factor

- The model is intended to be strategic and non-spatial. Therefore, any variation in the direction and shapes of fires on this landscape due to topographic features is irrelevant. Additionally, the topographic variation in north-eastern Alberta is minimal.

8. All forest stands in the Alberta Vegetation Inventory database returned to their original label after the stands have died

- Boreal forests are dynamic in both time and space. However, to parallel the timber supply analysis, the natural variation model simply assumed that what was there before the fire will be there after the fire.

stand areas for each of the five main forest cover types within ±25% of the mean of NRV on the entire forested area (productive and non-productive) of the FMA area.

NRV model (Andison 2003) estimations representing ± 25% range of the stratum's NRV mean for the Al-Pac FMA area are as follows:

- Deciduous 18%–32%: categorized as old forest @ 100 years
- Mixedwood 14%–24%: categorized as old forest @ 100 years
- White spruce 12%–20%: categorized as old forest @ 120 years
- Jack pine 13%–22%: categorized as old forest @ 100 years
- Black spruce 8%–14%: categorized as old forest @ 120 years.

Al-Pac utilized a timber supply model (WOODSTOCK; Remsoft Inc. 2007) to predict old-forest occurrence and distribution for all five major strata and track their abundance relative to the NRV ranges in the first 200 years of a modeling scenario (Andison 2003). In the absence of catastrophic fires, the timber supply model forecasts that levels of old forest will continue to increase over the next 50 years as the large, currently mature, cohort ages. Thus, over the next 50 years, Al-Pac can meet the old-forest NRV objective without constraining the current annual allowable cut targets. After approximately 60 years, our model indicated that the old-forest area of deciduous, white spruce, and mixedwood cover types would fall below the NRV. To ensure the old-forest seral stage remained within the target of ± 25% of the NRV mean, the annual allowable cut was designed to decrease at a designated time point in the modeling scenario so that a portion of the fiber supply is allowed to become old, prior to future harvest. This is a change from traditional harvest calculation strategies for Alberta. The reduced harvest allowance extends the rotation age of some stands and thus enables the old-forest levels to be maintained in the target range. From

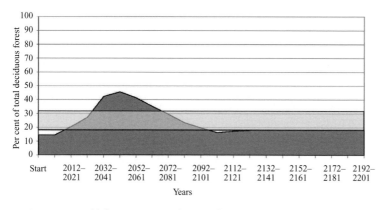

Figure 17.4. Old-forest retention from timber supply model analysis for deciduous strata. Note: light gray band represents the ±25% of mean NRV. A 10% reduction in annual allowable cut is forecast at year 60.

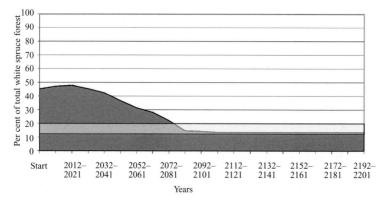

Figure 17.5. Old-forest retention from Woodstock analysis for white spruce strata. Note: light gray band represents the ±25% of mean NRV. A 10% reduction in annual allowable cut is forecast at year 60.

a modeling perspective, model year 60 (2061) was determined as the point to initiate a 10% reduction in annual allowable cut for white spruce, mixedwood, and deciduous in all 11 forest management units in the FMA area. Intervening at year 60 with a constrained harvest ensures that the amounts of old forest will be maintained within the NRV target zones. The timber supply model projections were not designed to account for wildfire and energy sector activities, which will undoubtedly result in changes to the old-forest forecasts. To acknowledge these omissions, the annual allowable cut will be recalculated every five to ten years, or after a significant wildfire event. See Figs. 17.4 and 17.5 for an example of the FMA area timber supply analysis forecast for old-forest retention in deciduous and white spruce strata.

TRIAD IMPLEMENTATION: ECOLOGICAL BENCHMARKS

Al-Pac's commitment to ecologically sustainable forest management is delivered through the adoption of the "TRIAD approach" (Hunter and Calhoun 1996; see also Chapter 14, this volume). This framework recognizes the importance of managing portions of the landscape for different values. The majority of the landscape is managed under a multiple-use sustainable forest management approach, where landscape patterns resulting from forestry activities are designed to approximate natural disturbances, and hence maintain biodiversity. The second portion of the TRIAD approach recognizes the importance of a network of large, representative protected areas that act as ecological benchmarks to compare to harvested areas. Finally, intensive management, which in Al-Pac's case consists of an agroforestry hybrid poplar program developed on privately owned farmland, is used to provide a secure, low-cost fiber source obtained from private land (see www.alpac.ca for more information on "poplar farming").

Assessing adequacy of representation of ecological benchmark areas

Gap analysis is used to measure the degree to which protected conservation networks are complete (Iacobelli *et al.* 2003). One approach to evaluation of the adequacy of conservation area networks is the evaluation of enduring feature representation; then gaps are filled by using a site-selection methodology. An enduring feature can be defined as "a landscape element or unit within a natural region characterized by relatively uniform origin of surficial material, texture of surficial material, and topography-relief" (Kavanagh and Iacobelli 1995). Each enduring feature is unique to each natural region, which is characterized, in part, by its climatic characteristics. The gap analysis measures the degree to which protected areas provide ecological representation within each enduring feature. Al-Pac, in collaboration with World Wildlife Fund (WWF) Canada, performed a gap analysis in north-eastern Alberta as part of Al-Pac's assessment of its TRIAD management approach. The WWF gap analysis tool is implemented as an automated GIS routine and can inform ecoregion-based conservation planning by testing reserve design options that have been developed by multicriterion methods, such as by overlay approaches or site-selection algorithms (Iacobelli *et al.* 2003). The large size of the Al-Pac FMA makes it suitable for conservation planning at this scale.

Criteria to assess the level of representation include sizes of protected areas, connectivity and adjacency to protected areas, habitat quality, and representation of environmental gradients. The WWF routine assesses each enduring feature based on the aforementioned criteria and size (ha) and then ranks each feature as having "adequate", "moderate", "partial", or "little or no" representation.

Incorporating additional information into ecological benchmark area selection

The High Conservation Value Forest Assessment framework that is part of Forest Stewardship Council certification (Forest Stewardship Council Canada Working Group 2004) provides additional information that can be incorporated into ecological benchmark area selection. Al-Pac has mapped High Conservation Value Forests within the Al-Pac FMA area (Dyer 2004) and used this information to complement the gap analysis approach. Other sources of information include vegetation inventory maps, previous Environmentally Significant Areas (ESA) analyses undertaken by the provincial government, and similar assessments carried out by local conservation organizations. Since ecological benchmark areas serve many purposes in addition to acting as reference areas to compare to working landscapes (e.g. traditional use areas and recreation sites), it is important to incorporate aboriginal and broader public input into identifying candidate sites.

In Alberta, existing land-use dispositions, particularly those granted to the oil and gas industry, make optimal establishment of ecological benchmark areas challenging. In order to identify benchmarks in areas that minimize conflict with other industrial land users, proposed benchmark areas were constrained not to overlap areas with existing energy leases. This is challenging in the Al-Pac FMA area, where more than 80% of the landscape is covered by oil and gas dispositions. An important lesson from this approach is that establishment of an effective ecological benchmark network is easier and would likely be more successful if decisions to protect areas were made before resource allocation decisions. Identification of important conservation areas after resource allocation decisions may require withdrawal of development rights and may involve conflict or need for compensation for affected parties. From a forestry perspective, establishment of ecological benchmark areas requires an investment of allocated wood fiber and a reduction in annual allowable cut. Regardless of these difficulties, the benchmark sites identified (see Fig. 17.6) were of High Conservation Value (in large part due to their current roadless state) and representative of the major enduring features found within the Al-Pac FMA area. Some

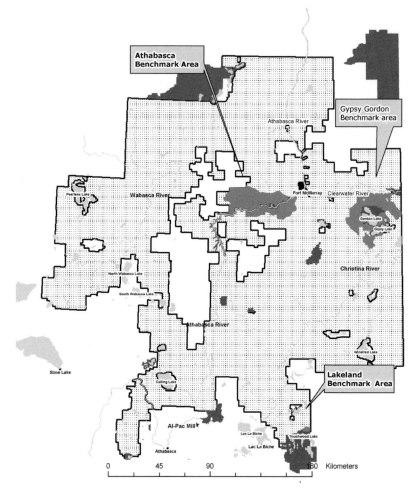

Figure 17.6. Proposed benchmark sites identified in gray medium on the Al-Pac FMA area; existing protected areas are shown in dark gray. Lakes and rivers are shown in light gray for geographic reference.

smaller enduring features were completely covered by petroleum disposi-tions and, consequently, not represented by ecological benchmark areas.

Al-Pac, in association with other stakeholders, identified approximately 200,000 ha of lands that are recommended as permanent representative benchmark areas to compare to the remainder of the landscape. Al-Pac has agreed not to harvest within these ecological benchmark areas and will invest 160,000 m³ of reduction in its timber allocation[16] if the areas are

---

[16] 60,000 m³ of conifer allocation and 100,000 m³ of deciduous allocation.

granted permanent protection by the provincial government. The WWF Gap Analysis tool was used to assess the increase in adequacy of representation of enduring features as a result of the proposed ecological benchmark areas. Assessment of representation after including the new ecological benchmark areas showed the proportion of the landscape "adequately" and "moderately" represented in conservation areas substantially increased under Al-Pac's proposed TRIAD approach. In a review of the proposed ecological benchmarks, Strittholt (2006) identified further gaps in representation. Al-Pac continues to evaluate options for representative benchmarks while not further reducing its timber allocation beyond the aforementioned investment level of a 160,000 m³ reduction in its annual allowable cut.

MANAGING CUMULATIVE EFFECTS

The rapid pace of industrial development makes north-eastern Alberta one of the busiest forest landscapes in the world (Schneider *et al.* 2003). The Athabasca oil sands are recognized as a major international oil supply area. New mines and well-based extraction facilities (e.g. steam-assisted gravity drainage (SAGD)) are being approved and developed each year. Presently there are over nine new open pit mines and 20 SAGD proposals seeking approval from regulatory agencies. Exploration for conventional oil and gas reserves also continues to grow, creating the need for electricity and hydrocarbon transmission corridors for electricity and hydrocarbons. Ecological/economic/social tradeoffs associated with overlapping tenures for resources in north-eastern Alberta are recognized, but tradeoff analyses and political decisions related to such tradeoffs are still largely at the discussion phase.

Integration of operations between different land users is one of the most powerful approaches available to improve stewardship of the boreal forest. Integrated land planning initiatives involve working closely with companies and government departments to ensure some degree of tradeoff analyses and conservation planning are being applied to land management decisions. The Alberta Chamber of Resources initiated its Integrated Land Management (ILM) Program in 2001, and an ILM research chair was developed at the University of Alberta (Boutin 2007). The Alberta government has identified integrated land management planning and the need for a land-use management framework to address issues related to overlapping land use as key items for action (Government of Alberta 2006; Kwong 2005, 2006). Using the TRIAD landscape management approach and an integrated planning process, forestry and oil and gas developers strive to successfully overlap approximately 30% of their operations to decrease the area disturbed in an already busy region of north-eastern Alberta (Alberta Chamber of Resources 2005a,b). ILM is now a component of core business at Al-Pac with objectives to reduce the amount, distribution, and duration of industrial footprint on the landscape, while also reducing costs through co-planning.

Managing industrial access development is important because the boreal forest of Alberta has levels of linear access[17] corridors that are unprecedented in forested ecosystems worldwide. Linear densities in the Al-Pac FMA area average approximately 1.5 $km\,km^{-2}$, with some areas reaching densities as high as 10 $km\,km^{-2}$. Seismic lines[18] are the dominant feature contributing to these high access densities. Simulations indicate that the existing linear footprint is insignificant compared with what is predicted under a "business as usual" approach to resource development in Alberta (Schneider *et al.* 2003). Seismic lines create access for humans, provide travel routes for predators such as wolves (James and Stuart-Smith 2000), and may result in habitat disruption beyond that associated with physical removal of vegetation on the line (e.g. Dyer *et al.* 2002; Bayne *et al.* 2005). Seismic lines in north-eastern Alberta were historically at least 5 m in width. In terms of area of forest removed, seismic lines represent a greater loss of forest than the combined footprint of existing oil sands mines in north-eastern Alberta. By 2002, approximately 82,000 km of "conventional" seismic lines had been cut in the Al-Pac FMA area (Schneider *et al.* 2003). Lack of demonstrated regeneration of these lines is probably due to a combination of reclearing and vehicle disturbance (Lee and Boutin 2006). Research indicates that cleared lines regenerate slowly, and represent a significant and cumulative loss of productive forest and reduction in annual allowable cut.

One of Al-Pac's earliest ILM programs focused on trying to reduce the effects associated with seismic lines. Although forest companies are compensated for loss of timber as a result of seismic clearing activities, this compensation fails to capture the true economic and ecological cost of the persistence of these lines on the landscape (Alberta Sustainable Resource Development 2006). In order to encourage the adoption of more ecologically beneficial seismic technologies in the FMA area and to minimize

---

[17] In Alberta linear access corridors are created by a variety of industrial and government operations. Linear access is created in the form of roads, power transmission lines, oil and gas pipelines, and seismic lines (see below).

[18] Seismic lines are linear corridors cut across the landscape for geophysical exploration in forested regions.

timber loss, Al-Pac agreed to waive compensation payments on all seismic lines less than 2.5 m in width. Line cutting that minimizes width may be initially more expensive than traditional methods, but compensation savings and the likely ecological benefits may make these techniques appear more attractive in the long term to seismic operators in north-eastern Alberta. Narrow seismic lines have a number of advantages over traditional lines. Narrow lines are less likely to facilitate human access, and it is hoped this will encourage timelier establishment of understory vegetation. Since the start of the rebate program in 2001, numerous companies have taken the challenge and attempted to cut lines less than 2.5 m wide in their operations. Over 5,000 km of narrow seismic lines have been cut over the past four winters. This approach is spreading as other forestry companies in Alberta have developed similar policies to encourage the adoption of more beneficial seismic practices within their FMA areas.

When forestry and energy operations occur in the same location, there are numerous ecological and economic benefits to the integration of activities. Preliminary analysis with Conoco-Phillips Canada demonstrated that plan integration in a specific region could result in a 50% reduction in road length, and cost savings of up to CA $3 million. In 2003, Al-Pac fully integrated development of the Opti-Nexen Canada, Long Lake SAGD project with a harvest operation on the project site. A joint road infrastructure, including a single access road, was developed that resulted in an 85% reduction of Al-Pac's road requirements compared with the development of two separate plans. Integration opportunities and ecological monitoring will continue.

MONITORING RESPONSES: THE ALBERTA BIODIVERSITY MONITORING PROGRAM

Although the need for a comprehensive provincial biodiversity monitoring program has been recognized for many years, such a program did not exist in Alberta. A change began in 1998 when a partnership including Al-Pac, other forest industries, oil and gas industries, governments, and research institutes developed the Alberta Biodiversity Monitoring Program (ABMP) (Schieck 2004; Stambaugh and Schieck 2005). The program goal was to provide credible scientific information to improve sustainable resource management and decision-making across Alberta. A team of more than 30 scientists identified protocols to measure and report on the status and temporal changes in a broad diversity of biota, habitat structures, vegetation communities, and landscape patterns within Alberta. These protocols and analyses were extensively peer-reviewed and have been amalgamated into an integrated design to effectively and efficiently survey landscapes, habitat elements, and biota.

Many species from a wide diversity of taxonomic groups were included in the ABMP (Table 17.3). The program focuses on species because these are the biotic units that stakeholders must manage (Bunnell 1998). To maximize the types of change that can be detected in the program, species were chosen from many different taxonomic groups, with many different terrestrial and aquatic habitat requirements, from a variety of trophic levels, and from a diversity of life-history strategies and life spans. When choosing survey methods, researchers reviewed many different potential protocols that sampled multiple species simultaneously, and could be conducted efficiently while achieving low measurement error. By combining information among species, the ABMP will assess changes in biotic communities; these are expected to provide stronger signals of biodiversity change than that found for individual species (Maes and Van Dyck 2005; Maxwell and Jennings 2005).

As an indirect means for monitoring species not included in the program, the ABMP also monitors terrestrial and aquatic habitats at a variety of spatial scales (Table 17.3). The use of habitats as coarse-filter measures of biodiversity is based on the assumption that if the amount and spatial distribution of habitats are similar to those found naturally, then the native biodiversity should also be similar (Attiwill 1994; Lindenmayer and Franklin 1997). To manage costs, habitats were included in the ABMP sampling protocols only if they had been shown in the literature to have direct effects on the presence and abundance of species, and if they could be sampled accurately and inexpensively. Finally, a variety of human land-use footprints were included so associations between changes in biota and changes in human land use could be evaluated. These correlative analyses are designed to focus supplementary research projects and facilitate adaptive management.

The ABMP is designed as a systematic grid of 1,656 sites spaced 20 km apart throughout Alberta. One hundred and forty-four (144) of these sites occur within Al-Pac's forest management area. To manage yearly costs, 20% of the ABMP sites are surveyed each year in a rotating panel design, resulting in all sites being surveyed during a 5-year period. The ABMP was designed to detect a 30% change after three complete cycles, with at least 90% ($\beta = 0.1$) certainty, and to have less than a 10% probability of declaring a difference when there really was none ($\alpha = 0.1$). Only species and habitats that could be surveyed effectively and efficiently were included in the final suite of protocols. To reduce measurement error, all field staff receives

Table 17.3. *Types of elements that are monitored as part of the Alberta Biodiversity Monitoring Program*

Terrestrial	Aquatic
Species Taxonomic Groups	
Mammals	Fish
Birds	Benthic macroinvertebrates
Springtails	Aquatic macroinvertebrates
Mites	Zooplankton
Vascular plants	Phytoplankton
Bryophytes	Benthic algae
Lichens	
Fungi	
Habitats	
At the local patch scale	
Live trees by species and size class	Basin characteristics
Dead tree and logs by size and decay class	Channel characteristics
Shrub cover by height	Submergent and emergent vegetation
Cover and composition of low ground vegetation	Vegetation at edge of water body
Cover and composition of litter	Amount of down wood
Soil amount and composition	Water physiochemistry
Vegetation diversity	
At the landscape scale	
Diversity of habitat types	Length by stream type/size
Area of >200 habitat types	Area by basin type/size
Patch size, shape, and connectivity for five major habitat types	Connectivity and sinuosity of aquatic elements
Human footprints	
Urban and/or industrial habitats	Bridges, culverts, and stream crossings
Rural residential	Residential and cottage
Roads	Agricultural habitats
Vegetation-covered trails and seismic lines	Harvested habitat
Agricultural habitats	
Harvested habitat	

extensive training prior to collecting data. In addition, a quality assurance team resurveys 2% of the sites each year, to assess error. A prototype of the ABMP was initiated in 2003, to collect data at 8% of the sites, test the statistical power of the program, refine the scientific components of the program, evaluate cost-effectiveness of the program, develop data analyses and communication methods, secure long-term funding, and develop a long-term business model for the program. Implementation of the program through the newly formed Alberta Biodiversity Monitoring Institute (ABMI) began in 2007.

The ABMI program is a proactive risk management tool that will provide early detection of biodiversity and ecological change, thus enabling Al-Pac, and other resource managers, to make choices and implement corrective actions before costly recovery programs are necessary. The ABMI establishes baselines so performance and change over time can be evaluated. In addition, the program facilitates sustainable forest management by enhancing the quality and timeliness of decision-making. The program will provide information that feeds into the harvest planning process, allows managers to assess various harvest practices (e.g. two-pass vs. aggregated harvest), and assesses the cumulative biodiversity and ecological effectiveness of activities. This monitoring program will help Al-Pac fulfill its stewardship and certification requirements, and thus help to maintain long-term fiber security and access to local and international markets.

CONCLUSION AND NEXT STEPS

"The only constant is change, continuing change, inevitable change, that is the dominant factor in society today. No sensible decision can be made any longer without taking into account not only the world as it is, but the world as it will be."   Isaac Asimov

Heraclitus made a similar comment about life in Greece 2,500 years ago, and its relevance holds true today. Global competitiveness, rising energy prices, climate change, and fluctuating currency are but a few of the international pressures affecting forest management. Existing across (or under, depending on your perspective) north-eastern Alberta is an oil and gas industry that will see significant expansion in the coming decades (Croft 2005; CAPP 2006). Al-Pac's commitment to innovation will continue to be exercised to remain engaged in the forest sector internationally.

Adaptive management is an important element of ecosystem-based management; Al-Pac's planning and operational practices continue to evolve. At the process level we know there are differences between fire and harvest. As we continue research and monitoring efforts to better understand fire and timber harvest and the ensuing ecological responses, we will be able to adapt our management planning and operational practices to minimize subsequent differences.

We will also continue to conduct research in the area of "mixedwood management". The forests of north-eastern Alberta are a complex mosaic of hardwood and softwood species. Prior to Al-Pac arriving on the scene in the early 1990s, the forest industry in this region focused on conifer harvesting. Many policies and practices that continue to influence forest management in Alberta promote the "unmixing" of these boreal mixed-woods. For example, the forested landbase in much of Alberta is designated either hardwood or softwood, depending on forest crown closure at the time of inventory classification. Reforestation following harvesting histor-ically directed managers to return it to that same type of forest as existed at the time of inventory. Such policy does not fully recognize the natural successional sequences of the boreal forest. As a result, silvicultural activ-ities, particularly for white spruce, are often forced to fight against nature and the ensuing competition (e.g. planting white spruce in a harvested area that naturally is coming back to hardwoods – aspen and poplar) results in costly management to control of competing grasses or hardwoods through chemical or mechanical methods. Early trials in harvesting techniques (e.g. high-effort understory protection[19]) and planting juvenile white spruce in the understory of mid-aged aspen stands are mixedwood management tech-niques showing promise both ecologically and economically. There are a number of key parameters in Al-Pac's old-forest strategy that will require continued collaborative research and development. Al-Pac's current old-forest strategy is largely aspatial and future research and planning direction on landscape and patch characteristics of old forest is working towards a spatially explicit old-forest plan. Examination of fire return intervals and the effect of fire control will better allow us to refine our old-forest strat-egy. Another matter in which refinement is required is the estimation of growth and yields rates on harvested sites, in-block roads, and reclaimed energy sector sites. Collectively, this suite of knowledge will provide us with a better understanding of boreal forest succession, structure, and age relationships that are the underpinnings of the natural disturbance model.

Managing human activities to maintain the quality and quantity of sur-face and subsurface water is becoming an increasingly important aspect of management for Al-Pac and other organizations locally and globally. Al-Pac is currently engaged in a proactive partnership with Ducks Unlimited

[19] High-effort understory protection is defined as a cutting pattern where harvesting equip-ment (fellerbuncher and skidder) is restricted to travel on pre-identified machine corridors 6 m wide. The fellerbuncher will reach 6 m to either side of the machine corridor and harvest deciduous stems only while protecting the immature spruce understory. Usually, 3 m or 5 m unharvested strips still containing the hardwood component are left between each or every second reach area to protect the understory conifer from blowdown.

Canada to develop a hydrology-based forest management approach. Knowledge generated through this partnership will be used to adjust our planning and operational practices to minimize hydrologic risk (Devito *et al.* 2005).

Monitoring differences in biodiversity between the working forest and benchmark areas is necessary in order to demonstrate the effectiveness of EBM forestry activities in maintaining biodiversity, or to demonstrate the need for changes in practices if unanticipated biodiversity changes occur. Al-Pac has voluntarily agreed not to harvest in the proposed ecological benchmark areas and continues to work with stakeholders and government to achieve legislative protection for these sites. We will also continue to explore opportunities, both inside and outside the Al-Pac FMA area, to complete the ecological benchmark network.

Another urgent need is to better understand the future cumulative effects of energy sector activities on boreal mixedwood spatial metrics, age structures, and succession. Despite the fact that over 1.5 million barrels of oil per day (and growing) are being extracted from oil sands deposits in north-eastern Alberta, the energy sector is still early in the development stage for one of the world's largest oil deposits. The ecological, social, and economic implications of such development are diverse. Under current policy frameworks, managing for cumulative effects is challenging. Ecologically there will be varying biotic responses and the Alberta Biodiversity Monitoring Institute is well positioned to document such changes at a regional and provincial scale. More uncertain is the social and political response as tradeoff implications become apparent. Some species will thrive in the changing landscape, while others face an uncertain future. Collaboration in a working landscape through integrated landscape management remains a priority for Al-Pac. However, managing for multiple values will grow increasingly more difficult as options are constrained by increasing cumulative effects. Since beginning operations in 1993, Al-Pac has pursued sustainable forest management that embraces ecological, economic, and social aspects. These efforts were validated in September 2005, when the company received FSC certification. At that time, the certification of 5.5 million hectares (13.6 million acres) of Al-Pac's FMA area represented the largest FSC-certified forest in the world.[20] In pursuit of continuous improvement and adaptive management, Al-Pac will continue its implementation of ecosystem-based management.

---

[20] The Athabasca oilsands of Al-Pac's FMA area (300,000 ha) was excluded from certification because it is not managed according to the company's ecosystem management approach.

References

Alberta Chamber of Resources. 2005a. *Integrated Landscape Management Program.* Available online at www.acr-alberta.com/.

Alberta Chamber of Resources. 2005b. *Integrated Landscape Management Program: Five-Year Supplemental Business Plan 2006–2011.* Calgary: Alberta Chamber of Resources.

Alberta Land and Forest Service. 2000. *Wildfire Historical Database.* Available online at www.govab.ca/env.forests/fpd.

(Al-Pac) Alberta-Pacific Forest Industries Inc. 2000a. *Operators Guide to Stand Structure.* Boyle, Alberta: Alberta-Pacific Forest Industries Inc.

(Al-Pac) Alberta-Pacific Forest Industries Inc. 2000b. *Alberta-Pacific's Detailed Forest Management Plan.* Boyle, Alberta: Alberta-Pacific Forest Industries Inc.

(Al-Pac) Alberta-Pacific Forest Industries Inc. 2001. *Alberta Vegetation Inventory for the Al-Pac Forest Management Agreement Area.* Approved by Alberta Sustainable Resource Development. Boyle, Alberta: Alberta-Pacific Forest Industries Inc.

(Al-Pac) Alberta-Pacific Forest Industries Inc. 2006. *Alberta-Pacific FMA Area Forest Management Plan.* Boyle, Alberta: Alberta-Pacific Forest Industries Inc.

Alberta Sustainable Resource Development. 2006. *Timber Damage Tables 2005/2006.* Available online at www.srd.gov.ab.ca/land/m_li_timberdamage. html. Last review/updated: October 21, 2005.

Andison, D. W. 2003. *Natural Levels of Forest Age-Class Variability on the Alberta-Pacific FMA.* Belcarra, BC: Bandaloop Landscape-Ecosystem Services. (Prepared for Alberta-Pacific Forest Industries Inc.)

Andison, D. W. and P. L. Marshall. 1998. Simulating the impacts of landscape-level biodiversity guidelines: a case study. *Forestry Chronicle* 75:655–65.

Attiwill, P. M. 1994. Disturbance of forest ecosystems: the ecological basis for conservation management. *Forest Ecology and Management* 63:247–300.

Bayne, E. M., S. L. Van Wilgenburg, S. Boutin and K. A. Hobson. 2005. Modelling and field-testing of Ovenbird (*Seiurus aurocapillus*) responses to boreal forest dissection by energy sector development at multiple scales. *Landscape Ecology* 20:203–16.

Bergeron, Y., A. Leduc, B. D. Harvey and S. Gauthier. 2002. Natural fire regime: a guide for sustainable management of the Canadian boreal forest. *Silva Fennica* 36:81–95.

Bourgeron, P. S. and M. G. Jensen. 1993. An overview of ecological principles for ecosystem management. Pp. 49–60 in M. E. Jensen and P. S. Bourgeron (eds.) *Eastside Forest Ecosystem Health Assessment*, Vol. II, *Ecosystem Management: Principles and Applications.* Portland, OR: USDA Forest Service.

Boutin, S. 2007. Integrated landscape management. Available online at www.biology.ualberta.ca/faculty/stan_boutin/ilm/ [viewed September 6, 2007].

Bradbury, S. 2002a. Response of understory vascular plants to wildfire and harvesting. Pp. 6-1–6-58 in S. J. Song (ed.) *Ecological Basis for Stand Management: A Synthesis of Ecological Responses to Wildfire and Harvesting.* Vegreville, AB: Alberta Research Council Inc.

Bradbury, S. 2002b. Response of nonvascular plants to wildfire and harvesting. Pp. 7-1 – 7-34 in S. J. Song (ed.) *Ecological Basis for Stand Management: A*

Synthesis of Ecological Responses to Wildfire and Harvesting. Vegreville, AB: Alberta Research Council Inc.

Bunnell, F. L. 1998. Overcoming paralysis by complexity when establishing operational goals for biodiversity. *Journal of Sustainable Forestry* 7:145–64.

(CAPP) Canadian Association of Petroleum Producers. 2006. *Oil Sands Resources, Production and Projects.* Available online at www.capp.ca/default.asp?V_DOC_ID=1162. (Accessed June 28, 2006.)

Carleton, T. J. and P. MacLellan. 1994. Woody vegetation response to fire versus clear-cut logging: a comparative survey in the central Canadian boreal forest. *Ecoscience* 1:141–52.

Christensen, N. L., A. M. Bartuska, J. H. Brown *et al.* 1996. The report of the Ecological Society of America committee on the scientific basis for ecosystem management. *Ecological Applications* 6:665–91.

Cissel, J. H., F. J. Swanson and P. J. Weisberg. 1999. Landscape management using historical fire regimes: Blue River, Oregon. *Ecological Applications* 4:1217–31.

Croft, D. 2005. Canada oil sands output may increase sixfold by 2030 (update 1). Available online at www.bloomberg.com/apps/news?pid=10000082&sid=aGEiywJ8Yr8s&refer=canada. (Accessed June 28, 2006.)

Cumming, S. G. 2001. Forest type and wildfire in the Alberta boreal mixedwood: what do fires burn? *Ecological Applications* 11:97–110.

Cumming, S. G., F. K. A. Schmiegelow and P. J. Burton. 2000. Gap dynamics in boreal aspen stands: is the forest older than we think? *Ecological Applications* 10:744–59.

Devito, K. J., I. Creed, T. Gan *et al.* 2005. A framework for broad scale classification of hydrologic response units on the Boreal Plain: is topography the last thing to consider? Invited Commentaries, HP Today. *Hydrological Processes* 19:1705–14.

Dyer, S. J. 2004. *High Conservation Value Forests (HCVF) Within the Alberta-Pacific Forest Management Agreement Area: A Summary Report.* Boyle, AB, Canada. Available online at www.alpac.ca.

Dyer, S. J., J. P. O'Neill, S. M. Wasel and S. Boutin. 2002. Quantifying barrier effects of roads and seismic lines on movements of female woodland caribou in northeastern Alberta. *Canadian Journal of Zoology* 80:839–45.

Eberhart, K. E. 1986. Distribution and composition of residual vegetation associated with large fires in Alberta. M.Sc. thesis, University of Alberta, Edmonton.

Eberhart, K. E. and P. M. Woodard. 1987. Distribution of residual vegetation associated with large fires in Alberta. *Canadian Journal of Forest Research* 17:1207–12.

Elkie, E. C. and R. S. Rempel. 2001. Detecting scales of pattern in boreal forest landscapes. *Forest Ecology and Management* 147:253–61.

Fisher, J. T. and L. Wilkinson. 2002. Mammalian response to wildfire and harvesting. Pp. 10-1–10-75 in S. J. Song (ed.) *Ecological Basis for Stand Management: A Synthesis of Ecological Responses to Wildfire and Harvesting.* Vegreville, AB: Alberta Research Council Inc.

Forest Stewardship Council Canada Working Group. 2004. *National Boreal Standard.* Toronto: FSC Canada.

Forestry Canada Fire Danger Group. 1992. *Development and Structure of the Canadian Forest Fire Behaviour Prediction System.* Information Report ST-X-3. Ottawa: Forestry Canada.

Forman, R. T. T. and M. Godron. 1986. *Landscape Ecology.* New York, NY: J. Wiley and Sons.

Franklin, J. F. 1989. Toward a new forestry. *American Forests* **95**:37–44.

Franklin, J. F. 1993. Preserving biodiversity species, ecosystems, or landscapes? *Ecological Applications* **3**:202–5.

Franklin, J. F., D. R. Berg, D. A. Thornburgh and J. C. Tappeiner. 1997. Alternative silvicultural approaches to timber harvesting: variable retention harvest systems. Pp. 111–39 in K. A. Kohm and J. F. Franklin (eds.) *Creating Forestry for the 21st Century.* Washington, D.C.: Island Press.

Government of Alberta. 2006. *Government of Alberta Strategic Business Plan and 2006–09 Business Plan.* March 22, 2006. Available online at www.finance.gov.ab.ca/publications/budget/budget2006/govbp.html. (Accessed July 18, 2006.)

Grumbine, R. E. 1994. What is ecosystem management? *Conservation Biology* **8**:27–38.

Hansen, A. J., T. A. Spies, F. J. Swanson and J. L. Ohmann. 1991. Conserving biodiversity in managed forests: lessons from natural forests. *BioScience* **41**:384–92.

Hebert, D., B. Harvey, S. Wasel *et al.* 2003. Implementing sustainable forest management: some case studies. Pp. 893–952 in P. J. Burton, C. Messier, D. W. Smith and W. L. Adamowicz (eds.) *Towards Sustainable Management of the Boreal Forest.* Ottawa, ON: National Research Council Research Press.

Hunter, M. L., Jr. and A. Calhoun. 1996. A triad approach to land-use allocation. Pp. 477–91 in R. A. Szaro and D. W. Johnston (eds.) *Biodiversity in Managed Landscapes.* London: Oxford University Press.

Iacobelli, A., H. Alidina, A. Blasutti and K. Kavanagh. 2003. *A Landscape-Based Protected Areas Gap Analysis and GIS Tool for Conservation Planning.* Toronto: World Wildlife Fund Canada.

James, A. and K. Stuart-Smith. 2000. Distribution of caribou and wolves in relation to linear corridors. *Journal of Wildlife Management* **64**:154–9.

Johnson, E. A. 1992. *Fire and Vegetation Dynamics: Studies from the North American Boreal Forest.* New York, NY: Cambridge University Press.

Johnson, E. A., K. Miyanishi and J. M. H. Weir. 1998. Wildfires in the western Canadian boreal forest: landscape patterns and ecosystem management. *Journal of Vegetation Science* **9**:603–10.

Kavanagh, K. and A. Iacobelli. 1995. *A Protected Areas Gap Analysis Methodology: Planning for the Conservation of Biodiversity.* Toronto, ON: World Wildlife Fund Canada.

Kessler, W. B., H. Salwasser, C. W. Cartwright and J. A. Caplan. 1992. New perspectives for sustainable natural resources management. *Ecological Applications* **2**:221–5.

Kimmins, J. P. 2002. Old growth forest. An ancient and stable sylvan equilibrium, or a relatively transitory ecosystem condition that offers people a visual and emotional feast? Answer – it depends. *Forestry Chronicle* **79**:429–40.

Kwong, N. L. 2005. *Speech from the Throne*. Government of Alberta, First Session of the Twenty-sixth Legislature. Available online at www.uofaweb.ualberta.ca/govrel//pdfs/FullText2005 SpeechFromTheThrone(PDF).pdf. (Accessed July 18, 2006.)

Kwong, N. L. 2006. *Speech from the Throne*. Government of Alberta, Second Session of the Twenty-sixth Legislature. Available online at www.gov.ab.ca/home/thronespeech/2006/. (Accessed July 18, 2006.)

Lee, P. 2002. Forest structure after wildfire and harvesting. Pp. 5-1–5-48 in S. J. Song (ed.) *Ecological Basis for Stand Management: A Synthesis of Ecological Responses to Wildfire and Harvesting*. Vegreville, AB: Alberta Research Council Inc.

Lee, P. and S. Boutin. 2006. Persistence and developmental transition of wide seismic lines in the western boreal plains of Canada. *Journal of Environmental Management* **78**: 240–50.

Lee, P. and S. Boutin. 2008. *Using Patterns of Live Tree Residuals After Natural Disturbances as a Template for Retention After Timber Harvest*. Edmonton, Alberta: SustainableForest Management Network.

Lee, P., S. Crites, L. Marinelli *et al.* 1999. *Fire and Harvest Residual (FAHR) Project: The Impact of Wildfire and Harvest Residuals on Forest Structure and Biodiversity in Aspen-Dominated Boreal Forests of Alberta*. Vegreville, AB: Alberta Research Council.

Lindenmayer, D. B. and J. F. Franklin. 1997. Managing stand structure as part of ecologically sustainable forest management in Australian mountain ash forests. *Conservation Biology* **11**:1053–68.

Maes, D. and H. Van Dyck. 2004. Habitat quality and biodiversity indicator performances of a threatened butterfly versus a multispecies group for wet heathlands in Belgium. *Biological Conservation* **123**:177–87.

Maxwell, D. and S. Jennings. 2005. Power of monitoring programs to detect decline and recovery of rare and vulnerable fish. *Journal of Applied Ecology* **42**:25–37.

Merrill, S. B., F. J. Cuthbert and G. Oehlert. 1998. Residual patches and their contribution to forest-bird diversity on northern Minnesota aspen clearcuts. *Conservation Biology* **12**:190–9.

Nelson, C. R. and C. B. Halpern. 2005. Short-term effects of timber harvest and forest edges on ground-layer mosses. *Canadian Journal of Botany* **83**:610–20.

Niemelä, J. 1999. Management in relation to disturbance in the boreal forest. *Forest Ecology and Management* **115**:127–34.

Norton, M. R. and S. J. Hannon. 1997. Songbird response to partial-cut logging in the boreal mixedwood forest of Alberta. *Canadian Journal of Forest Research* **27**:44–53.

Odum, E. P. 1969. The strategy of ecosystem development. *Science* **164**:262–70.

Ontario Ministry of Natural Resources. 2001. *Forest Management Guidelines for the Natural Disturbance Pattern Emulation*. Version 3.0. Toronto, ON: Ontario Ministry of Natural Resources.

Peck, J. E. and B. McCune. 1997. Remnant trees and canopy lichen communities in western Oregon: a retrospective approach. *Ecological Applications* **7**:1181–7.

Perera, A. H., L. J. Buse, M. G. Weber and T. R. Crow. 2004. Emulating natural forest landscape disturbances: a synthesis. Pp. 265–74 in A. H. Perera, L. J. Buse and M. G. Weber (eds.) *Emulating Natural Forest Landscape Disturbances: Concepts and Applications*. New York, NY: Columbia University Press.

Quinn, M. S. 2002. Ecosystem-based management. Pp. 370–82 in D. Thompson (ed.) *Tools for Environmental Management: A Practical Introduction and Guide*. Gabriola Island, BC: New Society Press.

Remsoft Inc. 2007. Spatial woodstock: flexible forest modelling. Available online at www.remsoft.com.

Schieck, J. 2004. *The Alberta Biodiversity Monitoring Program (ABMP): A Cost-effective, Multi-species, Broad-scale, Long-term, Biodiversity Monitoring Program*. Available online at www.abmp.arc.ab.ca/Documents/Prototype%20Summary.with%20fig.pdf.

Schieck, J. and K. A. Hobson. 2000. Bird communities associated with live residual tree patches within cut blocks and burned habitat in mixedwood boreal forests. *Canadian Journal of Forest Research* 30:1281–95.

Schieck, J. and S. J. Song. 2002. Responses of boreal birds to wildfire and harvesting. Pp. 9-1–9-100 in S. J. Song (ed.) *Ecological Basis for Stand Management: A Synthesis of Ecological Responses to Wildfire and Harvesting*. Vegreville, AB: Alberta Research Council Inc.

Schieck, J. and S. J. Song. 2006. Changes in bird communities throughout succession following fire and harvest in boreal forests of western North America: literature review and meta-analysis. *Canadian Journal of Forest Research* 36:1299–318.

Schieck, J., L. Marinelli, S. Crites *et al.* 2000a. Biodiversity in cutblocks with few large versus many small residual patches of trees and snags. Vegreville, AB: Alberta Research Council.

Schieck, J., K. Stuart-Smith and M. Norton. 2000b. Bird communities are affected by amount and dispersion of vegetation retained in mixedwood boreal forest harvest areas. *Forest Ecology and Management* 126:239–54.

Schneider, R. R. 2002. *Alternative Futures: Alberta's Boreal Forest at the Crossroads*. Edmonton, AB: Federation of Alberta Naturalists and the Alberta Centre for Boreal Research.

Schneider, R. R., J. B. Stelfox, S. Boutin and S. Wasel. 2003. Managing the cumulative impacts of land uses in the Western Canadian Sedimentary Basin: a modelling approach. *Conservation Ecology* 7. Available online at www.consecol.org/vol7/iss1/art8.

Schowalter, T. D. 1995. Canopy arthropod communities in relation to forest age and alternative harvest practices in western Oregon. *Forest Ecology and Management* 78:115–25.

Seymour, R. S. and M. L. Hunter, Jr. 1992. *New Forestry in Eastern Spruce-Fir Forests: Principles and Applications to Maine*. Maine Agricultural Experimental Station Miscellaneous Publications 716.

Smyth, C. 1999. Overstory composition of live residuals in fire affected landscapes of northern Alberta. M.Sc. thesis, University of Alberta, Edmonton.

Smyth, C. and P. Lee. 2001. *Distribution of Post-Wildfire Live Residuals Within Riparian Areas Within a Lower Foothills-Boreal Wildfire*. Report No. 2. Northern Watershed Project. Vegreville, AB: Alberta Research Council Inc.

Smyth, C., J. Schieck, S. Boutin S. and S. Wasel. 2005. Influence of stand size on pattern of live trees in mixedwood landscapes following wildfire. *Forestry Chronicle* **81**:125–32.

Song, S. J. (ed.) 2002. *Ecological Basis for Stand Management: A Synthesis of Ecological Responses to Wildfire and Harvesting.* Vegreville, AB: Alberta Research Council Inc.

Spies, T. A., W. J. Ripple and G. A. Bradshaw. 1994. Dynamics and pattern of a managed coniferous forest landscape in Oregon. *Ecological Applications* **4**:555–68.

Stambaugh, C. and J. Schieck. 2005. The Alberta Biodiversity Monitoring Program: a cost effective program for detecting biotic change in Alberta. Pp. 7–18 in H. Eppand and M. K. Brewin (eds.) *Prediction to Practice: Environmental Assessment Follow-up. Proceedings of the Alberta Society of Professional Biologists Conference.* Calgary, AB: Alberta Society of Professional Biologists.

Stelfox, J. B. (ed.) 1995. *Relationships between Stand Age, Stand Structure, and Biodiversity in Aspen Mixedwood Forests in Alberta.* Edmonton, AB: Alberta Environmental Centre (AECV95-R1) and Canadian Forest Service (Project No. 0001A). Available online at www.borealcentre.ca/reports/stelfox/aspen.html.

Steventon, J. D., K. L. MacKenzie and T. E. Mahon. 1998. Response of small mammals and birds to partial cutting and clearcutting in northwest British Columbia. *Forestry Chronicle* **74**:703–13.

Strittholt, J. R. 2006. *Al-Pac FMA – Adequacy of Proposed Protected Areas to Meet Requirements for FSC Certification.* A review prepared for Alberta-Pacific Forest Industries Inc. Corvallis, OR: Conservation Biology Institute.

Taylor, B., L. Kremsater and R. Ellis. 1997. Adaptive management of forests in British Columbia. BC Ministry of Forests, Forest Practices Branch, Victoria BC. Available online at www.for.gov.bc.ca/hfd/pubs/docs/sil/sil426.htm.

Wallin, D. O., F. J. Swanson and B. Marks. 1994. Landscape pattern response to changes in pattern generation rules: land use legacies in forestry. *Ecological Applications* **4**:569–80.

Walters, C. and C. S. Holling. 1990. Large-scale management experiments and learning by doing. *Ecology* **71**:2060–8.

Westworth, D. A. and E. S. Telfer. 1993. Summer and winter bird populations associated with five age-classes of aspen forest in Alberta. *Canadian Journal of Forest Research* **23**:1830–6.

Putting conservation target science to work

MARC-ANDRÉ VILLARD AND BENGT GUNNAR JONSSON

Target setting has become a familiar concept through the international policy debate on global climate change. In contrast with greenhouse gas emission targets, the type of targets we emphasize in this book must be developed from ecological knowledge rather than from a socio-economic analysis and a desired outcome. The focus on value-free, quantitative approaches to target setting we imposed from the start could not be applied to all chapters, however. Contributors to this book represent a wide array of professional backgrounds and, accordingly, they approached conservation target setting from a variety of perspectives. Hence, we were not surprised when some contributors argued that targets should integrate socio-economic considerations. Does this reflect insubordination on their part or, rather, the complex socio-economic ramifications of conservation issues? It would be naive to expect a large group of intellectuals to abide by a rule and, therefore, we suspect that both hypotheses may apply here! Including ourselves, most of this book's contributors work with forest managers and policy-makers on a weekly basis unless they are practitioners themselves. Thus, they are well aware of the practical limits to the development of conservation policy and its implementation. None the less, to paraphrase George Bush, we as co-editors decided to stay the course and separate ecological and socio-economic considerations in the target-setting approaches presented in the various chapters. Our stance on this issue generated interesting discussions, which provided insight for this synthesis.

This is not to say that the target-setting approaches presented in this book are purely objective. As a matter of fact, one of the main challenges of conservation target setting was described in Chapter 3 as inherently

Setting Conservation Targets for Managed Forest Landscapes, ed. M.-A. Villard and B. G. Jonsson. Published by Cambridge University Press.
© Cambridge University Press 2009.

subjective: agreeing on an appropriate benchmark condition for the focal ecosystem/landscape. Although various scientific methods (e.g. paleoecology) may come to the rescue, benchmarks must ultimately be agreed upon by all stakeholders. None the less, we reiterate the importance of keeping target setting as free as possible from value-driven pressures. It is important to recognize the difference between the process through which we set general conservation goals and the procedures used to develop specific targets to achieve these goals.

When critical ecological data are difficult or impossible to acquire, for example in the case of threatened species (Chapter 13), targets may have to be set through expert advice, using the best information available. Then, such targets must be frequently reassessed through active adaptive management. The inclusion of a chapter on tradeoffs between ecology and economics (Chapter 16) also seems to run counter to the "rule". However, we felt that the objective approach developed in Chapter 16 to assist managers making those tradeoffs was consistent with the rule in that it provides a generic tool rather than a specific course of action.

In the case of most forest landscapes and species, existing data can be analysed or new data collected in order to develop conservation targets. Even then, research teams are faced with a number of challenges when designing research oriented toward conservation target setting. These challenges were examined in Chapter 3 and addressed in many other chapters. Here, we aim to focus attention on broad research issues, which should be further explored if we are to make progress toward the development of conservation strategies articulated around sound targets.

CRITICAL ISSUES FOR THE DESIGN OF CONSERVATION STRATEGIES

Integrating targets from different levels of organization

A recurrent theme faced by forest management stakeholders is how to integrate information generated by scientific studies addressing a variety of taxa at different levels of organization. Our goal is not to stir up the debate on coarse- vs. fine-filter conservation strategies. There seems to be a consensus around the notion that combining information from both types of strategy (e.g. landscape planning based on rare ecosystem types and population-level targets) is preferable to focusing on either type of strategy alone. However, integrating these strategies is easier said than done. This book offers a wealth of examples of the different steps that should be taken to perform this integration. First, appropriate benchmark(s) must be decided upon using information on natural disturbance regimes and land-use history (Chapters 5 and 7). Then, large-scale survey data may be used to identify priority areas for biodiversity conservation while allowing for other forest values (Chapters 4 and 14). The landscape-level habitat requirements of particular species or taxa may also guide the spatial allocation of conservation and harvesting (Chapters 8 and 9). Landscape-scale considerations should also apply to the conservation of freshwater ecosystems (Chapter 12). Finally, at a finer scale, the requirements of focal taxa may be used to set targets for critical habitat components (Chapter 10) and to maintain or restore connectivity. However, some of these fine-scale components (e.g. dead wood within stands; "life-boats" in cutblocks; connections in the landscape) must be planned over a long time horizon.

Integrating information from several levels of organization requires appropriate tools. Modeling tools are developing rapidly and they increasingly allow linking the habitat requirements of individual species and landscape-level processes. Models describing both natural disturbances (e.g. Pennanen *et al.* 2004; Belleau *et al.* 2007; Chapter 7, this volume) and within-forest management planning (Chapter 15) are becoming more specific and spatially explicit. As future predictions on habitat distribution are provided by these models, they can potentially be linked to population models of indicator species to evaluate different management scenarios (Chapter 10). The links between forest management planning tools may also be refined to allow cost–benefit analyses of different long-term, landscape-level scenarios (Öhman and Lämås 2005; Jonsson *et al.* 2006; Chapter 16, this volume).

The spatial component: dispersion or aggregation?

Ecologists are still debating the relative influence of habitat amount and configuration on population viability (e.g. Fahrig 2003; Turner 2005; Koper *et al.* 2007). In the real world, habitat loss and fragmentation occur simultaneously and, therefore, it is a challenge to assess the relative role of each phenomenon in explaining the response of various species. In general, managed forest landscapes are relatively permeable to the movements of animals, or animal-dispersed seeds, compared with more sharply contrasted landscape types (e.g. forests fragmented by farmland or urban areas). However, the adoption of dispersed or aggregated harvest patterns (or protected areas) may have long-lasting effects on landscape structure and it may determine the fate of species with poor dispersal ability or those sensitive to edge effects. The choice between aggregated or dispersed harvest patterns may be informed through an analysis of natural disturbance regimes (see Chapter 17 for a case study). Knowing the extent, frequency, and severity of natural disturbances provides insight into the conditions in which species evolved. We must also acquire information on the dispersal ability of various taxa because in some forest regions, landscape structure is very different than it was prior to industrial forestry.

Several chapters address landscape influence on species occurrence patterns (see Chapters 8 and 9). We must also document species response in terms of fitness, as habitat requirements for survival or reproduction may be much higher than those associated with mere presence (e.g. Poulin *et al.* 2008). Finally, maintaining connectivity may be critical for the long-term occupancy of managed forest landscapes by various organisms (e.g. Jordan *et al.* 2007).

The temporal component: history and conservation strategies

Forest ecosystems and forest landscapes are dynamic. Indeed, many of the contributors strongly emphasized the role of disturbance in altering forest structure and landscape pattern. An understanding of landscape history may be important to refine predictions on biodiversity response to alternative harvest scenarios. Transient dynamics are important and some phenomena lag behind others. The most evident example is perhaps the fact that the distribution of extant species may be disconnected from current landscape configuration, resulting in so-called extinction debts and species credits (Hanski 2000). Species with negative population growth may be present in the landscape (debt) and there is still a possibility of ensuring their persistence (credit) if the causes of their decline are reversed.

The concept of *connectivity* needs to be expanded to include not only the spatial but also the temporal dimension. The longer the history of human influence, the more likely a system is to differ (be "disconnected") from its natural range of variation. The ability of the forest ecosystem to reorganize after a major disturbance event, such as harvesting, is called its resilience. This concept is closely linked to that of "ecological memory" (Holling 1986; Bengtsson *et al.* 2003). In a more concrete sense, this refers to the ability of a species to persist in a landscape in the form of remnant populations capable of (a) colonizing new habitat, or (b) maintaining genetic variation sufficient to adapt to new environmental conditions.

History also provides vital information on the conditions to which current biota are exposed. The long-term history represents the ecological context in which life-history characteristics of forest species have evolved. For example, species present in forest types subjected to frequent natural disturbances are more likely to have evolved to be efficient dispersers than species that evolved in more stable habitats. The short-term history of anthropogenic influence will tell us to what extent habitat loss and fragmentation may cause continued decline and extinction of species even if conditions improve.

The historical dimension undoubtedly adds a layer of complexity to the analysis of forest species' ecological requirements and, thus, to the development of efficient conservation targets. None the less, this complexity should be embraced: study areas may be compared along a gradient in land-use history so that potential effects of forest management trajectories can be projected into the future and areas with a short history of human influence may provide insight when setting restoration targets (Angelstam *et al.* 2004; Chapter 11, this volume).

The "practical" component: conservation targets, harvest planning, and operations

As mentioned in the opening, there may be a wide gap between targets deemed safe and sound from a research perspective and those that can actually be implemented on the ground. Reasons for this gap may or may not be justified, but a major one pertains to the layers of complexity added by the various agencies, institutions, and, ultimately, people involved in the management of forest lands. From research to policy to the forest operator, there must be a strong will to reach a given target, otherwise it will remain a theoretical construct on a conservation wish-list. The process through which policy can be implemented must follow a hierarchy of steps (Fig. 18.1).

The various factors influencing this procedure are clearly beyond the scope of this book. None the less, it is important to note that society as a whole ultimately determines what the broad conservation goals should be. Then comes the science, which should provide guidance on the establishment of targets, which are then entered into management plans and implemented on the ground. Conservation targets represent the interpretation of the goals in scientific terms that should be based on quantitative approaches and best available knowledge of the system. Tactical decisions may in turn conflict with targets if the latter turn out to be too costly given some societal constraint. However, it is not the role of science to negotiate the targets in relation to the goals, but a societal choice on what goals to set and what tradeoffs are ultimately acceptable at the implementation stage.

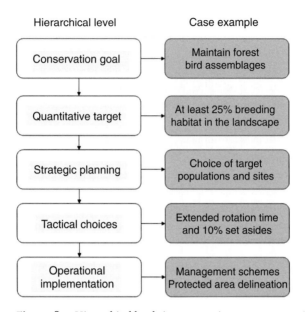

Figure 18.1. Hierarchical levels in conservation management. Note that the first level is a policy level, whereas the remaining levels are within the forest management domain, where quantitative target setting plays a central role.

The monitoring component

As we have argued throughout this book, setting quantitative conservation targets should be at the root of informed conservation strategies. None the less, it would be foolish not to recognize at the outset that targets need to be re-evaluated periodically as new information becomes available. Solid monitoring schemes should be included to allow for the development of truly adaptive management schemes (Fig. 18.2). Then, quantitative targets may reach their full potential; properly chosen, they will provide the guidance needed to evaluate progress towards the conservation goals.

Owing to the time required for their development, some forest components (e.g. density of large snags; percent cover of mature/old forest) may be less amenable to future target adjustments than others (e.g. percent cover of early-seral forest). Hence, target setting must be done carefully before large-scale implementation. None the less, periodical reassessment of targets should be encouraged and should not be viewed as a weakness in the target-setting process; rather, it indicates that we openly recognize the complexity of ecosystems and the limits of our knowledge.

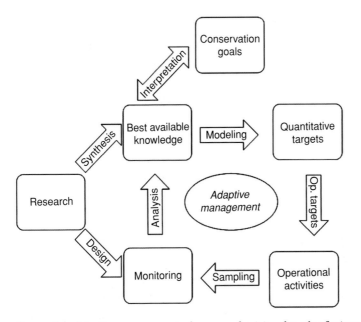

Figure 18.2. Adaptive management scheme emphasizing the role of science and quantitative input into the process. Although the conservation goals are set at a policy level, the input from research clearly shows that a value-free level of quantitative research is needed in the process.

The training component

Quantitative approaches call for quantitative training. Biology, ecology, genetics, forestry, soil science, social science, and other related fields are all important components of sustainable forest management. This is challenging and so maybe the reluctance to add yet another layer of science to the mix is understandable. However, quantitative analysis and modeling are critical in order to move from value-based goals to tractable targets. This calls for a much stronger involvement of quantitative scientists, willing both to share knowledge and to learn about the other aspects of sustainable forest management. There is by tradition a strong quantitative base in forestry on the economic side, able to translate various stand factors and management options into market values and logistics into optimal harvesting schedules. Recent developments suggest that some aspects of conservation may well be integrated into the equation (e.g. Chapter 15). However, many other conservation aspects are unlikely to be measurable in any human currency. Hence, the wisdom of land stewards will continue to be a critical component of the sustainable use of the planet's forests.

Another important aspect of training is to be able to learn from past successes or mistakes. This seemingly trivial observation may seem out of place in a "serious" book, but it became obvious to us, when co-editing this volume, that most of us forest ecologists, conservation biologists, and forestry practitioners tend to be myopic (and hard of hearing?) when it comes to compiling information. We are more or less trapped within our own region, study system, and group of collaborators. Even if many of us travel to meetings and try to keep up to date with new discoveries, we seem to sift incoming information through a geographic filter. One implicit feeling and sometimes explicit argument is that the potential for transfer of patterns and guidelines across forest regions is limited. This is, however, most likely only a lazy escape from having to consider the broader context of knowledge. Although parameter estimates in models, stand factors, and so on are site-specific, many approaches and patterns might have broad relevance. We strongly feel that not only does the interface between research and application need to be strengthened but also the exchange among researchers – perhaps even incorporating a higher degree of humility and openness towards research traditions outside our traditional spheres. If this book manages to open up disciplinary or geographical frontiers, we will consider it to be successful.

References

Angelstam, P., S. Boutin, F. Schmiegelow et al. 2004. Targets for biodiversity conservation – a rationale for macroecological research and adaptive management. Ecological Bulletins 51:487–509.

Belleau, A., Y. Bergeron, A. Leduc, S. Gauthier and A. Fall. 2007. Using spatially explicit simulations to explore size distribution and spacing of regenerating areas produced by wildfires: recommendations for designing harvest agglomerations for the Canadian boreal forest. Forestry Chronicle 83:72–83.

Bengtsson, J., P. Angelstam, T. Elmqvist et al. 2003. Reserves, resilience and dynamic landscapes. Ambio 32:389–96.

Fahrig, L. 2003. Effects of habitat fragmentation on biodiversity. Annual Review of Ecology Evolution and Systematics 34:487–515.

Hanski, I. 2000. Extinction debt and species credit in boreal forests: modelling the consequences of different approaches to biodiversity conservation. Annales Zoologici Fennici 37:271–80.

Holling, C. S. 1986. The resilience of terrestrial ecosystems, local surprise and global change. Pp. 292–317 in W. C. Clark and R. E. Munn (eds.) Sustainable Development of the Biosphere. Cambridge, UK: Cambridge University Press.

Jonsson, M., T. Ranius, H. Ekvall et al. 2006. Cost-effectiveness of silvicultural measures to increase substrate availability for redlisted wood-living organisms in Norway spruce forests. Biological Conservation 127:443–62.

Jordan, F., T. Magura, B. Tothmeresz, V. Vasas and V. Kodobocz. 2007. Carabids (Coleoptera: Carabidae) in a forest patchwork: a connectivity analysis of the Bereg Plain landscape graph. *Landscape Ecology* 22:1527–39.

Koper, N., F. K. A. Schmiegelow and E. H. Merrill. 2007. Residuals cannot distinguish between ecological effects of habitat amount and fragmentation: implications for the debate. *Landscape Ecology* 22:811–20.

Öhman, K. and T. Lämås. 2005. Reducing forest fragmentation in long-term forest planning by using the shape index. *Forest Ecology and Management* 212:346–57.

Pennanen, J., D. F. Greene, M.-J. Fortin and C. Messier. 2004. Spatially explicit simulation of long-term boreal forest landscape dynamics: incorporating quantitative stand attributes. *Ecological Modelling* 180:195–209.

Poulin, J.-F., M.-A. Villard, M. Edman, P. J. Goulet and A.-M. Eriksson. 2008. Thresholds in nesting habitat requirements of an old forest specialist, the Brown Creeper (*Certhia americana*), as conservation targets. *Biological Conservation* 141:1129–37.

Ranius, T. and O. Kindvall. 2006. Extinction risk of wood-living model species in forest landscapes as related to forest history and conservation strategy. *Landscape Ecology* 21:687–98.

Turner, M. G. 2005. Landscape ecology: what is the state of the science? *Annual Review of Ecology, Evolution and Systematics* 36:319–44.

Index